The Institute of Chartered Accountants in England and Wales

BUSINESS AND FINANCE

For exams in 2014

Study Manual

www.icaew.com

Business and Finance
The Institute of Chartered Accountants in England and Wales

ISBN: 978-0-85760-685-3

Previous ISBN: 978-0-85760-452-1

First edition 2007
Seventh edition 2013

British Library Cataloguing-in-Publication Data
A catalogue record for this book is available from the British Library

Printed in the United Kingdom by Polestar Wheatons

Polestar Wheatons
Hennock Road
Marsh Barton
Exeter
EX2 8RP

Your learning materials are printed on paper obtained from traceable sustainable sources.

Welcome to ICAEW

I am delighted that you have chosen to study for the ICAEW Certificate in Finance, Accounting and Business (ICAEW CFAB), or our world-leading chartered accountancy qualification, the ACA.

ICAEW CFAB provides key practical skills and essential knowledge for today's competitive business world. It is a stand-alone qualification that consists of the Certificate Level of the ACA qualification, so it can also be a stepping stone to achieving the ACA.

The ACA is one of the most advanced learning and professional development programmes available. Its integrated components provide an in-depth understanding across accountancy, finance and business. Combined, they help build the technical knowledge, professional skills and practical experience needed to become an ICAEW Chartered Accountant.

Accountants have been providing financial information to organisations for hundreds of years. Today, organisations of every size around the world depend on the skill and expertise of chartered accountants. They are respected for their understanding of complex financial information, and trusted for their strategic business advice.

As part of a worldwide network of over 19,000 students, you will have access to a range of resources and support as you progress through the ACA. Take a look at the key resources available to you on page x.

I wish you the very best of luck with your studies; we are with you every step of the way.

Michael Izza
Chief Executive
ICAEW

Contents

1 Introduction

ACA Overview

The ICAEW chartered accountancy qualification, the ACA, is one of the most advanced learning and professional development programmes available. Its integrated components provide you with an in-depth understanding across accountancy, finance and business. Combined, they help build the technical knowledge, professional skills and practical experience needed to become an ICAEW Chartered Accountant.

Each component is designed to complement each other, which means that students put theory into practice and can understand and apply what they learn to their day-to-day work. The components are:

Professional development

ICAEW Chartered Accountants are known for their professionalism and expertise. Professional development will prepare you to successfully handle a variety of different situations that you'll encounter throughout your career.

The ACA qualification improves your ability and performance in seven key areas:

- adding value
- communication
- consideration
- decision making
- problem solving
- team working
- technical competence.

Ethics and professional scepticism

Ethics is more than just knowing the rules around confidentiality, integrity, objectivity and independence.

It's about identifying ethical dilemmas, understanding the implications and behaving appropriately. We integrate ethics throughout the ACA qualification to develop your ethical capabilities – so you'll always know how to make the right decisions and justify them.

3-5 years practical work experience

Practical work experience is done as part of a training agreement with one of our 2,850 authorised training employers around the world. You need to complete 450 days, which normally takes between three and five years. The knowledge, skills and experience you gain as part of your training agreement are invaluable, giving you the opportunity to put what you're learning into practice.

15 accountancy, finance and business modules

You will gain in-depth knowledge across a broad range of topics in accountancy, finance and business. The modules are designed to fit with your practical experience, so you constantly progress through the qualification.

There are 15 modules over three levels. These can be taken in any order with the exception of the Case Study which has to be attempted last. You must pass every exam (or receive credit) – there are no options. This ensures that once qualified, all ICAEW Chartered Accountants have a consistent level of knowledge, skills and experience.

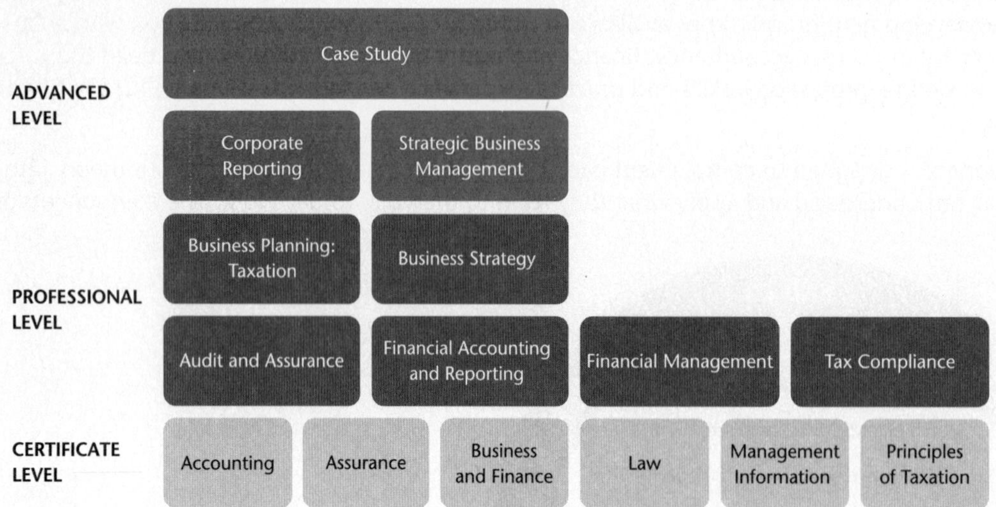

Certificate Level

There are six modules that will introduce the fundamentals of accountancy, finance and business.

They each have a 1.5 hour computer-based assessment which can be sat at any time. You may be eligible for credit for some modules if you have studied accounting, finance, law or business at degree level or through another professional qualification.

These six modules are also available as a stand-alone certificate, the ICAEW Certificate in Finance, Accounting and Business (ICAEW CFAB). If you are studying for this certificate, you will only complete the first six modules. On successful completion, the ICAEW CFAB can be used as a stepping stone to studying for the ACA.

Investment appraisal techniques are introduced at knowledge level in Management Information. An application of how businesses are set up and organised from a capital perspective is part of Business and Finance. These two Certificate Level modules are the foundations of Financial Management.

Professional Level

The next six modules build on the fundamentals and test your understanding and ability to use technical knowledge in real-life scenarios. Each module has a 2.5–3 hour exam, which are available to sit four times per year. These modules are flexible and can be taken in any order. The Business Planning: Taxation and Business Strategy modules in particular will help you to progress to the Advanced Level.

The knowledge base that is put into place at Certificate Level is developed further in the Financial Management module. Here, the aim is to enable you to recommend options for financing a business, recognise and manage links and make appropriate investment decisions.

Advanced Level

The Advanced Level module of Corporate Reporting requires you to apply the technical knowledge you have built at Professional Level, along with analytical techniques and professional skills, to resolve compliance and business issues that arise in the context of the preparation and evaluation of corporate reports and from providing audit services. At the Strategic Business Management module, you will need to demonstrate quantitative and qualitative skills to make realistic business recommendations in complex scenarios. You will also need to demonstrate business awareness at strategic, operating and transactional levels. These modules have a 3.5 hour exam and are available to sit twice a year.

The Case Study will require you to provide advice in respect of complex business issues, and will assess your ability to analyse financial and non-financial data, exercise professional and ethical judgement, and develop conclusions and recommendations. The Case Study is a 4 hour exam and is available to sit twice a year.

The above diagram illustrates how the knowledge of financial management principles gives a platform from which a progression of skills and accounting expertise is developed.

The Advanced Level exams are fully open book, so they replicate a real-life scenario where all the resources are at your fingertips.

For more information on the ACA qualification exam structure and syllabus, visit icaew.com/students

2 Business and Finance

2.1 Module aim

To provide students with an understanding of how businesses operate and how accounting and finance functions support businesses in achieving their objectives.

On completion of this module, students will be able to:

- identify the general objectives of businesses and the functions and tasks that businesses perform in order to meet their objectives
- specify the nature, characteristics, advantages and disadvantages of different forms of business and organisational structure
- identify the purpose of financial information produced by businesses, specify how accounting and finance functions support business operations, and identify sources and methods of financing for businesses and individuals
- specify the role of the accountancy profession and why the work of the profession is important
- identify the role that governance plays in the management of a business and specify how a business can promote corporate governance, sustainability, corporate responsibility and an ethical culture
- specify the impact on a business of the economic environment in which it operates.

2.2 Specification grid

This grid shows the relative weightings of subjects within this module and should guide the relative study time spent on each. Over time the marks available in the assessment will equate to the weightings below, while slight variations may occur in individual assessments to enable suitably rigorous questions to be set.

	Syllabus area	*Weighting (%)*
1	Business objectives and functions	} 30
2	Business and organisational structures	
3	The role of finance	25
4	The role of the accountancy profession	15
5	Governance, sustainability, corporate responsibility and ethics	15
6	External environment	15
		100

3 Key Resources

Student support team

Our student support team are here to help you as much as possible, providing full support throughout your studies.

T +44 (0)1908 248 250
F +44 (0)1908 248 069
E studentsupport@icaew.com

Student website

The student area of our website provides you with information on exam applications, deadlines, results and regulations as well as applying for credit for prior learning (CPL)/exemptions. The study resources section includes advice from the examiners, module syllabi, past papers and sample papers, webinars and study guides. The study guides are designed to help put the learning for each module into context and highlight the practical significance of what you'll learn. They also include the syllabus, technical knowledge grids and learning outcomes for each module, enabling you to gain an overview of how your learning links to the qualification. Visit icaew.com/students for these resources and more.

Online student community

The online student community is a forum to ask questions, gain study and exam advice from fellow ACA and CFAB students and access our free webinars. There are also regular Ask a Tutor sessions to help you with key technical topics and exam papers. Access the community at icaew.com/studentcommunity

Tuition

The ICAEW Partner in Learning scheme recognises tuition providers who comply with our core principles of quality course delivery. If you are receiving structured tuition with an ICAEW Partner in Learning, make sure you know how and when you can contact your tutors for extra help. If you are not receiving structured tuition and are interested in classroom, online or distance learning tuition, take a look at our recognised Partner in Learning tuition providers in your area, on our website icaew.com/students

Faculties and Special Interest Groups

Faculties and special interest groups support and develop members and students in areas of work and industry sectors that are of particular interest. There are seven faculties which provide knowledge, events and essential technical resources, including the Business and Finance faculty. Our 12 groups provide practical support, information and representation within a range of industry sectors including Charity and Voluntary, Entertainment and Media, Farming and Rural Business, Forensic, Healthcare, Insolvency, Valuation, Tourism and Hospitality, and more. Students can register free of charge for provisional membership of one special interest group and receive a monthly complimentary e-newsletter from one faculty of their choice. To find out more and to access a range of free resources, visit icaew.com/students

The Library & Information service (LIS)

The Library & Information service (LIS) is ICAEW's world-leading accountancy and business library. You have access to a range of resources free of charge via the library website, including the catalogue, LibCat. Visit icaew.com/library for more details.

CHAPTER 1

Introduction to business

Introduction

Learning objectives

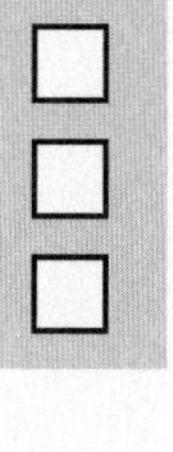

- State the general objectives of businesses
- State the general objectives of strategic management
- Specify the nature of sustainability and corporate responsibility

The specific syllabus references for this chapter are: 1a, 1b, 5g.

Syllabus links

The material in this chapter will be developed further in this paper, and then in the Business Strategy paper at the Professional level.

Examination context

While the material in this chapter is essentially introductory, questions on business objectives will be directly examined.

Questions are likely to be set in multiple choice format, either as a straight test of knowledge or in a scenario.

1 What is an organisation?

Section overview

- There are many different types of organisation in both the not-for-profit and business sectors.
- Organisations exist because the collective efforts of people are more productive as a result of them.
- All organisations share the feature that they are designed to get things done.
- Organisations differ in terms of ownership, control, activity, profit orientation, size, legal status and technology.

1.1 Introduction to organisations

Here are some examples of organisations, categorised as to whether they are profit-oriented or not-for-profit.

- A multinational car manufacturer (eg Ford)
- An accountancy firm (eg KPMG)

} Profit-oriented (private sector)

- A charity (eg UNICEF)
- A trade union
- A local authority
- An army
- A club

} Not-for-profit (charity/public sector)

1.2 Why do organisations exist?

Organisations exist because they:

- **Overcome people's individual limitations**, whether physical or intellectual
- **Enable people to specialise** in what they do best
- **Save time**, because people can work together or do two aspects of a different task at the same time
- **Accumulate** and share knowledge (eg about how best to build cars)
- Enable people to **pool their expertise**
- Enable **synergy**: the combined output of two or more individuals working together exceeds their individual output ('None of us is as smart as all of us').

In brief, organisations enable people to be **more productive**.

1.3 What do organisations have in common?

The definition below states broadly what all organisations have in common.

Definition

Organisation: A **social arrangement** for the controlled performance of collective **goals**, which has a **boundary** separating it from its environment.

The following table shows how this definition applies to two organisational examples: a car manufacturer and an army.

Characteristic	Car manufacturer (eg Ford)	Army
Social arrangement: individuals gathered together for a purpose	People work in different divisions, making different cars	Soldiers are in different regiments, and there is a chain of command from the top to the bottom
Controlled performance: performance is monitored against the goals and adjusted if necessary to ensure the goals are accomplished	Costs and quality are reviewed and controlled. Standards are constantly improved	Strict disciplinary procedures, training
Collective goals: the organisation has goals over and above the goals of the people within it	Sell cars, make money	Defend the country, defeat the enemy, international peace keeping
Boundary: the organisation is distinct from its environment	Physical: factory gates Social: employment status	Physical: barracks Social: different rules than for civilians

1.4 How do organisations differ?

Organisations also differ in many ways. Here are some possible differences.

Factor	Example
Ownership (public vs private)	*Private sector:* owned by private investors/shareholders *Public sector:* owned by the nation and managed by the government
Control	By the owners themselves, by people working on their behalf, or indirectly by government-sponsored regulators
Activity (ie what they do)	Manufacturing, healthcare, services (and so on)
Profit or non-profit **orientation**	Business exists to make a profit. An army or a charity, on the other hand, are not profit-oriented
Size	Small local business to multinational corporation
Legal status	Company, or an unincorporated body such as a club, association, partnership or sole trader
Sources of **finance**	Borrowing, government funding, share issues
Technology	High use of technology (eg computer firms) vs low use (eg corner shop)

1.4.1 Differences in what organisations do

Organisations do many different types of work (activity).

Industry	Activity
Agriculture	Producing and processing food
Manufacturing	Acquiring raw materials and, by the application of labour and technology, turning them into a product (eg a car)
Extractive/raw materials	Extracting and refining raw materials (eg mining)
Energy	Converting one resource (eg coal) into another (eg electricity)
Retailing/distribution	Delivering goods to the end consumer
Intellectual production	Producing intellectual property eg software, publishing, films, music etc
Service industries	These include banking, various business services (eg accountancy, advertising) and public services such as education and medicine

2 What is a business?

Section overview

- Organisations have secondary objectives that support their primary objectives.
- For a profit-making organisation, the primary objective is to maximise the wealth of its owners; for a non-profit organisation it is to provide goods and services for its beneficiaries.
- A business is an organisation which aims to maximise its owners' wealth but which can be regarded as an entity separate from its owners.

2.1 Profit vs non-profit orientation

The basic difference in orientation is expressed in Figure 1.1 below. Note the distinction between **primary** and **secondary** objectives. A primary objective is the most important: the other objectives support it. We shall come back to this.

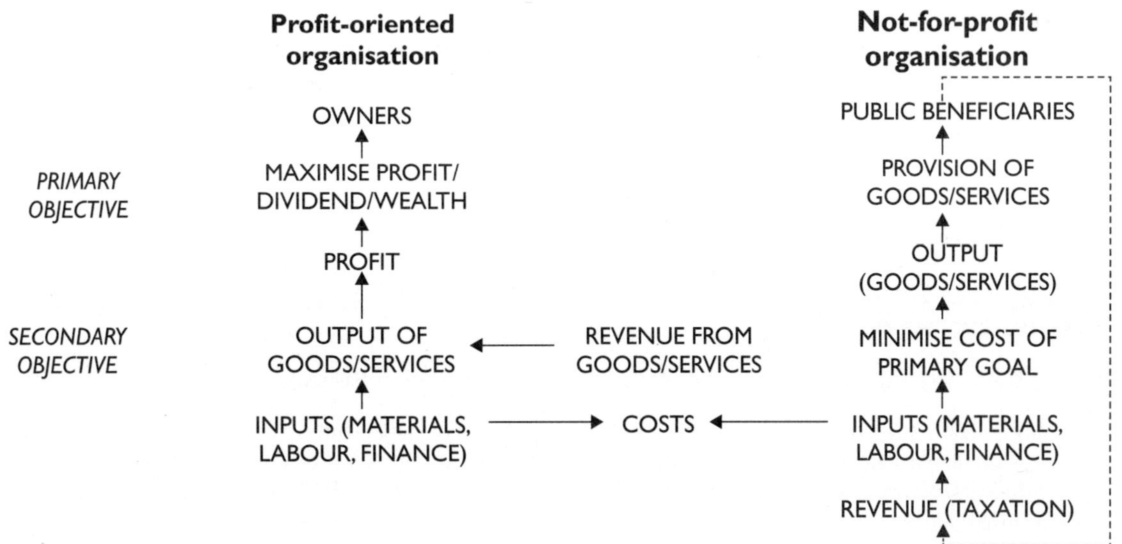

Figure 1.1: Profit-oriented and not-for-profit organisations

Profit-oriented organisations are generally referred to as **'businesses'**, though this is in fact a rather loose term.

- Businesses are profit-oriented but they encompass a variety of legal structures (as we shall see in Chapter 3):
  - Companies are owned by shareholders
  - A sole tradership is owned by one individual (usually called the proprietor), and
  - Partnerships are owned collectively by the partners
- Not-for-profit organisations are frequently structured and run on the lines of a business, so that they benefit from the economy, efficiency and effectiveness in using resources that profit orientation brings, but they are not generally owned by shareholders, proprietors or partners. They do not primarily aim to maximise profit or the wealth of their owners, but rather are focused on providing goods and services to their beneficiaries at minimised cost.
- The type of work engaged in by the organisation does not of itself determine whether it is a profit-orientated or not-for-profit organisation; a business can be involved in providing medical or education services just as much as can a charitable or government organisation.

Examples of **not-for-profit organisations**:

- Charities
- Clubs and associations
- Trade unions
- Professional bodies and institutes such as the ICAEW
- Government
- Governmental agencies
- Local authorities
- Hospitals
- Schools, colleges and universities

2.2 Definition of a business

It is the **primary objective** of the organisation that determines whether or not it is a business. Although as we have seen 'business' is a loose term which has no legal definition as such, it is useful to have a working definition at this point.

Definition

Business: An organisation (however small) that is oriented towards making a profit for its owners so as to maximise their wealth and that can be regarded as an entity separate from its owners.

3 Stakeholders in the business

Section overview

- A stakeholder is a person who has an interest of some kind in the business.
- A company's primary stakeholders are its shareholders. The primary stakeholders in a sole tradership or partnership also comprise the business's owners. Secondary stakeholders are directors/managers, employees, customers, suppliers and partners, lenders, government and its agencies, the local community, the public at large and the natural environment.
- Sustainability is the ability to meet the needs of the present without compromising the ability of future generations to meet their own needs. How far a business can operate sustainably using its tangible and intangible resources is a key issue, as is corporate responsibility: actions, activities and obligations of business in achieving sustainability.

You can see from Figure 1.1 that a profit-oriented business exists primarily in order to maximise wealth for its **owners**, while a not-for-profit organisation such as a charity or a government department exists primarily to provide services (and/or goods) for its **beneficiaries**.

In both cases the organisations have **stakeholders** who are interested in what the organisation does.

Definition

Stakeholder: Literally a person or group of persons who has a stake in the organisation. This means that they have an interest to protect in respect of what the organisation does and how it performs.

For a business formed as a company the primary stakeholders are its **shareholders**. It is their money, invested in the business, which is literally 'at stake'; it can be lost if the business performs badly, and it can earn a decent return if the business does well. The business owes it to the shareholders to look after their interests, but it has secondary stakeholders as well, to whom it also has responsibilities, and from whom it may receive pressure.

	Stakeholders in a business	What is at stake?	What do they typically expect of the business?
PRIMARY	Shareholders (or partners or proprietor)	Money invested	A return on their investment so that their wealth increases: • Steady, growing profits paid out by the business • Growth in capital value of their share of the business
SECONDARY	Directors/managers Employees and trade unions	Livelihoods, careers and reputations	Fair and growing remuneration Career progression Safe working environment Training Pension
	Customers	Their custom	Products/services that are of good quality and value Fair terms of trade Continuity of supply
	Suppliers and other business partners	The items they supply	Fair terms of trade Prompt payment Continuity of custom
	Lenders	Money lent	A return on their investment: • Interest • Repayment of capital
	Government and its agencies	National infrastructure used by business The welfare of employees Tax revenue	Reasonable employment and other business practices Steady or rising stream of tax revenue
	The local community and the public at large	National infrastructure used by business The welfare of employees	Reasonable employment and other business practices
	The natural environment	The environment shared by all	Reasonable environmental and other business practices

Interactive question 1: Social responsibility **[Difficulty level: Intermediate]**

What expectations would the local community have of a company operating a gas-fired power station within two miles of a medium-sized town?

See **Answer** at the end of this chapter.

Therefore there are wider areas of **social responsibility** of which the business must take account, such as its impact on the **natural environment**, how far its strategy is **sustainable** in terms of the world's resources in the long term, its **human resource management policies**, its **risk management** strategy and policies, its approach to contracts with **adverse political connotations**, the extent of its **charitable support**, and how far it goes beyond the minimum standards required by **laws and regulations**.

3.1 Sustainability and corporate responsibility

These ideas are all contained within two very important concepts for businesses today which we shall encounter several times in this Study Manual: **sustainability** and **corporate responsibility**.

Definitions

Sustainability: the ability to 'meet the needs of the present without compromising the ability of future generations to meet their own needs' (the UN's Brundtland Report 'Our Common Future', published in 1987). However today this definition reaches beyond the environmental and includes such concepts as social and economic justice, wellbeing, relationships and the creation of human capital.

Business sustainability: how far a business can operate in a sustainable way, and how it should interact with individuals and governments in doing so.

Corporate responsibility: the actions, activities and obligations of business in achieving sustainability

---

The emphasis of sustainability is thus on using **resources** that are sustainable, these being both:

- **tangible resources** such as raw materials and energy, and
- **intangible resources** such as human/intellectual capital, and relationships with stakeholders.

We shall come back to these topics in more detail in Chapters 7 and 11.

4 What are the business's objectives?

Section overview

- Every business has a hierarchy of objectives, from its primary objective down to its supporting secondary objectives. Together these form multiple objectives.
- Profit and wealth maximisation is usually the primary objective, though sometimes managers pursue a policy of profit satisficing only.

4.1 The hierarchy of objectives

The fact that a business is oriented towards making a profit means that the simple answer to the question 'what are the business's objectives?' is: **profit maximisation so as to increase shareholder wealth**.

In fact, however, there is a **hierarchy of objectives**, with one **primary objective** and a series of **secondary (subordinate) objectives** which should combine to ensure the achievement of the primary objective.

4.1.1 Primary objective

For a business the primary objective is the **financial objective** of **profit maximisation so as to increase shareholder wealth.**

- **Profit** is revenue less costs. It measures the creation of **value**, in terms of the relationship of inputs to outputs, with the cost of inputs (labour, materials and finance) being less than the ultimate output, which is the revenue generated. Profit thus integrates cost behaviour and revenue performance for the whole organisation.
- The link between profit and shareholder wealth is that the latter can only be maximised if profit is earned at an acceptable level of **risk**: focusing solely on maximising profit and ignoring risk can lead to decreased shareholder wealth (and financial collapse). Thus avoiding high risk should go hand-in-hand with making profits so as to maximise shareholder wealth.
- Profit cannot be pursued at any cost. Any business is subject to the **laws and regulations** of the country in which it operates, and it will also have **social responsibilities**, as we saw briefly above.

4.1.2 Secondary objectives

Secondary objectives support the primary objective. Here are some examples:

- **Market position**

  Total market share of each market; growth of sales, customers or potential customers; the need to avoid relying on a single customer for a large proportion of total sales; what markets should the business be in?
- **Product development**

  Bring in new products; develop a product range; invest in research and development; provide products of a certain quality at a certain price level
- **Technology**

  Improve productivity; reduce the cost per unit of output; exploit appropriate technology
- **Employees and management**

  Train employees in certain skills; reduce labour turnover; create an innovative, flexible culture; employ high quality leaders

4.2 Is wealth maximisation always the primary objective?

Making as much profit as possible at acceptable risk, or **wealth maximisation**, then, is assumed to be the primary objective of businesses. Where the person who has put their money at stake (the '**entrepreneur**') is in full managerial control of the firm, as in the case of a small owner-managed company or partnership, this assumption would seem to be very reasonable. Even in companies owned by shareholders, but run by non-shareholding managers, we might expect that the wealth maximisation assumption would be close to the truth.

But managers will not necessarily make decisions that will maximise shareholder wealth.

- They may have **no personal interest** in the creation of wealth, except insofar as they are accountable to shareholders
- There may be a **lack of competitive pressure** in the market to be efficient by minimising costs and maximising revenue, for example where there are few businesses in the market

4.2.1 Profit satisficing

Decisions might be taken by managers with **managerial objectives** in mind rather than the aim of wealth maximisation. The profit and risk levels must be satisfactory and so acceptable to shareholders, and they must provide enough profits retained in the business for future investment in growth, but rather than seeking to maximise profit and wealth, managers may choose to achieve simply a satisfactory profit for a business. This is called '**satisficing**', and is linked to a view of the strategy process called 'bounded rationality' by Herbert **Simon** – an issue we shall return to in Chapter 4.

4.2.2 Revenue maximisation

Baumol argued that the business acts to **maximise revenue** (not necessarily profit or wealth) in order to maintain or increase its market share, ensure survival, and discourage competition. Managers benefit personally because of the prestige of running a large and successful company, and also because salaries and other benefits are likely to be higher in bigger companies than in smaller ones.

4.2.3 Multiple objectives

Management writer Peter **Drucker** points out that:

'To manage a business is to balance a variety of needs and goals.... The very nature of business enterprise requires multiple objectives'. He suggests that objectives are needed in eight key areas.

- **Market standing**: this includes market share, customer satisfaction, size of product range and distribution resources
- **Innovation**: in all major aspects of the business
- **Productivity**: meeting targets for the number of outputs (items produced or tasks completed) within set timescales
- **Physical and financial resources**: efficient use (minimising waste) of limited resources (including people, space, materials, plant and equipment, finance and so on)
- **Profitability**: as discussed earlier
- **Manager performance and development**: managerial effectiveness in meeting objectives and creating a positive environment in the business; grooming of managers for continuity (managerial succession)
- **Worker performance and attitude**: labour productivity, stability (controlled labour turnover), motivation and morale, development of skills and so on
- **Social responsibility**: in areas such as community and environmental impacts, labour standards and employment protection, business ethics and so on (as discussed earlier).

4.2.4 Constraints theory

Simon has also pointed out that for some business areas decisions are taken without reference to the wealth objective at all. This is not because they are ignoring profit, but because profit is not the most important **constraint** in their business. This is perhaps seen most clearly in areas where ethical constraints apply, such as staff relations or environmental protection. It may also be seen in the need to satisfy customers with quality products and service – which may lower profitability.

5 Mission, goals, plans and standards

Section overview

- A business's planning and control cycle is designed to ensure that its objectives, mission and goals are met by setting plans, measuring actual performance against plans, and taking control action.
- The direction of the business is set by its mission, which sets out its basic function in society in terms of how it satisfies its stakeholders.
- The mission encompasses the business's purpose, strategy, policies, standards of behaviour and values.
- The business's goals can be classified as its aims (which are non-operational and qualitative) and its operational, quantitative objectives.
- Operational objectives should be SMART: specific, measurable, achievable, relevant and time-bound.
- Plans and standards set out what should be done to achieve the operational objectives.
- The organisation's plans are a result of its strategic planning process.

5.1 Planning and control system

Because businesses have primary and secondary objectives they want to satisfy, they need to direct their activities by:

- Deciding what they want to do to achieve the overall objective – these become detailed objectives that the business sets out to achieve, such as 'grow revenue by 20%' or 'reduce costs by 10%'
- Deciding how and when to do it and who is to do it (setting plans and standards)
- Checking that they achieve what they want, by measuring and monitoring what has been done and comparing it with the plan
- Taking control action to correct any deviation.

The overall framework for this is the system of **planning and control** in Figure 1.2.

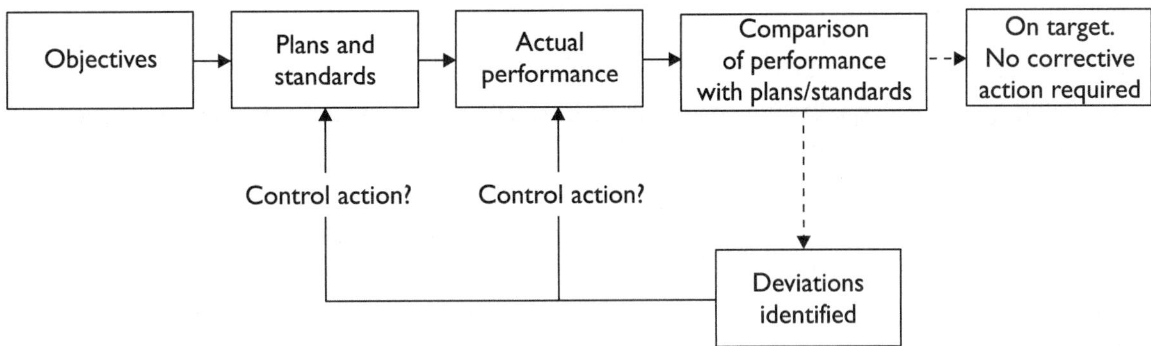

Figure 1.2: Planning and control system

Where there is a deviation from plan, a decision has to be made as to whether to adjust the plan (eg it was unachievable) or the performance (eg it was sub-standard).

It is the business's primary objective and how it is translated into plans and standards that underlie the planning and control system. The objective is incorporated in its mission, its goals (its aims and detailed objectives), plans and standards.

5.2 Mission

Overall, the main direction of a business is set by its mission.

Definition

Mission: 'The business's basic function in society', is expressed in terms of how it satisfies its stakeholders.

Elements of mission	Comments
Purpose	Why does the organisation exist and for whom (eg shareholders)?
Strategy	Mission provides the operational logic for the organisation: • What do we do? • How do we do it?
Policies and standards of behaviour	Mission should influence what people actually do and how they behave: the mission of a hospital is to save lives, and this affects how doctors and nurses interact with patients.
Values	What the organisation believes to be important: that is, its principles.

Even though the mission can be very general, you can see it should have real implications for the policies and activities of the organisation, and how individuals go about what they do.

5.2.1 Vision

Some businesses also set out their **vision** of the future state of the industry or business when determining what its mission should be. For instance, 'being the leading provider of X by 2016' is a **vision** of the future, which ties it in with a **mission** of 'providing high-quality environmentally-friendly X to all our customers'.

5.3 Goals: aims and objectives

Definition

Goals: 'The intentions behind decisions or actions' (Henry Mintzberg) or 'a desired end result' *(Shorter Oxford English Dictionary)*.

Goals give flesh to the mission. There are two types of goal:

- Non-operational, **qualitative** goals **(aims)**, for example, a university's aim may be: 'to seek truth'. (You would not see: 'increase truth by 5%')
- Operational, **quantitative** goals **(objectives)**, for example, 'to increase sales volume by 10%'.

Characteristics of operational goals (objectives)	Example
Objectives should be SMART • Specific • Measurable • Achievable • Relevant • Time-bound	• Operational aim: cut costs • Operational objective: reduce budgeted expenditure on office stationery by 5% by 31 December 2014

Interactive question 2: Goals [Difficulty level: Intermediate]

Most organisations establish quantifiable operational goals (objectives). Give reasons why non-operational goals (aims) might still be important.

See **Answer** at the end of this chapter.

5.3.1 The purpose of setting operational objectives in a business

'Objectives are needed in every area where performance and results directly and vitally affect the survival and prosperity of the business' (Drucker). Objectives in these key areas should enable management to:

- **Implement** the mission, by setting out what needs to be achieved.
- **Publicise** the direction of the organisation to managers and staff, so that they know where their efforts should be directed.
- **Appraise** the validity of decisions by assessing whether these are sufficient to achieve the stated objectives.
- **Assess and control actual performance**, as objectives can be used as targets for achievement.

5.4 Plans and standards

Definition

Plans: state what should be done to achieve the operational objectives. **Standards and targets** specify a desired level of performance.

- **Physical standards** eg units of raw material per unit produced.
- **Cost standards**. These convert physical standards into money measurement by the application of standard prices. For example, the standard labour cost of making product X might be 4 hours at £6 per hour = £24.
- **Quality standards**. These can take a variety of forms, such as percentage of phone calls answered within three rings (customer service quality standard).

5.5 How are plans set?

The **strategic planning process**, which we shall see in detail in Chapter 4, sets the overall mission, goals, plans and standards that the business will try to achieve.

Summary and Self-test

Summary

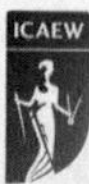

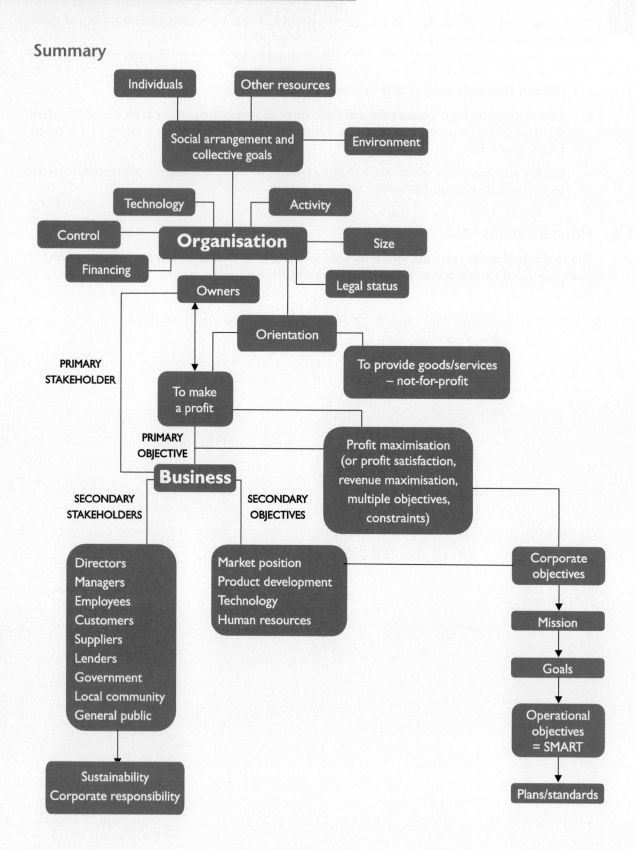

Self-test

Answer the following questions.

1 What is an organisation?

2 List four ways in which organisations may differ from each other.

3 A government funded agency exists to provide services to a group of beneficiaries. What would its secondary objective be?

4 What is a business?

5 What three things are normally expected of a business by its suppliers as stakeholders?

6 State two possible primary business objectives other than profit/wealth maximisation.

7 Define what is meant by a business's mission.

8 Inch plc's operational objective for its Yem manufacturing division is 'increasing manufacturing activities within a year'. On which **one** of the SMART criteria for objectives does this objective fall down?

A Specific
B Measurable
C Relevant
D Time-bounded

Now, go back to the Learning Objectives in the Introduction. If you are satisfied you have achieved these objectives, please tick them off.

Answers to Interactive questions

Answer to Interactive question 1

The local community would expect jobs and therefore prosperity to flow from the company, as well of course as electricity. It would also expect safe operating practices and a long term view taken of how the gas would be transported to the station, and any waste transported from the site. It would be concerned about direct pollution from gases etc, and would expect the company to minimise these. It would be concerned about the possibility of gas explosions, and would require reassurance about security procedures to deal with this risk. Some people would also be concerned about the overall effect on the world's environment, and would expect the company to make efforts to minimise its 'carbon footprint'.

Answer to Interactive question 2

Aims can be just as helpful as quantifiable objectives. Customer satisfaction, for example, is not something which is achieved just once. Some goals are hard to measure and quantify, for example 'to retain technological leadership'. Quantified objectives are hard to change when circumstances change, as changing them looks like an admission of defeat: qualitative aims may support greater flexibility.

Answers to Self-test

1 An organisation is a social arrangement for the controlled performance of collective goals, which has a boundary separating it from its environment

2 They may differ in terms of ownership (public or private), by whom their operations are controlled (by owners or managers), what they do, whether they are oriented towards making a profit, their size, their legal form (club, association, sole tradership, partnership, or company), where they get their money from and what technology they use

3 To minimise the costs of providing the services

4 A business is an organisation that is oriented towards making a profit for its owners but that can be regarded as an entity separate from its owners

5 Fair terms of trade; prompt payment; continuity of custom

6 **Two** of: profit satisficing; revenue maximisation; multiple objectives

7 A business's mission is its basic function in society expressed in terms of how it satisfies its stakeholders

8 B The objective is clearly time-bound and it is specific, as it is clear in which direction it wants activities to go. Being related to manufacturing it can be said to be relevant. However, it gives no indication of how the 'increase' is to be measured

CHAPTER 2

Managing a business

Introduction

Learning objectives

Tick off

- Identify the various functional areas within businesses ☐
- Show how the business functions assist in the achievement of business objectives ☐
- Identify the nature and functions of organisational management, human resources management and operations management ☐
- Show how the nature and functions of management are influenced by human behaviour ☐

Specific syllabus references for this chapter are: 1c, d.

Syllabus links

The material in this chapter will be developed further in this paper, and then in the Business Strategy paper at the Professional level.

Examination context

Questions on the nature of management, business functions and organisational behaviour could all easily appear in the exam.

Questions are likely to be set in multiple choice format; straight tests of knowledge and scenarios are equally likely.

1 What is management?

Section overview

- Management means getting things done through other people.
- Managers act on behalf of owners in the organisation.

Definition

Management: 'Getting things done through other people' (Stewart).

CHAPTER 2

We defined an organisation in Chapter 1 as 'a social arrangement for the controlled performance of collective goals.' This definition itself suggests the need for management.

- **Objectives** have to be set for the organisation
- Somebody has to **monitor progress and results** to ensure that objectives are met
- Somebody has to communicate and sustain **corporate values**, **ethics** and **operating principles**
- Somebody has to look after the interests of the **organisation's owners** and other **stakeholders**

In a **business** managers act, ultimately, on behalf of owners (shareholders). In practical terms, shareholders rarely interfere, as long as the business delivers profits year on year.

In a **public sector organisation**, management acts on behalf of the government. Politicians in a democracy are in turn accountable to the electorate. More of the objectives of a public sector organisation might be set by the 'owners' – ie the government – rather than by managers. The government might also tell senior managers to carry out certain policies or plans, thereby restricting their discretion.

2 Power, authority, responsibility, accountability and delegation

Section overview

- There are a number of significant forces at work in an organisation, which need to be managed. They include power, authority, responsibility, accountability and delegation.
- Power is the ability to get things done.
- Authority is the right to do something or to require someone else to do it.
- Responsibility is the obligation that someone has to do the thing that the person in authority over them has required.
- Accountability is the responsible person's liability to answer for what has happened to those with a legitimate interest in the matter.
- Delegation means giving someone else the responsibility and authority to do something, whilst remaining responsible and accountable for that thing being done properly.

2.1 What is needed for effective management?

Businesses have a large number of different activities to be co-ordinated, and large numbers of people whose co-operation and support is necessary for a manager to get anything done. As you have probably noticed if you have worked for any length of time, organisations rarely run like clockwork, and all depend on the directed energy of those within them. They need to be managed by **managers**.

To understand how managers can do their jobs effectively, we need to understand the differences between power, authority, responsibility, accountability and delegation.

2.2 Power

Definition

Power: The **ability** to get things done.

Power is not something a manager 'has' in isolation: it is exercised over other individuals or groups, and – to an extent – depends on their *recognising* the manager's power over them.

French and **Raven** (followed by Charles Handy) classified power into six types or sources.

Type of power	Description
Coercive power	The power of physical force or punishment. Physical power is rare in business organisations, but intimidation may feature, eg in workplace bullying.
Reward (or resource) power	Based on access to or control over valued resources. For example, managers have access to information, contacts and financial rewards for team members. The amount of resource power a manager has depends on the scarcity of the resource, how much the resource is valued by others, and how far the resource is under the manager's control.
Legitimate (or position) power	Associated with a particular position in the organisation. For example, a manager has the power to authorise certain expenses, or issue instructions, because the authority to do so has been formally delegated to her.
Expert power	Based on experience, qualifications or expertise. For example, accountants have expert power because of their knowledge of the tax system. Expert power depends on others recognising the expertise in an area which they need or value.
Referent (or personal) power	Based on force of personality, or 'charisma', which can attract, influence or inspire other people.
Negative power (*Handy*)	The power to disrupt operations: for example, by industrial action, refusal to communicate information, or sabotage.

Interactive question 1: Management power [Difficulty level: Intermediate]

Nisar Iqbal is a manager in the IT department of his firm. He has a degree in computer science and 14 staff reporting to him. What types of power can Nisar exert as a manager in order to make sure a project is completed on time?

See **Answer** at the end of this chapter.

2.3 Authority

Definition

Authority: The **right** to do something, or to ask someone else to do it and expect it to be done. Authority is thus another word for position or legitimate power.

Managerial authority is exercised in such areas as:

- **Making decisions within the scope of authority** given to the position. For example, a supervisor's authority is limited to his/her team and has certain limits. For items of expenditure more than a certain amount, the supervisor has to go to the manager
- **Assigning tasks** to subordinates, and expecting satisfactory performance of these tasks

2.4 Responsibility and accountability

Definitions

Responsibility: The **obligation** a person has to fulfil a task which s/he has been given.

Accountability: A person's **liability** to be called to account for the fulfilment of tasks s/he has been given by persons with a legitimate interest in the matter.

The terms reflect two sides of the same coin.

- A person is said to be **responsible for** a piece of work when he or she is required to ensure that the work is done
- The same person is said to be **accountable to** a superior when he or she is given work by that superior

One is thus accountable **to** a superior (or other persons with legitimate interest) **for** a piece of work for which one is responsible.

2.5 Delegation

The principle of **delegation** is that a manager may make subordinates **responsible for** work, but remains **accountable to** his or her own manager for ensuring that the work is done, that s/he retains overall responsibility. Appropriate decision-making **authority** must be delegated alongside responsibility.

We will come back to delegation at the end of this chapter.

3 Types of manager

Section overview

- Different types of manager have different types of authority.
- A manager may have line, staff, functional or project authority.

Types of manager in a business can be classified according to the types of **authority** they hold.

- A **line manager** has authority over a subordinate.
- A **staff manager** has authority in giving specialist advice to another manager or department, over which they have no line authority. Staff authority does not entail the right to make or influence decisions in the advisee department. An example might be a human resources manager advising a finance line manager on selection interviewing methods.
- A **functional manager** has functional authority, a hybrid of line and staff authority, whereby the manager has the authority, in certain circumstances, to direct, design or control activities or procedures in another department. An example is where a finance manager has authority to require timely reports from managers in other departments.
- A **project manager** has authority over project team members in respect of the project in progress; this authority is likely to be temporary (for the duration of the project) and the project team are likely still to have line managers who also have authority over them.

There are inevitable tensions involved in staff managers asserting staff authority in giving specialist advice to other managers.

Problem	Possible solution
The staff manager can **undermine** the **line manager's** authority, by empire building.	Clear demarcations for line, staff and functional managers should be created.
Lack of seniority: line managers may be more senior than staff managers.	Use functional authority (via policies and procedures). Experts should be seen as a resource, not a threat.
Expert staff managers may **lack realism**, going for technically perfect but commercially impractical solutions.	They should be fully aware of operational issues and communicate regularly with the line managers.
Staff managers **lack responsibility** for the success of their ideas.	They should be involved in implementing their suggestions and share accountability for outcomes.

4 The management hierarchy

Section overview

- The relationships of power, authority, responsibility, accountability and delegation together form a management hierarchy in most organisations, with a few managers holding the most power and authority towards the apex, with many managers holding less power and authority beneath them.
- Ultimately it is the manager at the very apex – the Chief Executive – who has ultimate authority and bears ultimate responsibility to the shareholders.

Businesses of any size develop a **management hierarchy**, with some management positions holding more power and authority than others, the less powerful managers being accountable to the more powerful ones, and the latter being responsible for the performance of the managers lower down the hierarchy. As in Figure 2.1, the hierarchy is usually represented as a pyramid, as top managers are far less numerous than direct operational staff.

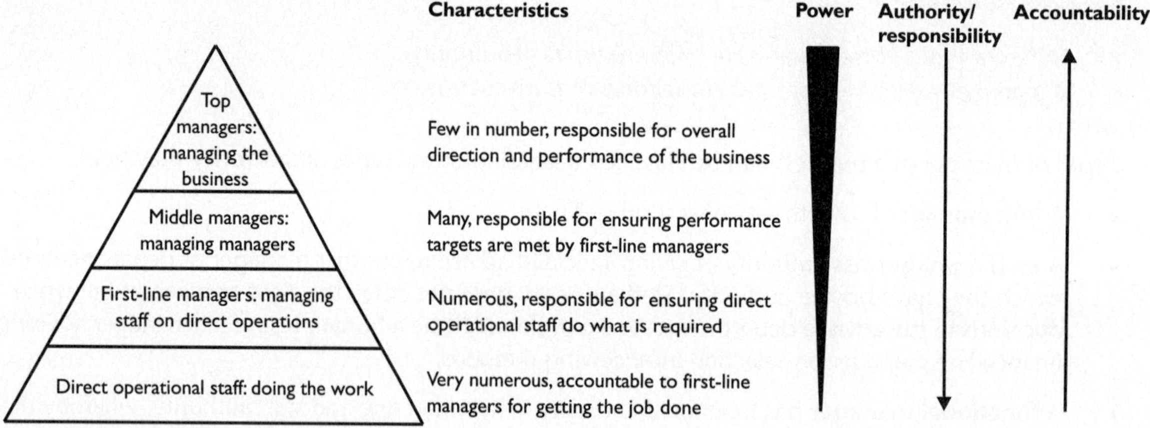

Figure 2.1: The management hierarchy

We shall see a great deal more about this in Chapter 3.

5 The management process

Section overview

- The process of management comprises planning, organising, controlling and leading.
- Planning involves setting detailed objectives and targets in the light of the overall objective, forecasts and resources.
- Plans should be constantly reviewed and updated in the light of actual performance.
- Organising involves identifying the processes, technology and people that are required and then allocating and co-ordinating the work.
- Controlling follows on from reviewing plans in the light of experience; control actions will often have to be taken to ensure that the overall objective can still be met.
- Leading means generating effort and commitment in a team.
- Feedback is an important part of the management process at every point.

5.1 The management process

The efforts of people in the business (in particular the activities of direct operational staff) need **organising**, and as we have seen it is the primary role of managers to 'get things done through other people' (according to Rosemary Stewart). This 'organising' role is actually part of a **management process** which comprises four main tasks: planning, organising, controlling and leading.

5.2 Planning

Following on from the business's overall objective, mission and goals, managers need to set the direction of the work to be done. This includes:

- Pinpointing specific aims
- Forecasting what is needed
- Looking at actual and potential resources
- Developing objectives, plans and targets
- Using feedback from the control part of the process to make necessary amendments to the plan (as we saw in Chapter 1 when we looked at Figure 1.2 Planning and control systems)

5.3 Organising

Managers allocate time and effort in such a way that the objectives, plans and targets are likely to be met. This includes:

- Defining what processes, technology and people are required
- Allocating and co-ordinating work

5.4 Controlling

Managers monitor events so they can be compared with the plan and remedial action can be taken if required.

5.5 Leading

Managers generate effort and commitment towards meeting objectives, including motivation of staff. We shall see more about this later in this chapter.

5.6 Putting the management process into action

Any problems foreseen at the **planning** stage, such as lack of staff, must be taken account of when deciding how activities should be **organised** so that, say, more staff are recruited. If, once the plan is put into action, it transpires that as well as too few staff there are not enough staff with the right skills, this **control** information must be **fed back** to the **planning** part of the cycle, where training programmes can be planned for implementation at the organising stage.

By means of this process, and the important element of leadership, the manager can take resources – staff, money, materials, equipment – and create the required outputs: goods, services, reputation, profit etc.

We shall look in more detail at the planning and control process in Chapter 7.

6 Managerial roles

Section overview

- Managers actually do a great many things in the course of the management process, namely handling data and information, dealing with people, and making decisions.
- Decisions have to be made regarding resource allocation, handling disturbances, negotiating, problem-solving and acting in an entrepreneurial way.

The management process sets out what managers have to achieve and how, but it does not as such describe what managers actually **do**. Mintzberg (1973) defined what managers do in terms of three key **roles**:

- The **informational** role (checking data received and passing it on to relevant people, as well as acting as the 'spokesperson' for his or her team in relation to other teams or his or her own manager)
- The **interpersonal** role (acting as leader for his or her own team, and linking with the managers of other teams)
- The **decisional** role. It is in this role that managers actually 'do' what we perceive as managing. In this role they:
  - **Allocate resources** to operations – for instance, deciding that three people are needed on an audit assignment
  - **Handle disturbances** – such as dealing with an awkward client, or sorting out a crisis in staffing caused by illness
  - **Negotiate** for what they need – this may be with more senior managers or with client staff
  - **Solve problems** that arise
  - **Act as entrepreneur** – spotting gaps in the market, or unmet needs in clients.

7 The importance of business culture to management

Section overview

- The organisation's culture has a very profound effect on how managers perform their roles.
- Culture incorporates the common assumptions, values and beliefs that people in an organisation share.
- Organisational culture varies depending on whether the business is inward or outward looking, and on whether there is a greater comparative need for flexibility or control.
- Internal process cultures look inwards and seek control over their environment.
- At the other extreme, open systems cultures look outwards and are very flexible about the effects of the environment.
- A human relations culture is inward-looking but is flexible as it focuses on the needs of people.
- A rational goal culture is very aware of the external environment but seeks to control it and its own processes.

CHAPTER 2

Managers have to operate within what is often referred to as the 'culture' of their particular business.

Definition

Culture: The common assumptions, values and beliefs that people share, 'the way we do things round here'.

Quinn (1995) emphasises two distinct tensions that affect the type of culture a particular business manifests:

- The tension between having **flexibility** and having **control**
- The tension between whether the business is **inward- or outward-looking**

Figure 2.2 allows us to identify four different cultural types, which may characterise entire businesses or just parts of businesses.

	Flexibility		
Inward-looking	Human relations culture	Open systems culture	**Outward-looking**
	Internal process culture	Rational goal culture	
	Control		

Figure 2.2: Types of business culture

Each cultural type can be briefly characterised as follows:

- **Internal process culture**: The business looks **inwards**, aiming to make its internal environment stable and **controlled**. Goals are known and unchanging, and there are defined methods, rules and procedures. Security, stability and order motivate staff. Example: public sector organisations.
- **Rational goal culture**: Effectiveness is defined as achieving goals that satisfy **external** requirements. The business is structured and controlled so as to deal effectively with the outside world. Competition and the achievement of goals motivate staff. Example: large established businesses.
- **Open systems culture**: The **external** environment is a source of energy and opportunity, but it is ever-changing and unpredictable. The business must be highly **flexible** and open to new ideas, so it is very adaptable in structure. Staff are motivated by growth, creativity and variety. Example: a new business unit working with fast-changing technology.
- **Human relations culture**: The business looks **inwards**, aiming to maintain its existence and the well-being of staff. Staff are motivated by a sense of belonging. Example: support service units

The type of culture manifested by an organisation affects the way in which it is managed, as we shall see.

Later in this study manual we shall consider how organisations can seek to ensure that they have an **ethical culture.**

8 Management models

Section overview

- Complex realities such as are found in any business of any size can be 'modelled' or described fully, so that their workings can be understood and the effects of future policies and decisions can be predicted.

8.1 What is a model?

Models are used in management theory to represent a complex reality, such as a client's business, which is then analysed and broken down into its constituent parts. Handy points out that management models:

- Help to explain the past, which in turn
- Helps us to understand the present, and thus
- To predict the future, leading to
- More influence over future events, and
- Less disturbance from the unexpected

Some management models are based on the fact that the culture of the business pervades everything it does. Of particular importance are the two control-oriented cultures that we saw above: rational goal and internal process.

8.2 The rational goal model of management

A business with a rational goal culture uses the reason *why* the business does something to make sure it is done as well as possible. This is a model of management that has been developed over about 100 years, since the days of Frederick Taylor's 'scientific management' model back in 1915. Taylor analysed factory work and came to the conclusion that in order for every worker to reach their state of maximum efficiency, managers needed to be in detailed control of every last part of the process. Individual initiative was not part of the equation; instead Taylor put forward **five 'principles' of scientific management**:

- Determine the one best way of doing a particular task
- Select the best person to do this task on the basis of their mental and physical capabilities
- Train the worker to follow the set procedure very precisely
- Give financial incentives to ensure the work is done in the prescribed way
- Give all responsibility to plan and organise work to the manager, not to the worker

Scientific management has come in and out of fashion over the years; there are strong elements of the model in some rational goal ideas commonly seen in organisations today:

- Systematic work methods
- Detailed division of labour
- Centralised planning and control
- 'Low involvement' employment relations, such as contract workers

We shall come back to scientific management ideas later in this chapter.

8.3 The internal process model of management

The internal process model looks at **how** the organisation is doing things, not at why. In businesses with an internal process model of management we tend to find:

- **Rationality** – use of the most efficient means to meet the business's objectives
- **Hierarchical lines of authority**; managers have closely defined areas of authority, and have none outside those areas

- Detailed **rules and procedures** – businesses which are subject to tight regulation and public scrutiny, such as those in the financial services sector, tend to have more rules and procedures
- **Division of labour** – tight limits are set on the areas of responsibility of staff
- **Impersonality** – appraisals of staff performance are based on objective criteria, not personal preference
- **Centralisation** (we shall come back to this in Chapter 3)

Businesses today operate in an environment which requires a high degree of control (because of regulations) but in which there is a high degree of competition. Therefore management will apply the principles of both the rational goal and the internal process models.

9 Business functions

Section overview

- The key functions in any business are marketing, operations/production, human resources and finance.

The functions that need to be performed in a business depend on many variables, such as what industry it is in, how geographically spread it is, and what its plans are for the future. Historically these functions have been identified generically as the following:

- **Marketing**, including sales and customer service
- **Operations** or **production**, usually including research and development (R&D), and procurement
- **Human resources**
- **Finance**

The finance function is a major focus of the *Business and Finance* syllabus and will be covered in Chapter 7 and throughout this Study Manual. Here we shall introduce a few of the principles that underlie the other functions.

10 Marketing management

Section overview

- Marketing is the management process which identifies, anticipates and supplies customer requirements efficiently and profitably. It forms one of the key functions in any business.
- A customer may buy goods and services but the person who uses them is called the consumer.
- Businesses may work in consumer or industrial markets.
- The elements of product marketing comprise the marketing mix, which entails price, product, place (distribution) and promotion. For services it also includes people, processes and physical evidence.
- Most markets require segmentation so that homogenous groups can be targeted.
- A business may have a marketing orientation, or it may be sales-, production- or product-orientated.
- Important issues related to product marketing include quality, reliability, packaging, branding, aesthetics, mix and servicing.
- The right price can make or break a product. Setting the price in the light of costs, competition, customers (demand) and corporate objectives is a key aspect of marketing management and one in which accountants very often play a supporting role.
- Making sure products are in the right place at the right time so that customers can buy them is vital.
- The key 'place' or distribution decision is whether to sell direct (higher margin, lower volume due to inaccessibility) or whether to go via intermediaries (lower margins, but higher volumes).

- Promotion incorporates advertising, sales promotions, public relations and personal selling via a sales team.
- Push techniques of promotion ensure that the product is there for the customer to buy; pull techniques persuade them to do so.

10.1 What is marketing?

Definition

Marketing: The set of human activities directed at facilitating and consummating exchanges. It therefore covers the whole range of a business's activities.

OR

Marketing: The management process which identifies, anticipates and supplies customer requirements efficiently and profitably.

A distinction can be made between:

- A **customer**, who purchases and pays for a good or service, and
- A **consumer**, who is the ultimate user of the good or service

Thus if a business is a manufacturer of corn flakes, its customers are wholesalers as well as supermarkets and small shops, but it is the consumer who eats the corn flakes.

10.2 Consumer and industrial markets

Markets can be analysed in terms of the product, or the end-user, or both. The most common distinction is between consumer and industrial markets.

Consumer markets are the markets for products and services bought by individuals for their own or family use. Goods bought by consumers in these markets can be categorised in several ways:

- **FMCGs** (fast-moving consumer goods). These are high volume, low unit value, fast repurchase, such as bread, baked beans.
- **Consumer durables**. These have low volume but high unit value. They may be further divided into
  - **White goods**, eg fridges, freezers
  - **Brown goods**, eg CD players, cars
  - **Soft goods**: these may be thought of as synonymous with consumer durables, eg clothes, bed linen
  - **Services**, eg dentist, doctor, holidays

A business which operates in the consumer market, selling to consumers, is often described as being in the 'business to consumers', or B2C market.

The main goods and services covered by **industrial markets** are shown below.

Raw materials	Processed materials and components	Capital goods	Supplies	Services
Iron ore	Steel	Machine tools	Stationery	Accountancy
Timber	Textiles	Computers	Carbide tips	Legal
Coal	Packing materials	Buildings	Lubricants	Distribution
Crude oil		Lorries		

Businesses operating in industrial markets are often described as 'business to business' or B2B.

10.3 The marketing mix and segmentation

Definition

Marketing mix: The set of controllable marketing variables that a firm blends to produce the response it wants in the target market (Kotler).

The most common way of presenting the marketing mix for tangible products is the **four 'P's**.

- **Product**: quality of the product as perceived by the potential customer. This involves an assessment of the product's suitability for its stated purpose (ie its features and benefits), its aesthetic factors, its durability, brand factors, packaging, associated services, etc.
- **Price**: prices to the customer, discount structures for the trade, promotion pricing, methods of purchase, alternatives to outright purchase.
- **Promotion**: advertisement of a product, its sales promotion, the company's public relations effort, salesmanship.
- **Place**: distribution channel decisions, website selling (e-tailing), location of outlets, position of warehouses, inventory levels, delivery frequency, geographic market definition, sales territory organisation.

Where the business is engaged in the provision of services, a further three Ps are involved, making 'the **seven Ps of services marketing**':

- **People:** the people employed by the service deliverer are uniquely important given they are likely to have regular interactions with customers. Service businesses therefore need to have excellent recruitment and selection policies, good training programmes (both in procedures and the service ethos), standard consistent operational procedures (eg airlines), the flexibility to enable staff to give good service, and effective motivational programmes.
- **Processes:** these often determine the structure of the 'service encounter'. There are some important 'moments of truth' that determine how effective a service is, such as enquiries and reservations before the service is granted, registration procedures, timing of when the service is consumed (the internet allows the purchase of many services to be done 24/7, for instance), and what happens after the service has been consumed.
- **Physical evidence**: this refers to items that give physical substance such as logos, staff uniforms and store layout/design – it gives the customer who buys a service 'something to show for it'.

How the elements are mixed varies enormously from product to product, and from business to business as can be seen below.

Company products/ Marketing mix variable	Internet clothes retailer	Major national drinks manufacturer	Mainframe computer manufacturer
Product	Similar to those of several other retailers, both internet and 'bricks and mortar'	Similar to those of several other manufacturers	Very advanced, subject to continual amendment, with a distinct place in the market
Price	A vital factor. Probably lower than similar physically retailed goods	Similar level and structure to that of several other manufacturers	Different from that of its broad competitors. Customer looks for service and 'value for money' rather than initial cost

Company products/ Marketing mix variable	Internet clothes retailer	Major national drinks manufacturer	Mainframe computer manufacturer
Promotion	Website is the sole source of orders and the major marketing expense	A high percentage of product cost. Use of TV and various press media. Sales promotions important	A low percentage of product cost. Use of trade press and up-market magazines and newspapers
	Sales. No sales people as such	A large team of selling-oriented, well-trained sales people	A large team of sales people trained to combine selling skills with good knowledge of the product and its use
Place (distribution)	No intermediaries. Distribution determined by postal and courier systems	Extensive use of wholesalers, retailers and licensees of premises. Frequent deliveries, regional warehouses, company owns its transport fleet	No intermediaries. Small vehicle fleet. Relatively infrequent deliveries. Little storage of finished items

A business operating in one market may vary the marketing mix for various **segments** of that market.

Definition

Market segmentation: The division of the market into homogeneous groups of potential customers who may be treated similarly for marketing purposes.

This segmentation allows the organisation to vary its marketing mix to each of the segments it caters for. For instance, Ford operates in the new car market but does not sell one car in one way to the whole market. It **segments** the market (separating it into various sub-markets which have shared characteristics) and then **targets** the consumers within the segment using varying marketing mixes. It places different emphasis on the mix variables depending on the segment targeted.

Segment of market	Target segment by placing most emphasis on
High income groups	Promotion – to create the image of quality, status
Families with children	Product – size, safety
Low income groups	Price – low: Product – reliability, economy

Interactive question 2: Product marketing [Difficulty level: Intermediate]

Pick a product that you see in the supermarket and try to identify how the various elements of the marketing mix have been used in marketing it to you.

See **Answer** at the end of this chapter.

10.4 Marketing orientation and its alternatives

Definition

Marketing orientation: a marketing-oriented business is one which accepts the needs of potential customers as the basis for its operations. Its success is seen as being dependent on developing and marketing products that satisfy those needs.

The implications of marketing orientation become much clearer when it is compared with alternatives.

- **Sales orientation**: Some businesses see their main purpose as being just to sell more of the product or services which they already have available. They may make full use of selling, pricing, promotion and distribution skills, but there is no systematic attempt to identify customer needs, nor to create products or services which will satisfy them.
- **Production orientation**: The business is just preoccupied with making as many units as possible. A classic instance is Henry Ford's statement 'you can have any colour [car] you like, so long as it's black'. Customer needs are subordinated to the desire to increase output.
- **Product orientation**: The company falls in love with its product, as is often seen with hi-tech industries, and it can no longer see that the sophisticated – and costly – specification is way beyond the needs of customers.

10.5 Product

Definition

Product: Anything that can be offered to a market for attention, acquisition, use or consumption that might satisfy a want or need. It includes physical objects, services, persons, places, organisations and ideas. Marketers tend to consider products not as 'things' with 'features' but packages of 'benefits' that satisfy a variety of consumer needs.

There are three main **elements of a product**:

- **Basic (or core) product** – a car. This looks at the perceived or real benefits to be gained from the product, eg Volvo cars satisfy safety/security needs, BMWs satisfy ego or status needs, etc
- **Actual product** – a Ford Focus
- **Augmented product** – Ford Focus with 0% finance or extended warranty. Essentially an augmented product can be thought of as having more features per £

General factors to be considered when taking a product from basic to actual and augmented include the following:

- **Quality and reliability** – often linked to the pricing decision, these are used for positioning the product. Level and consistency should be considered
- **Packaging** – is it functional (eg round a fridge) or part of the overall appeal (eg perfume)?
- **Branding** – this is often very important in highly competitive markets
- **Aesthetics** – smell, taste, appearance, etc
- **Product mix** – range of products, eg different Ford Focus models
- **Servicing/associated services** – are these required?

10.6 Price

At what level the product should be priced is highly relevant in any marketing mix. Price is particularly important as it is the only P producing revenue (the other three incur costs).

10.6.1 Influences on the business's pricing policy

- **Costs**: In order to make profits a business should ensure that its products are priced above their total cost, including their share of overheads. In the short term it may be acceptable to go below this if the price is still above the variable cost of producing one unit, thus ensuring a positive contribution towards the cost of overheads.
- **Competitors:** Only a monopoly can set any price it wants, and even this is often subject to government price controls and/or regulatory monitoring and approval. In very competitive markets the individual business has no choice, with the price being dictated by the market. The reality is usually somewhere between these two extremes. Relative pricing is extremely important in many markets, that is the price must be comparable to those of competitors.
- **Customers:** As with all other marketing decisions, a consideration of customer expectations is essential in setting prices. If possible, a business should try to determine exactly how customer demand is affected by changes in price (price elasticity), and therefore how many sales will result at a given price.
- **Corporate objectives**. Possible pricing objectives are:
  - To maximise profits
  - To achieve a target return on investment. This results in an approach based on adding something to the quantified cost to the business of providing the product
  - To achieve a target revenue figure
  - To achieve a target market share
  - To match the competition, rather than leading the market, where the market is very price-sensitive
  - To drive competitors out of the market through predatory pricing with a view to raising prices subsequently

We shall see more about market price and factors affecting demand in Chapter 13.

10.7 Place (distribution)

Providing customers with satisfying products at a price they like, while important, is not sufficient to ensure success. Such products must also be made available in adequate quantities, in the locations where customers expect to find them and at the times when customers want to buy them.

The basic decision to be made when considering distribution is whether to **sell direct**, often via the internet.

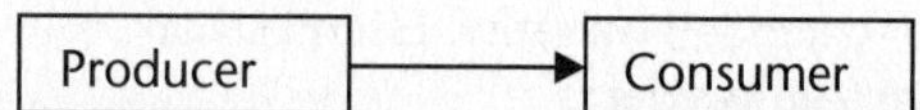

or to use intermediaries to give a longer distribution chain:

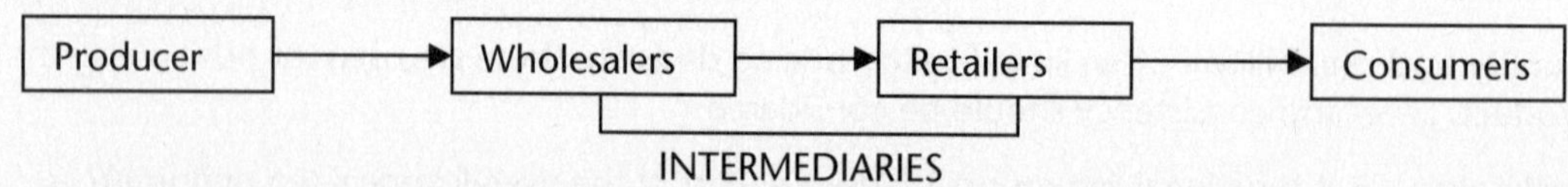

Advantages of selling direct	Advantages of using intermediaries
• No need to share profit margins	• More efficient logistically
• Control over ultimate sale	• Costs usually lower
• Speed of delivery to ultimate consumer likely to be quicker	• Consumers expect choice at point of sale
	• Producers may not have sufficient resources to sell direct

10.8 Promotion

Promotion is all about communication, thus informing customers about the product and persuading them to buy it. There are four main types of **promotion ('the communication mix')**:

- Advertising
- Sales promotion (such as 'buy one, get one free' offers)
- Public relations; and
- Personal selling.

We may distinguish two elements in promotion in Figure 2.3.

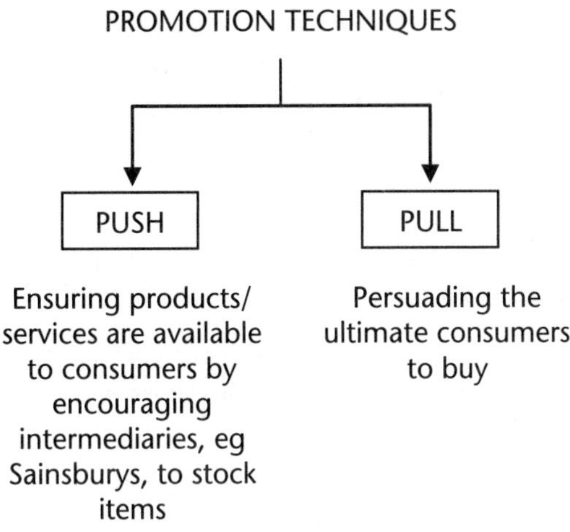

Figure 2.3 Push and pull promotion techniques

When determining its promotion package, the business should consider the customer and the ultimate consumer (in a B2C market). In a B2B market, the business needs to consider buyer, customer and user: these may be one and the same, but if not, all three have to be satisfied:

- The business = the customer
- Its purchasing manager = the buyer
- A direct operational worker = the user

11 Operations management

Section overview

- Operations management (or production management) means creating the goods or services that the business supplies to customers by transforming inputs into outputs.
- The key dimensions are the Four Vs: volume, variety, variation in demand and visibility
- The key variables that must be balanced in order to deliver effective operations are the overall level of demand for the goods and services, resources, capacity, inventory levels and performance levels of the processes required.
- R&D involves pure and/or applied research, and/or development. Applied research and development may be into products or processes.
- Procurement involves acquiring goods and services in the right procurement mix, as to: quantity, quality, price and lead time.

11.1 Operations and production management

Definition

Operations (or production) management: Creating as required the goods or services that the business is engaged in supplying to customers by being concerned with the design, implementation and control of the business's processes so that inputs (materials, labour, other resources, information) are transformed into output products and services.

All operations involve a transformation process, but they can differ in four different ways or dimensions, referred to as the 'four Vs' of operations: **volume, variety, variation** in demand and **visibility**. Each of these affects the way in which an operation will be organised and managed.

Volume: Operations differ in the volume of inputs they handle and the volume of output they produce.

- High volume might lend itself to a capital-intensive operation, with specialisation of work and well-established systems for getting the work done. Unit costs should be low.
- Low volume means that each member of staff will have to perform more than one task, so that specialisation is not achievable. Unit costs of output will be higher than with a high volume operation.

Variety: This refers to the range of products or services an operation provides, or the range of inputs handled. For example, an operation might produce goods to customer specification, or it might produce a small range of standard items.

- High variety: the operation needs to be flexible and capable of adapting to individual customer needs. The work may therefore be complex, and unit costs will be high.
- Low variety: the operation should be well-defined, with standardisation, regular operational routines and low unit costs.

Variation in demand: Demand might vary with the time of the year (eg in the tourist industry) or even the time of day (eg telecoms traffic, commuter travel services). Variations in demand might be predictable, or unexpected, and in degree it may be highly variable or not so variable at all.

- High variation (fluctuating demand): the operation has a problem with capacity utilisation so it will try to anticipate variations in demand and alter its capacity accordingly (eg the tourist industry takes on part-time staff during peak demand periods). Unit costs are likely to be high because facilities and staff are under-utilised in off-peak periods.
- Low variation (stable demand): the operation should achieve a high level of capacity utilisation, and unit costs will accordingly be lower.

Visibility: This is the extent to which an operation is exposed to its customers, and can be seen by them. Some operations are partly visible to the customer and partly invisible: this distinction is often made in terms of 'front office' and 'back office' operations.

- High visibility calls for staff with good communication and inter-personal skills. More staff are needed and so the operation is more expensive to run. Customer satisfaction with the operation will be heavily influenced by perception (eg customers will be dissatisfied if they have to wait), and staff need high customer contact skills. Unit costs of a visible operation are likely to be high.
- Low visibility means that there is a time lag between production and consumption, allowing the operation to utilise its capacity more efficiently. Customer contact skills are not important, and unit costs should be low.

Operations management is concerned therefore with **balancing** key variables:

- External and internal **demand** for goods and services
- **Resources**
- **Capacity** of the long-term assets of the business such as machinery, buildings and computer systems, and of the other assets of the business such as people (staff)
- **Inventory** levels
- Performance of the **process** which creates the goods or services

11.2 Research and development (R&D)

The research and development (R&D) function may involve **pure research** and/or **applied research** and/or **development.**

Definitions

Pure research: original research to obtain new scientific or technical knowledge or understanding. There is no obvious commercial or practical end in view.

Applied research: research which has an obvious commercial or practical end in view.

Development: the use of existing scientific and technical knowledge to produce new (or substantially improved) products or systems, prior to starting commercial production operations.

Applied research and also development may be intended to improve **products** or **processes.**

- **Product research:** finding new and improved products for the market. The new product development (NPD) process must be carefully controlled; although new products are a major source of competitive advantage, they can cost a great deal of money to bring to market.
- **Process research: developing new and better ways of producing** the goods/services

The R&D function is sometimes seen as part of the operations function (say if its focus is on process research), sometimes as part of the marketing function (especially if its focus is NPD), and sometimes as a separate function entirely.

11.3 Procurement

Definition

Procurement: the acquisition of goods and/or services at the best possible total cost of ownership, in the right quantity and quality, at the right time, in the right place and from the right source for the direct benefit or use of the business.

Procurement may be part of the operations function of a business or it may be a function on its own. Its object should be to obtain the best **procurement mix,** comprising four elements.

- **Quantity**: the size and timing of purchase orders will be dictated by the balance between:
  - **Time:** delays in production caused by insufficient inventories
  - **Cost of holding inventories**: tied up capital, storage space, deterioration, insurance, risk of pilferage
- **Quality**: The quality of input resources affects the quality of outputs and the efficiency of the operations/production function. For instance the production department will need to be consulted about the quality of goods required for a manufacturing process, and the marketing department about the quality of goods acceptable to customers of a shop.

- **Price**: Favourable short-term trends in prices may influence the procurement decision, but it should really have an eye to the best value over a period of time – considering quality, delivery, urgency of order, inventory-holding requirements and so on.
- **'Lead time'**: this is the time between placing and delivery of an order, and it can be crucial to efficient inventory control and production planning. The reliability of suppliers' delivery arrangements must therefore be assessed.

12 Human resource management

Section overview

- Managing human resources means creating, developing and maintaining an effective workforce which matches the business's requirements and which responds effectively to the environment.
- HRM functions include planning and control of personnel levels; job design; recruitment and selection; training and development; performance appraisal; disciplinary procedures; remuneration decisions; grievance and dispute handling; compliance with legal and other standards, including those related to health and safety; communication with employees; counselling employees; maintaining information and records on personnel; encouraging workforce diversity.
- Hard approaches to HRM focus on workers as resources; soft approaches emphasise that they are human, with short- and long-term needs and goals.
- Harvard's four Cs model of HRM suggests that it should achieve: commitment, competence, congruence and cost-effectiveness in the workforce.

12.1 What is human resource management (HRM)?

Definition

Human resource management: 'The creation, development and maintenance of an effective workforce, matching the requirements of the business and responding to the environment' (Naylor).

Some workforce-related functions are likely to be the responsibility of a human resource department alone, such as:

- Personnel planning and control
- Production of job descriptions and person specifications in terms of what is needed regarding experience, skills and education
- Development of policies for compliance with legal and other employment standards
- Development of training courses
- Designing remuneration packages and drawing up employment contracts

Many aspects of human resource management however are also the responsibility of line managers in charge of employees' day-to-day work. These include:

- Performance appraisal
- Discipline
- Identifying training needs
- Recruitment and selection

12.2 Different approaches to HRM

Hard and **soft** approaches to HRM have been identified, representing opposite ends of the spectrum.

- The **hard approach** emphasises the **resources** element of HRM. Human resources are planned and developed to meet the wider objectives of the business, as with any other resource such as materials or money. It involves managing the functions of HRM (set out below) to maximise employee effectiveness and control staff costs.
- The **soft approach** emphasises the **human** element of HRM. It is concerned with employee relations, the development of individual skills and the welfare of staff. It is exemplified in developing:
  - **Short-term** commitment, competence, congruence and cost-effectiveness (the four Cs model, see below)
  - **Long-term** individual well-being, organisational effectiveness and societal well-being

12.3 The Harvard four Cs model of HRM

The four Cs model was developed at Harvard as a means of investigating HRM issues in a wider environmental context rather than merely as a set of functions as listed above. It argues that HRM policies need to be derived from a critical analysis of:

- **Stakeholder demands**, including employees as one legitimate stakeholder group
- **Situational factors** (eg labour market conditions, management style, technology, ownership, competitive conditions)

The model suggests that the effectiveness of HRM should be evaluated under four headings:

1 **Commitment**. Assesses employees' motivation, loyalty and job satisfaction. These factors are likely to measure an employee's commitment to a business. Measures can include labour turnover (how many people leave in a period compared with how many on average are employed), absenteeism, exit interviews, and satisfaction surveys.

2 **Competence**. Relates to employees' skills, abilities and potential. These may be measured by a skills inventory and appraisal system. The objective of HRM policies in this area should be to attract, retain, motivate, train and promote the right people.

3 **Congruence**. This is a measure of the extent to which management and employees share a common vision for the business and act consistently to attain that vision. Evidence of congruence can include absence of grievances, conflicts and strikes, and the state of industrial relations.

4 **Cost-effectiveness**. Concerns operational efficiency and productivity. Outputs are aimed to be achieved at the lowest input cost. Labour cost and effectiveness by comparison to competitors may be a measure of HRM achievement in this area.

13 Introduction to organisational behaviour

Section overview

- Organisational behaviour describes individual and group behaviour in organisations.
- Organisational behaviour is affected by many variables, only some of which have obvious manifestations (they appear above the waterline in the organisational iceberg). These overt variables include customers, organisational goals, technology, physical facilities, organisational design, financial resources, overt competence and skills, and rules and regulations.
- There are also some very important variables which are not usually physically manifested but which are capable of undermining an organisation. These covert variables include attitudes, patterns of communication, informal team processes, personalities, conflict, political behaviour and underlying competencies and skills.
- It can be helpful to see an organisation in terms of one or more of Morgan's metaphors: a machine, an organism, a brain, a culture, a political system, a psychic prison, flux and transformation, and an instrument of domination.
- Important models of human behaviour in organisations include Taylor's scientific management theory, and McGregor's Theory X and Theory Y. Taylor and Theory X both emphasise the importance of remuneration as a key need and therefore motivator of people.
- Maslow's more complex content theory of the hierarchy of people's needs specifies that people's behaviour stems from their desire to fulfil their needs, but that once certain needs (eg for a good level of pay) are fulfilled they no longer motivate.
- Herzberg goes one further to say that remuneration is simply a hygiene factor: it can demotivate but does not of itself motivate people to fulfil their true potential. This can only be achieved by motivator factors, such as recognition, challenge, responsibility and advancement.
- Teams or groups of people in organisations who communicate with each other and who have a leader, a common sense of identity, a common aim, group norms of behaviour are often very effective.
- Groups go through a number of stages as they develop: forming, storming, norming and performing (Tuckman).
- In an active work group there are a number of key roles, including those of the leader, shaper, 'plant', evaluator, resource-investigator, company worker, team worker and finisher (Belbin).
- The effectiveness of a manager is determined by the degree of autonomy and authority they have, and what sort of leadership style they manifest.
- Leadership style varies from being exploitative and authoritative to being participative. A manager who subscribes to McGregor's Theory X will favour the former, while a manager who favours Theory Y will veer towards the latter.
- Delegation is a very important means by which managers get things done but it has drawbacks as well as advantages.

13.1 What is organisational behaviour?

Definition

Organisational behaviour: The study and understanding of individual and group behaviour in an organisational setting in order to help improve organisational performance and effectiveness (Mullins).

Organisational behaviour is not about **human behaviour** alone, but about how people's behaviour interlinks with the business's **formal structure**, the **tasks** to be undertaken, the **technology** and **processes** used, the **management process** and the **external environment.**

13.2 The organisational iceberg

A useful image for how human behaviour is affected by many variables and is manifested in organisational behaviour is put forward by Hellriegel, Slocum and Woodman as the '**organisational iceberg**' (see figure 2.4 below).

'One way to recognise why people behave as they do at work is to view an organisation as an iceberg. What sinks ships isn't always what sailors can see, but what they can't see.'

In other words, as well as the **formal aspects** of a business which one can see 'above the waterline' (they are 'overt'), there are many **behavioural aspects** which one cannot see as such (they are 'covert', or under the water). It is these covert aspects which tend to cause the most problems!

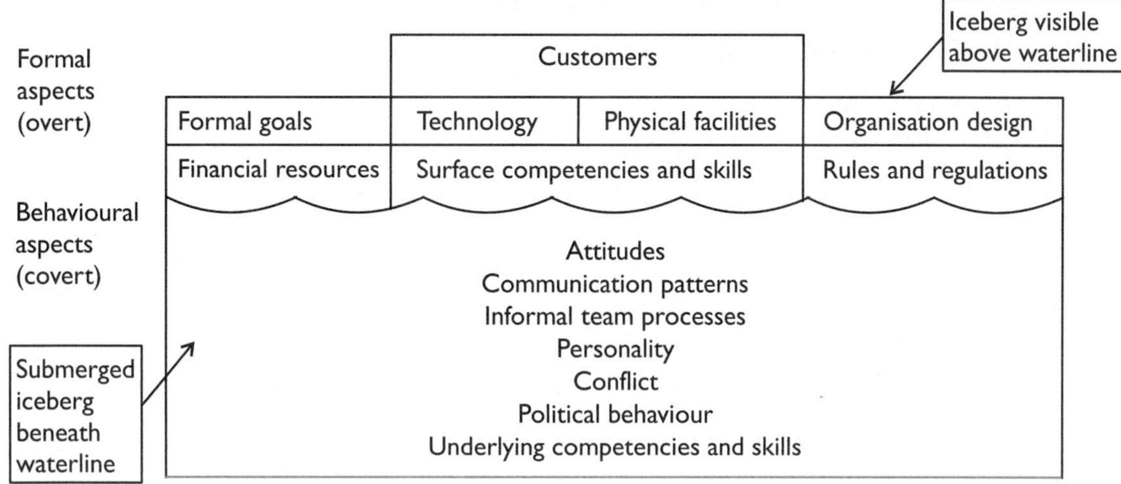

Figure 2.4 The organisational iceberg

13.3 Organisational metaphors

In order to help us understand the complex nature of life in businesses, Morgan developed a range of metaphors, likening the business to a number of different things in order to bring out certain characteristics of organisational behaviour. Note that some or all of the metaphors may be applied to the same business – they are mostly not mutually exclusive.

View the business as:	The business is seen as:
A machine	A set of efficient operations in a routine, reliable and predictable context; effective when business has a stable and protected environment
An organism	A living, highly adaptable system; effective when business operates in a turbulent and dynamic environment
A brain	Inventive, rational, flexible and creative; effective when business needs intelligent changes and the ability to learn
A culture	A complex system made up of unique combinations of ideologies, values, rituals and systems of belief and practice; effective particularly when contemplating changes to the business
A political system	A pattern of authority, power, superior-subordinate relationships and conflicting interests; helps to understand the practical reality of getting things done, or often not getting things done, in a business
A psychic prison	A set of illusions about what has happened and is happening; helps to understand why businesses do not always act rationally
Flux and transformation	A combination of permanent and changing features; effective particularly when contemplating changes to the business
An instrument of domination	Power struggles which lead to the business pursuing the goals of the few, not the many; again, helpful in understanding why things do or do not get done

13.4 Models of human behaviour

Early writers, such as Taylor, stated that people were similar and could be treated in a standardised fashion. McGregor, in contrast to Taylor, found that individuals did behave differently from each other. As individuals are different, what motivates each individual will differ from person to person.

13.4.1 Taylor's model: scientific management

Taylor made three basic assumptions about human behaviour at work:

- People are rational economic animals concerned with maximising their economic gain
- People respond as individuals, not groups
- People can be treated in a standardised fashion, like machines

Taylor's conclusions were as follows:

- Main motivator: high wages
- Manager's job: tell workers what to do
- Workers' jobs: do what they are told and get paid

Interactive question 3: Human behaviour **[Difficulty level: Intermediate]**

Taylor wrote his *Principles of Scientific Management* in 1911. How relevant is it today?

See **Answer** at the end of this chapter.

13.4.2 McGregor's model: Theory X and Theory Y

McGregor developed two theories, X and Y. Each one represents a different set of assumptions about how people are. He did not imply that one or other theory typifies all people. X and Y are two extremes with a whole spectrum of values between the two.

Theory X

- Individuals dislike work and avoid it where possible
- Individuals lack ambition, dislike responsibility and prefer to be led
- A system of coercion, control and punishment is needed to achieve business objectives
- Above all, the individual desires security

Theory Y

- Physical and mental effort in work is as natural as rest or play
- Commitment to objectives is driven by rewards – self-actualisation is the most important reward (see Maslow's hierarchy below)
- External control and threats are not the only way to achieve objectives – self-control and direction are very important
- People learn to like responsibility
- The intellectual potential of the average human is only partially utilised – it needs to develop further

In order to understand 'what' motivates people we shall look first at content theories of motivation, then focus on creating conditions that meet individuals' needs.

13.5 Motivation

Definition

Motivation: The degree to which a person wants certain behaviours and chooses to engage in them.

Motivated workers are characterised by:

- Higher productivity
- Better quality work with less waste
- A greater sense of urgency
- More feedback and suggestions made for improvement
- More feedback demanded from superiors

Clearly these are desirable features to have. Research has shown that motivated employees will work at 80–95% of their ability whereas employees lacking motivation will typically work at 30% of their ability. Demotivated workers are likely to become alienated.

13.5.1 Maslow's content theory: the hierarchy of needs

One way of understanding individual behaviour is in terms of the individual's **needs**, which may be conscious or subconscious. The basic model is in Figure 2.5.

Figure 2.5: Basic model of need-driven behaviour

Abraham Maslow (*Motivation and Personality* (1954)) suggested a **hierarchy** of such needs to explain an individual's motivation.

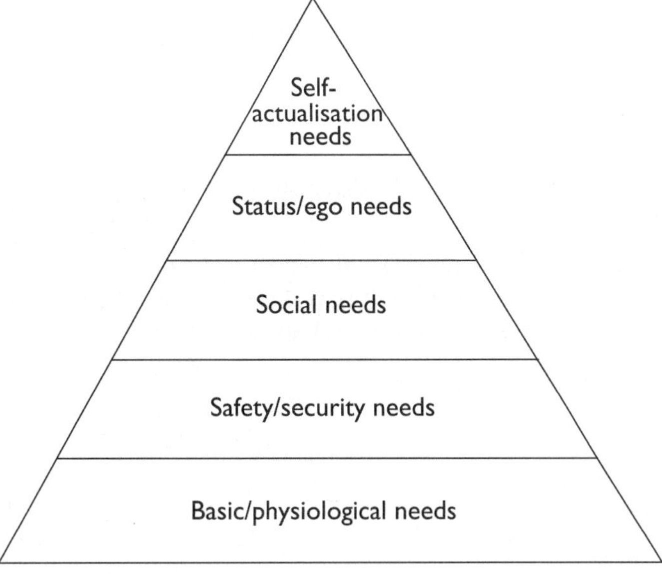

Figure 2.6: Maslow's hierarchy of needs

CHAPTER 2

- A person will start at the bottom of the hierarchy or pyramid and will initially seek to satisfy basic physiological needs – food, shelter, clothing etc
- Once these needs are satisfied they no longer motivate and the individual concerned moves up to the next level; safety/security needs
- Safety needs could encompass physical safety (eg wearing a hard hat on a building site) and/or protection against unemployment and the consequences of sickness, as well as being safeguarded against unfair treatment
- Again, once these needs are satisfied (eg by company rules re dismissal, health and safety, pension policies etc) they no longer motivate and the person moves up to the next level in the hierarchy
- Social needs recognise that people want to belong to a group. Being a member of an effective team, or enjoying good social interaction with colleagues, satisfies these needs so they no longer motivate, and the individual moves up to the next level in the hierarchy
- Status/ego needs involve the desire to have the respect and esteem of others. This could be satisfied, for example, by gaining a promotion
- Self-actualisation needs are concerned with what people think about themselves, whether they feel that their lives are worthwhile and that they have meaning. For many this can only be satisfied by ongoing success and new challenges

Needs may be met in or out of the workplace. For example, a person who is captain of a local sports team may not feel the need to engage so much in social activities at work.

Maslow's hierarchy does not mention money in its list of specific factors (social needs etc). One of the important emphases of the theory was on the significance of non-financial motivators. However, Maslow did see money as a contributory factor – ie money itself is not important except where it helps one satisfy the basic and safety needs.

While money is likely to be very important in satisfying basic physiological needs it is only important regarding status needs if status symbols such as BMWs, Rolex watches, etc are valued by others.

13.5.2 Herzberg's content theory: hygiene and motivating factors

Herzberg (*Work and the Nature of Man*) found that the factors causing motivation and positive job satisfaction were not simply the opposites of factors causing demotivation and dissatisfaction.

This led him to suggest a two-step approach to motivation and satisfaction, as shown in Figure 2.7.

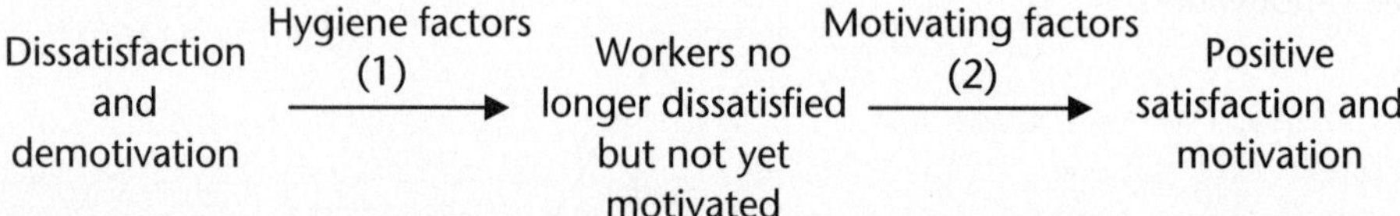

Figure 2.7: Hygiene (1) and motivating (2) factors

Hygiene factors are involved in dealing with dissatisfaction (step (1)) but **motivating factors** are needed to ensure actual motivation (step (2)).

Just as hygiene may prevent disease but is insufficient to make people healthy, so dealing with 'hygiene factors' will prevent dissatisfaction but will not necessarily lead to motivated workers. **Hygiene factors** are concerned with the context of the job rather than its content:

- Company policy and administration
- Supervision
- Salary
- Relationship with other staff
- Working conditions

Motivating factors are concerned with the content of people's jobs and need to be addressed to ensure motivation. They include:

- A sense of achievement
- Recognition
- Challenging work
- Responsibility
- Advancement
- The job itself

One of the most significant aspects of Herzberg's findings was the classification of salary as a hygiene factor, that is that increasing salary would reduce dissatisfaction but would not motivate workers other than perhaps as a short-term KITA ('kick in the ass'). Like Maslow, Herzberg emphasised the importance of **non-financial motivators.**

This was in contrast to the prevailing thought of the time that would attempt to deal with problems regarding motivation by paying people more.

Note that hygiene factors are concerned with satisfying lower-level Maslow needs (basic, safety, social) whereas motivating factors are more concerned with higher Maslow needs (status and self-actualisation).

13.6 Group behaviour

Definition

Group: A collection of people with the following characteristics:

- Common sense of identity
- Common aim or purpose
- Existence of group norms (ie expected/accepted standards of behaviour)
- Communication within the group
- The presence of a leader

13.6.1 The usefulness of groups

As far as businesses are concerned, groups are used to:

- Bring together several skills
- Plan and organise
- Solve problems/take decisions
- Distribute information
- Arbitrate or make awards
- Co-ordinate between departments

As far as individuals in businesses are concerned, groups are useful to:

- Satisfy social and status needs (Maslow)
- Give support, and
- Provide social contact and personal relationships

13.6.2 Stages of group development

Tuckman formulated four stages through which groups proceed.

- **Forming**. At this initial stage, the group is no more than a collection of individuals who are seeking to define the purpose of the group and how it will operate
- **Storming**. Most groups go through this **conflict** stage. Here, preconceptions are challenged, and norms of attitude, behaviour etc are challenged and rejected. Members compete for chosen roles within the group (eg leader, comedian). If successful, this stage will have forged a stronger team with greater knowledge of each other and their objectives
- **Norming.** This stage establishes the norms under which the group will operate. Members experiment and test group reaction as the norms become established. Typically, the norming stage will establish how the group will take decisions, behaviour patterns, level of trust and openness, individuals' roles, and so on
- **Performing**. Once this final stage has been reached the group is capable of operating to full potential, since the difficulties of adjustment, leadership contests etc should have been resolved

Tuckman suggested that groups are inefficient at the forming and storming stages, become more efficient at the norming stage but really need to reach the performing stage for maximum efficiency.

13.6.3 Team roles

Belbin observed that people adopt one or more of the following eight roles when placed within a particular type of group context, this is a team.

- **The leader** – co-ordinating (not imposing) and operating through others
- **The shaper** – committed to the task; may be aggressive and challenging; will also always promote activity
- **The plant** – thoughtful and thought-provoking
- **The evaluator** – analytically criticises others' ideas; brings team down to earth
- **The resource-investigator** – not a new ideas person but tends to pick up others' ideas and adds to them; is usually a social type of person who often acts as a bridge to the outside world
- **The company worker** – turns general ideas into specifics; is practical and efficient; tends to be an administrator handling the scheduling aspects
- **The team worker** – concerned with the relationships within the team; is supportive and defuses potential conflict situations
- **The finisher** – unpopular, but a necessary individual: the progress chaser ensuring that timetables are met

Belbin suggested that an effective team will have each personality type represented, subject to the following:

- Only one leader and/or shaper is required
- Equal numbers of plants and evaluators
- Equal numbers of company workers and team workers
- Not too many finishers (probably one is enough)

Belbin later suggested an additional role: **the specialist**, brought in from outside the team.

13.7 Leadership style

The effectiveness of any given manager will be influenced by their:

- **Authority**: having sufficient rights to control and judge the actions of subordinates
- **Autonomy**: giving subordinates necessary and reasonable freedom of action to carry out their roles
- **Leadership**: exercising the power conferred by right in such a way as to win a willing and positive response from subordinates

There has been extensive research into 'managerial effectiveness' and numerous attempts to describe/identify the 'best' leadership 'style' to adopt.

13.7.1 Likert's authoritative – participative continuum

Likert identified four basic leadership styles, in Figure 2.8.

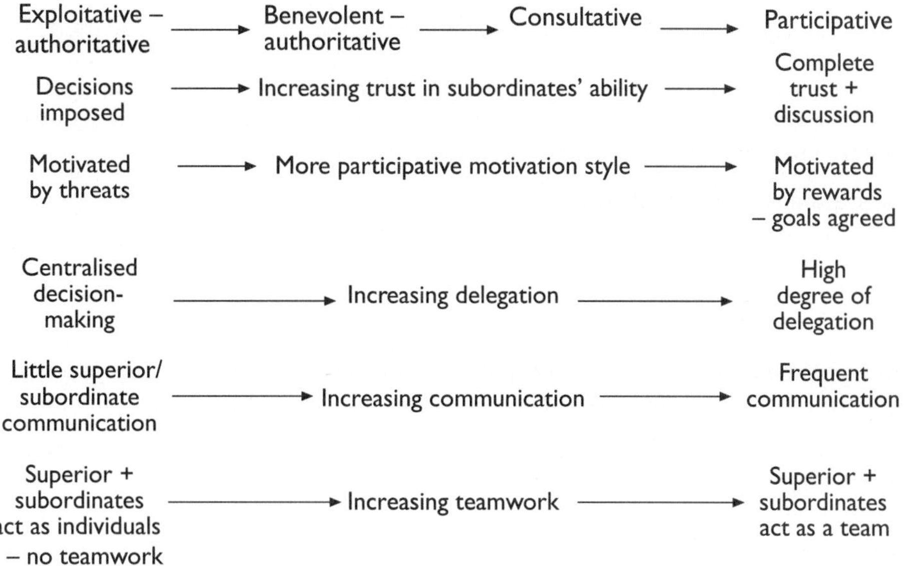

Figure 2.8: Likert's four leadership styles

- **Exploitative-authoritative**
  - Decisions are imposed by managers on subordinates
  - Subordinates are motivated by threats
  - Authority is centralised with minimal delegation
  - There is little communication between superior and subordinate
  - There is no teamwork (ie managers and subordinates do not act as a team)
- **Benevolent-authoritative**
  - Leadership is by a condescending form of the master–servant relationship
  - Subordinates are motivated by rewards
  - There is some degree of delegation of responsibility
  - There is little communication between superior and subordinate
  - There is relatively little teamwork
- **Consultative**
  - Superiors have substantial but not complete trust in their subordinates
  - Motivation is by rewards and some involvement in objective-setting
  - There is an increasing degree of delegation
  - There is some communication between superior and subordinate
  - There is a moderate amount of teamwork
- **Participative**
  - Superiors have complete confidence in subordinates
  - Motivation is by rewards and participation in objective-setting
  - There is a high degree of delegation
  - There is much communication between superior and subordinate
  - There is a substantial amount of teamwork

Likert considered the participative style to be ideal for the profit-oriented and human-conscious business, and said that all businesses should adopt this style. Other writers disagree, arguing that under certain circumstances a form of authoritarian management works best, eg in the small entrepreneurial business.

Likert also identified four **characteristics of effective managers.**

1 **Employee-centred** rather than work-oriented
2 Set **high standards** but are **flexible** in terms of methods to use to achieve those standards
3 Natural **delegators** with high levels of **trust**
4 Encourage **participative** management

Interactive question 4: Management effectiveness [Difficulty level: Intermediate]

Consider a manager for whom you have worked in the past, or perhaps the manager of the audit on which you are currently engaged. Consider objectively how effective that manager was, and try to identify what in particular the manager was/is good/bad at.

See **Answer** at the end of this chapter.

13.7.2 McGregor's Theory X/Theory Y

If a manager believes McGregor's Theory X, then he or she is more likely to adopt a **coercive, dictatorial approach** to leadership. Employees will be seen as a barrier to be overcome.

If Theory Y is believed, then employees are seen as having great potential and the manager's role is to help people to realise that potential.

13.7.3 Blake & Mouton's managerial grid

The **managerial grid** put forward by Blake and Mouton allows us to map a particular manager's leadership style according to where it features on two scales: concern for people, and concern for getting the task done.

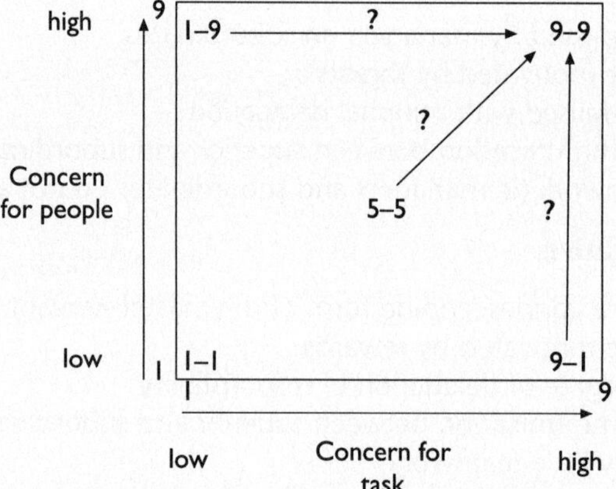

Figure 2.9: Blake and Mouton's Managerial Grid® (republished in 1991 as the Leadership Grid)

Managers at each of the five points marked can be characterised as follows:

9–9 Participative (team manager). High productivity as a result of the integration of task and human requirements.

9–1 Authoritarian. People are treated like machines to get the task done.

1–9 'Country club'. Keep everyone happy, don't worry about the task.

5–5 Average. No-one over-exerting themselves.

1–1 Impoverished. No concern for either people or getting the task done. Should these people be managers?

13.8 Delegation

Definition

Delegation: Delegation involves giving a subordinate responsibility and authority to carry out a given task, while the manager retains overall responsibility.

Advantages of delegation:

- Manager can be relieved of less important activities
- It enables decisions to be taken nearer to the point of impact and without the delays caused by reference upwards
- It gives businesses a chance to meet changing conditions more flexibly
- It makes the subordinate's job more interesting
- It allows for career development and succession planning
- It brings together skills and ideas
- Team aspect is motivational
- It allows performance appraisal

Problems caused by poor delegation:

- Too much supervision can waste time and be demotivating for the subordinate
- Too little supervision can lead to subordinates feeling abandoned and may result in an inferior outcome if they are not completely happy with what they are doing
- Manager tries to delegate full responsibility, that is s/he uses delegation to 'pass the buck'
- Manager only delegates boring work
- Manager tries to delegate impossible tasks because s/he cannot do it themselves
- Managers may not delegate enough because they fear their status is being undermined, and they want to stay in control
- Subordinates may lack the skills and training required

Summary and Self-test

Summary (1/2)

Procurement
Quality
Quantity
Price
Lead time

R&D
Pure
Applied
Development

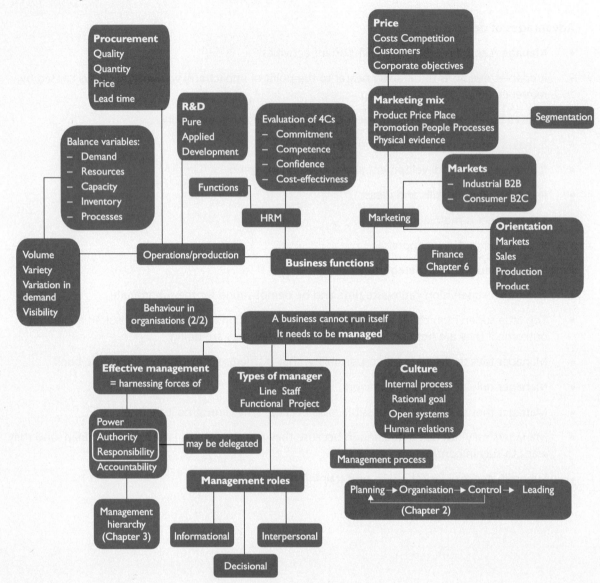

Price
Costs Competition
Customers
Corporate objectives

Marketing mix
Product Price Place
Promotion People Processes
Physical evidence

Segmentation

Balance variables:
- Demand
- Resources
- Capacity
- Inventory
- Processes

Evaluation of 4Cs
- Commitment
- Competence
- Confidence
- Cost-effectivness

Functions

HRM

Markets
- Industrial B2B
- Consumer B2C

Marketing

Orientation
Markets
Sales
Production
Product

Volume
Variety
Variation in demand
Visibility

Operations/production

Business functions

Finance
Chapter 6

Behaviour in organisations (2/2)

A business cannot run itself
It needs to be **managed**

Effective management
= harnessing forces of

Types of manager
Line Staff
Functional Project

Culture
Internal process
Rational goal
Open systems
Human relations

Power
Authority
Responsibility
Accountability

may be delegated

Management process

Planning → Organisation → Control → Leading
(Chapter 2)

Management roles

Management hierarchy (Chapter 3)

Informational

Interpersonal

Decisional

Summary (2/2)

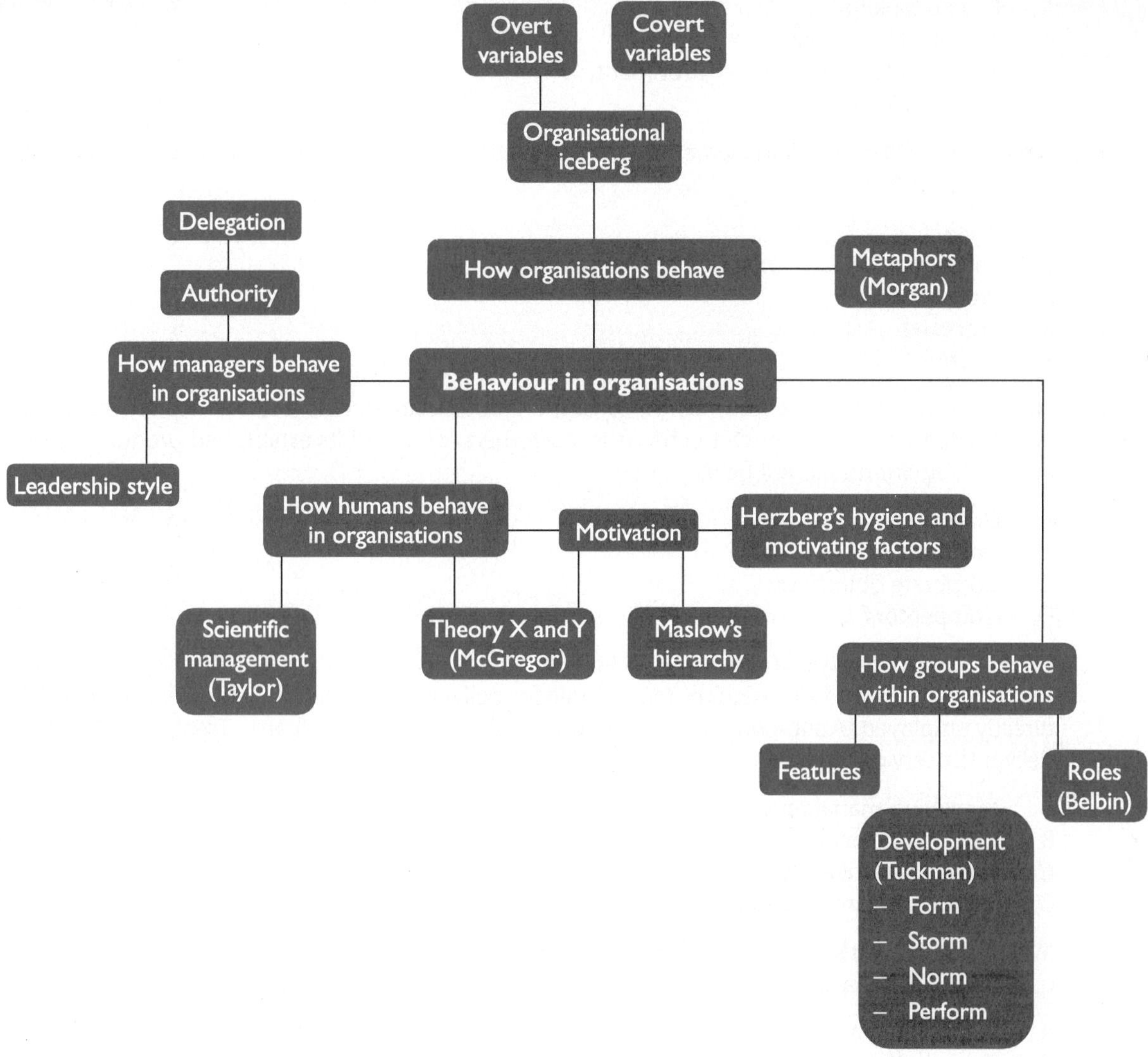

Self-test

Answer the following questions.

1 When a manager delegates authority and responsibility for a task, they also delegate full accountability. True or false?

2 Cedric is an IT specialist responsible for a new database which is used by all functions in the organisation. If Kara, a human resources manager, attempted to alter the database parameters Cedric could prevent her from doing so by exercising:

A Line authority
B Staff authority
C Functional authority
D Project authority

3 Ethel has been given responsibility for identifying the processes, technology and up to five people required to complete a particular project, and then to allocate the work and co-ordinate it. In terms of the management process, Ethel is

A Planning
B Organising
C Controlling
D Leading

4 Which **two** of the following qualities are typical of a rational goal culture?

A Inward looking
B The need to be flexible
C The need to control the environment
D Outward looking

5 Which **two** of the following elements of the marketing mix are peculiar to services marketing?

A Price
B Place
C People
D Promotion
E Processes
F Place

6 Strand plc operates in the fast moving consumer goods market, where it is a medium-sized player. When determining how much to charge its customers for one of its established products, the main influence on Strand plc will be its

A Customers
B Costs
C Corporate objectives
D Competitors

7 Randalf, a manager with Trent plc, is faced with a decision about a service that is being marketed to consumers. The service requires four people for delivery and costs £1,000 when these people are directly employed. A sub-contractor has told Randalf that he would charge Trent plc £1,000 to deliver the service to customers. This decision is one about

A Marketing management (place)
B Operations management (procurement)
C Finance (relative costs)
D Human resources management

8 In terms of the organisational iceberg, which of the following is a covert variable affecting organisational behaviour?

A Political behaviour
B Organisational design
C Organisational goals
D Regulations

9 The model of human behaviour that states that humans seeks security above all else is called

A Theory X
B Scientific management
C The hygiene factor
D Theory Y

10 Sitin's team leader has told him that as a member of the team he is very committed to the team's task and always promotes activity, but that sometimes he can be too aggressive and challenging. In terms of Belbin's roles, Sitin is the team's

A Plant
B Evaluator
C Shaper
D Finisher

Now, go back to the Learning Objectives in the Introduction. If you are satisfied you have achieved these objectives, please tick them off.

Answers to Interactive questions

Answer to Interactive question 1

Nisar has resource power by virtue of the fact he manages 14 IT staff, and he has position power as their manager. He has expert power by virtue of his qualification. There is no information on which to base an assessment of his coercive, personal or negative power.

Answer to Interactive question 2

In FMCG, such as you see in a supermarket, the supplier will have made tremendous efforts to use all aspects of the marketing mix to persuade you to buy and use the product. In terms of product it will have been designed to satisfy a range of your needs, including how you may feel about packaging and the look of it. Its price will have been designed to be affordable to its target market whilst securing both a profit and an edge over competitors for both the manufacturer and the supermarket. The product has been placed in the supermarket via a network of intermediaries, although large chains like Tesco frequently deal direct with producers and handle the distribution (inbound logistics) themselves too. It will be placed in a position in the supermarket such that you are encouraged to see it and want it; products vie for shelf space at eye level in the supermarket, and where ranges are situated is a key element of supermarket marketing. Fresh produce is often placed at the entrance to be appealing to the eye and draw you in; the fragrance of fresh bread is often piped over from the bakery to appeal to your sense of smell at the entrance too. Promotion extends beyond placement on the shelves to include offers such as BOGOF (buy one get one free) and advertising in various media.

Answer to Interactive question 3

Large hotel chains make use of standard recipes and performance standards manuals. Housekeeping staff have a prescribed layout for each room with training based on detailed, ordered procedures and 'one best way' to service a room. Staff are expected to clean a set number of rooms per shift with bonuses for extra rooms.

This is just one example of the systematic work methods and detailed direction of labour that Taylor advocated, and which are still much in evidence in today's businesses.

Answer to Interactive question 4

The manager's style – the degree to which they are authoritative or participative – should be evaluated by considering how they made decisions, delegated, communicated, motivated and operated the team. If you found the manager was good it was probably because they focused on employees, set high standards for output but were flexible about methods, trusted you and delegated happily, and encouraged you to join in with decisions and generally feel involved.

Answers to Self-test

1 False. The manager remains accountable to senior management for the task

2 C Cedric has line authority only over his immediate subordinates. He has general staff authority by which he can advise other line managers on using the database, but in an issue such as this where he is responsible for the database, he can exercise functional authority to prevent Kara from changing the parameters

3 B

4 C and D

5 C and E

6 D FMCG are highly competitive markets so the prices charged by competitors will in the end be the greatest influence

7 B

8 A

9 A

10 C

CHAPTER 3

Organisational and business structures

Introduction

Learning objectives

Tick off

- Identify the various functional areas within businesses ☐
- Identify the nature and functions of organisational management ☐
- Identify different organisational structures and specify their advantages and disadvantages ☐
- Identify the differences between businesses carried out by sole traders, partnerships, limited liability partnerships, alliances and groups ☐
- Show the advantages and disadvantages of each business structure ☐
- Identify the differences between unincorporated businesses and companies, and show the advantages and disadvantages of incorporation ☐

Specific syllabus references are: 1c, d; 2a, b, c.

Syllabus links

Detailed legal aspects of partnerships and companies are developed further in Law at Certificate level. Accounting for sole traders, partnerships and companies is covered in Accounting at Certificate level. Groups are covered in Financial Accounting and Reporting at Professional level. Choosing the right organisational and business structures from a strategic perspective is developed in Business Strategy at Professional level. Optimising the financial aspects of organisational and business structures are covered in Financial Management at Professional level.

Examination context

Questions on both organisational and business structures could easily appear in the exam.

Questions are likely to be set in multiple choice format and in a scenario context. Knowledge-type questions are also likely, based on particular principles, theories or models.

1 Introduction to organisational structure

Section overview

- Organisational structure sets out how the various functions in the organisation are arranged.
- Organisational structure comprises six building blocks (Mintzberg): the operating core over which the middle line has authority; together these are facilitated by the technostructure and support staff. The strategic apex controls the entire organisation, and in turn it is guided by the organisation's overarching ideology.
- Classical principles of organisational structure emphasised: division of work, the scalar chain, the identity of authority and responsibility, centralisation, unity of command and direction, initiative, subordination of individual interests, discipline and order, stability, equity, fair remuneration and *esprit de corps.*
- While some classical principles still apply, in practice the values of multi-skilling and flexibility are very important.
- The organisation's structure is conveyed via an organisation chart or manual, and/or in job descriptions.

1.1 What is organisational structure?

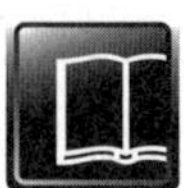

Definition

Organisational structure: Formed by the grouping of people into departments or sections and the allocation of responsibility and authority, organisational structure sets out how the various functions (operations, marketing, HR, finance etc) are formally arranged.

Organisational structure is a framework intended to:

- **Link individuals** in an established network of relationships so that authority, responsibility and communications can be controlled
- **Allocate the tasks** to be done to suitable individuals or groups
- Give each individual or group the **authority** required to perform the allocated tasks, while controlling their behaviour and use of resources in the interests of the business as a whole
- **Co-ordinate** the objectives and activities of separate groups, so that overall aims are achieved without gaps or overlaps in the flow of work
- Facilitate the **flow of work**, information and other resources through the business

1.2 The building blocks and co-ordinating mechanisms of organisational structure

Mintzberg suggests that all businesses can be analysed into six 'building blocks', as shown in Figure 3.1: the operating core, middle line and strategic apex (the management hierarchy that we saw in Chapter 2) plus support staff and the technostructure, all taking place within an overall ideology.

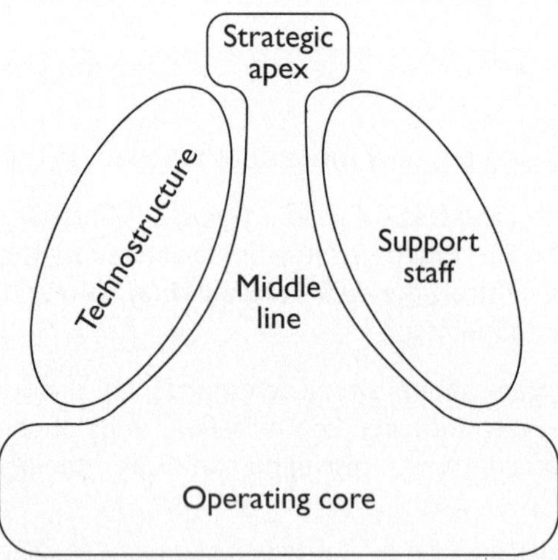

Figure 3.1: Mintzberg's building blocks

Building block	Function
Operating core	People *directly* involved in the process of obtaining inputs, and converting them into outputs, ie direct operational staff.
Middle line	Conveys the goals set by the strategic apex and controls the work of the operating core in pursuit of those goals, ie middle and first-line managers.
Strategic apex	Ensures the organisation follows its mission. Manages the organisation's relationship with the environment. Top managers.
Support staff	Ancillary services such as PR, legal counsel, the cafeteria and security staff. Support staff do not plan or standardise operations. They function independently of the operating core.
Technostructure	Analysts determine and standardise work processes and techniques. Planners determine and standardise outputs (eg goods must achieve a specified level of quality). Personnel analysts standardise skills (eg through training programmes).
Ideology	Values, beliefs and traditions, ie the business culture.

Interactive question 1: Ideology

[Difficulty level: Intermediate]

Where do you fit into the organisational structure of your firm? Try to identify the point at which the firm narrows to form the 'middle line' and also those departments which are part of the technostructure and support. What do you think the overarching ideology of the firm is?

See **Answer** at the end of this chapter.

Co-ordinating mechanisms integrate these building blocks into a cohesive unit, as follows:

- **Direct supervision**: giving of orders by a superior to a subordinate
- **Standardisation of work**: laying down standard operating procedures
- **Standardisation of skills**: requiring workers to have particular skills or qualifications
- **Standardisation of outputs**: specification of results such as the setting of targets
- **Mutual adjustment**: informal communication and self-government

1.3 Classical principles of organisational structure (Fayol)

Classical theories state that organisations are based on the principle of **hierarchy** which we saw in outline in Chapter 2. There is a line of decision-making power from the top of the organisation to the bottom.

Henri **Fayol**, an early ('classical') management theorist, suggested that all organisations should follow the 14 guiding principles outlined in the table below, based on the principles of **hierarchy**, in order to function effectively and efficiently.

Principle	Comment
Division of work	Work should be divided and allocated rationally, based on **specialisation**.
Scalar chain	Authority should flow vertically down a clear **chain of command** from highest to lowest rank. This principle is linked to the concept of **span of control**, which is the number of individuals under the direct supervision of any one person. (This is discussed further below.)
Correspondence of **authority** and **responsibility**	The holder of an office should have **enough authority** to carry out all the responsibilities assigned to them.
Appropriate **centralisation**	Decisions should be taken **at the top** of the organisation where appropriate.
Unity of **command** (for people)	For any action, a subordinate should receive orders from **one boss** only. Fayol saw dual command as a disease, whether it is caused by imperfect demarcation between departments, or by a superior giving orders directly to an employee without going via the intermediate superior.
Unity of **direction** (for the organisation)	There should be one head and **one plan** for each activity.
Initiative	Employees should be encouraged to use **discretion**, within the bounds of their authority.
Subordination of individual interests	The interest of one employee or group of employees should not prevail over that of the **general interest** of the organisation.
Discipline	A **fair disciplinary system** can be a strength in an organisation. Members of the organisation should behave in agreed ways.
Order	People and resources should **reliably** be where they are supposed to be.
Stability of personnel	There should be **continuity** of employment where possible.
Equity	Organisational policies should be **just**.
Remuneration	**Rewards** should be 'fair', satisfying both employer and employee alike.
Esprit de corps	**Harmony and teamwork** are essential to promote discipline and contentment.

1.4 Modern approaches to organisational structure

Modern management theorists emphasise values such as:

- **Multi-skilling**. Contrary to the idea of specialisation, multi-skilled teams (where individuals are trained to perform a variety of team tasks, as required) enable tasks to be performed more flexibly, using labour more efficiently.
- **Flexibility**. This is perhaps the major value in modern management theory. Arising from the competitive need to respond swiftly (and without organisational trauma) to rapidly-changing customer demands and technological changes, organisations and processes are being re-engineered to flexible structures such as the following:

- Smaller, multi-skilled, temporary structures, such as **project or task-force teams**.
- Multi-functional units, facilitating communication and co-ordination across departmental boundaries. This is called **matrix organisation** (which we shall see more about later), and it blurs the principle of 'unity of command', since an employee may report both to their departmental superior *and* to a project or product manager whose job is to manage all areas of activity related to the product or project.
- **Flexible deployment of the labour resource**, for example through part-time and temporary working, contracting out tasks, flexitime, annual (rather than daily) hours contracts and so on.

1.5 Communicating the organisational structure

There are three main methods of communicating the structure of the business. These are outlined in Figure 3.2.

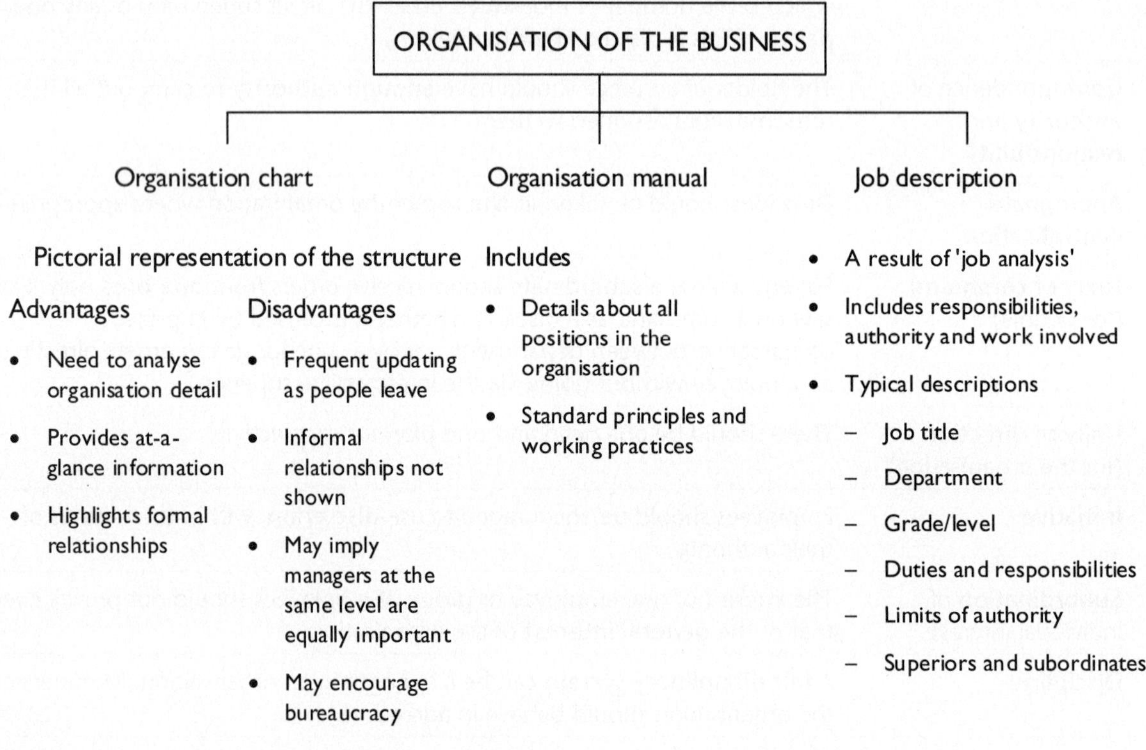

Figure 3.2: Communicating organisational structure

2 Types of organisational structure

Section overview

- Mintzberg's six building blocks can be combined to form five different organisational structures: a simple structure, a machine bureaucracy, a professional bureaucracy, a divisionalised structure (geographic or product/brand) or an adhocracy.
- These organisational structures are typified in part by whether the external environment is either simple or complex, and either static or dynamic.

Mintzberg's building blocks and coordinating mechanisms in Figure 3.1 are generally combined in one of five different types of organisational structure. Each is characterised by different types of external environmental and internal factors.

Types of organisational structure	External environment	Internal factors	Key building block	Key co-ordinating mechanism
Simple structure	Simple Dynamic	Small Young Simple tasks	Strategic apex	Direct supervision
Machine bureaucracy	Simple Static	Large Old Regulated	Technostructure	Standardisation of work
Professional bureaucracy	Complex Static	Professional Simple systems	Operating core	Standardisation of skills
Divisionalised	Simple Static Diverse	Very large Old Divisible tasks	Middle line	Standardisation of outputs
Adhocracy/ Innovative	Complex Dynamic	Young Complex tasks	Operating core	Mutual adjustment

We shall look at what simple, complex, static and dynamic mean in the context of external environment in Chapter 4.

We will study four of these organisational structures in depth.

- Simple organisational structure – known as the entrepreneurial structure
- Machine bureaucracy organisational structure – known as the functional or bureaucratic structure
- Divisionalised organisational structure (by product/brand or by geography)
- *Ad hoc* organisational structure – known as the matrix structure

The suitability of each structure will be dependent on the size of the business; generally speaking, as a business grows it will progress from entrepreneurial to functional to divisional structure. A matrix structure may occur independently or within a functional or divisional structure.

2.1 Entrepreneurial structure

Features

- Entrepreneur has specialist knowledge of product/service
- Entrepreneur has total control over running of the business

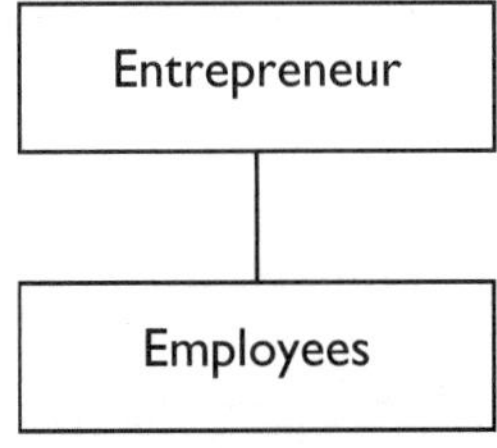

Figure 3.3 Entrepreneurial structure

The entrepreneurial structure is most suitable where there is one product or a group of similar products.

Advantages

- Quick decisions can be made with skill and flair
- Goal congruence – the entrepreneur's objectives are pursued exclusively
- Flexible/adaptable to change

Disadvantages

- Cannot expand beyond a certain size (too many decisions need to be made and too many people need to be managed)
- Cannot easily cope with diversification into new products/services about which the entrepreneur does not have specialist skills/knowledge
- Lack of career structure for lower level employees
- May be too centralised, ie too much decision-making power retained by entrepreneur

2.2 Functional structure (bureaucratic structure)

Features

- Jobs grouped by common feature, eg production, and ranked in hierarchy, eg managers, supervisors, employees etc
- Clear lines of reporting and authority exist
- Formal procedures and paperwork characterise this type of structure
- The vertical flow of authority (scalar chain) can go up and down through the structure from top to bottom

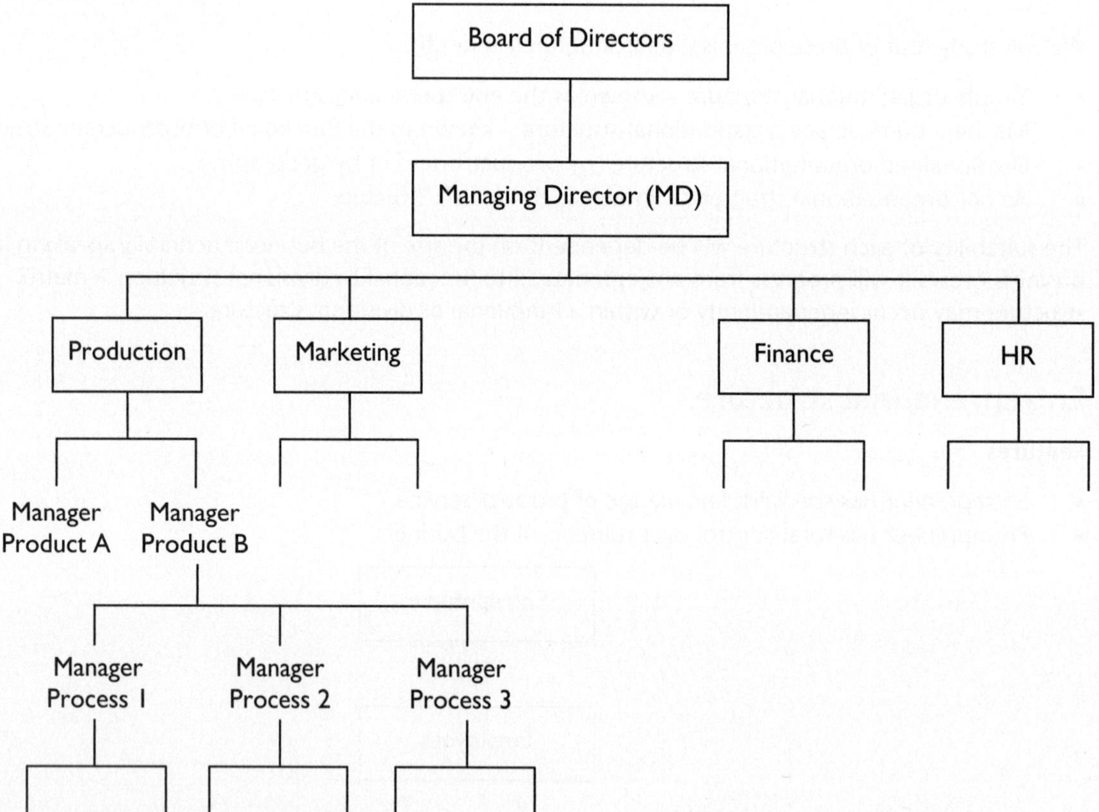

Figure 3.4 Functional structure (bureaucratic)

The **functional bureaucratic structure** is most suitable where there is

- Single product/closely-related product forms
- Relatively stable environment, ie one not subject to rapid change
- A smaller enterprise

Advantages

- Good career opportunities, employees can progress 'up through the ranks'
- Can be efficient as functional tasks are well-known and understood by individuals
- Exploits specialist functional skills

Disadvantages

- Structure is very rigid and unsuitable for
  - Growth
  - Diversification
- Tendency towards authoritative non-participative management style as clear levels of authority are enforced
- Poor decisions/slow decisions which have to pass along a line of authority
- Functional heads may build empires and interfunctional disputes may result

2.3 Divisional structure

Definition

Divisionalisation: The division of a business into autonomous regions (geographic divisionalisation) or product businesses (product/brand divisionalisation), each with its own revenues, expenditures and capital asset purchase programmes, and therefore each with its own profit responsibility.

Features

- Business is split into divisions – division is usually by product/brand or by geography/location
- Divisions are typically given responsibility for their profits and assessed in terms of profit (profit centre)
- In the UK the typical approach is to use a holding or parent company and subsidiaries (a group structure – we shall come back to this later in this chapter)

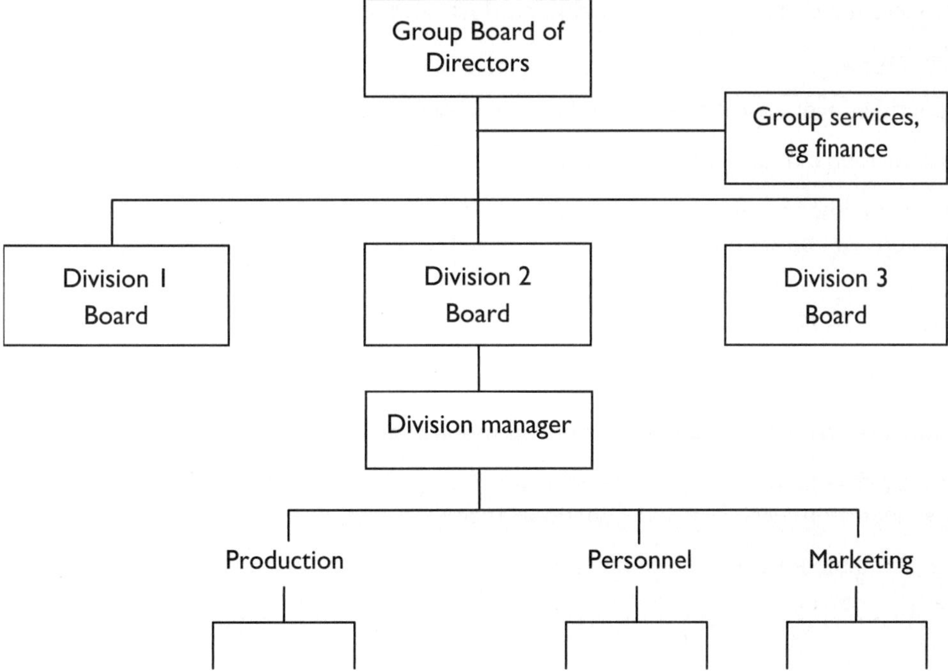

Figure 3.5: Divisional structure

Each division of the organisation might be:

- A subsidiary company under the holding company (we shall come back to this)
- A profit centre within a single business

CHAPTER 3

Successful divisionalisation requires certain key conditions.

- Each division must have **properly delegated authority**, and must be held properly accountable to the group board (eg for profits earned).
- Each division must be **large enough** to support the quantity and quality of management it needs.
- The division must not rely on head office for excessive **management support**.
- Each division must have a **potential for growth** in its own area of operations.
- There should be scope and challenge in the job for the management of each division.
- If divisions deal with each other, it should be as 'arm's length' transactions. There should be no insistence on preferential treatment to be given to a 'fellow division' by another division of the overall organisation.

The divisional structure is most suitable when:

- There are larger, more diversified businesses
- There is diversity by product and/or location

Advantages

- Flexible in adapting to growth and diversification – extra divisions can simply be added into the structure
- Good for developing managers as they are given responsibility for divisional profit
- Reduces the number of levels of management
- Encourages a greater attention to efficiency, lower costs and higher profits
- Better decisions on performance made by managers 'in the know'
- Releases top management to concentrate on strategic issues
- Reduces the likelihood of unprofitable products and activities being continued

Disadvantages

- Squabbles over allocation of central costs can occur
- Interdivisional trading problems, ie at what transfer price should the trades take place?
- It may be impossible to identify completely independent products or markets for which separate divisions can be set up

2.4 Matrix structure

Features

- Formalises vertical and lateral lines of communication
- Managers appointed for projects or customers – project or customer managers liaise with managers from each function (functional managers)
- May be temporary, ie for one-off contract

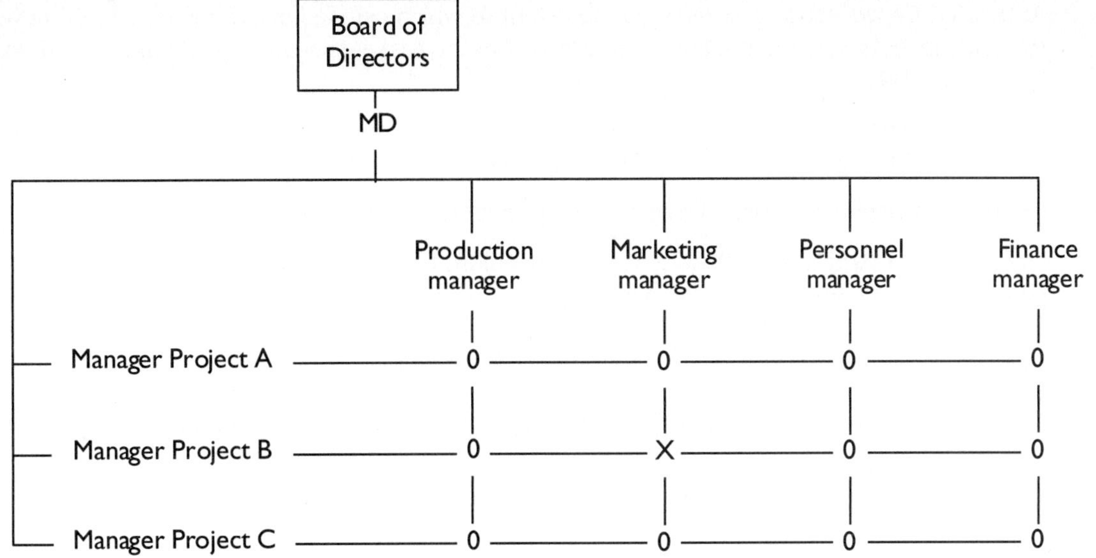

0 = individual in structure
X = reports both to marketing manager and Project B manager

Figure 3.6 Matrix structure showing project managers

The matrix structure is most suitable to

- Complex/hi-tech industries
- Educational establishments where there may be lecturers reporting to both subject and course heads
- R&D departments

Advantages

- Reflects importance of project or customer, so may improve relationships and sales
- Business co-ordinated with regard to technology, information, etc

Disadvantages

- Conflicting demands on staff time (staff have to serve two bosses)
- Conflicting demands over allocation of other resources
- Dilution of authority of functional heads

3 Centralisation and decentralisation

Section overview

- An organisational structure is centralised when decision-making authority is concentrated in its strategic apex.
- Centralisation offers greater control and coordination.
- Decentralisation offers greater flexibility.

3.1 What is centralisation?

We can look at centralisation in two ways.

- **Geography**. Some functions may be centralised rather than 'scattered' in different offices, departments or locations.

  So, for example, secretarial support, IT support and information storage (filing) may be centralised in specialist departments (whose services are shared by other functions) rather than carried out by staff/equipment duplicated in each division.

- **Authority**. Centralisation also refers to the extent to which people have to refer decisions upwards to their superiors. Decentralisation therefore implies increased delegation, and autonomy at lower levels of the business.

We shall use the terms centralisation/decentralisation to refer to how much authority/decision-making ability is diffused throughout the organisational structure.

- **Centralised structures**: upper levels retain authority to make decisions
- **Decentralised structures**: authority to make decisions (ie commit people, money and resources) is passed down to lower levels of the hierarchy

Definition

Centralised organisation: One in which decision-making authority is concentrated in one place, that is the strategic apex.

3.2 Factors affecting the amount of decentralisation in a business

- **Leadership style**: if it is authoritative, the business will be more centralised
- **Size of organisation**: as size increases, decentralisation tends to increase
- **Extent of activity diversification**: the more diversified, the more decentralised
- **Effectiveness of communication**: decentralisation will not work if information is not communicated downwards
- **Ability of management**: the more able, the more decentralisation
- **Speed of technological advancement**: lower managers are likely to be more familiar with changing technology, therefore decentralise
- **Geography of locations**: if spread, decentralise
- **Extent of local knowledge needed**: if required, decentralise

3.3 Which is better – centralisation or decentralisation?

Generally, centralisation offers greater **control and co-ordination**, while decentralisation offers greater **flexibility** as authority is delegated.

Pro centralisation	Pro decentralisation (delegation of authority)
Decisions are made at one point and so are easier to co-ordinate.	Avoids overburdening top managers, in terms of workload and stress.
Senior managers can take a wider view of problems and consequences.	Improves motivation of more junior managers who are given responsibility and authority.
Senior management can balance the interests of different functions, eg by deciding on the resources to allocate to each.	Greater awareness of local problems by decision makers. (Geographically dispersed organisations are often decentralised on a regional/area basis for this reason.)
Senior managers keep control.	Greater speed of decision making, and response to changing events, since no need to refer decisions upwards. This is particularly important in rapidly changing markets.
Quality of decisions is (theoretically) better due to senior managers' skills and experience.	Helps develop the skills of junior managers: supports managerial succession.

Pro centralisation	Pro decentralisation (delegation of authority)
More likely to produce congruent decisions as decision-makers are more likely to pursue same objectives.	Separate spheres of responsibility can be identified: controls, performance measurement and accountability are better.
Possibly cheaper, by reducing number of managers needed and so reduced costs of overheads – simpler structure.	Communication technology allows decisions to be made locally, with information and input from head office if required.
Crisis decisions are taken more quickly at the centre, without need to refer back.	
Policies, procedures and documentation can be standardised business-wide.	
Transfer pricing is less of a problem.	

4 Span of control: tall and flat businesses

Section overview

- A manager's span of control quantifies how many people are reporting directly to them.
- The scalar chain describes the series of links between the most senior managers and the direct operational staff in an organisation.
- Wide spans of control/short scalar chains create flat management hierarchies.
- Narrow spans of control/long scalar chains create tall management hierarchies.

CHAPTER 3

4.1 Span of control

Definition

Span of control: The number of people (subordinates) reporting to one person.

The classical theorist Urwich held that:

- There needs to be **tight managerial control** from the top of a business downwards
- The span of control should therefore be **restricted**, to allow maximum control consistent with the manager's capabilities: usually between three and six subordinates
- If the span of control **is too wide** (there are too many subordinates), too much of the manager's time will be taken up with routine problems and supervision, leaving less time for planning. Even so, subordinates may not get the supervision, control and communication that they require
- If the span of control **is too narrow** (there are too few subordinates), the manager may fail to delegate, keeping too much routine work to himself and depriving subordinates of decision-making authority and responsibility. There may be a tendency to interfere in or over-supervise the work that is delegated to subordinates – and the relative costs of supervision will thus be unnecessarily high. Subordinates tend to be dissatisfied in such situations, having too little challenge and responsibility and perhaps feeling that the superior does not trust them

Influences on the span of control:

- A manager's **capabilities** limit the span of control: there are physical and mental limitations to any single manager's ability to control people and activities
- The **nature of the manager's workload**: the more non-supervisory work in a manager's workload, the narrower the span of control and the greater the delegation of authority to subordinates should be

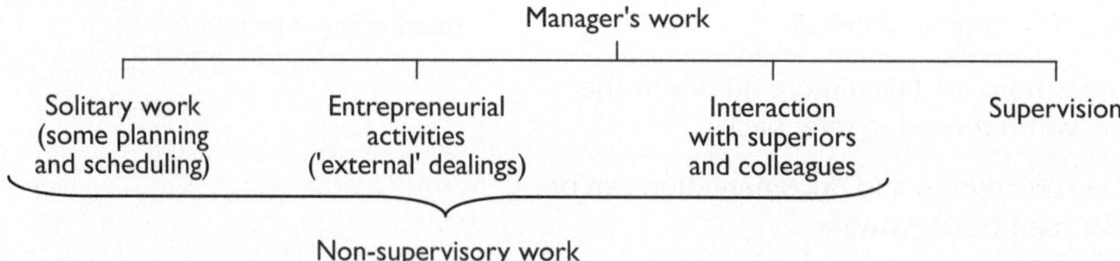

Figure 3.7 The manager's workload

- The **geographical dispersion** of subordinates: dispersed teams take more effort to supervise
- **Subordinates' work**: if all subordinates do similar tasks, a wider span is possible. If **close group cohesion** is desirable, a narrower span of control might be needed
- The **nature of problems** that a manager might have to help subordinates with. Time consuming problems suggest a narrower span of control
- The degree of **interaction between subordinates**. If subordinates can help each other, a wider span is possible
- The amount of **support** that supervisors receive from other parts of the organisation or from **technology** (eg computerised work monitoring, or 'virtual meetings' with dispersed team members)

Interactive question 2: Work loads **[Difficulty level: Intermediate]**

For your own firm or perhaps for one of your audit clients, select a manager who you believe may be overworked. Think about what amount of time that manager seems to spend 'doing' their own work, and how much time they spend supervising staff. How far do you think the manager's problems are caused by having too wide a span of control, and what effect does this have?

See **Answer** at the end of this chapter.

4.2 Tall and flat businesses

The management hierarchy determines the 'shape' of the organisation; longer scalar chains create taller businesses.

Definitions

Scalar chain: The chain of command from the most senior to the most junior.

Tall business: One which, in relation to its size, has a large number of levels in its management hierarchy, normally because there are **narrow spans of control**.

Flat business: One which, in relation to its size, has a small number of hierarchical levels, normally because there are **wide spans of control**.

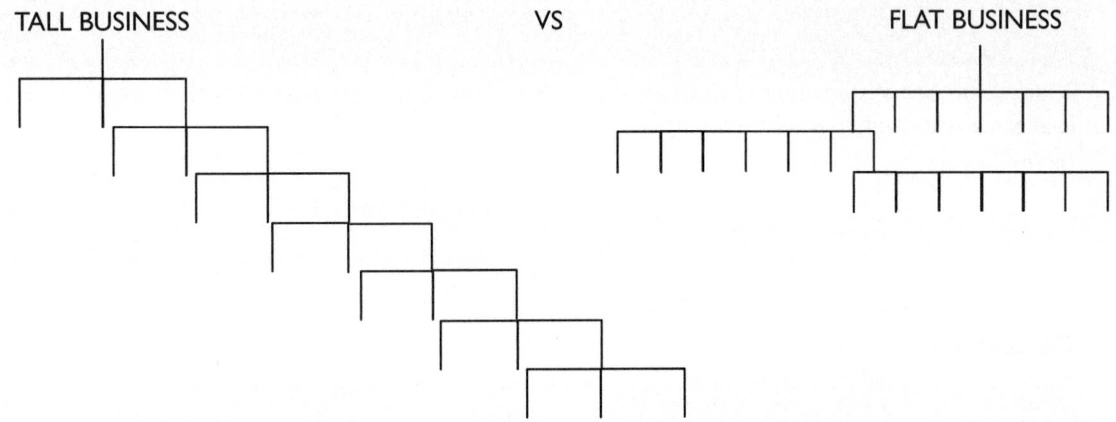

Figure 3.8: Tall and flat organisational structures

- In the tall business (seven layers), each manager has only three subordinates
- In the flat business (three layers) each manager has seven subordinates

The span of control concept therefore has implications for the length of the **scalar chain** (Figure 3.9).

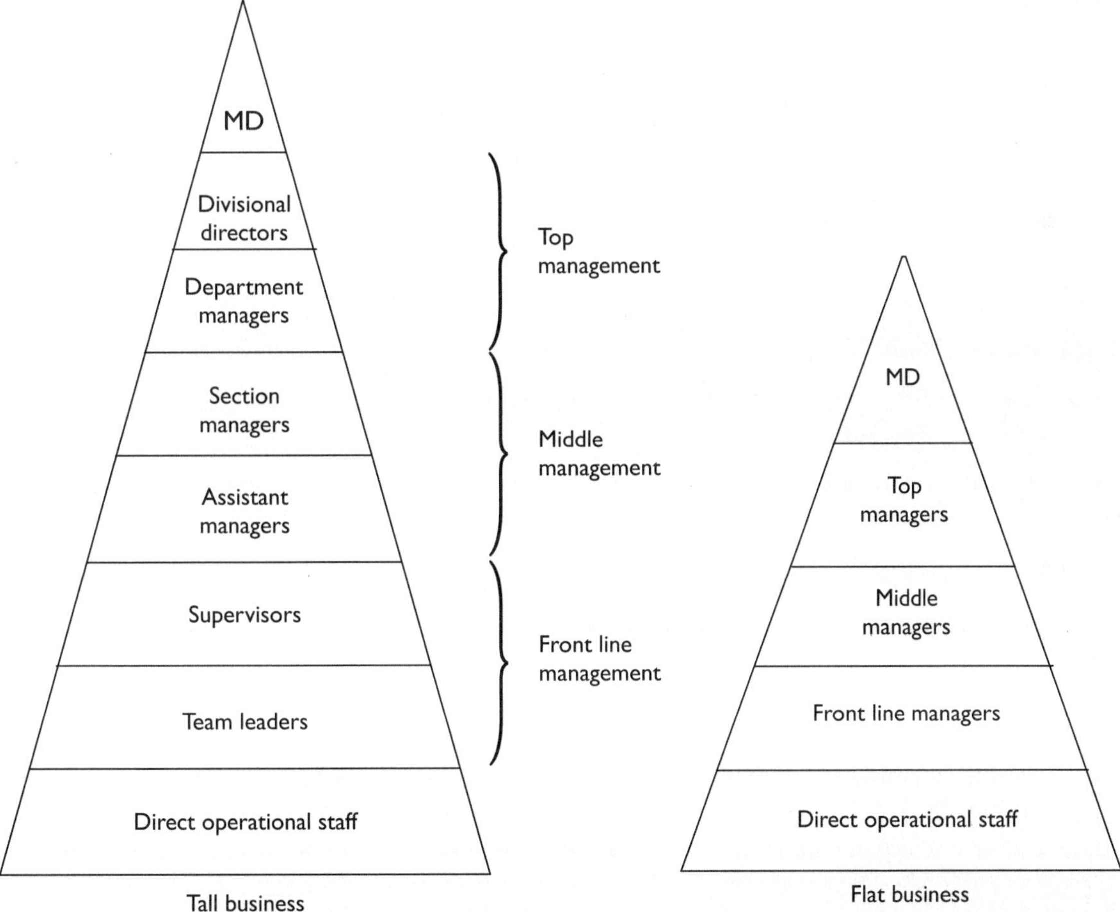

Figure 3.9: Scalar chain in tall and flat businesses

4.2.1 Are tall or flat businesses better?

Tall business

For	Against
Narrow control spans	Inhibits delegation
Small groups enable team members to participate in decisions	Rigid supervision can be imposed, blocking initiative

For	Against
A large number of steps on the promotional ladder – assists management training and career planning	The same work passes through too many hands
	Increases administration and overhead costs
	Slow decision making and responses, as the strategic apex is further away

Flat business

For	Against
More opportunity for delegation	Requires that jobs *can* be delegated. If managers are overworked they are more likely to be involved in crisis management
	Managers may only get a superficial idea of what goes on
Relatively cheap	Sacrifices control
In theory, speeds up communication between strategic apex and operating core	Middle managers are often necessary to convert the grand vision of the strategic apex into operational terms

5 Mechanistic and organic structures

Section overview

- Bureaucracies or mechanistic organisational structures suit relatively static, slow-changing operating environments.
- Organic organisational structures are suited to relatively dynamic operating environments.

5.1 What are mechanistic and organic structures?

The terms 'mechanistic' and 'organic' were coined by Burns and Stalker to describe organisational structures which are:

- Stable, efficient and suitable for slow-changing operating environments (**mechanistic businesses**, or 'bureaucracies'), and
- Flexible, adaptive and suitable for fast-changing or dynamic operating environments (**organic businesses**).

Mechanistic and organic structures can be distinguished from each other on a number of factors.

Factor	Mechanistic business	Organic business
The task	Tasks are specialised and broken down into sub-tasks.	Specialist knowledge and expertise contribute to the common task of the organisation.
How the task fits in	People are concerned with completing the task efficiently, rather than how the task can improve organisational effectiveness.	Each task is seen and understood to be set by the total situation of the business: focus is on the task's contribution to organisational effectiveness.

Factor	Mechanistic business	Organic business
Co-ordination	Managers are responsible for co-ordinating tasks.	People adjust and redefine their tasks through interaction and mutual adjustment with others.
Job description	There are precise job descriptions and delineations of responsibility.	Job descriptions are less precise: people do what is necessary to complete the task.
Legal contract v common interest	Hierarchical structure of control. An individual's performance and conduct derive from a contractual relationship with an impersonal business.	Network structure of control. An individual's performance and conduct derive from a supposed community of interest between the individual and the business, and the individual's colleagues.
Decisions	Decisions are taken by senior managers who are assumed to know everything.	Relevant technical and commercial knowledge and decision-making authority can be located anywhere.
Mission	Insistence on loyalty to the concern and obedience to superiors.	Commitment to the business's mission is more highly valued than loyalty as such.

5.2 Mechanistic structures: bureaucracy

Definition

Bureaucracy: 'A continuous organisation of official functions bound by rules' (Weber).

- Continuous organisation: The business does not disappear if people leave: new people will fill their shoes
- Official functions: The business is divided into areas (eg operations, marketing) with specified duties. Authority to carry them out is given to the managers in charge
- Rules: A rule defines and specifies a course of action that must be taken under given circumstances

CHAPTER 3

5.2.1 Characteristics of bureaucracy

Characteristic	Description
Hierarchy of roles	Each lower office is under the control and supervision of a higher one.
Specialisation and training	There is a high degree of specialisation of labour.
Professional nature of employment	Managers are employees; promotion is according to seniority and achievement; pay scales are prescribed according to the position or office held in the organisation structure.
Impersonal nature	Employees work within impersonal rules and regulations and act according to formal, impersonal procedures.
Rationality	The hierarchy of authority and office structure is clearly defined. Duties are established and measures of performance set.
Uniformity in the performance of tasks	Procedures ensure that, regardless of who carries out tasks, they should be executed in the same way.
Technical competence	All managers are technically competent. Their competence within the area of their expertise is rarely questioned.
Stability	The business rarely changes in response to environmental pressures.

5.2.2 Advantages of bureaucracies

- Ideal for **standardised, routine tasks**. For example, processing driving licence applications is fairly routine, requiring systematic work
- They can be very **efficient** in stable environments
- Rigid adherence to procedures may be necessary for **fairness**, adherence to the **law**, **safety** and **security** (eg procedures for data protection)
- Some people are **suited** to the structured, predictable environment. Bureaucracies tend to be long-lived because they select and retain bureaucratically-minded people

5.2.3 Disadvantages of bureaucracies

- **Slow decision-making**, because of the rigidity and length of authority networks.
- Uniformity creates **conformity**, inhibiting the personal development of staff.
- They suppress **innovation**: they can inhibit creativity, initiative and openness to new ideas and ways of doing things.
- They find it hard to **learn** from their mistakes, because of the lack of feedback (especially upwards).
- **Slow to change:** environmental change therefore causes severe trauma.
- **Communication** is restricted to established channels, ignoring opportunities for networking, upward feedback and suggestions that may contribute to customer service and innovation.

5.3 Organic organisations

Organic structures have their own control mechanisms.

Control mechanism	Description
Status	Although organic businesses are not hierarchical in the way that bureaucracies are, there are **differences of status**, determined by people's greater expertise, experience and so forth.
Commitment	The degree of **commitment** employees have to the goals of the business and the team is more **extensive** in organic than in mechanistic systems.
Shared values and culture	Hierarchical control is replaced by the development of **shared beliefs and values**. In other words, corporate **culture** becomes a powerful guide to behaviour.

6 Introduction to business structure

Section overview

- A business may take the business structure of a sole tradership (one owner), a partnership (more than one owner) or a limited company (usually many more than one owner).
- All businesses have unlimited liability for their own debts.

So far we have considered various factors affecting organisational structure. A key influence in practice is the **business structure** it takes. In fact this means what **legal form** the business takes.

Businesses may take one of three basic legal forms.

- Sole tradership
- Partnership
- Companies

In addition any business may form an **alliance** with other businesses, or it may form a **group structure**. We shall look at each of these points in turn.

7 Sole tradership

Section overview

- In a sole tradership there is unlimited liability of the owner for the business's debts.
- There is no legal distinction between the owner and the business, but separate ledger accounts and financial statements should be maintained for tax purposes.
- Sole traders may borrow money and employ people, but they have unlimited risk.
- A sole tradership ceases to exist on the death of the owner, though assets (including goodwill) and liabilities can be sold by their estate.

Definition

Sole tradership: A single proprietor owns the business, taking all the risks and enjoying all the rewards of the business.

C H A P T E R 3

7.1 Features of a sole tradership

- There is no legal distinction between the proprietor and the business
- The proprietor is wholly liable for the debts of the business, borrowing money in his/her own name
- The business is usually financed by a mixture of owner's capital (including retained earnings), loans and short-term credit
- While a sole trader can offer a lender a fixed charge over assets such as buildings and machinery as security, they cannot use floating charges over all the business assets as a company can
- Sole traders take drawings from the business
- Many sole traders employ people to do some or all of the actual work in the business, but it is usual for the proprietor to take a very active role, doing many different tasks and managing the business in a very 'hands-on' way
- A sole tradership business can be sold as a going concern by its owner
- If a sole trader dies, the business's assets and liabilities form part of their estate but the sole tradership as such ceases to exist – there is no perpetual succession

7.2 Advantages and disadvantages of sole tradership

A sole trader has the flexibility of 'being their own boss', taking all the decisions and getting things done in their own preferred way. There is no publicity requirement of sole traders beyond the requirement to prepare financial statements for taxation purposes, and this offers both privacy and cost savings.

However, the fact that they have sole charge can be a disadvantage as there are limits to the skills and the time of one individual. While no-one shares the profits there is also no-one to share the load. Frequently sole traders overwork and find it difficult to take a holiday. It is also hard to expand unless there are new ideas and new capital.

Sole traders who have employees have the same responsibilities in respect of them as any other business, and of course the sole trader also has the significant responsibility of unlimited liability for the business's debts.

8 Partnerships

Section overview

- In a general partnership there is unlimited liability of the partners for the business's debts.
- The partnership does not have a separate legal existence.
- General partnerships may borrow money and employ people, but they have unlimited risk and cease to exist on the death of one partner.
- Some partners in a limited partnership may have limited liability.
- All partners in a limited liability partnership may have limited liability.

Definition

Partnership: The relation which subsists between persons carrying on a business in common with a view of profit.

Two or more people who own a business, agreeing to take all the risks and enjoy all the rewards of the business, are called a partnership. They agree between themselves how the risks, rewards and property are shared. They may agree to contribute different amounts of capital, to take different shares of profits and losses, to own partnership property in different shares, or to guarantee salaries to certain partners. It is up to them.

Partnership is a common form of business structure. It is **flexible**, because it can either be a **formal** or **informal** arrangement, so it can be used for large organisations or for a small husband and wife operation.

Partnership is normal practice in the **professions** as historically professions prohibited their members from carrying on practice through limited companies. In some professions this has been relaxed, and other professions permit their members to trade as limited liability partnerships (LLPs) which have many of the characteristics of companies. Non-professional businesses have never been restricted in this way and generally prefer to trade through a limited company for the advantages this can bring.

8.1 Features of a partnership

In many ways trading as a partnership is not so different from trading as a sole trader.

- How far the business is legally distinct from its owners depends on the form of partnership used, but frequently the partners are jointly and severally liable for the debts of the partnership.
- The financing issues that face sole traders also face many general and limited partnerships.
- Partners take drawings from the business.
- While all the partners may be as actively involved in the business as the typical sole trader, there is more scope for partners to specialise, and/or to 'take a back seat' in the business.
- A share in a partnership is not a form of property as such and selling it can be difficult.
- If a partner dies, a general or limited partnership (see below) is dissolved – there is no 'perpetual succession'.

There are three forms of partnership: general, limited and limited liability partnerships.

8.2 General partnerships

In a general partnership regulated by the Partnership Act 1890, the partnership has no separate legal identity. All partners are jointly and severally liable for the partnership's debts. If one partner becomes personally insolvent, for instance, the others must take on his or her own 'share' of the partnership's debts themselves.

8.3 Limited partnerships

In a limited partnership regulated by the Limited Partnerships Act 1907, the partnership has no separate legal identity. One or more partners however may have limited liability for the partnership's debts provided there is at least one, fully liable partner. This means that, provided they have fully paid the amount of capital that the partnership agreement stipulates, the limited partners do not have to make any further contribution to partnership assets even if the partnership is insolvent. Limited partners cannot take their capital out of the partnership and they may not take part in management.

8.4 Advantages and disadvantages of general and limited partnerships

Partners have the flexibility of 'being their own boss', taking all the decisions and getting things done in their own preferred way, but without the loneliness and pressure of the sole trader. There is no publicity requirement of general and limited partnerships beyond the requirement to prepare financial statements for taxation purposes.

Multiple partners will have different skills and more time to devote to management and expansion than one individual. There is someone to share the load and less chance of overwork. New ideas and new capital are more readily available.

Partners with employees have the same responsibilities in respect of them as any other business. In a general partnership they each have unlimited liability for the business's debts, but they have to share profits.

The relationship between the partners is of crucial importance to whether the partnership realises its potential. It is based on **trust**; if the relationship fails and partners fall out, the agreement is at an end and the partnership essentially ceases to exist. Moreover, partners can be left with liability for debts run up by another partner, sometimes without their knowledge.

8.5 Limited liability partnerships

Professionals are frequently bound by professional rules to operate as partnerships, of a limited size in some cases. This historically meant that the partners had to trade with unlimited liability for partnership debts, which represented a significant restriction on the amount of risk that the partners were willing to take on. It is possible to form limited liability partnerships (LLPs) under the Limited Liability Partnership Act 2000; these are little different from limited liability companies, which we shall see next. In particular, LLPs have a legal identity separate from their owners. Because of this, some of the funding restrictions suffered by general and limited partnerships are relaxed.

9 Companies

Section overview

- In a limited company the owners (shareholders) have limited liability for the unpaid debts of the company.
- The company is legally distinct from its owners.
- The death of a shareholder has no effect on the company; their shares are personal property which can be transferred to another person.
- Private companies, unlike public companies, may not offer their securities for sale to the public. They are generally smaller as well.

Definition

Company: A legal entity registered as such under the Companies Act 2006.

A business which trades as a company may be no different from a partnership or sole trader in any other way than in one important fact: while sole traders and partners as owners take all the risks in the business, having (generally) unlimited liability for the debts of the business, the owners of a limited company (its shareholders) have limited liability for its debts beyond any amount they may still owe for the shares they hold. **The company has unlimited liability for its own debts.**

9.1 Features of a limited company

- The company is legally distinct from its owners
- As well as a fixed charge, the company can offer a floating charge over its changing assets as security for lending
- Shareholders take dividends, not drawings, from the business
- Directors run the company; shareholders do not take part in the management of the business unless they are also directors and/or employees, but they have no automatic right to be directors
- Shares are a form of property that can easily be sold by their owners, especially if the company has a public listing of shares on a public stock exchange; transferring ownership of shares to another person has no direct effect on the company
- If a shareholder dies, their shares are transferred to another person without any effect on the company at all – there is what is known as 'perpetual succession'

As the company's shareholders enjoy the benefit of limited liability for the company's debts, there are stringent rules in place which protect the capital contributed by shareholders as a 'buffer' for creditors. If the company becomes insolvent, shareholders cannot receive any of their capital back until creditors are paid in full.

A company's constitution is contained primarily in its Articles of Association, which are open to public scrutiny. The constitution sets out the company's relations with the external world and also how shareholders relate to the company, its directors and each other, that is how the company is run.

9.2 Types of company

Definitions

Public company: A company whose memorandum states that it is public and that it has complied with the registration procedures for such a company. It may offer its shares and other securities for sale to the public at large.

Private company: A company which has not been registered as a public company under the Companies Act 2006. It may **not** offer its securities to the public at large.

In the UK a **public** company is a company registered as such under the Companies Act 2006 with the Registrar of Companies. **Any company not registered as public is a private company**.

Public companies (plcs) do not necessarily have their shares listed on a public stock exchange.

A company must have at least one shareholder. Unless there are clauses in the constitution to the contrary, there are no limits to the number of shares or shareholders a company can have, but generally directors are limited in the number of shares they can issue in the company by the requirement that they have shareholder approval for issues. Public companies must have at least two directors and must have at least £12,500 in share capital paid up at registration.

9.3 Advantages of companies

- The **separate legal personality** of the company.
- The **limited liability of its members** (shareholders).
- **Perpetual succession.** A change in the ownership of a company does not affect its continued existence.
- **Transferability of interests**. Shareholders in a company can sell their shares either to other shareholders or to outsiders, subject to the provisions of the company's constitution and the Companies Act 2006. It is not possible for partners to assign or transfer their interest in a partnership (unless the other partners consent). They would have to retire from the partnership, hence causing its dissolution.
- **Security for loans** includes floating as well as fixed charges.

9.4 Disadvantages of companies

- **Separation of ownership and control**. A sole trader and the partners in a firm can all participate in the day-to-day management of the entity: it is effectively 'their' business. The shareholders of a company, however, do not have such a right, and their input is limited to what can be achieved by the passing of resolutions.
- **Ownership of assets**. Due to the concept of separate legal personality, a company owns its own assets and a shareholder does not have any right to just take a share in them. A sole trader owns his or her own business's assets, and the partners in a firm own the assets jointly, so that when a partner leaves he or she is entitled to the value of their share of the assets.
- **Accounting records and returns**. Sole traders and (non-limited liability) partnerships do not have to keep their accounting records in any format prescribed by the Companies Act 2006, and they do not have to undergo an audit. Companies, both private and public, are subject to stringent legal rules governing the keeping of accounting records, the filing of financial statements and the annual return with the Registrar of Companies and, in the case of larger companies, the requirement to have an audit. This degree of bureaucracy can deter businesses from incorporation.
- **Publicity**. Due to the need to file financial statements, discussed above, it is possible for third parties, such as competitors and creditors, to obtain information about the company's financial position and such sensitive issues as the remuneration of directors. Partnerships and sole traders do not need to make any of this information publicly available.

- **Regulations and expense**. The law – primarily the Companies Act 2006 – sets out very stringent rules that all companies must follow, on areas as diverse as the maintenance of capital, the contents of the constitution and the amount that can be lent to directors. This adds to the bureaucracy encountered by companies, and can be expensive.

Interactive question 3: Incorporation [Difficulty level: Intermediate]

In what circumstances can you see that the disadvantages of incorporation may outweigh the advantages?

See **Answer** at the end of this chapter.

10 Which business structure should a business take?

Section overview

- Many operational, business, legal, practical and financial factors must be considered when deciding which business structure should be adopted for a particular business.

The following factors should be considered when deciding whether a general (non-LLP) partnership should become a company.

Factor	Company	Partnership (non-LLP)
Entity	Is a legal entity separate to its members	Has no existence outside of its members
Liability	Members' liability can be limited	Partners' liability is usually unlimited
Succession	Perpetual succession – change in ownership does not affect existence	Traditional partnerships are dissolved when any of the partners leaves
Owners' interests	Members own transferable shares	Partners cannot transfer their interests in a partnership
Assets	Company owns the assets	Partners own assets jointly
Management	Company must have at least one or two director(s)	All partners can participate in management
Constitution	Company must have a written constitution	A partnership may have a written partnership agreement, or the agreement may just be verbal
Financial statements	A company must deliver financial statements to the Registrar	Partners do not have to send their financial statements to the Registrar
Security	A company may offer a floating charge over its assets	A partnership may not give a floating charge on assets
Withdrawal of capital	Strict rules concerning repayment of subscribed capital	More straightforward for a partner to withdraw capital

11 Alliances

Section overview

- A business of whatever form may enter into various types of alliance with other businesses, creating business structures in the form of joint ventures, licences, strategic alliances, agency or a group structure.

There are various ways in which businesses (of whatever legal business structure: sole trader, partnership or company) can work together.

11.1 Joint venture

A separate business – usually but not always a limited company – can be formed in which the businesses take a financial stake (usually, but not always, as shareholders) and management is provided as agreed.

Benefits

- Less capital is required than if the businesses were on their own, so there is less risk
- Reduces competition
- Enables firms to gain access to restricted markets
- Access to the skills of each party

Disadvantages

- Disputes over how the business should be run, costs incurred, management charges, etc
- If the joint venture breaks down, the special skills of a business may be used against it by its former joint venture partner
- Possible lack of financial support

11.2 Licences

A licensing agreement is a permission to another company to manufacture or sell a product, or to use a brand name.

Most licences are restricted geographically so in the case of a sales licence, the licensor (who grants the licence) can retain control over where the product is sold, and can prevent competition with his own products or those of other licensees. The most common form of licensing agreement is the **franchise**, which usually involves an annual fee plus a minimum order for goods, usually at a discount.

11.3 Strategic alliances

A strategic alliance is an informal or weak contractual agreement between parties or a minority cross-shareholding arrangement (a cross-shareholding is where each party takes a small number of shares in the other parties). Normally no separate company is formed. National airlines have created such alliances to cross-book passengers. Similarly, some European telecom companies have created alliances to aid international expansion.

The benefits and disadvantages are similar to those of joint ventures.

In addition:

- The looser arrangement is easier to break
- They may contravene competition laws, eg be viewed as an illegal cartel (we shall see more about cartels in Chapter 14)
- There may be less commitment than to a joint venture, so the benefits are not as great

11.4 Agents

Agents can be used as the distribution channel where local knowledge and contacts are important, eg exporting. The agreements may be restricted to marketing and product support.

Other situations where agents are used include:

- Sales of cosmetics (Avon), clothes etc (Ann Summers)
- Holidays
- Financial services, eg insurance brokers

The main problem for a business that uses agents is that it is cut off from direct contact with the customer.

11.5 Groups

As companies are entitled to own shares, groups of companies may form. In its simplest form, a group of companies might look like Figure 3.10.

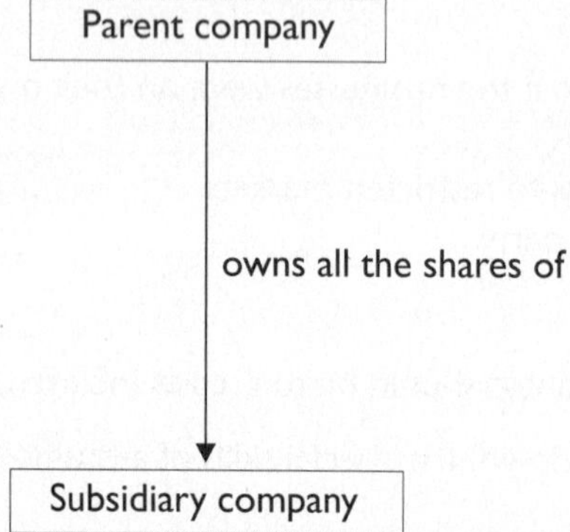

Figure 3.10 Simple group structure

In practice, groups are usually much larger and much more complex. There is no necessity for all the subsidiary company's shares to be held by the parent company and in many groups there are significant minority shareholders of subsidiary company shares.

Advantages

- Funds can be moved around a group of companies as required as can people and tax losses
- Having distinct parts (in separate companies) or one whole (the group) allows different structures and cultures to be developed as appropriate to each business in the group
- Risk of failure is spread; provided the parent company has paid fully for the shares it holds in the subsidiary, the insolvency of the subsidiary will not necessarily involve any liability for the parent company
- Minority shareholdings can be retained in subsidiaries by the entrepreneurs who set up each business. This can help to keep the entrepreneur in the business
- Skills, expertise, equipment and administration matters can be shared and/or centralised

Disadvantages

- Financial reporting for groups can become extremely complex
- Groups of companies require a great deal of administration in terms of annual returns etc
- While legally the risk is spread, the failure of a group company can have very detrimental effects on all the other companies in the group

Summary and Self-test

Summary (1/2)

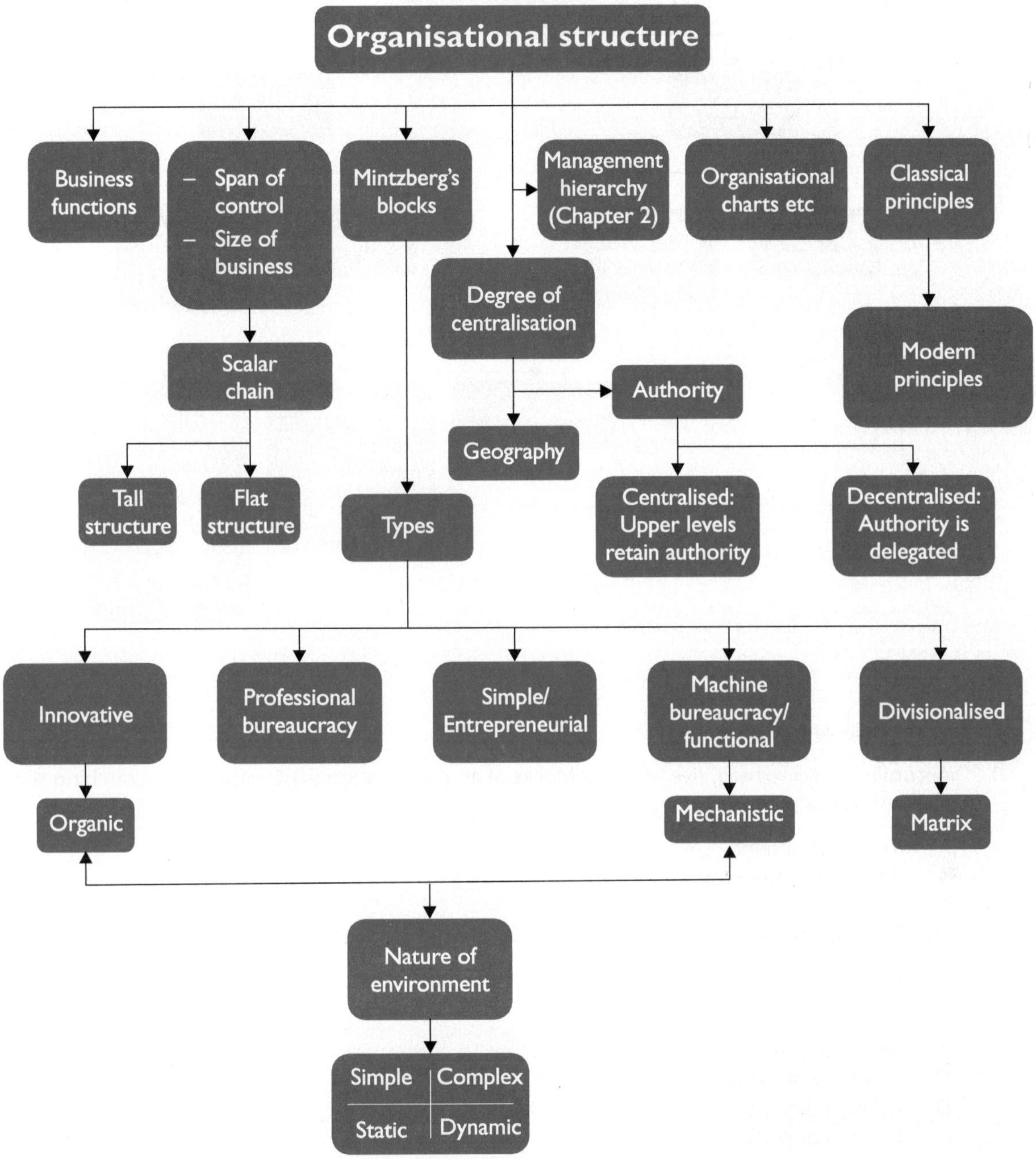

CHAPTER 3

Summary (2/2)

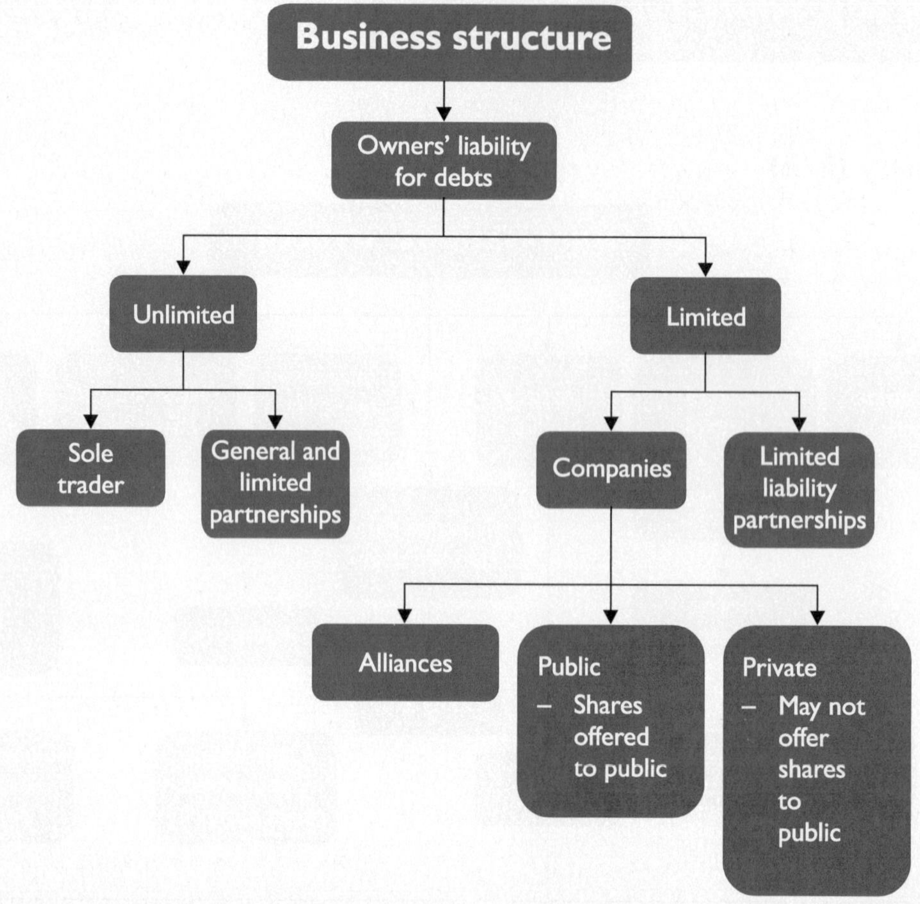

Self-test

Answer the following questions.

1 According to Mintzberg, five building blocks of an organisation exist within an overarching sixth element. He called this sixth element:

A The environment
B The technostructure
C The ideology
D The strategic apex

2 Which of the following are classical principles of organisational structure according to Fayol?

A The scalar chain
B Matrix structure
C Flexibility of personnel
D Unity of direction
E Division of work

3 Tranche Ltd is a company that was set up by Rosa Tranche, a 25 year old entrepreneur, in 2013. It operates in a sector in which innovation is key and which changes very quickly. There are a great many factors that drive both supply and demand. Tranche Ltd's three staff are together engaged in varying and complex tasks which require a high degree of intelligence, flexibility and self-direction. Tranche Ltd would be expected to have

A An adhocracy structure
B A divisionalised structure
C A machine bureaucracy structure
D A simple structure

4 The board of Cranford plc has decided that its existing organisational structure is unsuited to the demands of its current environment and strategy, and wish to change to one that is more decentralised. Which of the following aspects of Cranford plc and its management would hamper decentralisation?

A It has many employees working in various locations
B It operates in several different sectors
C It has senior and junior managers who are technically able
D It has senior managers who have an authoritative leadership style

5 Which of the following factors directly limits how many subordinates should report to a single manager?

A The size of the business
B Where the manager is situated in the management hierarchy
C How far the manager is engaged in dealings with customers and suppliers
D The length of the scalar chain

6 A bureaucracy is suited to a situation where the business's environment is

A Dynamic and complex
B Static and complex
C Static and simple
D Dynamic and simple

7 Which of the following statements about sole tradership is correct?

A The business has perpetual succession
B The owner has limited liability for unpaid business debts
C The owner must do all the work
D The business may borrow money against a fixed charge on the sole trader's assets

8 Pedro, Lynn and Shilpa wish to go into business together. They all wish to take an active role in management. None of them wishes to publicise whether or not they make a financial success of the business. Which business structure should it take?

A A general partnership
B A limited partnership
C A limited liability partnership
D A limited company

9 Which, if any, of the following businesses has limited liability for its debts?

A A general partnership
B A limited company
C A limited liability partnership
D None of them

10 A franchise is a form of

A Joint venture
B Licensing agreement
C Strategic alliance
D Agency

Now, go back to the Learning Objectives in the Introduction. If you are satisfied you have achieved these objectives, please tick them off.

Answers to Interactive questions

Answer to Interactive question 1

You are likely to be part of the operating core of your firm, along with other unqualified and part-qualified accountants. The organisational structure probably narrows at the level of senior managers, who report upwards to a small number of partners. At the strategic apex will be not only key fee-earning partners but also other senior partners who are responsible for strategic aspects of the firm. The technostructure will comprise the systems and processes that allow the business to function, such as the financial system and ICT. Support staff will include administrative staff plus finance and HR staff, plus the training department. The overarching ideology is perhaps one of professionalism, expertise, ethical values and commercial awareness.

Answer to Interactive question 2

Often managers are expected to supervise a large number of staff, say 10 or 15, while still doing a great deal of their 'own' work, such as planning and scheduling, dealing with clients and suppliers, performing technical work and having meetings with colleagues and senior managers. At some point some aspect of their work will suffer, and very often it is all aspects. Staff suffer from too wide a span of control by having too little of the right kind of supervision, and too much of the wrong kind, by feeling neglected, and by having to deal with a stressed manager.

Answer to Interactive question 3

Where a sole trader or some partners have historically been used to taking all the risks and having all the rewards of a business, having to share control with other shareholders in a formal way can be problematic. Often they don't like the publicity and the administration that incorporation involves, and in particular don't like the fact that customers, competitors and suppliers have access to financial information on the business. The expense and disruption of an audit is often felt to be disproportionate to the benefit gained by the business itself.

Answers to Self-test

1	C	
2	A, D, E	Flexibility is a more modern approach, while the matrix structure cuts across the classical principle of unity of command
3	A	Both the divisionalised and the bureaucratic organisational structure would be unsuitable as the business is so small and young. The simple structure is unsuitable as the tasks involved are complex.
4	D	
5	C	
6	C	
7	D	
8	A	As they all wish to be involved they cannot form a limited partnership; their desire to avoid publicity prevents them from operating as either a company or a limited liability partnership as both forms must file details with the Registrar
9	D	
10	B	

CHAPTER 4

Introduction to business strategy

Introduction

Learning objectives

Tick off

- State the general objectives of strategic management ☐
- Specify the strategic management process ☐
- Specify the interrelationship between a business's vision, mission and strategic objectives ☐
- Identify the relationship between a business's overall strategy and its functional strategies ☐
- Identify the nature and purpose of strategic plans, business plans and operational plans ☐
- Specify how a strategic plan is converted into fully-integrated business and operational plans ☐

Specific syllabus references are: 1b, e, f, g.

Syllabus links

The topics covered in this introduction to strategic management are developed further in Business Strategy at the Professional level, and in the Advanced level.

Examination context

Questions on the strategic management process and on the differences between strategies and plans at different levels in the business could easily appear in the exam.

Questions are likely to be set in multiple choice format and in a scenario context. Knowledge-type questions are also likely, based on particular principles, theories or models.

1 What is strategy?

Section overview

- A business's strategy is concerned with its long-term direction and objectives, its environment, the resources it has and the return it makes for its owners. It can be seen as a plan, a ploy, a pattern, a position and a perspective.
- Strategies exist at corporate, business and functional/operational levels in the business.
- Corporate strategy covers the business as a whole.
- Business strategies exist for each strategic business unit (SBU), including their competitive strategies.
- Functional strategies exist for production/operations, marketing, finance and HR within each SBU.

1.1 What is meant by 'strategy'?

There are probably as many different definitions of 'strategy' (or 'corporate strategy') as there are textbooks on the subject. Three possible definitions are as follows:

Definition

'**Strategy** is the direction and scope of an organisation over the long term, which achieves advantage for the organisation through its configuration of resources within a changing environment, to meet the needs of markets and to fulfil stakeholder expectations.' Johnson & Scholes (2002).

'**Strategy** is concerned with an organisation's basic direction for the future, its purpose, its ambitions, its resources and how it interacts with the world in which it operates.' Lynch (2000).

'**Strategy** is a course of action, including specification of the resources required, to achieve a specific objective.' (CIMA *Official Terminology*)

From these definitions we can say that strategy is concerned with:

- The long-term **direction** (objectives) of the business
- The **environment** in which it operates
- The **resources** at its disposal
- The **return** it makes to stakeholders

1.1.1 Mintzberg's 5Ps of strategy

Mintzberg looked at how the word 'strategy' has been used by people who have written about the subject, and identified what has come to be known as the 5 Ps:

- **Strategy as plan**: a **strategic plan** is a document produced at the end of a planning process. It is explicit, written down and contains targets and instructions for people to follow.
- **Strategy as ploy**: a ploy is a manoeuvre in a competitive game with the intention of winning a victory over, or disadvantaging somehow, a competitor.
- **Strategy as pattern**: strategy may become apparent by a stream of actions, a pattern of behaviour or a consistency in what the business does. This arises from the culture of the management team.
- **Strategy as position**: how does the business fit with its environment? How does it 'match' its internal resources and competences (strengths and weaknesses) with environmental conditions (opportunities and threats)? What is its market position in relation to other businesses (eg offering a product/service to a particular segment or satisfying customer needs in a particular way such as high price/high quality versus low price/lower quality)?

- **Strategy as perspective**: its strategy is the business's unique way of looking at the world and interpreting it (eg Apple Inc believing ICT to be a lifestyle accessory while Dell sees it more as a functional business tool).

1.2 Levels of strategy

Strategy can exist at several levels in a business as shown in Figure 4.1.

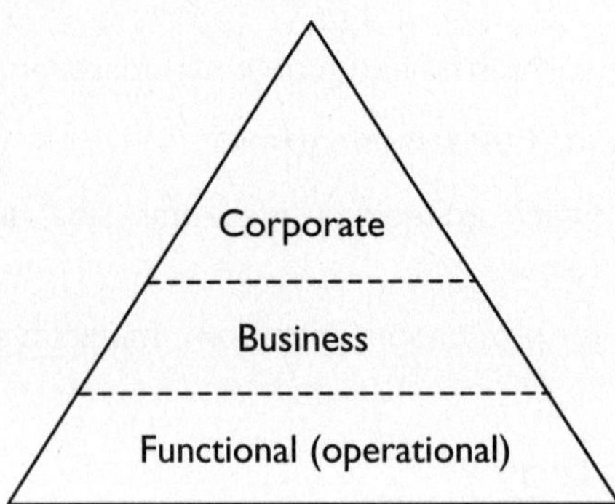

Figure 4.1: Levels of strategy

1.3 Corporate strategy

Corporate strategy is generally determined at main board level for the business as a whole. The types of matter dealt with include:

- Determining the overall corporate mission and objectives
- Overall product/market decisions, for example to expand, close down, enter a new market, develop a new product etc via methods such as organic growth, merger and acquisition or joint venture etc
- Other major investment decisions besides those for products/markets, such as information systems, IT development
- Overall financing decisions – obtaining sufficient funds at lowest cost to meet the needs of the business
- Relations with external stakeholders, such as shareholders, lenders, government, etc

1.4 Business strategies

These normally form in **strategic business units** (SBUs), and relate to how a particular market is approached, or a particular SBU acts.

Definition

Strategic business unit (SBU): A section, within a larger business, which is responsible for planning, developing, producing and marketing its own products or services.

Competitive strategy is normally determined at this level covering such matters as:

- How advantage over competitors can be achieved
- Marketing issues, such as the marketing mix

1.5 Functional (operational) strategies

These refer to the main functions within each SBU, such as production/operations, finance, human resources and marketing, and how they deliver effectively the strategies determined at the corporate and business levels.

2 Introduction to strategic management

Section overview

- Strategic management involves making decisions on the business's scope and long-term direction, and resource allocation.
- Strategic planning involves a planning and control process at the strategic level.
- A formal approach to strategic planning involves strategic analysis, strategic choice, implementation of the strategy chosen, and review and control. It is often seen as too rational and logical, and too focused on the long-term so that short-term changes upset it completely.
- The 'emergent' approach to strategy aims to evolve strategy continuously and incrementally. It therefore involves strategic analysis and review/control as with the formal approach, but strategic choice and implementation are concurrent.

2.1 What is strategic management?

The formal approach to strategic management, on which we shall largely be concentrating in this chapter states that all organisations need to plan if they are not to drift. Strategic management involves:

- Taking decisions about the scope of a business's activities
- The long-term direction of the business, and
- The allocation of resources

It involves an entire cycle of **planning and control** at a strategic level, that is **strategic planning**.

2.1.1 Formal strategic planning

A formal or rational approach to strategic planning involves four key stages:

- Strategic analysis
- Strategic choice
- Implementation of chosen strategies
- Review and control

We shall look at each stage in detail later.

Definitions

Planning: The establishment of objectives and the formulation, evaluation and selection of the policies, strategies, tactics and action required to achieve them. Planning comprises long-term/strategic planning, and short-term/operational planning.

Strategic plan: A statement of long-term goals along with a definition of the strategies and policies which will ensure achievement of these goals.

The formal approach to strategic management in a process of strategic planning has frequently been criticised because:

- It assumes that human activities are **rational** and **logical**, which is very often not the case. Managers have psychological limitations so they cannot weigh up the consequences of options or be the objective analysts that the formal, rational approach expects. Instead, they do the best they can within the limits of their circumstances, knowledge and experience in a process described as '**bounded rationality**' by **Simon**.
- It produces **prescriptive solutions for the long-term** which are rarely achieved because **changes in the environment in the short term**, such as competitors bringing out new products, necessitate immediate changes to the strategy.

2.1.2 The emergent approach to the strategy process

The **emergent approach** to the strategy process addresses these two problems by:

- **Accepting** the final goal is often unclear, and therefore
- **Adapting** to human needs and
- **Evolving** continuously and incrementally

The emergent approach to strategy can include the same degree of strategic analysis as the formal approach but strategic choice and implementation go on at the same time in a continuous process. It therefore involves three stages.

- Strategic analysis
- Strategic choice and implementation
- Review and control

In this 'suck it and see' approach, objectives and strategies are a result of negotiation and discussion, taking into account the human element in the system (particularly culture and organisational politics). A strategy is likely to be tried and developed as it is implemented. If it fails, alternative strategies will be tried. It is likely to be more short term than the traditional process, which tends to result in 'here's the strategy for the next three years, now we implement it'.

Worked example: Honda motorbikes in the US

Honda dominates the US (and UK) markets for motorcycles but its success in the US was something of an accident. Honda entered the US market with a full range of bikes, from small scooters to large powerful bikes. The initial strategy was to take on US manufacturers of large bikes. The strategy failed because, despite Honda having more reliable and better performing bikes, the US brands were far better known.

Honda had made no real effort to sell its scooters as they did not meet the needs of its target segment – men buying large bikes. After the failure of its initial strategy Honda needed cash, so it turned to selling scooters as an 'about town' bike. Small bikes were a success – particularly with those who had never bought a bike before – and this gave Honda a platform from which it later achieved dominance over the whole market.

On the face of it the initial strategy was developed along traditional lines but failure turned it into an emergent approach and a successful one.

2.2 Making strategic decisions

If we assume that strategic management follows the formal model with a logical sequence which involves analysing the current situation, generating choices relating to competitors, products and markets (strategic choice) and implementing the chosen strategies (strategy implementation), then to develop a strategy a business has to answer the following questions.

- What is it **good at**?
- How might the market **change**?
- How can **customer satisfaction** be delivered?
- What might **prevent** the plan from coming into being?
- What should be done to **minimise risk**?
- What **actions** should be followed?

In answering these questions the business needs to make a series of **strategic decisions**.

2.2.1 Characteristics of strategic decisions

Johnson and Scholes (*Exploring Corporate Strategy*) have summarised the characteristics of strategic decisions for a business as follows.

- They concern the **scope** of the business's activities
- They match a business's activities to its **capabilities** and the **environment** in which it operates
- They revolve around the allocation of **resources**
- They set off a chain of 'lesser' **operational decisions**
- They are based on the **values** and expectations of senior management
- They dictate the long-term **direction** that the business takes
- They lead **to change** in the business

3 The strategic planning process

Section overview

- Strategic planning incorporates internal and external analysis then corporate appraisal, which together inform the business's choice of mission, goals and strategic objectives. Any resulting gap between where the business is currently headed and where the strategy process has indicated it should be headed is addressed by making appropriate strategic choices, which are then implemented, reviewed and controlled.
- Strategic choice involves generating strategic options and evaluating these, then selecting the most appropriate.
- The business needs to choose competitive, product/market and institutional strategies.
- Implementing strategies involves planning resources and operations, structuring the business effectively and using appropriate control systems.

3.1 The stages of strategic planning

Using the rational model we can divide strategic planning into a number of different stages: strategic **analysis**, strategic **choice**, strategic **implementation** and ongoing **review and control** (see Figure 4.2).

The order in which the stages of strategic planning are carried out depends on whether the business takes a positioning-based or a resource-based view:

- The **positioning-based view** takes it that the forces at work in an industry, sector or market are the most important factors for strategy, so strategy development is about identifying opportunities in the environment and developing strategic capability to take advantage of them.
- The **resource-based view** takes it that the business's strategic capabilities are most important, because they explain differences between businesses and the superior performance of some over others. Strategies therefore are developed on the unique capabilities of the business, and opportunities should be sought to allow the business to exploit these capabilities to achieve competitive advantage.

In what follows we shall be taking the **positioning-based** view.

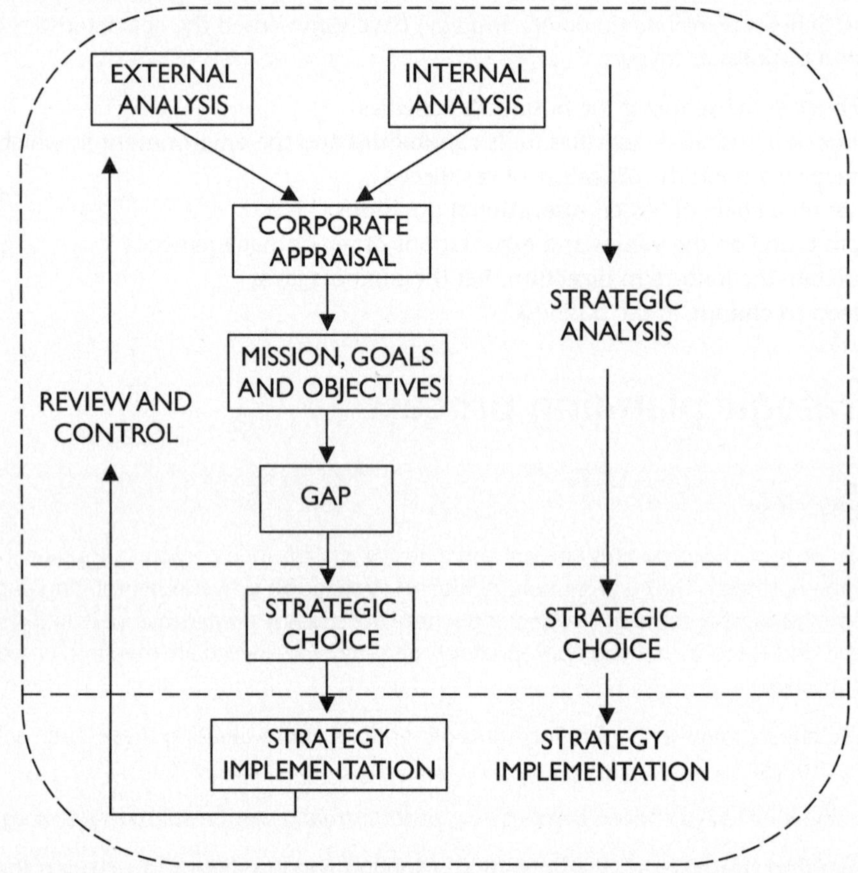

Figure 4.2: Positioning-based strategic planning process

3.2 Strategic analysis

	Stage	Comment	Key tools, models, techniques
Step 1	External analysis (analysing the environment)	Identify opportunities and threats in the business's external environment	• PESTEL analysis • Industry life cycle • Porter's five forces analysis • Competitor analysis
Step 2	Internal analysis (analysing the business)	Identify strengths and weaknesses. Analyse the business's current resources, products, customers, systems, structure, results, efficiency, effectiveness	• Resource audit • Distinctive competences • Value chain • Supply chain • Product life cycle • BCG matrix
Step 3	Corporate appraisal	Combines Steps 1 and 2	• SWOT analysis
Step 4	Mission, goals and objectives	Mission denotes values, the business's rationale for existing; goals interpret the mission for different stakeholders; objectives are quantified embodiments of the mission	• Stakeholder analysis • Mission statement
Step 5	Gap analysis	Compares outcomes of Step 3 with Step 4	• Gap analysis

3.3 Strategic choice

Stage	Comment	Key tools, models, techniques
Strategic options generation	Come up with new ideas: • How to compete (secure **competitive advantage**) in the market • Where to compete • Method of growth	• Resource-based strategies • Positioning-based strategies – Porter's generic strategies – Ansoff's product/market strategies
Strategic options evaluation	Normally, each strategy has to be evaluated on the basis of 'SFA': • Acceptability to stakeholders • Suitability to the business operational circumstances • Feasibility in terms of available finance, resources, time and competences	• Stakeholder analysis • Risk analysis (see Chapter 5)
Strategy selection	Choosing between the alternative strategies	

At the end of the process, the business should have three types of strategy:

- **Competitive strategies**: the generic strategies for competitive advantage a business will pursue. They determine **how it competes**
- **Product-market strategies** determine **where it competes** and the direction of growth (which markets a business should enter or leave)
- **Institutional strategies** determine the **method of growth** (ie relationships with other businesses)

3.4 Strategy implementation

Strategy implementation is the **conversion** of the strategies chosen into detailed **plans** or **objectives** for operating units.

The planning of implementation has several aspects.

- **Resource** planning
- **Operations** planning
- **Organisation** structure and control systems

4 Analysing the environment

Section overview

- The business's external environment incorporates the physical, the general and the task environments.
- The task environment may be simple or complex.
- Each environment may be static or dynamic.
- PESTEL analysis is used to analyse the general environment, namely its political, economic, social/demographic, technological, ecological and legal factors.
- Political factors: capacity expansion, demand, divestment/rationalisation, emerging industries, entry barriers and competition.
- Economic factors: wealth (changes in GDP), inflation, interest rates, tax, government spending, the business cycle and productivity.
- Social factors (demography): growth, age and geography of population, household and social structure, employment and wealth.
- Legal factors: changes in civil and criminal laws, employment and health/safety regulations, data protection, consumer protection, environmental regulation.
- The industry in which the business operates has a history which can be analysed using industry life cycle analysis: introduction, growth, maturity and decline.
- Porter's five forces analysis of the business's competitive environment: potential entrants, customers, suppliers, substitute goods/services, and competitors. The relative bargaining power of customers and suppliers together with the degree of threat from the others determines how much rivalry there is between businesses and therefore how profitable the industry is likely to be.
- Competitor analysis involves looking at the business's different types of competitor: brand, industry, generic and form. For each type, their strategy, assumptions about the industry, situation and capability should be analysed to determine how they will respond to the business's competitive strategy (their reaction profile): laid back, tiger, selective or stochastic.

4.1 What is in the business's external environment?

Businesses exist within an environment which strongly influences what they do and whether they survive and develop. Strategic planners must take account of potential environmental impacts in order to produce plans that are realistic and achievable.

Definition

Environment of a business: Everything outside its boundaries. It may be segmented according to Figure 4.3 into the physical, the general and the task environment.

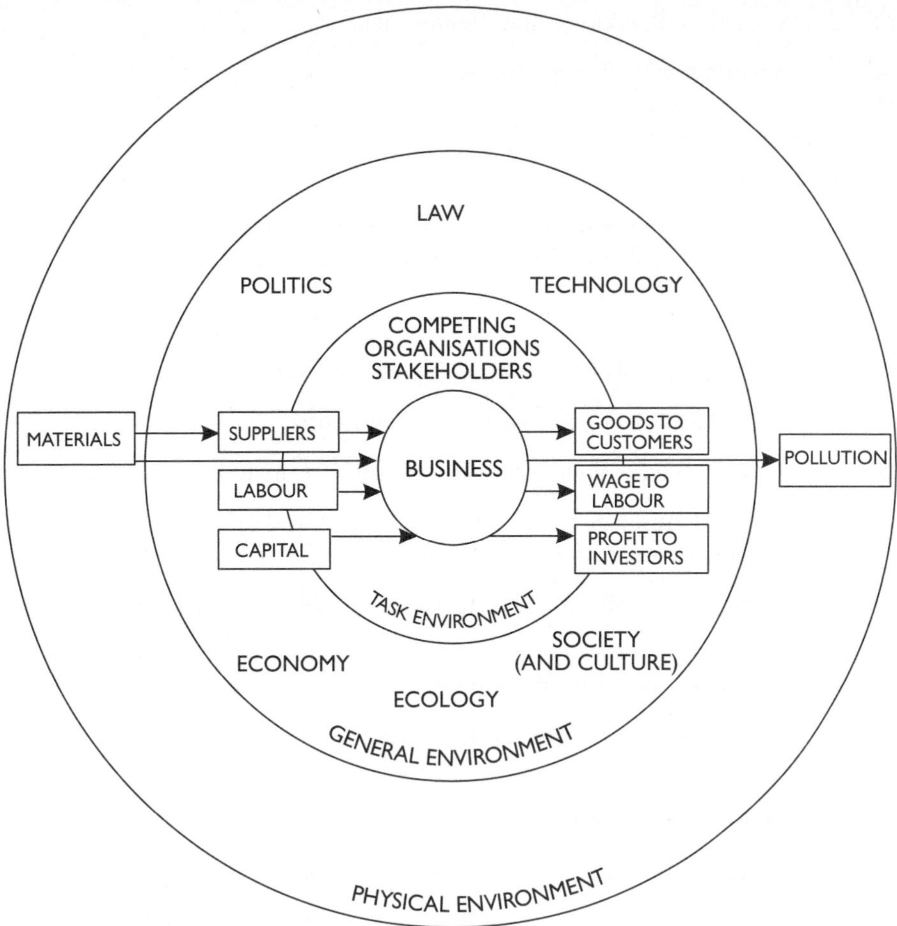

Figure 4.3: The business's external environment

Definitions

General environment: Covers all the political, legal, economic, social/cultural, ecological and technological (**PESTEL**) influences in the countries a business operates in.

Task environment: Relates to factors of particular relevance to the business, such as its competitors, customers and suppliers of resources.

The task environment may be **simple**, for instance where there are few competitors and predictable outcomes and suppliers, or highly **complex**.

With regard to environmental issues there is a further variable to be dealt with: the **time horizon** of changes in the external environment. Some have **long-term impact**, which can be dealt with by careful planning, but some have **short-term** or **immediate impact**, which require **crisis management**.

4.2 Environmental uncertainty

No business can predict the future with absolute certainty. Strategic planning has to take place in the context of an uncertain future environment – competitors may enter or leave markets, new technologies may be discovered, governments may change, etc.

A business needs to think about how **static** or **dynamic** its future environment is likely to be. We have already seen in Chapter 3 that these qualities can affect the business's structure.

4.2.1 Static environments

Some businesses exist in relatively static environments. For example, raw material producers such as farmers often experience only slow environmental change. Other businesses are insulated from change by institutional factors. Solicitors, for example, have traditionally felt themselves to be protected from competition by regulation.

The 'Four Ss' can be used to describe a static environment:

- **Static** – environmental change is slow
- **Single** – product/market
- **Simple** – technology
- **Safe**

In static situations there is often great value in studying the business's historic and current environment. As change is only slow the past can be a useful predictor of the future.

4.2.2 Dynamic environments

Most businesses face environments characterised by rapid change and complexity.

The 'four Ds' can be used to describe a dynamic environment:

- **Dynamic** – the speed of environmental change appears to increase through time
- **Diverse** – many businesses are now multiproduct and operate in many markets; business is also increasingly international
- **Difficult** – because of the above factors analysis of the environment is not easy
- **Dangerous** – because of the above factors ignoring the environment can have serious consequences for the business

In dynamic environments the past is often a poor guide to the future.

4.3 Analysing the general environment: PESTEL analysis

Using PESTEL analysis we can consider the environmental factors affecting a business under six general headings as seen in Figure 4.4:

- Political factors
- Economic factors
- Social/demographic factors
- Technological factors
- Ecological factors
- Legal factors

ECONOMIC FACTORS

- Globalisation
- Business cycles
- Interest rates
- Inflation
- Unemployment
- Exchange rates

ECOLOGICAL FACTORS

- Sustainability issues, eg energy, natural resources
- Pollution
- Green issues

TECHNOLOGICAL FACTORS

- Government investment and R&D policy
- New discoveries: products and methods of production
- Speed of technology transfer
- Levels of R&D spending by competitors
- Developments in other industries that could transfer across

PESTEL ANALYSIS

SOCIAL/DEMOGRAPHIC FACTORS

- Income distribution
- Social mobility
- Levels of education/health
- Size of population
- Location
- Age distribution
- Lifestyle changes
- Consumerism
- Attitudes to work and leisure
- Green consumers

POLITICAL FACTORS

- Social welfare policy
- Taxation policy
- Regulations
- Government stability

LEGAL FACTORS

- Competition legislation
- Environmental protection laws
- Employment law
- Consumer protection
- Health and safety regulations

Figure 4.4: Possible items in a PESTEL analysis

The aim is to identify the factors which are currently affecting the business and those which are likely to become significant in the future. To avoid this becoming merely a listing exercise, the business must identify the few key influences from all those identified by the analysis, that is, the key **opportunities** available to it in the external environment, and the key **threats** which it faces.

Interactive question 1: Business environment [Difficulty level: Intermediate]

You have developed an idea to set up a business publishing brief study notes for student accountants when you qualify. Have a try at analysing the external environment in which such a business would exist.

See **Answer** at the end of this chapter.

4.3.1 Political influences

Political influences on businesses are dominated by the influence of **government**, which can and very often does have a profound effect on the structure of entire industries.

Capacity expansion	Government policy can encourage businesses to increase or cut their capacity. • Direct taxes can reduce demand and hence supply • The tax system offers 'capital allowances' to encourage investment in equipment • A variety of **incentives** exist for locating capacity in a **particular area** • Incentives are used to encourage investment by **foreign businesses**
Demand	• The government is a major customer • Government can also influence demand by legislation, taxes or subsidies
Divestment and rationalisation	The state may take decisions regarding the selling off or closure of businesses, especially in sensitive areas such as defence.
Emerging industries	These can be promoted by the government or damaged by it.
Entry barriers	Government policy can discourage firms from entering an industry, by restricting investment or competition or by making it harder, by use of quotas and tariffs, for overseas firms to compete in the domestic market.
Competition	• The government's **purchasing decisions** will have a strong influence on the strength of one business relative to another in the market (eg armaments) • **Regulations and controls** in an industry will affect the growth and profits of the industry, eg minimum product quality standards • As a supplier of **infrastructure** (eg roads), the government is also in a position to influence competition in an industry • Governments and supra-national institutions such as the EU might impose policies which keep an industry **fragmented**, and prevent the concentration of too much market share in the hands of one or two producers

We shall see more about the effect of regulation and other government interventions on businesses in Chapters 13 and 14 of this Study Manual.

4.3.2 Economic factors

The economic environment is an important influence at local and national level. Here are some factors to which businesses must attend.

Factor	Impact
Local economic trends:	Type of industry in the area. Office/factory rents. Labour rates. House prices.
National economic trends:	
Overall growth or fall in wealth (Gross Domestic Product or GDP)	Increased/decreased demand for goods (eg dishwashers) and services (eg holidays).
Inflation	Low in most countries; distorts business decisions; wage inflation compensates for price inflation.
Interest rates	How much it costs to borrow money (the interest rate) affects **cash flow**. Some businesses carry a high level of debt. How much customers can afford to spend is also affected as rises in interest rates affect people's mortgage and other debt payments.
Tax levels	Corporation tax affects how much businesses can invest or return to shareholders. Income tax and VAT affect how much consumers have to spend, hence their demand.

Factor	Impact
Government spending	Suppliers to the government (eg construction firms) are affected by government spending.
The business cycle	Economic activity is always punctuated by periods of growth followed by decline, simply because of the nature of trade. The UK economy has been characterised by periods of 'boom' and 'bust'. Government policy can cause, exacerbate or mitigate such trends, but cannot abolish the business cycle. (Industries which prosper when others are declining are called counter-cyclical industries.)
Productivity	An economy cannot grow faster than underlying growth in productivity without risking inflation.

We shall look at the economic environment in more detail in Chapter 13.

4.3.3 Social factors

How a country's population is made up – its **demography** – gives rise to factors that are important in strategic planning.

Factor	Comment
Growth	The rate of growth or decline in a national population and in regional populations.
Age	Changes in the age distribution of the population.
Geography	The concentration of population into certain geographical areas.
Household and family structure	A household is the basic social unit and its size might be determined by the number of children, whether elderly parents live at home etc. In the UK, there has been an increase in single-person households and lone parent families.
Social structure	The population of a society can be broken down into a number of subgroups, with different attitudes and access to economic resources.
Employment	In part, this is related to changes in the workplace and in legislation. Many people believe that there is a move to a casual flexible workforce; factories have a group of core employees, supplemented by a group of insecure peripheral employees, on part-time or temporary contracts, working as and when required.
Wealth	Rising standards of living lead to increased demand for certain types of consumer good.

Social factors are also important in the context of society's changing attitudes to certain issues such as marriage, crime etc. Very often these attitudes are voiced by the media (newspapers, TV, radio).

4.3.4 Technological factors

Technological change is rapid, and businesses must adapt themselves to it. It affects activities as follows.

- The **type** of products or services that are made and sold.
- The way in which products are **made**: equipment, new raw materials.
- The way in which **services** are provided, for example the internet.
- The way in which **markets are identified**.
- The way in which businesses are **managed**.
- The means and extent of **communications with external clients**.

4.3.5 Ecological factors

Factor	Example
Resource inputs	Managing physical resources sustainably (eg replanting forests)
Waste output	Managing more efficiently so as not to attract fines
Legislation	The effect of transport on the natural environment, 'food miles'
Government	Pollution and recycling regulations
Disasters	Increasing levels of natural disasters eg mudslides, drought due to global warming
Demand	Consumers demanding environmentally friendly products and disapproving of excessive waste packaging etc
Pressure groups	Green activities have huge influence

4.3.6 Legal factors

Factor	Example
General legal framework: contract, tort, agency	Basic ways of doing business, negligence proceedings
Criminal law	Theft of industrial secrets, insider dealing, bribery, fraud, fraudulent trading, market abuse, money laundering
Company law	Directors and their duties, reporting requirements, takeover proceedings, shareholders' rights, insolvency, corporate governance
Employment law	Trade Union recognition, minimum wage, unfair dismissal, redundancy, maternity, equality
Health and safety law	Fire precautions, safety procedures
Data protection	Use of information about employees and customers
Consumer protection	Laws to protect consumers (eg refunds and replacement, 'cooling off' period after credit agreements), what is or isn't allowed in advertising
Environment	Pollution control, waste disposal
Tax law	Corporation tax payment, collection of income tax (PAYE) and National Insurance contributions, VAT

4.4 Industry life cycle

The concept of **life cycle analysis** is popular in strategic management. It reflects the fact that, just as humans are born, develop, mature, decline and finally die, so too do products, businesses, markets and – at the largest scale – whole industries.

The stages of the industry life cycle are:

- **Introduction** – newly-invented product or service is made available for purchase
- **Growth** – a period of rapid expansion of demand or activity as the industry finds a market
- **Maturity** – a relatively stable period of time where there is little change in sales volumes year to year but competition between businesses intensifies
- **Decline** – a falling-off in activity levels as businesses leave the industry and the industry ceases to exist or is absorbed into some other industry.

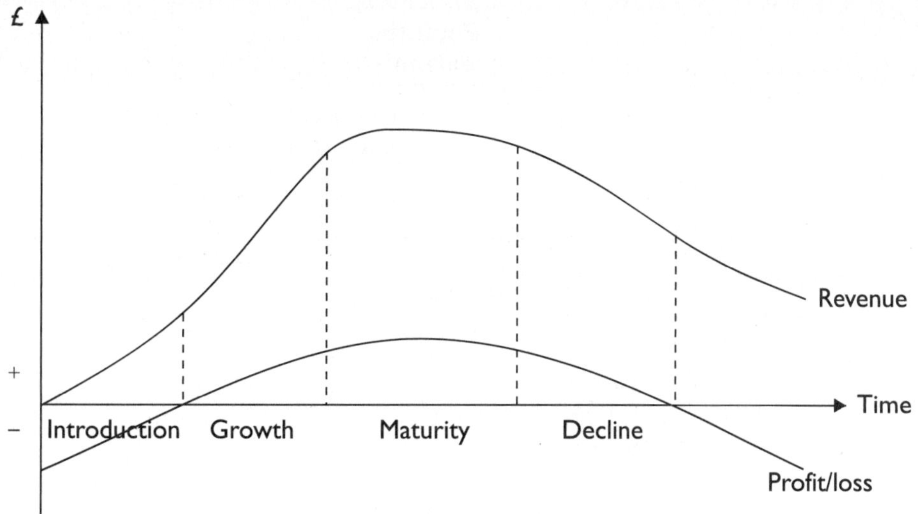

Figure 4.5: Industry life cycle

Some industry life cycles are identical in pattern and timing to that of their product (eg in the steel industry). Others have longer life cycles than the particular products, eg the music industry which has endured from sheet music to downloads, merely releasing (and re-releasing) its music as new products as the format changes.

4.5 Analysing the competitive (task) environment: Porter's five forces analysis of an industry

When looking at the competitive aspect of the task environment of the business, a very useful model is the five forces analysis put forward by Michael Porter. To understand this model we need to distinguish between a market and an industry.

Definitions

Market: Comprises the customers or potential customers who have needs which are satisfied by a product or service.

Industry: Comprises those businesses which use a particular competence, technology, product or service to satisfy customer needs, and which therefore compete with each other.

Porter states that there are five **competitive forces** which influence the state of competition in an **industry as a whole**, illustrated in Figure 4.6:

- new entrants
- customers
- substitutes
- suppliers
- industry competitors.

Collectively these determine the profit potential of the industry as a whole, because of the **threats** they represent (new entrants and substitutes), the **bargaining power** they hold (customers and suppliers), and the **degree of rivalry** that exists among current competitors in the industry.

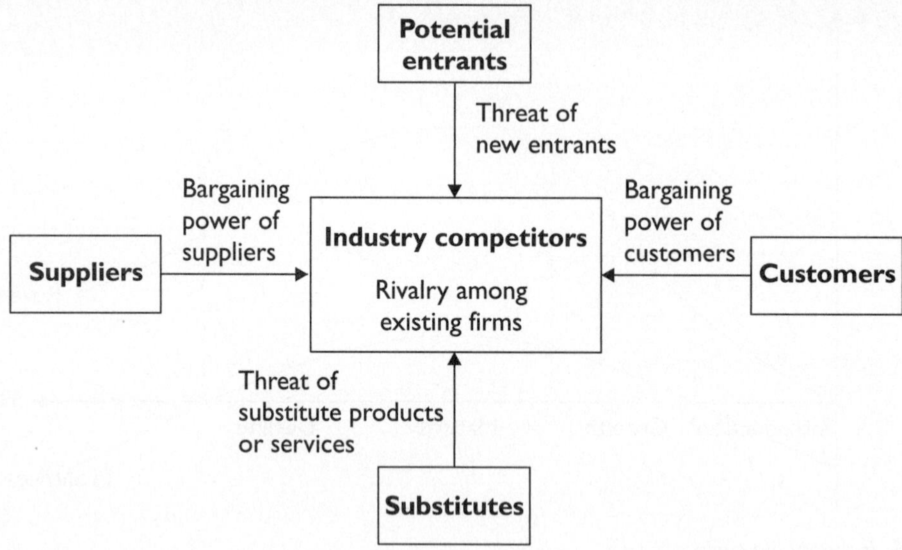

Source: adapted from Porter (*Competitive Strategy*)

Figure 4.6: Porter's Five Forces

4.5.1 The threat of new entrants (and barriers to entry to keep them out)

A new entrant into an industry will bring extra capacity and more competition. The strength of this threat is likely to vary from industry to industry, depending on:

- The strength of the **barriers to entry** which discourage new entrants
- The **likely response of existing competitors** to the new entrant

Barriers to entry	Comment
Scale economies	As scale of operations increases, the cost per unit of the product or service falls. This means that new entrants must start their operations on a large scale or suffer a vast disadvantage. A high level of fixed costs also requires entry on a large scale.
Static market	If the market as a whole is not growing, the new entrant has to capture a large slice of the market from existing competitors.
Product differentiation	Existing firms in an industry may have built up a good brand image and strong customer loyalty over a long period of time; they may promote a large number of brands to crowd out the competition.
Investment requirements	When investment requirements are high, the barrier against new entrants will be strong, particularly when the investment would possibly be high-risk.
Switching costs	Switching costs refer to the costs (time, money, convenience) that a customer would have to incur by switching from one supplier's products to another's. Although it might cost a consumer nothing to switch from one brand of frozen peas to another, the potential costs for the retailer or distributor might be high.
Access to distribution channels	Distribution channels carry products to the end-buyer. New distribution channels are difficult to establish, and existing distribution channels are hard to gain access to.
Cost advantages of existing producers, independent of scale economies	Include: • Patent rights • Experience and know-how (the learning curve) • Government subsidies and regulations • Favoured access to raw materials

We shall look at economies of scale in more detail in Chapters 13 and 14.

Entry barriers might be **lowered** by:

- Changes in the environment
- Technological changes
- Novel distribution channels for products or services

4.5.2 The threat from substitute products

A **substitute product** is a good/service produced by **another industry** which satisfies the same customer needs.

Worked example: The Channel Tunnel

Passengers have several ways of getting from London to Paris, and the pricing policies of the various industries transporting them there reflect this.

(a) 'Le Shuttle' carries cars in the Channel Tunnel. Its main competitors are the *ferry* companies, offering a substitute service. Therefore, you will find that Le Shuttle sets its prices with reference to ferry company prices, and *vice versa.*

(b) Eurostar is the passenger rail service from London to Paris/Brussels. Its main competitors are not the ferry companies but the *airlines.* Initially, prices on the London-Paris air routes fell with the commencement of Eurostar services, and some airlines curtailed the number of flights they offered. Low-cost airlines changed this equation by offering a cheaper alternative.

4.5.3 The bargaining power of customers

Customers include both the **ultimate consumer** and the buyers forming the **distribution channel**. Customers want better quality products and services at a lower price. Satisfying this might force down the profitability of suppliers in the industry. Just how strong the bargaining of customers is depends on several factors.

- How much the **customer buys**
- How **critical** the product is to the customer's own business
- **Switching costs (the cost to the customer of switching supplier)**
- Whether the products are **standard items** (hence easily copied) or **specialised**
- The **customer's own profitability**
- Customer's **ability to bypass** the supplier or to take over the supplier
- The **skills** of the customer's **purchasing staff**, or the price-awareness of consumers
- The importance of **product quality** to the customer

4.5.4 The bargaining power of suppliers

Suppliers can exert pressure for higher prices in the industry but their bargaining power is dependent on several factors:

- Whether there are just **one or two dominant suppliers** to the industry, able to charge monopoly or oligopoly prices (we shall see more about this in Chapter 13)
- The threat of **new entrants** or substitute products to the **supplier's industry**
- Whether the suppliers have **other customers** outside the industry, and so do not rely on the industry for the majority of their sales
- The **importance of the supplier's product** to the customer's business
- Whether the supplier has a **specialised product** which buyers need to obtain
- Whether **switching costs** for their customers would be high

4.5.5 The rivalry amongst current competitors in the industry

The **intensity of competitive rivalry** within an industry will affect the profitability of the industry as a whole. Competitive actions might take the form of price competition, advertising battles, sales promotion campaigns, introducing new products for the market, improving after sales service or providing guarantees or warranties.

The intensity of competition will depend on the following factors.

Factor	Comment
Market growth	Rivalry is intensified when firms are competing for a greater market share in a total market where growth is slow or stagnant.
Cost structure	High fixed costs are a temptation to compete on price, as in the short run any sales are better than none at all.
Switching	Suppliers will compete more fiercely if buyers switch easily (eg Coke v Pepsi).
Capacity	A supplier might need to achieve a substantial increase in output *capacity*, in order to obtain reductions in costs per unit.
Uncertainty	When one firm is not sure what another is up to, there is a tendency to respond to the uncertainty by formulating a more competitive strategy.
Strategic importance	If success is a prime strategic objective, firms will be likely to act very competitively to meet their targets.
Exit barriers	Make it difficult for an existing supplier to leave the industry. • Long-term assets with a low break-up value (eg there may be no other use for them, or they may be old) • The cost of redundancy payments to employees • If the business is a division or subsidiary of a larger enterprise, the effect of withdrawal on the other operations within the group

Interactive question 2: Product rivalry **[Difficulty level: Intermediate]**

Select an industry with which you are very familiar, such as fashionable clothing. Try to identify whether or not there is rivalry among the competing businesses in the industry.

See **Answer** at the end of this chapter.

4.6 Analysing the competitive (task) environment: competitor analysis

To analyse the situation and potential activities of industry competitors (the fifth force in Porter's model) we can use competitor **analysis**. The objective of this is to draw out those areas where the business competes well and has a competitive advantage, and those where this is held by the business's rivals.

A business must **define who its current competitors actually are**. This group may be larger than is immediately apparent. Coca-Cola, for example, competes against the following.

- Pepsi in the cola market, and retailers' own brands
- All other soft drinks
- Tea and coffee
- Coca-Cola's chief executive has declared that 'the main competitor is tap water: any other definition is too narrow'

4.6.1 Types of competitor

Kotler lists four **types of competitor** depending on the relative level at which the competitor operates.

- **Brand competitors** are similar firms offering similar products: for example, *McDonald's* and *Burger King*.
- **Industry competitors** have similar products but are different in other ways, such as geographical market or range of products: for example, online retailing (eg *Amazon)* and traditional retailing
- **Generic competitors** compete for the same disposable income with different products: for example, a music store which sells CDs and DVDs, and a book store on the opposite side of the same street
- **Form competitors** offer distinctly different products that satisfy the same needs: for example, manufacturers of matches and those of cigarette lighters

For each competitor, the following factors can be analysed.

Factor to be analysed	Comment
Competitor's strategy (for the business as a whole and the relevant business unit)	• What are the business's **stated financial goals**? What trade-offs are made between long-term and short-term objectives? • Do **managerial beliefs** (eg that the firm should be a market leader) affect its goals? • **Organisation structure**: what is the relative status of functional areas? • What are the **managers** like? Do they favour one particular type of strategy? • To what extent does the business **cross-subsidise** others in the group if the business is part of a group? What is the **purpose of the business**: to raise money for the group?
The **competitor's assumptions** about the industry	• What does a competitor believe to be its **relative position** in the industry (in terms of cost, product quality)? • Are there any **cultural or regional differences** that indicate the way the competitors' managers are likely to respond? • What does the competitor believe about the future for the industry? • Does the competitor accept the industry's '**conventional wisdom**'?
The **competitor's current and potential situation** with regard to:	• Distribution • Operations • Overall costs • Marketing and selling • Financial strengths • Organisation • Research and engineering • Managerial ability • Products
Competitor's capability	• What does the competitor do distinctively well - what are its **core competences**? • Does the competitor have the **ability to expand** in a particular market? • What **competitive advantages and disadvantages** does the competitor possess?

All these are combined in a **competitor reaction profile.** This indicates the competitor's vulnerability and the right 'battleground' on which to fight.

Kotler lists four reaction profiles.

- The **laid back** competitor does not respond to moves by its competitors
- The **tiger** competitor responds aggressively to all opposing moves
- The **selective** competitor reacts to some threats in some markets but not to all
- The **stochastic** competitor is unpredictable

5 Analysing the business

Section overview

- Internal analysis encompasses the business's resources and competences, value chain, supply chain and products/markets.
- A resource audit looks at the business's machinery, culture, structure and intangible assets, management and the information they use, markets, materials, people, processes and finance.
- Activities in the value chain are designed to create value: the extra amount or margin that the customer is prepared to pay for a product/service over and above its input costs.
- Primary value-adding activities: inbound and outbound logistics, operations, marketing and service. Secondary activities support the value-adding ones: infrastructure, HRM, technology and procurement.
- The business's supply chain describes all the suppliers and partners who together support the mutual effort to produce goods and services for customers. This integrated supply chain needs to be managed effectively.
- The product life cycle describes how a product shows different levels of profitability and investment over the different phases during which it is on the market: introduction, growth, maturity and decline.
- The Boston Consulting Group (BCG) matrix analyses product and SBUs in terms of their relative market share and potential for market growth, and identified appropriate strategies for each one.

5.1 What aspects of the business should be analysed?

Having completed its analysis of the external general and task environment, the business should next analyse itself. This primarily involves analysis of:

- Its resources and competencies, using a position and resource audit
- Its 'value chain'
- Its supply chain
- Its products and markets, using the product life cycle and the BCG matrix

5.2 Analysing resources and competencies (the position audit)

To develop a strategic plan, an organisation's management must be aware of its current position.

Definition

Position audit: Part of the planning process which examines the current state of the entity in respect of:

- Resources of tangible and intangible assets and finance
- Its competencies, that is what it has the ability to do well via its combination of resources, skills etc
- Products, brands and markets
- Operating systems such as production and distribution
- Internal organisation
- Current results
- Returns to shareholders

The **Ms model** categorises the factors to be reviewed in a **resource audit** as follows.

Resource	Example
Machinery	Age. Condition. Utilisation rate. Value. Replacement. Technologically up-to-date? Cost.

Resource	Example
Make-up	Culture and structure. Patents. Goodwill. Brands.
Management	Size. Skills. Loyalty. Career progression. Structure.
Management information	Ability to generate and disseminate ideas. Innovation. Information systems.
Markets	Products and customers.
Materials	Source. Suppliers and partnering. Waste. New materials. Cost. Availability. Future provision.
Men and women	Number. Skills. Wage costs. Proportion of total costs. Efficiency. Labour turnover. Industrial relations. Succession plans.
Methods	How are activities carried out?
Money	Credit and turnover periods. Cash surpluses/deficits. Short-term and long-term finance. Gearing levels.

A resource audit should go on to consider how well or how badly resources have been utilised, and whether the business's systems are effective and efficient.

Every business operates under resource **constraints**, that is, **limited resources**.

Definition

Limiting factor or **key factor**: Anything which limits the activity of an entity. An entity seeks to optimise the benefit it obtains from the limiting factor. Examples are a shortage of supply of a resource or a restriction on sales demand at a particular price.

Once the limiting factor has been identified, the planners should:

- In the short term, make best use of the resources available
- Try to reduce the limitation in the long term

Limiting factor analysis is part of management accounting as we shall see in Chapter 7.

5.3 Analysing Porter's value chain

The **value chain** model of corporate activities, developed by Porter, offers a bird's eye view of the business and what it does. Competitive advantage, says Porter, arises out of the way in which businesses organise and perform **activities**.

Definition

Activities: The means by which a business creates value in its products. (They are sometimes referred to as **value activities**.)

Activities incur **costs**, and, in combination with other activities, provide a product or service which earns **revenue**.

Worked example: Value chain in a restaurant

A restaurant's activities can be divided into buying food, cooking it, and serving it (to customers). There is no reason, in theory, why the customers should not do all these things themselves, at home. The customer, however, is not only prepared to **pay for someone else** to do all this but is also prepared to **pay more than the cost of** the individual resources (food, wages etc). The ultimate value a business creates is measured as the amount customers are willing to pay for its products or services above the

cost of carrying out value activities. A business is profitable if the realised value to customers exceeds the collective cost of performing the activities.

- Customers **purchase value,** which they measure by comparing a business's products and services with similar offerings by competitors.
- The business **creates value** by carrying out its activities either more efficiently than other businesses, or by combining them in such a way as to provide a unique product or service.

Interactive question 3: Creating value [Difficulty level: Intermediate]

Outline different ways in which the restaurant can 'create' value.

See **Answer** at the end of this chapter.

5.3.1 Activities in the value chain

Porter (in *Competitive Advantage*) grouped the various activities of an organisation into a value chain (Figure 4.7).

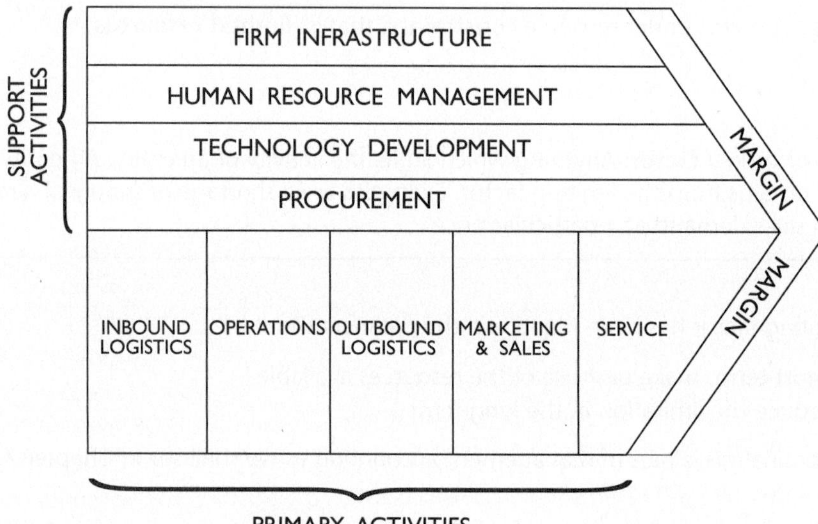

Figure 4.7: Value chain

The **margin** is the excess the customer is prepared to **pay** over the **cost** to the business of obtaining resource inputs and providing value activities.

Definition

Value chain: The sequence of business activities by which, in the perspective of the end-user, value is added to the products or services produced by an entity.

Primary activities are directly related to production, operations, sales, marketing, delivery and service.

Primary activity	Comment
Inbound logistics	Receiving, handling and storing inputs to the production system (ie warehousing, transport, inventory control etc).
Operations	Convert resource inputs into a final product. Resource inputs are not only materials. 'People' are a 'resource', especially in service industries.
Outbound logistics	Storing the product and its distribution to customers: packaging, warehousing, testing etc.

Primary activity	Comment
Marketing and sales	Informing customers about the product, persuading them to buy it, and enabling them to do so: advertising, promotion etc.
Service	Installing products, repairing them, upgrading them, providing spare parts and so forth.

Support activities provide purchased inputs, human resources, technology and infrastructural functions to support the primary activities.

Support activity	Comment
Procurement	Acquire the resource inputs to the primary activities (eg purchase of materials, subcomponents, equipment). See the section on analysing the supply chain below.
Human resource management	Recruiting, training, developing and rewarding people.
Technology development	Product design, improving processes and/or resource utilisation.
Firm infrastructure	Planning, finance, quality control: Porter believes these are crucially important to an organisation's strategic capability in all primary activities.

Linkages connect the activities of the value chain.

- **Activities in the value chain affect one another**. For example, more costly product design or better quality production might reduce the need for after-sales service.
- **Linkages require co-ordination**. For example, reducing the level of inventory held requires smooth functioning of operations, outbound logistics and service activities such as installation.

5.3.2 Using the value chain

A business can secure competitive advantage by:

- Inventing **new or better ways** to do activities
- **Combining** activities in new or better ways
- Managing the **linkages in its own value chain** to increase efficiency and reduce costs
- Managing the **linkages in the value system**

5.4 Analysing the supply chain

A simple view of the support activity of procurement would be to state that it is just about getting the best price from suppliers for the best quality goods and services, based on an arm's length relationship with the supplier. Increasingly, however, a business looks beyond their immediate supplier to the whole supply chain supporting the business in a mutual effort to produce goods and services.

The business therefore needs to analyse the parties in its supply chain and see whether the principles of **integrated supply chain management** can be applied to improve efficiency.

Definition

Integrated supply chain management (SCM): Optimising the activities of businesses working together to produce goods and services.

Integrated SCM is a means by which the business aims to manage the chain from input resources to the consumer. It can involve the following aspects.

- Reduction in the number of suppliers and much closer '**partnership**' relationships with those that remain

- Reduction in customers served for the sake of focus, and concentration of the company's resources on customers of high potential value
- Price and inventory co-ordination. Businesses co-ordinate their price and inventory policies to avoid problems and bottlenecks caused by short-term surges in demand, such as promotions
- Linked computer systems – electronic data interchange saves on paperwork and warehousing expense
- Early supplier involvement in product development and component design
- Carefully designed distribution system
- Joint problem-solving among supply chain partners
- Supplier representative on site

The aim is to co-ordinate the whole chain, from raw material suppliers to end customers. The chain should be considered as a **network** rather than a **pipeline** – a network of vendors support a network of customers, with third parties such as transport firms helping to link the businesses.

5.5 Analysing products and markets: the product life cycle

Definition

Product life cycle: How a product demonstrates different characteristics of profit and investment over time. Analysing it enables a business to examine its portfolio of goods and services as a whole.

Just as with industries, so too can the profitability and sales of a product be expected to change over time. The **product life cycle** is an attempt to recognise distinct stages in a product's history. Marketing managers distinguish between different aspects of the product.

- **Product class:** this is a broad category of product, such as cars, washing machines, newspapers (also referred to as the **generic product**).
- **Product form:** within a product class there are different forms that the product can take, for example five-door hatchback cars or two-seater sports cars; twin tub or front loading automatic washing machines; national daily newspapers or weekly local papers, and so on.
- **Brand:** the particular type of the product form (eg Ford Focus).

The product life cycle applies in differing degrees to each of the three aspects. A product class (eg cars) may have a long maturity stage, and a particular brand *might* have an erratic life cycle (eg Rolls Royce) or not. Product forms however tend to conform to the classic life cycle pattern in Figure 4.8.

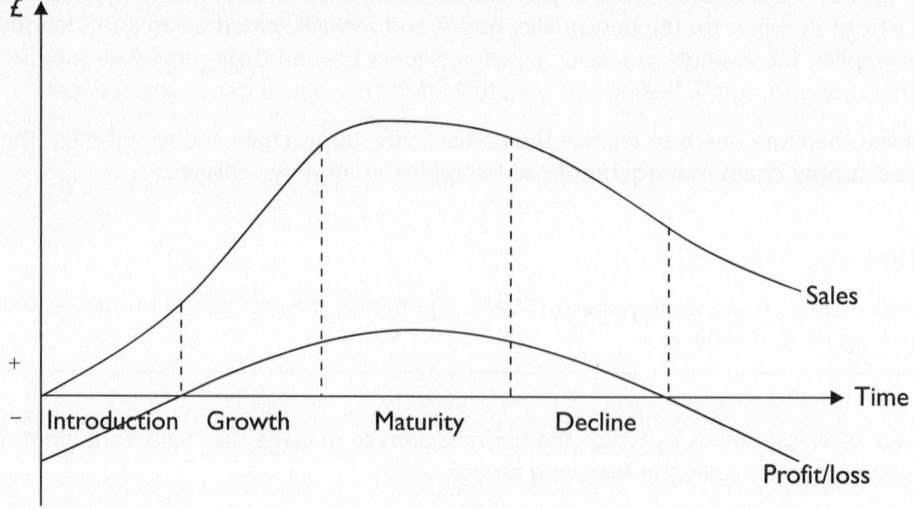

Figure 4.8: Product life cycle

Stage in life cycle	Comments
Introduction	A new product takes time to find acceptance by would-be purchasers and there is a slow growth in sales. Unit costs are high because of low output and expensive sales promotion. There may be early teething troubles with production technology. The product for the time being is a loss-maker.
Growth	If the new product gains market acceptance, sales will eventually rise more sharply and the product will start to make profits. Competitors are attracted and as sales and production rise, unit costs fall.
Maturity	The rate of sales growth slows down and the product reaches a period of maturity which is probably the longest period of a successful product's life. Most products on the market will be at the mature stage of their life. Profits are good.
Decline	Eventually, sales will begin to decline so that there is over-capacity of production in the industry. Severe competition occurs, profits fall and some producers leave the market. The remaining producers seek means of prolonging the product life by modifying it and searching for new market segments. Many producers are reluctant to leave the market, although some inevitably do because of falling profits. Some producers may continue even where there are losses, perhaps to support complementary products.

In the strategic analysis process, planners should assess:

- The **stage of its life cycle** that any product has reached.
- Each **product's remaining life**, ie how much longer the product will contribute to profits.
- How **urgent is the need to innovate**, to develop new and improved products?

5.6 Planning products and markets: the BCG matrix

Another useful way to look at the products/services the business is engaged in and the markets it services is to analyse them using the Boston Consulting Group (BCG) matrix.

BCG developed a matrix (Figure 4.9) based on research that assesses a business's products in terms of potential **cash generation** and **cash expenditure** requirements. Products, or SBUs, are categorised in terms of **market growth rate** and **relative market share**.

Definition

Market share: One entity's sale of a product or service in a specified market expressed as a percentage of total sales by all entities offering that product or service.

- Assessing **rate of market growth** as high or low depends on the conditions in the market.
- **Market share** is assessed as a ratio: it is market share compared with the market share of the **largest competitor**. Thus a relative market share greater than 1 indicates that the product or SBU is the market leader.

		Market share	
		High	*Low*
Market growth	*High*	**Stars** ⇨ Build	**Question marks** ⇨ Build OR Harvest
	Low	**Cash cows** ⇨ Hold OR Harvest	**Dogs** ⇨ Hold OR Divest

Figure 4.9: BCG matrix

- **Stars**. In the short term, these require capital expenditure (investment) in excess of the cash they generate, in order to maintain their market position, but they promise high returns in the future. Strategy: **build** (forgo short-term earnings and profits to build market share).
- In due course, stars will become **cash cows**. These need very little capital expenditure and generate high levels of cash income. However, it is important to remember that apparently mature products can

be invigorated, possibly by competitors, who could thus come to dominate the market. Cash cows can be used to finance the stars. Strategy: **hold** (maintain the market position) or **harvest** (take maximum earnings in the short term at the expense of long-term development) if weak.

- **Question marks**. Do the products justify considerable capital expenditure in the hope of increasing their market share, or should they be allowed to die quietly as they are squeezed out of the expanding market by rival products? Strategy: **build** or **harvest**.
- **Dogs**. These may be ex-cash cows that have now fallen on hard times. Although they will show only a modest net cash outflow, or even a modest net cash inflow, they are cash traps which tie up funds and provide a poor return on investment. However, they may have a useful role, either to complete a product range or to keep competitors out. Strategy: **divest** (release resources for use elsewhere) or **hold**.

A business's portfolio of products should be balanced, with cash cows providing finance for stars and question marks, and a minimum of dogs.

6 Corporate appraisal

Section overview

- Corporate appraisal brings together the results of the external and internal analyses so that the business can assess its strengths, weaknesses, opportunities and threats (SWOT analysis).
- Key areas for SWOT analysis are marketing, products/brands, distribution/logistics, research and development of new products, finance, production capacity, inventory, management, staff and organisational structure.

Corporate appraisal brings together the analyses to date.

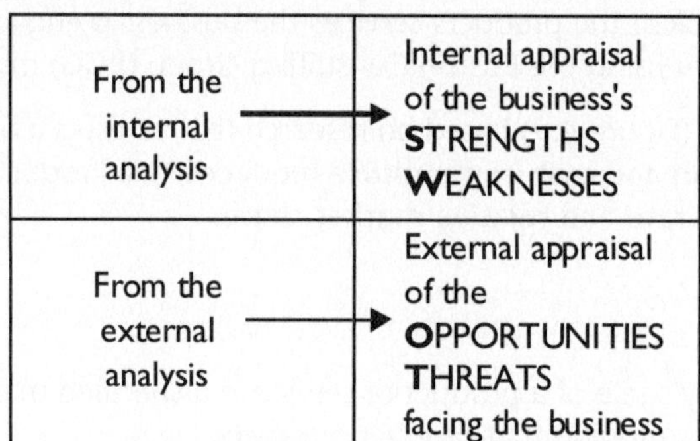

From the internal analysis →	Internal appraisal of the business's STRENGTHS WEAKNESSES
From the external analysis →	External appraisal of the OPPORTUNITIES THREATS facing the business

The business's unique strengths, weaknesses, opportunities and threats are analysed using **SWOT analysis**.

6.1 SWOT analysis

Definition

Corporate appraisal: A 'critical assessment of the strengths and weaknesses, opportunities and threats (**SWOT analysis**) in relation to the internal and environmental factors affecting an entity in order to establish its condition prior to the preparation of the long-term plan'. (CIMA *Official Terminology*)

It is important to remember the phrase 'critical assessment' used in the definition above. A simple listing of four types of factor is not likely to produce a robust and workable strategy. The managers involved must have a detailed and intimate understanding of the nature and implications of the factors. In particular, it is important to be **realistic**, erring neither towards optimism nor towards pessimism.

6.1.1 SWOT: positioning-based or resource-based views?

As stated earlier in this Study Manual, we have so far used a **positioning-based approach** to our strategic analysis of the business, so we discuss SWOT at this stage as a kind of summary or synthesis of our prior examination of resources and environment.

The alternative **resource-based approach** to strategic analysis would use SWOT as the first stage of the strategy making process, seeking to establish the nature of the business's core competences before deciding what the objectives of strategy should be.

6.1.2 Strengths and weaknesses

The internal appraisal seeks to identify:

- **Shortcomings** in the business's present skills and resources
- **Strengths** in its skills and resources which it should seek to exploit

The precise content of the SWOT analysis will depend on the business. Here are some ideas.

Area	Issues
Marketing	Fate of new product launches Use of advertising Market shares and market sizes Growth markets Success rate of the sales team Level of customer/client service
Products and brands	Analysis of sales Margin, and contribution to fixed costs Product quality Reputation of brands Age and future life of products Price elasticity of demand (see Chapter 13)
Distribution/logistics	Service standards Delivery fleet facilities Geographical availability
Research and development	Relevance Costs Benefits Workload
Finance	Availability of funds Contribution Returns on investment Accounting ratios
Plant and equipment/ production	Production capacity Value of assets Land and buildings Economies of scale (see Chapter 13)
Raw material and finished inventory	Sources of supply Turnover periods Storage capacity Obsolescence and deterioration

Area	Issues
Management and staff	Age Skills Industrial relations Training Recruitment Communications
Business management and organisation	Organisation structure Leadership style Communication links Information systems

6.1.3 Opportunities and threats

The **external appraisal** should identify:

- Profit-making **opportunities** which can be exploited by the business's strengths
- Environmental **threats** (a declining economy, competitors' actions, government legislation, industrial unrest etc) against which the business must protect itself

For **opportunities**, it is necessary to decide:

- What opportunities exist in the business environment?
- What is the capability profile of competitors? Are they better placed to exploit these opportunities?
- What is the company's comparative performance potential in this field of opportunity?

For **threats**, it is necessary to decide:

- What threats might arise, to the business or its environment?
- How will competitors be affected?

Opportunities and threats might relate to any or all of the items covered in the PESTEL analysis plus those in the five forces analysis (customers, suppliers, new entrants, substitutes, and of course competitors).

Interactive question 4: Opportunities and threats **[Difficulty level: Intermediate]**

Consider your career as a chartered accountant. How well-placed are you to make a success of it?

See **Answer** at the end of this chapter.

6.2 Combining the elements of the SWOT analysis

SWOT analysis indicates the **types of strategy** that appear to be available, to exploit strengths and opportunities and to deal with weaknesses and defend against threats.

- Major strengths and profitable opportunities can be exploited, especially if strengths and opportunities are matched with each other.
- Major weaknesses and threats should be countered, or a contingency strategy or corrective strategy developed.

The SWOT analysis is summarised on a **cruciform chart**. In the example below, the development of potential strategies from the analysis is illustrated.

Strengths	Weaknesses
£10 million of capital available. Production expertise and appropriate marketing skills.	Heavy reliance on a small number of customers. Limited product range, with no new products and expected market decline. Small marketing organisation.
Opportunities	**Threats**
Government tax incentives for new investment. Growing demand in a new market, although customers so far relatively small in number.	Major competitor has already entered the new market.

The business seems to be in imminent danger of losing its existing markets. A new market opportunity exists to be exploited and since the number of customers is currently few, the relatively small size of the existing marketing force would not be an immediate hindrance.

In practice, **a combination of financial, competition and institutional strategies** will be required, as we shall see.

7 Setting strategic objectives

Section overview

- Analysis of the business's mission and objectives allows it to determine exactly what it is trying to achieve.
- Stakeholder analysis – ie what the business's stakeholders are trying to achieve – informs this analysis.
- Stakeholders have internal and external sources of power, and have varying levels of interest in the business. Relative power and interest are assessed via stakeholder mapping, which determines how far the business should reflect what the stakeholders want. This should be incorporated in its mission statement.
- The business's mission feeds down to its corporate strategy (strategic objectives), then its competitive, investment and financial strategies/goals/targets, its business strategies and its functional/operational strategies, plans and standards.

7.1 What are we trying to achieve?

In our positioning-based model of the strategic planning process it is at this point that we look at the business mission and objectives. What is the business about, who is it for, and what is it aiming to achieve? To answer these questions, we need to conduct a detailed **stakeholder analysis**, before formulating the business's **mission** and **objectives**.

7.2 Stakeholder analysis

In Chapter 1 we outlined what a stakeholder is. We now need to look at how stakeholders' goals and objectives for the business are balanced in order to determine what the business's goals and objectives should be, in the light of corporate appraisal.

Because of the different interests at stake, the needs and objectives of each set of stakeholders are bound not to correspond; indeed, they often conflict.

Stakeholders	Conflict
Shareholders vs Managers/directors	Profit vs Growth
Shareholders vs Managers/directors	Growth via merger vs Independence
Shareholders vs Employees	Cost efficiency vs Jobs
Customers vs Shareholders and managers/directors	Service levels vs Profits and costs
Shareholders vs Bankers	Return vs Risk

Ultimately the business's objectives tend to follow the wishes of the most dominant stakeholders, its directors/managers, but they are constrained by those of other stakeholders, notably shareholders. The business needs to pay attention to all stakeholders, whether their needs determine or indeed have any effect on the business's objectives depends on the relative power of the stakeholder groups.

7.2.1 Stakeholder mapping: power and interest

Mendelow maps stakeholders on a matrix (Figure 4.10) whose axes are **power held** and the **level of interest** in the business's activities. These factors help define the type of relationship the business should seek with its stakeholders.

Level of interest

Power	Low (interest)	High (interest)
Low	A Minimal effort	B Keep informed
High	C Keep satisfied	D Key players

Figure 4.10: Mendelow's power/interest matrix

Power is the means by which stakeholders can influence a business's objectives. Sources of power may be internal or external.

Internal sources of power (for directors/managers and employees)	Comment
Hierarchy	Formal power over others in the business shown by span of control
Influence/reputation	Informal power from either charismatic leadership or group consensus on a particular issue
Relative pay	Better paid employees such as directors and managers have more position power as a result
Control of strategic resources	For example trade unions when demand for output is high and labour is scarce, or size of budget allocation
Knowledge skills	Individuals deriving power from their specialist knowledge or skills
Environmental control	Finance and marketing staff may have a more detailed knowledge of the external environment than other functional staff, such as production
Strategic implementation involvement	Many people are involved in implementing strategy, and the use of personal discretion in decision-making can give some element of power

External sources of power	Comment
Control over strategic resources	Major suppliers, banks (finance) and shareholders (finance) can exert this form of power
Involvement in implementation	Distribution outlets have greater knowledge of customer requirements than manufacturers and can therefore dictate to manufacturers, rather than *vice versa*
Knowledge and skills	Subcontractors have power if they perform vital activities for a business
External links	Public services often consult a wide variety of external stakeholders in decision making and therefore these stakeholders have an informal influence over the organisation
Legal rights	Eg government, planning authorities

The **interests of stakeholders** involve consideration of two factors.

- **Where their interest rests**, eg shareholders want dividends and capital growth, employees want higher pay and good conditions, customers want low prices, reliable supplies, and so on
- **How interested they are**, for instance they will be interested if there are alternatives (job, supplier, customer etc), if they are the industry regulator, or if there is a significant capital investment

When considering a potential strategy, the stakeholder should be placed in the appropriate quadrant depending on their power and their level of interest. The quadrant where they are placed – A, B, C or D – determines how they should be approached.

- **Key players** are found in segment D: strategy must be *acceptable* to them, at least and ideally they should **participate** in it. An example would be a major customer.
- Stakeholders in segment C must be treated with care. While often passive, they are capable of moving to segment D. The business should intervene with these stakeholders and keep them **satisfied**. Large institutional shareholders might fall into segment C.
- Stakeholders in segment B do not have great ability to influence strategy, but their views can be important in influencing more powerful stakeholders, perhaps by lobbying. They should therefore be **kept informed** by **education** and **communication**. Community representatives and charities might fall into segment B.
- Minimal effort is expended on segment A – they can simply be directed.

A single stakeholder map is unlikely to be appropriate for all circumstances. In particular, stakeholders may move from quadrant to quadrant when different potential future strategies are considered.

7.3 Determining the mission and strategic objectives

As we saw in Chapter 1, the business's '**mission**' describes its basic function in society. The mission can be set at the beginning of the strategic planning process, or it can derive from it after the corporate appraisal. It can include the business's **vision** of its future state, or the future state of the industry.

The mission feeds down into a set of **strategic objectives**, which are statements of intent to particular stakeholders such as shareholders or employees, building on stakeholder analysis. These are broken down further into **goals**, expressed as **targets** for the business as a whole and for SBUs in it. In this way, the targets for SBUs are designed with the business's strategic objectives and mission in mind, so there is **goal congruence**. This '**top down**' approach to formulating the final strategic plan can be expressed as a hierarchy (Figure 4.11).

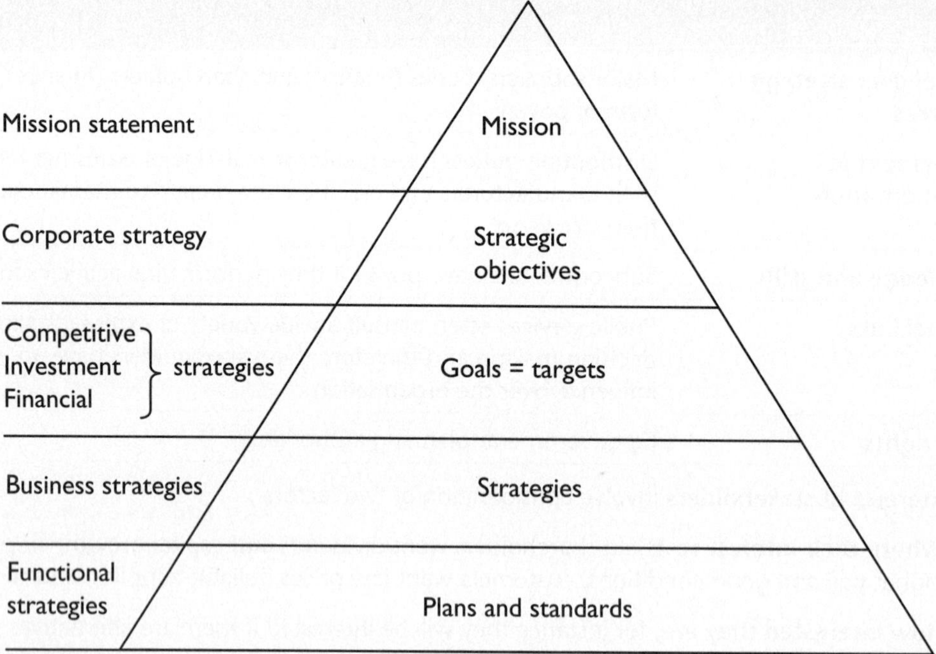

Figure 4.11: Hierarchy of objectives and strategies (top down approach)

For each SBU in the business, **business and functional (or operational) strategies** need to be determined which will ensure that targets are met. These are then broken down into detailed **plans** to be implemented according to specified **standards**.

7.3.1 Mission statement

Definition

Mission statement: A formal document that states the business's basic function in society expressed in terms of how it satisfies its stakeholders.

There is no standard format for a mission statement, but a good basis is to include the four elements we saw in Chapter 1: **purpose** of the business, **strategy** (what it does and how), **values** and **policies and standards of behaviour**.

7.3.2 Strategic objectives

Definition

Strategic objectives: The primary strategic objective – in the case of a business, to make a profit for shareholders – plus other major objectives addressed to the stakeholders.

An example of a statement of strategic objectives is as follows:

'Our primary aims are to provide a sound investment for our shareholders by increasing shareholder value and also worthwhile job prospects for our employees. Our objectives are increasing levels of customer satisfaction, real growth in earnings per share and a competitive return on capital employed.'

In Chapter 5 we shall see how the business's attitude to and appetite for **risk** feeds into the strategic planning process at this point.

7.3.3 Goals and targets

For the business as a whole and for SBUs in it, the strategic objectives should be translated into quantified and specific goals. In relation to the statement of strategic objectives above, for the business concerned these could be as follows.

Area	Goals	Target
Revenue	Growth	£3m from £2.5m this year
Gross margin	Increase	Cost of sales represents 65% of revenue, down from 70%
Expenses	Reduce	Overheads cut to £300,000 from £450,000
Earnings per share	Growth	From £300,000/1.2m = 25p To £660,000/1.2m = 55p
Return on capital employed	More competitive	From £300,000/6m = 5% To £660,000/6.6m = 10%
Shareholder value	Increase	Move from share price of £2 per share to £2.20
Employee job prospects	Worthwhile	Ensure fewer employees leave the business and more enter training to ensure career progression
Customer loyalty	Ensure customers are increasingly satisfied	Raise customer service levels

We shall see more about targets in Chapter 7.

7.3.4 Strategies, plans and standards

The strategies that are chosen by the business need to be ones which can achieve the targets set out, for instance to increase sales, reduce costs and raise capital. As we saw in Section 2 of this chapter, these are initially specific **business strategies** that tie in with the overall **corporate strategy** of the business, comprising:

- The competitive strategy – which products and markets do we operate in?
- The investment strategy – what systems, structure and assets do we need to invest in?
- The financial strategy – how are we going to raise the necessary funds?

A **financial strategy** for each area – operations, marketing, HR and finance – plus detailed **plans** and **standards** are then developed that will ensure the targets are met. Usually these plans will at some stage take the quantified form of a **budget**, as we shall see in Chapter 7.

We shall see more about selecting a corporate strategy and translating it into the various types of sub-strategy a little later. Before this level of detail is reached, the business needs to check the size of the gap between its desired strategic objectives and what it would achieve if it carried on with no changes in strategy. This is called **gap analysis**.

8 Gap analysis

Section overview

- Gap analysis looks at the gap between what the business would achieve if it continued on its existing course, and what it needs to achieve as demonstrated by its strategic planning process, measured in terms of profit.
- A gap in profit could be filled by strategies for improved efficiency, new products/markets, and acquisitions/mergers.

Definition

Gap analysis: 'A comparison between an entity's desired future performance level (expressed in terms of profit) and the expected performance of projects both planned and underway. Differences are classified in a way which aids the understanding of performance, and which facilitates improvement.'

(CIMA *Official Terminology*)

The **gap** is **not** between the current position of the business and the desired future position. It is the gap between the position forecast if the business continues with current activities, and the desired future position as set out in the strategic objectives.

Gap analysis is based on two questions.

- What are the business's objectives?
- What would the business be expected to achieve if it 'did nothing' – it did not develop any new strategies, but simply carried on in the current way with the same products and selling to the same markets?

This difference is the gap. New strategies should close this gap, so that the business can expect to achieve its objectives.

The **profit gap** (Figure 4.12) is the difference between the target profit and the profit forecast.

- The business estimates the effects on the gap of any projects or strategies in the pipeline. Some of the gap might be filled by a new project already underway
- Then, if a gap remains, new strategies have to be developed to close it

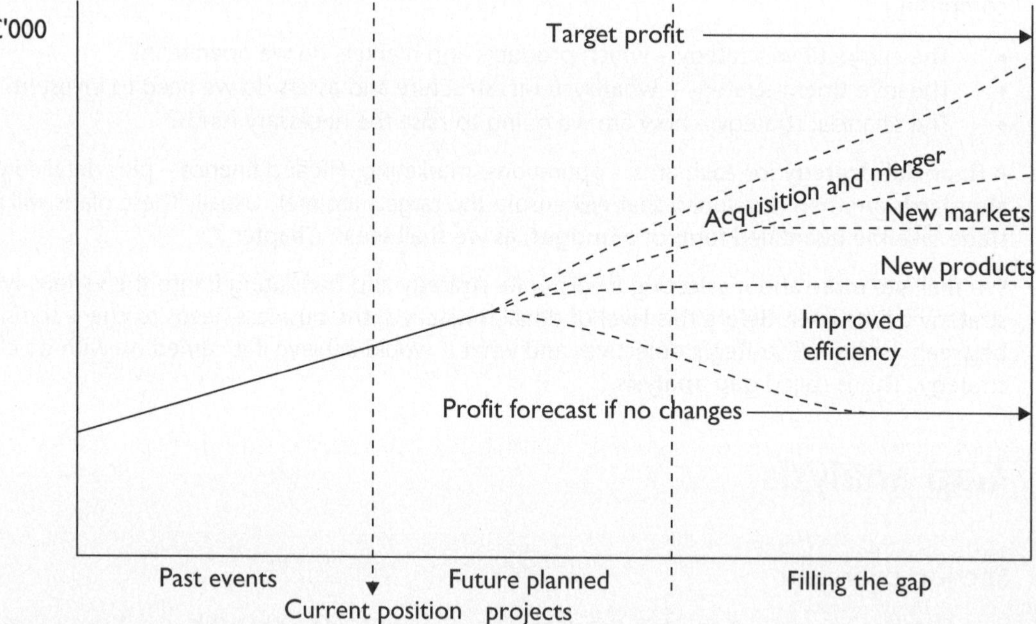

Figure 4.12: Gap analysis

9 Choosing a corporate strategy

Section overview

- The business needs a competitive, an investment and a financial strategy: it does not always need a new one, if gap analysis shows that it can simply continue on its existing path.
- Generic competitive strategies are cost leadership (being the producer at the lowest cost, *not* necessarily the producer who charges the lowest prices to consumers), differentiation (being the producer of unique and desirable products) and focus (being a niche producer for part only of a market, concentrating either on cost or on differentiation in that niche).
- Product/market strategies comprise market penetration (sell more of the current product in the current market), product development (sell new product in the current market), market development (sell the current product in a new market) and diversification (sell new product in a new market).
- Corporate strategies should be evaluated using SFA analysis in terms of Suitability, Feasibility and Acceptability to stakeholders.

9.1 Do we have to choose a new corporate strategy?

If there is no gap then the business can simply choose to continue with its current corporate strategy. Assuming there is a gap, however, the business needs to select competitive, financial and investment strategies that will ensure the strategic objectives are met.

We shall concentrate here on two models for competitive strategy: Porter's generic competitive strategies, and Ansoff's matrix. These provide suggested competitive strategies from which the business selects on the basis of how effectively they close the profit gap.

9.2 Porter's generic competitive strategies

Definition

Competitive strategy: 'Taking offensive or defensive actions to create a defendable position in an industry; to cope successfully with… competitive forces and thereby give a superior return on investment for the business' (Porter).

Porter believes there are three **generic competitive strategies**: cost leadership, differentiation and focus (niche).

Definitions

Cost leadership: Producing at the **lowest cost** in the industry as a whole (not necessarily being the producer offering the lowest prices to the consumer, though the cost leader can compete freely on price in the marketing mix).

Differentiation: The provision of a product or service which the industry as a whole believes to be **unique**.

Focus (or niche) involves a restriction of activities to only part of the market (a segment) through:

- Providing goods and/or services at lower cost in that segment (**cost-focus**)
- Providing a differentiated product or service to that segment (**differentiation-focus**)

Cost leadership and differentiation are industry-wide strategies. Focus involves segmenting the market but involves pursuing, within one or just a few segments only, a strategy of cost leadership or differentiation.

9.2.1 Cost leadership

By producing at the lowest cost, the cost leader can compete on price with every other producer in the industry, and earn higher unit profits, if it so chooses.

How to be the cost leader

- Set up production facilities to obtain **economies of scale**
- Use the **latest technology**
- Concentrate on **improving productivity**
- **Minimise overhead costs**
- **Get favourable access to sources of supply**
- Relocate operations to **cheaper countries**

9.2.2 Differentiation

The business competes on the basis of **particular characteristics** of its products. Products may be categorised as follows.

- **Breakthrough products** offer a radical performance advantage over competition, perhaps at a drastically lower price.
- **Improved products** offer better performance at a competitive price.
- **Competitive products** offer a particular combination of price and performance.

How to differentiate

- **Build up a brand image**
- **Give the product special features** to make it stand out
- **Exploit other activities of the value chain** such as marketing and sales or service
- Use **IT** to create new **services** or **product features**

9.2.3 Focus (or niche) strategy

The business concentrates its attention on one or more particular segments or niches of the market, and does not try to serve the entire market with a single product.

- A **cost-focus strategy:** aim to be a cost leader in a particular niche
- A **differentiation-focus strategy:** pursue differentiation for a chosen niche

9.3 Ansoff's matrix: product/market strategies

Ansoff drew up a **matrix** (Figure 4.13) describing how a combination of a business's activities in current and new markets, with existing and new products, can lead to four different competitive strategies for **growth**.

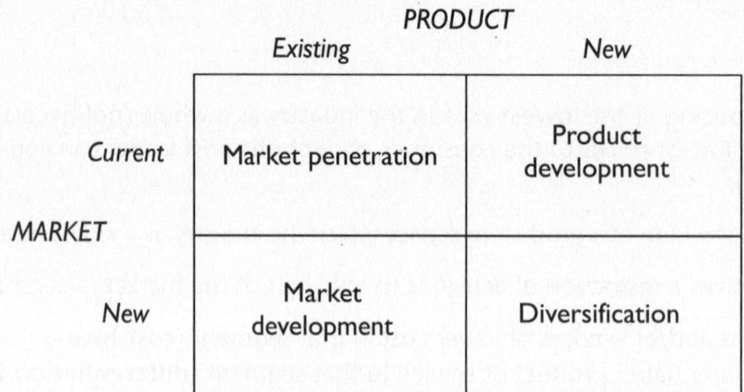

PRODUCT
Existing
New
MARKET
Current
New
Market penetration
Product development
Market development
Diversification

Figure 4.13: Ansoff's product/market matrix

9.3.1 Existing products in current markets: pursue market penetration

- **Maintain or increase share** of current markets with existing products, eg through competitive pricing, advertising, sales promotion
- Secure **dominance of growth markets**
- Restructure a mature market by **driving out competitors**
- Increase usage by **existing customers** (eg airmiles, loyalty cards, differential pricing)

9.3.2 Existing products in new markets: pursue market development

- **New geographical areas** and export markets
- **Different package sizes** for products eg food and other domestic items
- **New distribution channels** to attract new customers
- **Differential pricing policies** to attract different types of customer and create **new market segments**

9.3.3 New products in current markets: pursue product development

- Introduce new products to **existing and new customers** in current markets
- Product development **forces competitors to innovate**
- **Newcomers** to the market might be discouraged

9.3.4 New products in new markets: pursue diversification

The business should have a clear idea about what it expects to gain from diversifying to new products and new markets at the same time.

- **Growth.** New products and new markets should be selected offering prospects for growth which the existing product-market mix does not
- **Surplus** funds not required for other expansion needs can be invested in diversification, or they could be returned to shareholders

9.4 SFA analysis

If a business is faced with a gap and has developed alternative corporate strategies, each of which could in theory fill the gap, it needs to:

- Evaluate each strategy, then
- Choose the best one.

Johnson and Scholes set three criteria for evaluating and choosing strategies, to be applied in a process known as SFA analysis: **S**uitability, **F**easibility and **A**cceptability.

9.4.1 Suitability of the strategy

Does the strategy fit the business's operational circumstances? Does it:

- **Exploit** strengths?
- Rectify **weaknesses**?
- **Neutralise** or deflect environmental **threats**?
- Help the business to seize **opportunities**?
- **Satisfy** the business's objectives?
- **Fill the gap** identified by gap analysis?
- Generate/maintain **competitive advantage**?
- Involve an acceptable level of **risk**?

9.4.2 Feasibility of the strategy

Can the strategy in fact be implemented?

- Is there enough **money**?
- Is there the **ability** to deliver the goods/services specified in the strategy?
- Can we deal with the likely **responses that competitors** will make?
- Do we have access to **technology, materials and resources**?
- Do we have enough **time** to implement the strategy?

Strategies which do not make use of existing competences, and which therefore call for new competences to be acquired, might not be as feasible as alternative strategies because:

- Gaining competences via organic growth takes time
- Acquiring new competences can be costly

9.4.3 Acceptability of the strategy to stakeholders

The **acceptability** of a strategy relates to people's expectations of it. It is here that stakeholder analysis can be brought in, which we saw earlier in this chapter.

- **Financial considerations**. How far do alternative strategies contribute to meeting the dominant objective of increasing shareholder wealth?
- **Customers** may object to a strategy if it means reducing service, but on the other hand they may have no choice.
- **Government**. A strategy involving a takeover may be prohibited under competition law (see Chapter 14). Similarly, the environmental impact may cause key stakeholders to withhold consent.
- **The public**. The environmental impact may cause key stakeholders to protest.
- **Risk**. Different shareholders have different attitudes to risk. A strategy which changed the risk/return profile, for whatever reason, may not be acceptable. We shall look at risk in more detail in Chapter 5.

10 Implementing the strategy

Section overview

- To implement the chosen corporate strategy, the competitive, investment and financial strategies need to be broken down so there are business strategies and plans for each SBU, and within these there are functional strategies and operational plans. These are then expressed in budgets.

10.1 Breaking the strategy down

The selected corporate strategy comprises competitive, investment and financial strategies (see Figure 4.9). there are then further broken down as we have seen into **business** and **functional strategies.**

- **Business strategies** determine how competitive advantage is gained by a particular SBU, and in particular how the marketing mix must be adjusted to achieve this
- **Functional strategies** develop the business strategy for an SBU as it affects the:
  - Marketing function
  - Production/operations function
  - Human resources function, and
  - Finance function

10.2 Levels of plan

To implement the strategies, plans need to be produced.

- The **strategic plan** as we have seen, embodies the corporate strategy and strategic objectives. It sets out the general direction that will be taken to achieve the corporate objectives but it is not itself very detailed
- The **business plan** for the business as a whole or for an SBU sets out the market(s) to be served, how the business/SBU will serve the market(s), and what finance is required (based on the business strategy)
- The **operational plan** specifies what is expected of each function in the business as a whole or an SBU, based on the relevant functional strategy, and how specific actions will be taken in order to meet that expectation

Finally, **budgets** are prepared that set out the business's plan for a defined period, expressed in money terms. Usually a business has a variety of budgets at different levels of detail. The **board of directors** has a **summarised or master budget** for the whole entity that expresses the entire strategic plan, while separate functions in an SBU of that entity have **detailed budgets** for what each particular function needs to do to ensure that the master budget is achieved.

We shall look in more detail at budgets and the budgetary process in Chapter 7.

Summary and Self-test

Summary

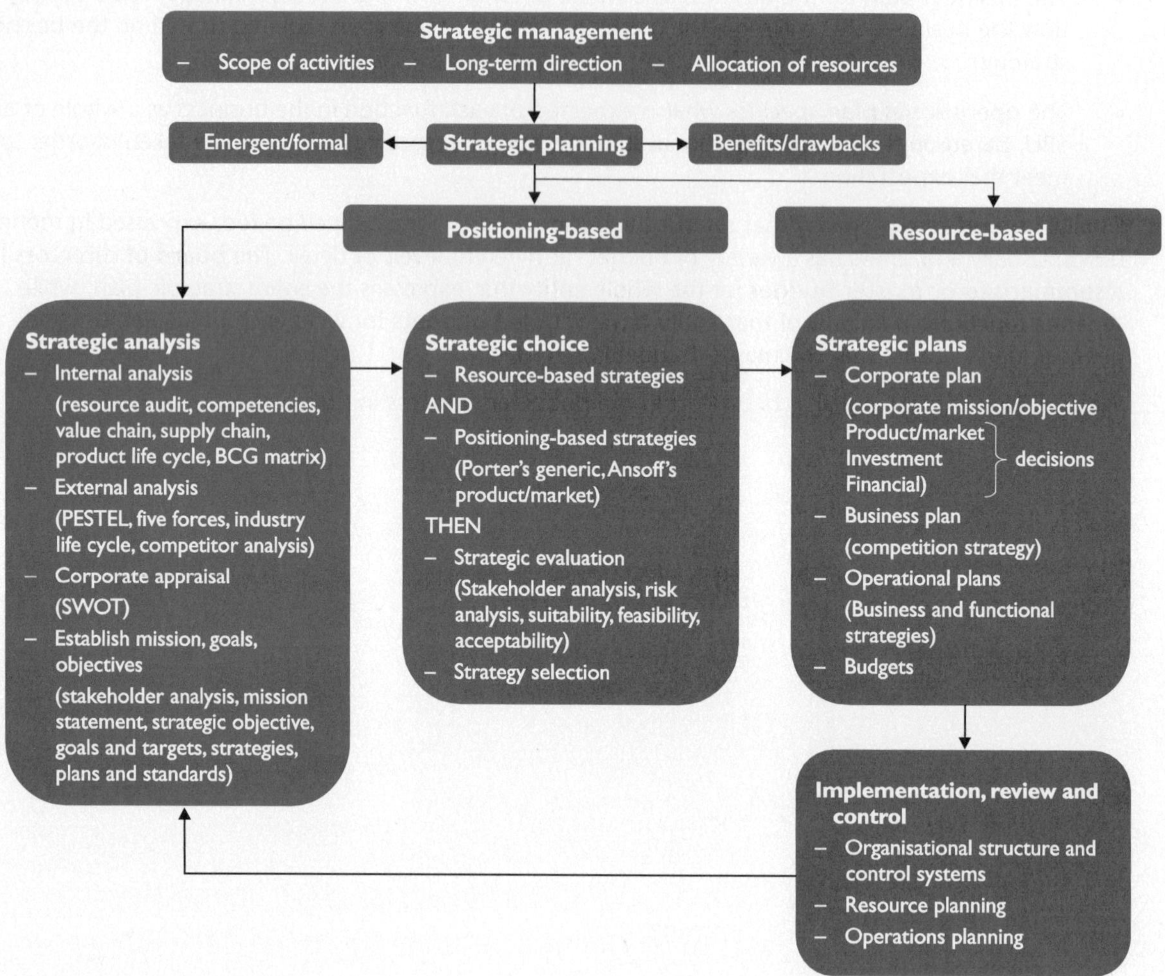

Self-test

Answer the following questions.

1 The emergent approach to the strategic planning process combines which **two** of the following stages into a single process?

A Strategic analysis
B Gap analysis
C Strategic choice
D Strategic implementation
E Review and control

2 In a resource-based approach to strategic planning, the business's mission, goals and objectives are determined

A following stakeholder analysis at the start of the process
B following stakeholder analysis and the corporate appraisal stage
C following SWOT analysis in the corporate appraisal stage
D following competitor analysis at the strategic choice stage

3 Competitors exist in the business's

A Physical environment
B General environment
C Task environment
D Internal environment

4 Linker plc has just been informed of a significant new regulation with which it needs to comply immediately. In relation to this, which of the following statements is true?

A There has been a change in Linker plc's task environment which it can cope with using planning

B There has been a change in Linker plc's general environment which it can cope with using crisis management

C There has been a change in Linker plc's task environment which it can cope with using crisis management

D There has been a change in Linker plc's general environment which it can cope with using planning

5 Minion plc has conducted a five forces analysis of its industry. This states that competition in the industry will become less intense in the medium term. Which of the following factors alone would explain this?

A The government has set a minimum capital requirement for anyone entering the industry
B A product which claims to eliminate the need for Minion plc's product has been launched
C The income levels of Minion plc's target market are being eroded by inflation
D A key raw material is now in short supply

6 Xenon plc runs restaurants while Zenos plc operates a chain of cinemas. The two companies are

A Industry competitors
B Generic competitors
C Form competitors
D Brand competitors

7 A competitor with a stochastic reaction profile

A reacts aggressively to all opposing moves by competitors
B does not react to any moves by competitors
C reacts to some moves by competitors, but not all
D reacts unpredictably to competitor moves

8 Which of the following is a primary activity in Porter's value chain?

A HRM
B Procurement
C Outbound logistics
D Technology

9 Penpen plc's 'freb' product has high market share in a market that is fully saturated. In terms of the BCG matrix, for Penpen plc the 'freb' is

A A star
B A cash cow
C A question mark
D A dog

10 Hubert is a stakeholder in Vipe plc. The company has selected a strategy which is acceptable to Hubert and in which the company is keen to secure his participation. In respect to Vipe plc Hubert has

A High power and high interest
B Low power and low interest
C High power and low interest
D Low power and high interest

Now, go back to the Learning Objectives in the Introduction. If you are satisfied you have achieved these objectives, please tick them off.

Answers to Interactive questions

Answer to Interactive question 1

You may have thought of some of these factors, or maybe some others. You should have structured your analysis using the PESTEL framework.

- **Political factors**: status/value of professional exams in education and employment system, potential regulation of tuition and study methods, effect of laws on the future of the accountancy profession as a whole, possible political instability
- **Economic factors**: effect of business cycle on recruitment of student accountants, effect of interest and exchange rates on business, potential for global market
- **Social factors**: acceptability of accountancy as a profession, levels of education of entry level accountants, size of population and therefore number of student accountants
- **Technological factors**: in what format will study notes be published, and how accessible is the technology to the target market? Can technology help to prevent copyright infringements?
- **Ecological factors**: how to produce and market study notes in a 'green' way
- **Legal factors**: employment and health and safety issues; how can the study notes keep up with changes to the law that need to be included in them?

Answer to Interactive question 2

You should have attempted an analysis of the industry from the perspective of the five forces that together determine the degree of competition in it: buyers' and suppliers' bargaining power, the threat of substitutes and new entrants, and the number and power of industry competitors. If you selected one business in an industry such as fashion clothing then you will quickly have realised that it is highly competitive. There are relatively low barriers to entry and a very high level of substitutes available, so competition is intense. Customers are notoriously fickle and have strong bargaining power, though suppliers have less power so the industry is able to push costs lower all the time.

Answer to Interactive question 3

Each of these options is a way of organising the activities of buying, cooking and serving food in a way that customers will value.

(a) It can become more efficient, by automating the production of food, as in a fast food chain.

(b) The chef can develop commercial relationships with growers, so he or she can obtain the best quality fresh produce at a good price.

(c) The chef can specialise in a particular type of cuisine (eg Nepalese, Korean).

(d) The restaurant can be sumptuously decorated for those customers who value 'atmosphere' and a sense of occasion in addition to a restaurant's purely gastronomic pleasures.

(e) The restaurant can serve a particular type of customer (eg celebrities).

Answer to Interactive question 4

You should have answered this question by using SWOT analysis in terms of your strengths and weaknesses, and the opportunities and threats that face you. It should naturally have led you onto considering how you can overcome your weaknesses and build on your strengths. It should have made you think about whether you know enough about where the opportunities for doing what you want with your career really lie, and about what potential threats to these may lie ahead.

Answers to Self-test

1	C, D	Note that gap analysis is part of the strategic analysis process; strategic analysis and review and control are separate processes under both the formal and the emergent models
2	A	Options B and C describe the planned strategy approach; Option D describes neither approach
3	C	
4	B	A regulation is a political/legal factor in the general environment; a regulation taking effect in a short timescale requires crisis management, while one taking place in the long term requires planning
5	A	A minimum capital requirement is a barrier to entry, so new entrants will be deterred and competition will decrease. Each of the other factors should lead to increased competition: B is a new substitute, C increases the bargaining power of customers, and D increases the bargaining power of suppliers
6	B	Restaurants and cinemas compete for the part of consumers' income that is allocated to leisure/entertainment
7	D	A, B and C describe tiger, laid back and selective reactions respectively
8	C	All the others are secondary, support activities
9	B	
10	A	From its reaction, we can see that Hubert is being treated as a key player

CHAPTER 5

Introduction to risk management

Introduction

Learning objectives

Tick off

- Identify the main components of the risk management process ☐
- Show how the main components of the risk management process operate ☐
- Identify the key issues in relation to risk and crisis management ☐

Specific syllabus references are: 1h, i.

Syllabus links

The topics covered in this introduction to risk management are developed as well in Assurance at Certificate level, in Audit and Assurance, Business Strategy and Financial Management at Professional level, and in the Advanced level exams.

Examination context

Questions on risk management could easily appear in the exam.

Questions are likely to be set in multiple choice format and in a scenario context. Knowledge-type questions are also likely, set on particular principles or definitions.

1 Introduction to risk

Section overview

- Risk means that something can turn out differently to what you expected, or wanted.
- Risk exists in any situation, while uncertainty arises only because there is inadequate information.
- Pure risk is the possibility that something will go wrong, and speculative risk is the possibility that it will go well.
- Downside or pure risk represents a threat: things may turn out worse than expected.
- Upside or speculative risk represents an opportunity: things may turn out better than expected.

1.1 What is risk?

You know what risk is in **everyday terms**. You know it is **risky** to climb a tall ladder, no matter what you may think there is at the top. You know it is **risky** to bet your life savings on a horse race, no matter how much you think you might win.

These things are **risky** because at the point when you decide to do them you cannot be sure **how bad** the outcome will be. You may fall off the ladder and injure yourself when you are half-way up. The horse you back may be beaten at the winning post.

On the other hand, you cannot be sure **how good** the outcome may be, either: you cannot be sure that the **opportunities** won't ever amount to anything. If you don't risk climbing the ladder you will never be the owner of whatever it is at the top. Most people would think it is too risky to throw away their life savings on a race, but there is **always the chance** that your horse will win. If you don't place the bet you will miss the **opportunity**.

Risks and opportunities exist because nobody knows what will happen in the future, and nobody can control it. Of course you can **control** whether or not you climb the ladder, but you **cannot stop others** from doing so, and you **cannot stop entirely unexpected things** from happening.

These issues can be summarised in the following definition of risk.

Definition

Risk: The possible **variation** in an **outcome** from what is **expected** to happen.

We can break this definition down to highlight the following issues to do with risk:

- **Variability**: events in the future cannot be predicted with certainty
- **Expectation**: we expect something to happen, or perhaps hope that it will not happen
- **Outcomes**: this is what actually happens compared with what is intended or expected to happen

1.2 What is uncertainty?

Risk and uncertainty are not the same things:

- **Risk** (the possibility of variation) exists in any situation
- **Uncertainty** arises only because we are ignorant of all the facts: we lack information

Definition

Uncertainty: The inability to predict the outcome from an activity due to a lack of information.

CHAPTER 5

You can never avoid this uncertainty, in anything you do: it is something that you have to **make decisions** about, or something you need to **manage**. If you decide to take a risk, or follow up an opportunity, the outcome may be hugely beneficial – or it may ruin you.

1.3 What are upside and downside risks?

Because events could turn out either better or worse than expected, sometimes we refer to **two-way risk** or **symmetrical risk.**

The risk that something will go wrong is called '**downside risk**', if it is likely that things will go right the term '**upside risk**' is used.

1.4 How far does risk affect a business achieving its objectives?

When considering whether a business will be successful and achieve its objectives, the term '**pure risk**' describes the possibility that something will go wrong, **speculative risk** is the possibility that something could go better than expected (though it could go worse). If we all focused on pure risk then there would be little point in taking a risk; the fact that something could go well is the basis on which business flourishes.

It is helpful for businesses to think about risk in the context of **managing events** with an eye on **achieving objectives**. This has long been the objective of COSO, an international organisation dedicated to improving the quality of financial reporting through business ethics, effective internal controls and corporate governance. Here are the definitions given in the COSO *Enterprise Risk Management Framework* (2004).

Definitions

Risk: The possibility that an event will occur and **adversely** affect the achievement of objectives.

Opportunity: The possibility that an event will occur and **positively** affect the achievement of objectives.

In this chapter we shall be concentrating on risk as defined by COSO.

2 Risks for businesses and their investors

Section overview

- Risks for a business include poor market conditions, poor control and poor outcomes of investments. Often businesses look particularly at the risks that they will fail to achieve their critical success factors (CSFs). How far the business is prepared to take on these risks is a measure of its risk appetite.
- The risk to those who finance the business (owners and lenders) is that they will suffer poor rather than high returns on their investment.
- Both businesses and financiers have particular attitudes to the level of risk they are prepared to endure: risk averse, risk neutral and risk seeking.

2.1 Risks for the business

If the objective of a business is to maximise shareholder value then risks for the business are **risks of losses**, resulting (directly or indirectly) in negative cash flows. When losses become severe, there might be a risk of insolvency, leading to the liquidation of the business.

The activities of certain businesses are inherently risky because they are potentially dangerous to public well-being: transport and pharmaceutical businesses are obvious examples.

The risks faced by **businesses in general** are as follows.

- There are risks that **trade conditions might be poor**, and **sales might fall** or **costs might rise**. A new product launch might be unsuccessful, or an expensive research and development project might fail to produce a new commercial product
- There is a risk that **inadequate controls** (quality controls, administrative controls, controls over people etc) within the business may result in losses through inefficiency, damage to business reputation, or deliberate fraud
- A business might face risks of a **financial nature**, and losses might occur because of the way it has financed an operation

The larger the business, the more varied are the risks.

Interactive question 1: Business risk [Difficulty level: Intermediate]

Try to identify a small business with which you have some familiarity, such as an audit client or one you have worked for in a vacation. What risks does the business, as opposed to its owner(s), face?

See **Answer** at the end of this chapter.

2.2 Risks for investors

Lenders have to bear the risk that the business will default on its debt obligations, and fail to make an interest payment or even become insolvent and be unable to repay the loan principal. A lender will expect a higher return than that offered on, say, Government securities or gilts (commonly taken to be a risk-free investment), to compensate for the added risk.

Shareholders are the ultimate bearers of risk. If a company becomes insolvent, they will lose all their investment. More important, if company profits fall, dividends and the share price are also likely to fall. Lenders are entitled to interest before any profits can be paid as dividend, so that the risk to income is much less for lenders than for equity shareholders.

Risk for shareholders is two-way: there is the possibility of poor returns (no dividends or low dividends, and a fall in the share price), or profits and dividends might be higher than expected, and the share price might rise by more than anticipated. Risk is greater for shareholders when there is a greater possibility of wide variations in profits, dividends and share prices from year to year. The range of potential variation in returns is known as the **volatility of returns**.

2.3 Risk and strategic planning

In the strategic planning analysis process it is important to focus on risks that are specific to the business, or the industry sector in which it operates, rather than general ones. They should be mapped to the relevant threats and opportunities that they represent to the business. A plan for managing each specific risk can then be formulated.

It is often useful to relate risks to the business's **critical success factors** (CSFs), as a significant risk is one that would create an obstacle to any of the CSFs.

Definition

Critical success factor (CSF): 'those product features that are particularly valued by a group of customers and, therefore, where the organisation must excel to outperform the competition' (Johnson & Scholes, 2002).

2.3.1 Risk appetite

Not all risk is bad, and returns are generally higher for higher-risk projects. As part of the planning process, the business needs to decide what its 'appetite' for risk is, and apply this in choosing appropriate strategies.

Definition

Risk appetite: The extent to which a business is prepared to take on risks in order to achieve its objectives.

The approach should be as follows.

1. Decide what the business wants to achieve (the **strategic objective**).
2. Decide what the business's '**risk appetite**' is, in other words the extent to which it is prepared to take on risks in order to achieve its objective.
3. Find **strategies** to achieve the objectives that do not involve more risk than the business is willing to accept.
4. If there are no methods of reducing the risk to an acceptable level, the objective needs to be **amended**.

2.3.2 Attitudes to risk

- A **risk averse attitude** is that an investment would be chosen if it has a more certain but possibly lower return than an alternative less certain, potentially higher return investment.
- A **risk neutral attitude** is that an investment would be chosen according to its expected return, irrespective of the risk.
- A **risk seeking attitude** is that an investment would be chosen on the basis of it offering higher levels of risk, even if its expected return is lower than an alternative no-risk investment with a higher expected return.

2.3.3 Expected returns

When a business looks at an investment it has to judge what return is expected from it. For instance, an investment of £100,000 at a rate of 5% has an expected return of £5,000.

When the business starts considering risk in relation to an investment it is also likely to derive a range of possible returns from the investment, given best-case, worst case and most likely scenarios. These can be combined in a weighted average to give the overall expected return.

Worked example: Expected return

Jack plc has the opportunity to invest £100,000 in a project. The project manager has estimated three scenarios for the project's annual return, and the related returns and probabilities:

	Probability of scenario occurring	*Annual return under the scenario*
		£
Worst case scenario	0.3	2,000
Most likely scenario	0.6	5,000
Best case scenario	0.1	10,000

The expected return for the project can be calculated using a weighted average:

	Probability	Annual return under the scenario	Expected return (probability x return)
		£	£
Worst case scenario	0.3	2,000	600
Most likely scenario	0.6	5,000	3,000
Best case scenario	0.1	10,000	1,000
Expected return			4,600

Note that the expected return of £4,600 is not actually predicted as a return; it is used instead as an overall measure of the investment for decision making and risk evaluation purposes.

3 Types of risk

Section overview

- Risk is either business risk or non-business risk.
- Business risks arise from the business's nature, operations and environment.
- Business risks are: strategy, enterprise, product, economic, technology and property risks.
- Non-business risks are any other type of risk: financial (credit and market risk) and operational (process, people, systems, legal and (single) event risks).

3.1 Risk classifications

There are several ways in which risks can be classified according to their source or characteristics as shown in Figure 5.1. The main distinction is between business and non-business (financial and operational) risk.

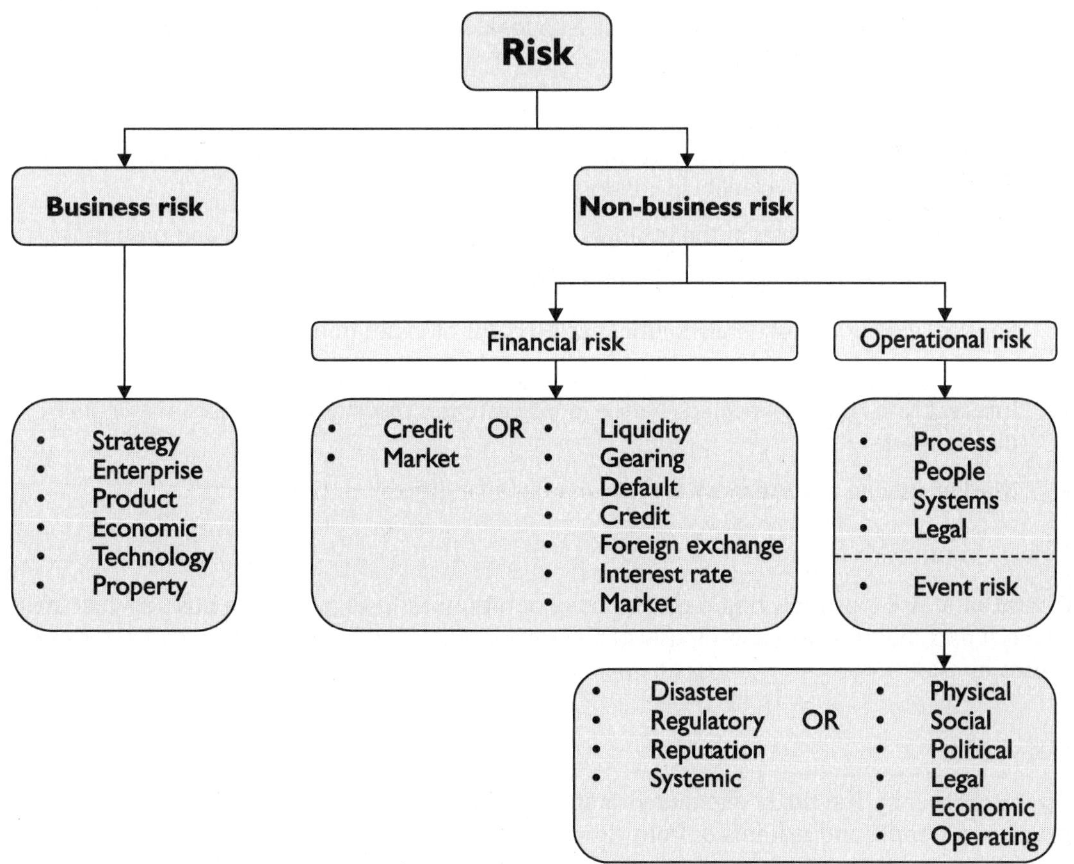

Figure 5.1 Risk classifications

CHAPTER 5

3.2 Business risk

Business risk arises from the nature of the business, its operations and the conditions it operates in. It includes:

- **Strategy risk**: the risk of choosing the wrong corporate business or functional strategy
- **Enterprise risk**: the success or failure of a business operation and whether it should have been undertaken in the first place
- **Product risk**: the chance that customers will not buy the company's products or services in the expected quantities
- **Economic risk**: the effect of unexpected changing economic conditions
- **Technology risk**: the risk that the market or industry is affected by some change in production or delivery technology
- **Property risk**: the risk of loss of property or losses arising from accidents

3.3 Non-business risk

Non-business risk is any other type of risk, usually classified as **financial risk** and **operational risk** (or **event** risks).

3.3.1 Financial risk

Lam, in *Enterprise Risk Management*, divides **financial risk** into credit risk and market risk.

- **Credit risk** is 'the economic loss suffered due to the default of a borrower, customer or supplier'. In other words it is the risk that customers or borrowers will not pay, or will not pay quickly enough, or that suppliers will cease to supply.
- **Market risk** is 'the exposure to potential loss that would result from changes in market prices or rates', which might include share prices, commodity prices, interest rates and foreign exchange rates.

Another way of breaking down financial risk is to look in more detail at the sources of risk that are external to the business, including:

- **Liquidity risk**: an unexpected shortage of cash
- **Gearing risk**: high borrowing in relation to the amount of shareholders' capital in the business, increasing the risk of volatility in earnings, and insolvency
- **Default risk**: receivables of the business fail to pay what they owe in full and on time
- **Credit risk**: the company's credit rating is downgraded
- **Foreign exchange risk**: making unexpected gains or losses from changes in a foreign exchange rate
- **Interest rate risk**: unexpected change in interest rates placing the business at a financial disadvantage
- **Market risk**: an adverse movement in share market prices

3.3.2 Operational risk

Operational risk is possibly best regarded as all non-business risks faced by a business that are not financial risks, but this is an enormously **broad** definition. We could define it instead in terms of what **causes** it.

Definition

Operational risk: 'The risk of direct or indirect loss resulting from inadequate or failed internal **processes, people** and **systems** or from external **events**' (*Basel Committee on Banking Supervision*).

- **Process risk** is the risk that a business's processes may be **ineffective** (fail to achieve their objectives) or **inefficient** (achieve their objectives but at excessive cost).
- **People risk** is the risk arising from staff constraints (for example insufficient staff, or inability to pay good enough wages to attract the right quality of staff), incompetence, dishonesty, or a corporate culture that does not cultivate risk awareness, or encourages profits without regard to the methods used to make them.
- **Systems risk** is a term that is usually used in the sense of the risks arising from information and communication systems such as systems capacity and availability, data integrity, and unauthorised access and use. IT is so central to almost all businesses that it certainly merits a category to itself.
- **Legal risk** is the risk of loss from the fact that a contract cannot be legally enforced. It arises through uncertainty in laws, regulations and legal actions. Sources of legal risk include enforceability issues as well as exposure to unanticipated changes in laws and regulations.
- **Event risk** is the operational risk of loss due to **single events** that are unlikely but may have serious consequences. Natural or man-made disasters are the most obvious examples of event risk. These may include:
  - **Disaster risk**: a catastrophe occurs, such as fire, flood, ill health or death of key people, terrorism and so on
  - **Regulatory risk**: new laws or regulations are introduced, affecting the business's operations and profitability
  - **Reputation risk**: the business's activities damage its reputation in the eyes of stakeholders.
  - **Systemic risk**: failure by a participant in the business's supply chain or system to meet its contractual obligations, so the system itself is at risk

  Another way of classifying **event risks** is according to their sources in the external environment:
  - **Physical risks**: such as climate and geology
  - **Social risks**: changes in tastes, attitudes and demography
  - **Political risks**: changes determined by government, or by a change of government
  - **Legal risks**: changes in legislation and regulations, including the consequences of breaking the law or otherwise failing to meet legal duties or obligations
  - **Economic risks**: changing economic conditions
  - **Operating environment risks**: technological changes

4 Risk concepts

Section overview

- How big a risk a business is facing is measured in terms of exposure, volatility, impact and probability.

The scale of any risk for a business depends upon four key **risk concepts**.

- **Exposure** is the measure of the way in which a business is faced by risks. Some businesses will by their very nature be less exposed than others. A transport company such as an airline or a railway operator is considerably more exposed to the operational risk that its customers will be injured whilst using its services than is a bank or a firm of accountants. A business that has minimal debt finance and no overseas customers or suppliers has little or no exposure to the financial risks of either interest rate movements or exchange rate movements.
- **Volatility** is how the factor to which a business is exposed is likely to alter. A coffee producer is dependent on good weather; businesses like fashion and music are subject to changes in public taste. Some businesses operate in regions that are politically unstable.

- **Impact** (or consequence) refers to measures of the amount of the loss if the undesired outcome occurs. Impact might be measured purely in financial terms, or in terms of delay, injuries/loss of life or other ways depending on the type of risk.
- **Probability** (or likelihood) means how likely it is that a particular outcome will occur. In some cases it is possible to estimate probability on the basis of **past experience** (historical records) combined with **information** about all the variables involved and how they interact. In others it is much harder to estimate probability because no historical data exists. The development of an entirely **new product** is an example.

The greatest risks for a particular business will arise when:

- Exposure is high
- The underlying factor is volatile
- The impact is severe, and
- The probability of occurrence is high

Different combinations of these four risk concepts result in different levels of response from the business.

5 The objectives of risk management

Section overview

- Risk management involves identifying, analysing and controlling those risks that threaten the assets or earning capacity of the business so as to reduce the business's exposure by either reducing the probability or limiting the impact, or both.

5.1 What is risk management?

Definition

Risk management: The identification, analysis and economic control of risks which threaten the assets or earning capacity of a business.

Risk management is actively used by many businesses, some of which employ risk managers. Smaller businesses and individuals may not recognise a specific task of risk management but will nevertheless have developed their own methods of analysing and managing risk.

The purpose of risk management is to understand and then to minimise cost-effectively the business's **exposure** to risk and the adverse effect of risks, by:

- Reducing the **probability** of risks occurring in the first place, and then if they do occur
- Limiting the **impact** they will have on the business

5.2 When is risk management necessary?

- There may be **legal requirements** to manage risk: you are required by law to insure your car, for instance
- Risk management (in the form of insurance) may be required by **licensing authorities** and **regulatory bodies**. For example a football stadium would not be allowed to operate if it did not have **public liability insurance**: ICAEW members in public practice must have **professional indemnity insurance** (PII)
- **Financial organisations** may require risk management: if you have a mortgage your lender no doubt requires you to have **buildings insurance** to protect its security

Interactive question 2: Indemnity insurance [Difficulty level: Intermediate]

Find out if you can, the basis of the requirement that chartered accountants should have to have professional indemnity insurance (PII), and what it is designed to achieve.

See **Answer** at the end of this chapter.

Large listed companies in the UK are required to determine the nature and extent of their significant risks and to maintain sound risk management systems.

- A **risk-based management approach** is a requirement for all UK companies listed in the FTSE 350 under the **UK Corporate Governance Code 2012**. The Code includes guidelines on consideration, management and reporting of risk. We shall see more about this in Chapter 12.
- EU regulations stipulate that a European listed company's published financial statements must contain a description of the principal risks and uncertainties facing the company. This is subject to audit by external auditors.

6 The risk management process

Section overview

- Risk management involves identifying risk, assessing and measuring it in terms of exposure, volatility, impact and probability, controlling it by means of avoidance, transfer and reduction, accepting what remains and then monitoring and reporting on events.
- Risks can be identified by considering what losses would ensue: property, liability, personnel, pecuniary and interruption loss.
- Once identified, the gross risk is measured by multiplying its probability (a value between 0 and 1) by the impact (the value of the loss that would arise). The aim of risk management is to minimise gross risk.
- Some risk can be avoided by not doing the risky activity, and some can be reduced by taking precautionary measures. Some of what remains of the gross risk can be transferred to someone else, especially by insurance. The remaining gross risk must be accepted or retained.
- All the elements of the risk management process must be monitored and reported on to an appropriate person.

6.1 What is involved in the risk management process?

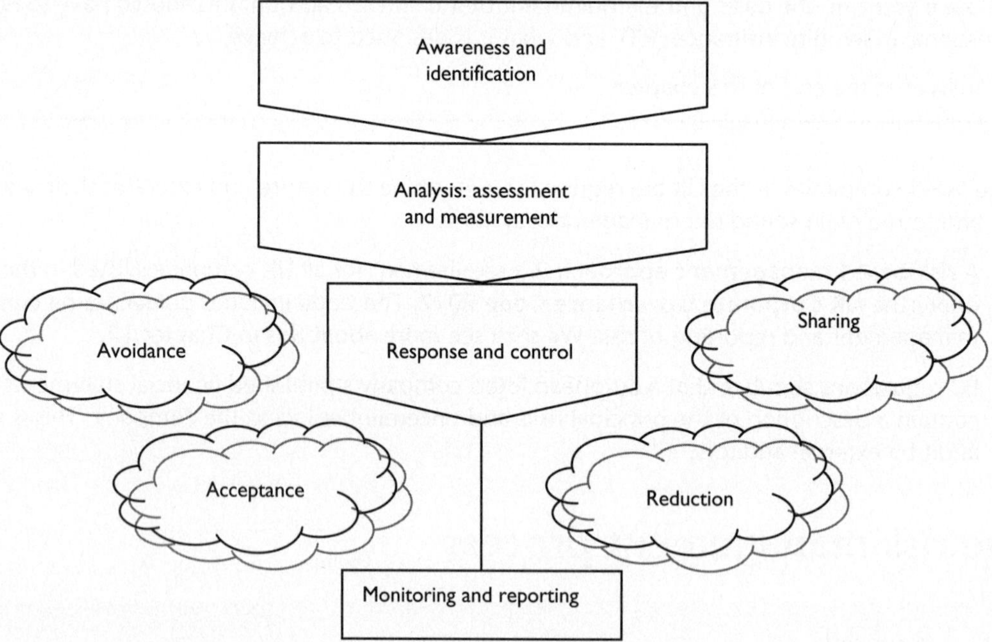

Figure 5.2: Risk management process

- Risk **awareness** and **identification**, using techniques such as brainstorming and analysis of past experience to identify the business's **exposure** to risks.
- Risk **analysis (assessment and measurement)**: this considers the **volatility** of particular factors, the *probability* of an event occurring and the severity of the *impact* if it does. Measurement may be qualitative or quantitative.
- Risk **response** and **control**: in essence a risk can be *avoided* (do not do the risky activity), *reduced* (eg by strictly controlling processes), *shared* (eg with an insurer) or simply *accepted*.
- Risk **monitoring** and **reporting** is a continuous process.

We shall look at each element of the risk management process in turn.

6.2 Risk awareness and identification

Risk **awareness** is partly a state of mind, but it is also dependent on how well the matter under consideration is **understood**.

Suppose a UK business was considering launching a new product in China but knew absolutely nothing about doing business in China. It is highly likely that it will not be aware of the many risks to which the business could be exposed because of factors such as different regulations, different ways of approaching customers, differences in disposable income and so on. The risks remain to be **identified**.

Definition

Risk identification: Identifying the whole range of possible risks and the likelihood of losses occurring as a result of these risks.

Risk identification must be a continuous process, based on awareness and knowledge that:

- Potential new risks may arise
- Existing risks may change

Exposure to both new and altered risks must be identified quickly and managed appropriately.

There are two approaches to identifying risks, which operate most effectively when combined.

- A **top-down approach** is led by the senior management/board of the business, spending time on attempting to identify key risks. Often, this is linked to the business's CSFs: what might happen to prevent us from achieving each CSF?
- A **bottom-up approach** involves a group of employees, with an expert in risk management, working together to identify risks at the operational level upwards

Categories **of loss**:

- **Property loss** – possible loss, theft or damage of any static or moveable assets
- **Liability loss** – loss occurring from legal liability to third parties, personal injury or damage to property
- **Personnel loss** – due to injury, sickness or death of employees
- **Pecuniary loss** – as a result of defaulting receivables
- **Interruption loss** – a business being unable to operate due to one of the other types of loss occurring

Identifying too many risks can make the risk management process overly complex. The business should focus its efforts on **significant risks**: those that are potentially damaging to the business's value.

6.3 Risk analysis: assessment and measurement

After risks have been identified, there should be a process of judging whether each risk is serious, and which risks are more serious than others.

Definitions

Risk assessment: For each risk its nature is considered, and the implications it might have for the business; an initial judgement is then made about the seriousness of the risk.

Risk measurement: Identifying the **probability** (likelihood) of the risk occurring, quantifying the resultant **impact** (consequence) and calculating the amount of the potential loss using expected values for **gross risk**.

Gross risk is the potential loss associated with the risk, calculated by combining the impact and the probability of the risk, before taking any control measures into account.

An aim of risk assessment should be to identify those risks that have the greatest significance, and so should receive the closest management attention.

Significance can be measured in terms of the potential loss arising as a result of the risk, that is its gross risk. This depends on:

- The potential **impact,** quantified as an expected value (usually using weighted averages as we saw earlier in relation to expected returns)
- The **probability of occurrence,** measured mathematically, as a decimal between 0 and 1

Gross risk = Probability × Impact

A method that is frequently used to assess risks is to plot each one on a risk map, showing impact on a scale of 1 to 10 (or just low to high) on one axis, and probability on a similar scale on the other axis.

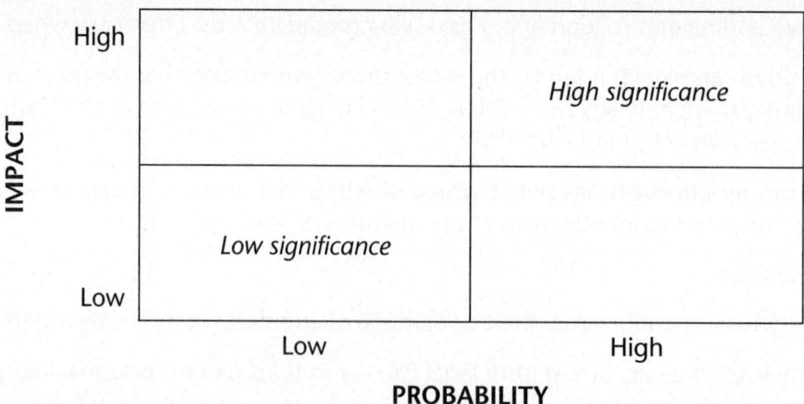

Figure 5.3: Risk assessment map

With regard to controlling risk the greatest attention may then be paid to risks that fall in the high significance (high impact/high probability quadrant), bearing in mind that the quantum of each in terms of gross risk should also be considered: a 'high significance' gross risk of only £10,000 will probably draw less attention than a medium significance risk of £1million, for example.

In Chapter 12 we shall look at corporate governance and risk assessment relevant to large listed companies in the UK (the UK Corporate Governance Code 2012 and the Turnbull Guidance).

6.4 Risk response and control

Measurement (qualitative or quantitative) and assessment establish **priorities** that determine the amount of management time that should be spent developing and implementing a **response** to control any particular risk: obviously, large gross risks in the high significance quadrant should be considered first.

The **possible responses** to a risk, so as to control it, are as follows.

- **Avoidance**: not doing the risky activity. This may not be an option, but the first question should always be 'Do we need to do this risky activity at all?'
- **Reduction**: doing the activity, but using whatever means are available to ensure that the probability of the event occurring and the impact if it does are as small as possible
- **Sharing**: for example taking out **insurance** against the risk, but only **after** every effort has been made to reduce it, so that insurance premiums are kept as low as possible. Another sharing strategy might be to enter an agreement with one or more other companies (joint ventures, outsourcing arrangements and partnerships with suppliers are all examples). **Hedging** is a means of sharing market risk. Risk sharing is sometimes called risk **transfer**, but it is rare to be able to transfer all the risk.
- **Acceptance** (sometimes called **retention**): this should only be considered if the other options are not viable, for example if the costs of extra control activities and the costs of insuring against the risk are greater than the cost of the losses that will occur if the event happens. The concept of **materiality** should apply: immaterial risks can be accepted. Nevertheless, risks that have been accepted should still be **kept under review**: new developments may mean that a different response becomes more appropriate.

The risk map can be expanded to include risk responses depending on the assessment and measurement of the risk.

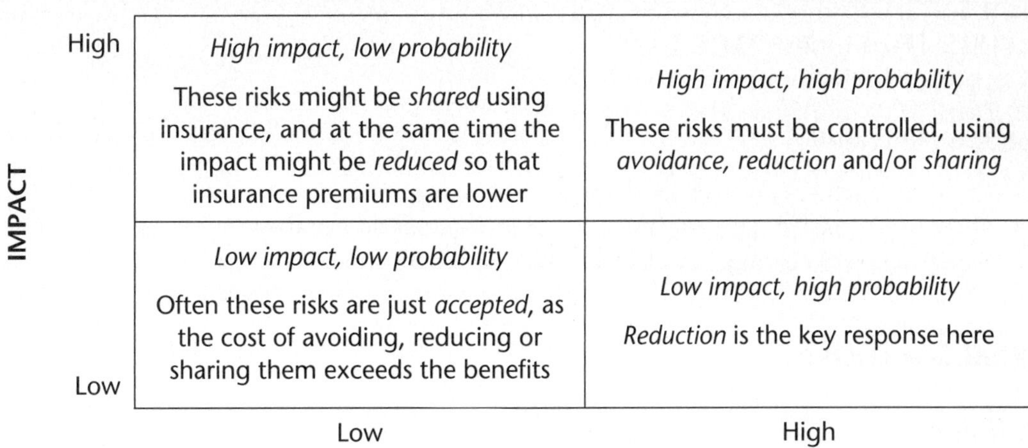

High
Low
IMPACT
High impact, low probability
These risks might be shared using insurance, and at the same time the impact might be reduced so that insurance premiums are lower
High impact, high probability
These risks must be controlled, using avoidance, reduction and/or sharing
Low impact, low probability
Often these risks are just accepted, as the cost of avoiding, reducing or sharing them exceeds the benefits
Low impact, high probability
Reduction is the key response here
Low
High
PROBABILITY

Figure 5.4: Risk responses

The controls that are put in place in response to risks can take a variety of forms.

- **Physical controls** such as locks, speed limits and clothing protect people, assets and money.
- **Financial controls** such as credit checks, credit limits and customer deposits protect money and other financial assets.
- **System controls** include procedural controls, so that processes are carried out in the right way, software controls in computer systems, and organisation controls on people so that, for instance, they do not exceed their authority. Together system controls protect the business's ability to perform its work.
- **Management controls** include all aspects of management that ensure the business is properly planned, controlled and led, such as the organisation's structure, and the annual budget.

We shall see more about controls later in this Study Manual.

6.5 Monitoring and reporting risk

Monitoring risk should be a continuous, ongoing process, such that if a risky event does occur then the action taken should include an immediate **review** of the management of that risk, followed by changes as necessary. In this sense 'monitoring' is a form of **control**.

- Has **corrective action** now been taken? Has it been effective?
- Was the risk **identified** in the first place, and if not why not?
- If the risk was identified and planned for but the event still occurred is it because **early warning indicators** were not monitored?
- If the **response and/or controls** were **ineffective** what changes or new procedures are necessary?

All identified risk management problems that could affect the organisation's ability to achieve its objectives should be **reported** to those in a position to take necessary action.

- The **chief executive** regarding serious problems.
- **Senior managers** regarding risk management problems that affect their units.
- **Managers** in increasing levels of detail as the process moves down the organisational structure.

The board of directors or audit committee should also be informed. The board or committee may ask to be made aware only of problems that meet a **specified threshold** of seriousness or importance.

Listed companies which are required to follow the main principles of the UK Corporate Governance Code 2012 have particular requirements as to:

- determining the nature and extent of the significant risks the company is willing to take in achieving its strategic objectives, and
- reporting risk management issues.

We shall see more about this in Chapter 12.

7 Crisis management

Section overview

- Crisis management involves identifying a crisis and planning a response to it.
- Three main types of crisis are financial, public relations and strategic.
- Businesses need contingency plans to deal with a crisis should it occur.

7.1 What is a crisis?

Definition

Crisis: An unexpected event that threatens the wellbeing of a business, or a significant disruption to the business and its normal operations which impacts on its customers, employees, investors and other stakeholders.

Crises can be fairly **predictable and quantifiable**, or totally **unexpected**.

7.2 What is crisis management?

Definition

Crisis management: Identifying a crisis, planning a response to the crisis and confronting and resolving the crisis.

Crisis management is much more commonly used in businesses now:

- Crises such as natural disasters and terrorism have been seen to have an even more extreme effect in the context of global trade, so businesses are more motivated to manage crises better
- Society is more litigious than it used to be, and businesses are expected to be able to deal better with crises now than in the past
- Better IT and other technology systems allow businesses to be able to do more to avert and/or manage a crisis
- Social media means that publicity surrounding any sort of crisis is widespread and can feed on itself, raising the potential for very severe reputational consequences if damage limitation does not swing into action quickly

7.3 Types of crisis

There are three main types of crisis in terms of their **effects** on the business:

- **Financial crisis** – short-term liquidity or cash flow problems, and long-term solvency problems
- **Public relations crisis** – negative publicity that could adversely affect the success of the business
- **Strategic crisis** – changes in the business environment that call the viability of the business into question, such as new technology making old products or processes obsolete

There are many types of crisis in terms of their **cause**.

- **Natural event:** physical, especially environmental, destruction due to natural causes such as earthquake
- **Industrial accident:** buildings collapse, fire, release of toxic fumes, sinking or leaking of a ship

- **Product or service failure:** product recall of faulty or dangerous goods; communications, systems or machine failure causing massive reduction in capacity; health scare related to the product or industry
- **Public relations disaster:** pressure group or unwelcome media attention; adverse publicity in the media; removal/loss/prosecution of CEO or other key management
- **Business crisis:** sudden strike by workforce; sudden collapse of key supplier; withdrawal of support by major customer; competitor launches new product; sudden shortfall in demand
- **Management crisis:** hostile takeover bid; death of key management; managers poached by main competitor; boardroom battles
- **Legal/regulatory crisis:** product liability; new regulations increase costs or remove competitive edge; employee or other fraud

Worked example: Industrial accident

In 2005 the oil storage depot at Buncefield, Hemel Hempstead suffered a major explosion and fire. The result was:

- Loss of product
- Significant loss of capacity
- Disruption to supplies
- Loss of business
- Physical damage to neighbouring houses and commercial premises
- Environmental damage
- Damage to reputation
- Claims for compensation
- Legal action

Worked example: Public relations disaster

In 1991 Gerald Ratner, head of the chain of high street jewellers that bore his name, explained why his products were so inexpensive. He said that a product sold in his shop was cheap because it was 'total rubbish'. He 'sold a pair of earrings for under £1, which was cheaper than a prawn sandwich, but probably wouldn't last as long'. The result: share values fell substantially, Mr Ratner left the company and it was sold.

7.4 Managing a crisis

A crisis happens when a **risk becomes a reality**. The business should seek to prevent crises, and to have contingency plans should a crisis occur. It should also act to resolve an actual crisis in the most effective way.

7.4.1 Crisis prevention

The business should always seek to **prevent** a crisis by **planning ahead** and **projecting likely outcomes**; it should avoid decisions that have the potential to turn into a crisis.

7.4.2 Contingency planning

The business should make **a contingency plan** for the worst and/or most likely crises to occur. This must be kept up to date, and staff should be trained in how it should be implemented in the event of a crisis.

7.4.3 Effective action in the event of a crisis

- Assess objectively the cause(s) of the crisis
- Determine whether the cause(s) will have a long-term or short-term effect
- Project the most likely course of events
- Focus resources on activities that mitigate or eliminate the crisis
- Look for opportunities

In the event of a **public relations crisis**

- Act immediately to prevent or counter the spread of negative information; this may require intense media activities.
- Use media to provide a counter-argument or question the credibility of the original negative publicity.

Interactive question 3: Contingency planning **[Difficulty level: Intermediate]**

Consider what you would do if, at a time when your business has a small overdraft and very little money expected in shortly, it is faced with a large demand from a government body which requires settlement in one month.

See **Answer** at the end of the chapter.

8 Disaster recovery

Section overview

- A disaster is a major crisis or event which causes a breakdown in the business's operations and resultant losses.
- A business needs to recover from a disaster as quickly as possible. This is helped if the business has a disaster recovery plan covering standby and recovery procedures and personnel management.

8.1 What is a disaster?

Definition

Disaster: The business's operations, or a significant part of them, break down for some reason, leading to potential **losses** of equipment, data or funds.

We have seen that **event risk** is the operational risk of loss due to single events that are unlikely but that may have serious consequences. Political risk is one example and is often associated especially with less developed countries where events such as wars or military coups may result in an industry or a business being taken over by the government and having its assets seized.

Here are some examples, along with some responses and controls, based on reduction and sharing of the risk of the disaster where it cannot be avoided.

- A **fire safety plan** is an essential feature of security procedures, in order to prevent fire, detect fire and put out the fire. Fire safety includes:
  - **Site preparation** (for example, appropriate **building materials, fire doors**)
  - **Detection** (for example, **smoke detectors**)
  - **Extinguishing** (for example, **sprinklers**)
  - **Training** for staff in observing **fire safety procedures**
- **Flooding** and water damage can be countered by the use of **waterproof ceilings and floors** together with the provision of **adequate drainage**.

- Keeping up maintenance programmes can counter the leaking roofs or dripping pipes that result from **adverse weather conditions**. The problems caused by power surges resulting from lightning can be countered by the use of **uninterruptible (protected) power supplies**. This will protect equipment from fluctuations in the supply. Power failure can be protected against by the use of a **separate generator**.
- Threats from terrorism can be countered by **physical access controls** and consultation with police and fire authorities.
- Accidental damage can be avoided by **sensible attitudes to behaviour** while at work and **good layout** of workspaces.

Any system which has suffered a disaster **must recover as soon as possible** so that further losses are not incurred, and current losses can be rectified.

What is considered a disaster is relative to the size of the business and the significance of the item that breaks down. The failure of a hard drive in a single PC could be extremely serious for a small business which depended on that one computer, but in a large business it might cause minimal inconvenience, so long as backup copies of data files are maintained.

Minor breakdowns occur regularly and require **short-term** recovery plans such as agreements with a maintenance company for same or next-day on site repairs. Disasters which result in the destruction of a major facility or installation require a **long-term** plan.

A long-term **disaster recovery plan** will typically provide for:

- **Standby procedures** so that some operations can be performed while normal services are disrupted
- **Recovery procedures** once the cause of the breakdown has been discovered or corrected
- **Personnel management** policies to ensure that the above are implemented properly

The plan must cover all activities from the **initial response** to the disaster (crisis management), through to **damage limitation** and **full recovery**. Responsibilities must be clearly spelt out for all tasks. The contents of the plan will include the following.

Section	Comment
Definition of responsibilities	It is important that somebody (a manager or co-ordinator) is designated to take control in a crisis. This individual can then delegate specific tasks or responsibilities to other designated people.
Priorities	Limited resources may be available for processing. Some tasks are more important than others. These must be established in advance. Similarly, the recovery plan may indicate that certain areas must be tackled first.
Backup and standby arrangements	These may be with other installations, or with a business that provides such services (eg maybe the hardware vendor). Alternatively, other processes may be possible, for instance taking cash when credit/debit card processing is interrupted.
Communication with staff	The problems of a disaster can be compounded by poor communication between members of staff.
Public relations	If the disaster has a public impact, the recovery team may come under pressure from the public or from the media.
Risk assessment	Some way must be found of assessing the particular requirements of the problem.

Summary and Self-test

Summary

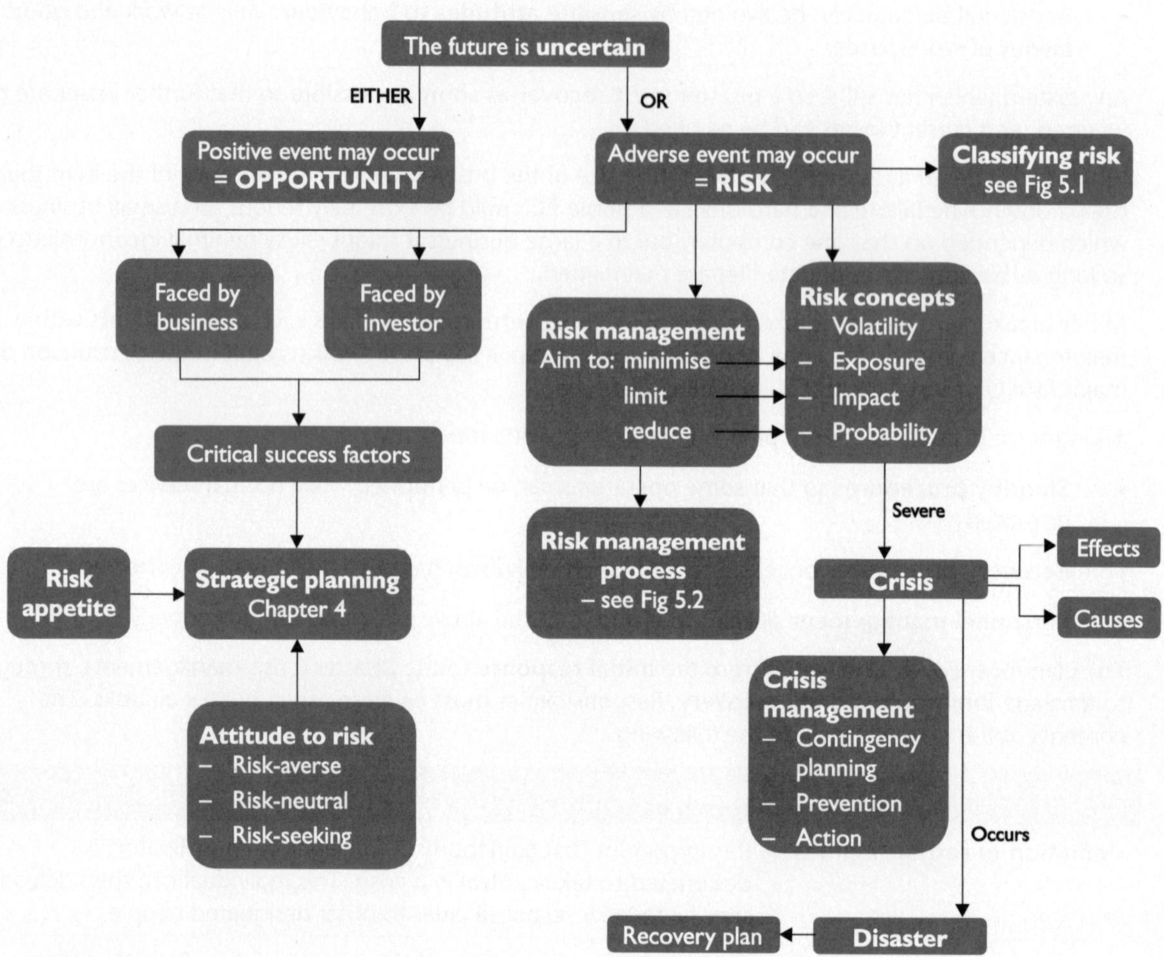

Self-test

Answer the following questions.

1 Which of the following is COSO's definition of risk?

- A That events in the future cannot be predicted with certainty
- B The possible variation in an outcome from what is expected to happen
- C The inability to predict the outcome of an activity due to a lack of information
- D The possibility that an event will occur and adversely affect the achievement of objectives

2 Which of the following is a downside risk for a business?

- A That costs might rise
- B That revenue might rise
- C That controls may succeed
- D That quality might improve

3 Benbuck plc has had a wide range of returns to shareholders in recent years. This means that as an investment Benbuck plc shares are

- A Volatile and low risk
- B Non-volatile and low risk
- C Volatile and high risk
- D Non-volatile and high risk

4 Strang plc has identified that the new production machinery in which it is considering an investment may soon become obsolete on the grounds of low productivity. This business risk could be identified as

A A product risk
B A technology risk
C An enterprise risk
D A property risk

5 Mimso Bank plc's staff appear to be oblivious to the importance of risk. For Mimso Bank plc this is

A A business risk
B An enterprise risk
C A financial risk
D An operational risk

6 The size of the gross risk facing a business is measured as

A Volatility × exposure
B Impact × exposure
C Impact × probability
D Volatility × probability

7 In terms of risk management, choosing to transfer some risk is part of

A Risk awareness
B Risk response
C Risk assessment
D Risk monitoring

8 Brando plc has 40 employees engaged in an activity that has been identified as having a high element of risk to the company's reputation. The company decides that the activity is necessary but that only 10 staff should be engaged in it in future, and these staff should receive extra training. The risk responses that Brando plc has applied are

A Avoidance and reduction
B Transfer and acceptance
C Reduction and acceptance
D Avoidance and transfer

9 Heller & Co is a firm of solicitors which has long been aware that the departure of one partner, Mike Heller, would constitute a crisis for the firm. It has therefore ensured that he is highly paid and that Sue Jones, another partner, shadows his work and knows his clients. On 15 June Mike walks out of the firm and provokes a serious crisis which the firm's very expensive PR consultants handle. The area of crisis management which Heller & Co has neglected to address in their management of the crisis is

A Crisis prevention
B Contingency planning
C Analysis of the causes of Mike's actions on 15 June
D Taking action to mitigate the crisis

10 Klib plc operates in a politically unstable country. It has arranged that a consultancy firm with access to similar facilities as Klib plc has a complete set of backup files for Klib plc. This strategy is part of Klib plc's

A Risk management
B Crisis management
C Disaster recovery planning
D Operational planning

Now, go back to the Learning Objectives in the Introduction. If you are satisfied you have achieved these objectives, please tick them off.

Answers to Interactive questions

Answer to Interactive question 1

For many small businesses the most evident risk is that customers do not buy what they supply, whether because of competition, fashion or an economic downturn. This is also the risk that is most difficult to deal with, though being well-informed and innovative help to ensure that the business can react adequately. There is a real risk too that the costs of providing the goods or service will rise, which again is hard to contend with as the business may have little or no bargaining power. The risks from inadequate controls are less likely though more catastrophic; most small business owners are very closely involved in the running of it and keep close control of quality, administration and staff, but there are plenty of businesses which have gone under due to one fraud, or one lapse of quality. Finance is also a serious risk; bank overdrafts can be called in on demand, and cashflow has often caused very severe problems, even winding up, in otherwise successful businesses.

Answer to Interactive question 2

PII is a requirement not of the law but of the ICAEW itself, which acts as regulator of its members both in and out of public practice. The work of the ICAEW in regulating members is overseen by Financial Reporting Council, which we shall see more about in Chapter 10. PII is intended to provide funds to persons who have suffered financial loss as a result of the negligence of a chartered accountant; this is paid to the injured party, not to the chartered accountant, but it is an example of how a person (the chartered accountant) may transfer some of the risks they face to another entity, in this case the insurance company.

Answer to Interactive question 3

You should not wait for further evidence before acting. Immediately take action to maintain or increase cash flow:

- Accelerate receipts from customers even if this requires the granting of discounts
- Decelerate payments to suppliers even if this means losing discounts
- Increase short-term sales but maintain or increase margins on sales if possible
- Reduce expenses:
  - eliminate non-essential expenses
  - sell surplus long-term assets
  - reduce payroll if possible
  - renegotiate the overdraft and other debts

Answers to Self-test

1	D	Option A describes variability, option B is not COSO's definition and option C defines uncertainty
2	A	All the other options are upside risks
3	C	Volatility measures the variation of returns in terms of profits, dividends and share prices; the more volatile the return, the higher the risk
4	B	
5	D	This is a people risk, which is a kind of operational, non-business risk
6	C	
7	B	
8	A	Reducing the number of staff is a form of avoidance; training the remaining ones is a form of risk reduction
9	C	
10	C	

CHAPTER 6

Introduction to financial information

Introduction

Learning objectives

Tick off

- Specify the extent to which financial information:
  - Provides for accountability of management to shareholders and other stakeholders ☐
  - Reflects business performance ☐
  - Is useful to users in making decisions ☐
  - Meets the information needs of national, social and economic contexts (eg national statistical information) ☐
- Identify, in the context of accounting and other systems, the issues surrounding:
  - Information processing ☐
  - Information security ☐
  - Information management ☐
- Specify why the management of a business require information about performance measurement including non-routine areas such as in supporting an entity's sustainability management ☐

Specific syllabus references are: 3a, d, e.

Syllabus links

The topics covered in this introduction to financial information are developed as well in Management Information at Certificate level, Business Strategy and Financial Management at Professional level, and in the Advanced level.

Examination context

Questions on financial information could easily appear in the exam.

Questions are likely to be set in multiple choice format in a scenario context. Knowledge-type questions are also likely on particular definitions or principles.

1 Why is business finance important?

Section overview

- Finance plays a central role in a business, so financial information does as well.

Without **money** a business could not exist: it could not pay its expenses, it could not acquire inventory, and it could not employ labour. It would not want to exist: businesses exist to make money, that is, a profit. All businesses require a level of finance to get started, and then a balance of money coming in and going out in order to stay in existence.

We have seen several times so far in this text that a business's finances play an important, indeed, central role in what it does.

- Most of a business's **stakeholders** have finance at stake in the business; shareholders and lenders obviously invest directly in the business, but in addition managers' and other employees' personal finances depend on it, suppliers need to be paid by it, customers depends on it for goods and services that will in turn support their finances, and the government wants tax revenue from it (see Chapter 1)
- The **primary objective** of a business is a financial one: to increase shareholders' wealth by creating shareholder value (see Chapter 1)
- Finance is a **separate function** in the organisational structure of most businesses (as we shall see in far more detail in Chapter 7)
- How much finance the business needs and how this can be raised often determine the **business structure/legal form** it takes (see Chapter 3)
- Together with its competitive strategy and its investment strategy, the business's financial strategy is central to its overall **corporate strategy** (see Chapter 4)
- Businesses are exposed to financial **risks** of various kinds and must find ways of managing these risks (see Chapter 5)

Because of the central importance of finance in a business it follows that **information** on the business's finances will be needed.

2 Uses and types of financial information

Section overview

- Information on the business's finances is used for planning, controlling, recording transactions, measuring performance and making decisions.
- Planning, operational, tactical and strategic information are all required.

2.1 Why do businesses and managers need financial information?

Businesses and managers require **financial information** for:

- Planning
- Controlling
- Recording transactions
- Performance measurement
- Decision making

2.1.1 Planning

Once a decision has been made, say on what competitive strategy to follow, it is necessary to plan **how to implement** the steps necessary to make it effective. Planning requires a knowledge of, among other things, available **resources**, possible **time-scales** for implementation and the likely **outcome under alternative scenarios**.

2.1.2 Controlling

Once a plan is implemented, its actual performance must be controlled. Information is required to assess **whether implementation is proceeding as planned** or whether there is some unexpected deviation from plan. It may consequently be necessary to take some form of corrective action.

2.1.3 Recording transactions

Information about **each transaction or event** is required for a number of reasons.

- Documentation of transactions can be used as **evidence** in a case of dispute
- There may be a **legal requirement** to record transactions, for example for accounting and audit purposes
- Detailed information on production costs can be built up, allowing a better **assessment of profitability**
- The efficiency of labour utilised in providing a particular service can be measured

2.1.4 Performance measurement

Just as individual operations need to be controlled, so overall performance must be measured in order to enable **comparisons of the actual outcome with the plan**. This may involve collecting information on, for example, costs, revenues, volumes, time-scale, profitability and long-term sustainability.

2.1.5 Decision making

Information is required as a basis on which to make informed decisions. This completes the full circle of the business management process.

2.2 Type of information

Information can be classified according to the use to which it is put. The same type of information will not be provided to a front-line manager of a team of machine operatives as to the board of directors. This is because the front-line manager needs to know how many operatives can be employed on one shift, for instance, while the board of directors want to know whether enough skilled operatives can be available in the medium-term to resource increased production of a successful new product.

Information can thus be classified as follows.

- **Planning information** helps people involved in the planning process
- **Operational information** helps people carry out their day-to-day activities, eg how many operatives are needed on one shift
- **Tactical information** helps people deal with short-term issues and opportunities, eg monthly variance reports for the factory
- **Strategic information** supports major long-term decision-making, eg can resources be made available to expand production?

3 Qualities of good information

Section overview

- Information should be ACCURATE and complete. It should have a benefit that is in proportion to its cost, and it should be targeted at its user. It should be relevant and from an authoritative source. It should be provided at the time when it is needed, and it should be easy to use.
- What makes information valuable is its source, its ease of assimilation, its accessibility and its relevance.
- The cost of obtaining information should be less than the benefits it brings.

Information of whatever type is of good quality if it has eight key characteristics, which are easiest to remember if you use the mnemonic ACCURATE.

Note that the second A here stands for '**Authoritative**', an increasingly important concern given the huge **proliferation of information sources** available online today.

Quality	Example
Accurate	Figures should **add up**, the degree of **rounding** should be appropriate, there should be **no typographical errors**, items should be allocated to the **correct category**, and **assumptions should be stated** for uncertain information (no spurious accuracy).
Complete	Information should include everything that it **needs** to include, for example external data if relevant, or comparative information.
Cost-beneficial	It should not **cost more** to obtain the information than the **benefit** derived from having it. Providers of information should be given **efficient** means of collecting and analysing it. Presentation should be such that users do not waste time working out what it means.
User-targeted	The **needs of the user** should be borne in mind, for instance senior managers may require summaries, whereas junior ones may require detail.
Relevant	Information that is **not needed** for a decision should be omitted, no matter how 'interesting' it may be.
Authoritative	The **source** of the information should be a reliable one (**not**, for instance, 'Joe Bloggs' Predictions Page' on the internet unless Joe Bloggs is known to be a reliable source for that type of information).
Timely	The information should be available **when it is needed**.
Easy to use	Information should be **clearly presented**, **not excessively long**, and sent using the **right medium** and **communication channel** (e-mail, telephone, hard-copy report etc).

Interactive question 1: Good information [Difficulty level: Exam standard]

Managers often complain that they are weighed down by information which they struggle to make sense of and to use. Which of the ACCURATE qualities of good information are most often ignored in information given to managers?

See **Answer** at the end of this chapter.

3.1 What makes information valuable?

- **Its source**

  If external information comes from a source that is widely known and respected for quality, thoroughness and accuracy (Reuters, say, or the BBC) it will be more valuable to users than information from an unknown or untested source, because it can be relied upon with confidence. If an internal source is known to be accurate, efficient and reliable, the information it produces will be more valuable to its users.

- **Ease of assimilation**

  Information can be presented using not only words and figures but also **colour, graphics, sound and movement**. This makes the receipt of information a richer and so more valuable experience, and it means that information can be more easily, and more quickly, understood.

- **Accessibility**

  If information can be made available in an easily accessible place (such as the **internet**) users do not have to commit too much time and effort to retrieving it.

- **Relevance**

  Unlike certain commodities the value of information in general is not based on scarcity: indeed the most frequent complaint of many modern managers is that there is far too much of it. Instead the value of information is **in the eyes of the beholder** to some extent: information about a new type of plastic may be of keen interest and value to a car manufacturer because it is relevant – but of no value whatsoever to a software house.

3.2 Assessing the cost and value of information

Information which is **obtained but not used** has no actual value to the person that obtains it. It is only the **action taken** as a result of a decision based on information which has actual value for a business. An item of information which leads to an actual increase in profit of £90 is not worth having if it cost £100 to collect. Whether it is worthwhile having more information therefore depends on:

- The **extra benefits** expected from getting it, and
- The **extra costs** of obtaining it

Its value can be measured in terms of the difference it would make to management decisions if the information were made available.

As we shall see shortly, a management information system (MIS) is used to produce a wide variety of information so the cost of an individual item of information is **not always easy to quantify**.

Interactive question 2: Information cost [Difficulty level: Intermediate]

A manager uses particular enquiry software to enquire into her company's MIS. What is the cost of this enquiry?

See **Answer** at the end of this chapter.

Just as the costs of an item of information are harder to assess than might appear superficially, so too the **benefits are often hard to quantify**. While nobody doubts that information is valuable, it is not always easy to construct an economic assessment of this value.

- A monthly variance analysis report will only generate economically consequential decisions if there is some **control failure** leading to variances, but control failures are not easy to predict.
- The economic consequences of a decision are also **not always easy to predict**.

4 Sources of data and information

Section overview

- Useful data/information comes from both inside and outside the organisation, from a variety of sources.

CHAPTER 6

4.1 What are data and information?

These two terms are often used interchangeably and it is useful at this point to make sure you are clear about the distinction between them.

Definitions

Data (plural; singular is 'datum'): Distinct pieces of information, which can exist in a variety of forms – as numbers or text on pieces of paper, as bits or bytes stored in electronic memory, or as facts stored in a person's mind.

Information: The output of whatever system is used to process data. This may be a computer system, turning single pieces of data into a report, for instance.

Database: a structured collection of records or **data** that is stored in a **computer system** along with rules as to the information that will be sought from it, so that queries may be answered by interrogating the database.

4.2 Internal data sources

Capturing data/information from **inside** the organisation involves the following.

- A **system** for collecting or measuring **transactions** data – for example sales, purchases, inventory etc – which sets out procedures for **what** data is **collected**, how frequently, by whom, and by what methods, and how it is **processed**, **filed** or **communicated**.
- **Informal communication** of information between **managers and staff** (for example, by word-of-mouth or at meetings).
- **Communication between managers.**

Inside the business, data/information come from the following internal sources.

- **The accounting records**: sales ledgers, purchase ledgers, nominal ledgers and cash books etc hold information that may be of great value outside the finance function, for example, sales information for the marketing function. To maintain the integrity of its accounting records, a business operates **controls** over transactions. These also give rise to valuable information. An inventory control system, for example, will include details of purchase orders, goods received notes, goods returned notes and so on, which can be analysed to **provide management information** about speed of delivery, say, or the quality of supplies
- **Human resources and payroll records**, holding information on people, their skills and aspirations, and so on
- **Machine logs and computer systems** in **production/operations** containing information about machine capacity, fuel consumption, movement of people, materials, and work in progress, set up times, maintenance requirements and so on
- **Timesheets in service businesses**, notably accountants and solicitors, containing data on the **time spent** on various activities, both to justify fees to clients and to assess the efficiency and profitability of operations
- **Staff**. Information may be obtained either informally in the course of day-to-day business or through meetings, interviews or questionnaires

4.3 External data sources

Capturing data information from **outside** the business may be formal or informal.

Formal collection of data from outside sources includes the following.

- A business's **tax specialists** will gather information about changes in tax law and how this will affect the business
- Obtaining information about any **new legislation** on health and safety at work, or employment regulations, must be the responsibility of a particular person who must then pass on the information to managers affected by it
- **Research and development (R&D)** work often relies on information about other R&D work being done by another business or by government institutions
- **Marketing managers** need to know about the opinions and buying attitudes of potential customers. To obtain this information, they carry out marketing research exercises

Informal gathering of information from the environment **goes on all the time, consciously or unconsciously**, because the employees of an organisation learn **what is going on in the world around them** – perhaps from the internet, newspapers, television reports, meetings with business associates or the trade press.

A business's files (paper and computerised) include information from external sources such as invoices, letters, e-mails, advertisements and so on **received from customers and suppliers**. Sometimes additional external information is required, requiring an active search outside the business. The following sources may be identified.

- The internet in general
- The government
- Advice or information bureaux, such as Reuters or Bloomberg
- Consultancies of all sorts
- Newspaper and magazine publishers
- Specific reference works which are used in a particular line of work
- Libraries and information services
- The systems of other businesses via electronic data interchange (EDI)

5 Information processing and management

Section overview

- In the information processing system data is input, processed and then output as information.
- Information processing needs to be complete, accurate, timely, inalterable, verifiable and assessable (CATIVA).
- The transaction processing system (TPS) performs, records and processes routine information for marketing, production/operations, finance and HR functions.
- The management information system (MIS) processes data into information that supports and facilitates decision making by managers.
- Information management systems comprise: executive support/information systems; decisions support systems; expert systems; knowledge work systems; office automation systems
- The internet, intranets and extranets are becoming increasingly important as parts of the information management system.

5.1 How is data/information processed?

Definition

Information processing: Data once collected is converted into information for communicating more widely within the business.

To be effective, information processing should meet the following CATIVA criteria:

Completeness	Everything that needs to be processed should be processed.
Accuracy	Processing should be done so that the data remains true to its sources, and the information produced contains no errors.
Timeliness	Processing should occur in line with data availability and information needs, which means real time (instantaneously) in many cases.
Inalterability	The process should be open to neither unauthorised intervention whilst in action nor alteration once completed (this aids accuracy and security).
Verifiability	The sources of the data and the trail from data through processing to information should be capable of being followed through.
Assessability	The effectiveness of the processing should be open to scrutiny so that its quality can be judged.

5.2 Information systems

Just as materials and labour are processed into outputs by the business's production or operations system, so are data processed into information by the business's information systems.

Definitions

A system: A set of interacting components that operate together to accomplish a purpose.

A business system: A collection of people, machines and methods organised to accomplish a set of specific functions.

Information systems (IS): All systems and procedures involved in the collection, storage, production and distribution of information.

Information technology (IT): The equipment used to capture, store, transmit or present information. IT provides a large part of the information systems infrastructure.

Information management: The approach that a business takes towards the management of its information including planning IS/IT developments, the organisational environment of IS, control and technology.

A system has three component parts: **inputs**, **processes** and **outputs**. Other key characteristics of a system are the environment and the system boundary – as shown in Figure 6.1.

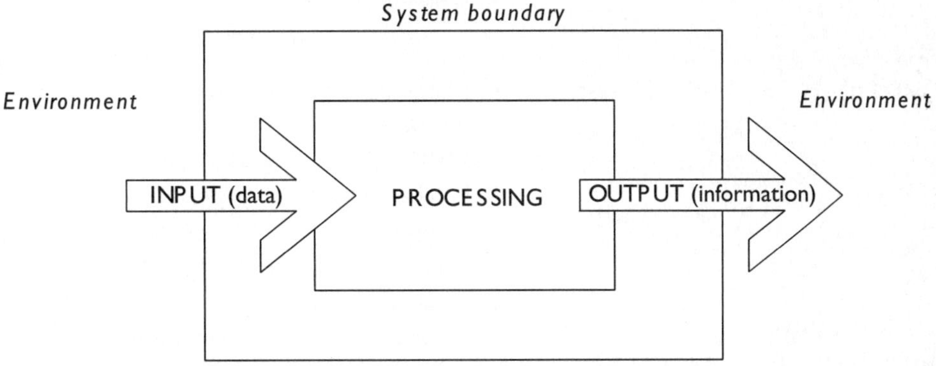

Figure 6.1 Information system

- **The data input** may be **output from other systems**: for example, the output from a transactions processing system forms the input for a management information system (as we shall see)
- **Processing** transforms input data into output information. There is **not necessarily a clear relationship** between the number of inputs to a process and the number of outputs
- **Output information** is the **result of the processing**
- A **system boundary** separates the information system from its environment. For example, the marketing information system and the accounting information system are generally separate, but there may be an **interface** between the two systems to allow the exchange of resources. There may also be interfaces between internal and external information systems, for instance between a processing system and the sales system of its major suppliers
- Anything which is outside the system boundary belongs to the system's **environment** and not to the system itself. A system **accepts inputs** from the environment and **provides outputs** into the environment. The parts of the environment from which the system receives inputs may not be the same as those to which it delivers outputs. The environment exerts a considerable influence on the behaviour of a system; but the system can do little to **control** the behaviour of the environment

In relation to financial information, the two information processing systems in which we are most interested are:

- The transaction processing system, and
- The management information system

5.3 The transaction processing system (TPS)

Definition

Transaction processing system (TPS): A system which performs, records and processes routine transactions.

A TPS is used for **routine tasks** in which data items or transactions must be processed so that operations can continue. A TPS supports most business functions in most types of businesses.

Transaction processing systems				
	Sales/marketing system	Manufacturing/ production system	Finance/ accounting system	Human resources system
Major functions of system	• Sales management • Marketing research • Promotion pricing • New products	• Scheduling • Purchasing • Shipping/ receiving • Engineering • Operations	• Budgeting • Nominal ledger • Invoicing • Management accounting	• Personnel records • Benefits • Salaries • Labour relations • Training
Major parts of systems	• Sales order system • Marketing research system • Pricing system	• Materials resource planning • Purchase order control • Engineering • Quality control	• Nominal ledger • Accounts receivable /payable • Budgeting • Treasury management	• Payroll • Employee records • Employee benefits • Career path systems

5.4 The management information system (MIS)

Definition

Management information system (MIS): Converts data from mainly internal sources into information (eg summary reports, exception reports). This information enables managers to make timely and effective decisions for planning, directing and controlling the activities for which they are responsible.

An MIS provides regular reports and (usually) on-line access to the business's current and historical performance. The MIS transforms data from underlying TPS into summarised files that are used as the basis for management reports. It:

- Supports **structured** decisions at operational and management control levels
- Is designed to report on **existing** operations
- Has little analytical capability
- Is relatively **inflexible**
- Has an **internal** focus

5.5 Information management systems

There is a wide range of systems available to support a business's information management.

Definitions

Executive support system (ESS) or Executive information system (EIS): a sophisticated database that pools data from internal and external sources and makes information available to senior managers in an easy-to-use form. ESS help senior managers make strategic, unstructured decisions

Decision support system (DSS): combines data and analytical models or data analysis tools to support semi-structured and unstructured decision making.

Expert system: captures human expertise in a limited domain of knowledge to allow users to benefit from expert knowledge and information. The system will consist of a database holding specialised data and rules about what to do in, or how to interpret, a given set of circumstances.

Knowledge work systems (KWS): facilitate the creation and integration of new knowledge into an organisation.

Office automation systems (OAS): systems that increase the productivity of data and information workers.

Worked example: Information management systems for the medical profession

Executive support systems (ESS)	The general managers of hospitals will have information on bed usage, costs of procedures, the demographics of the hospital catchment area, the priorities of government, the care provided nearby and the potential for epidemics or other issues. They will use this to set priorities and decide the levels of provision for the coming years.
Management information systems (MIS)	Managers exist at many levels such as practices, wards, clinics, procurement divisions etc. They will use information on demand and resource availability, costs and revenues etc to ensure care is given within budget.
Decision support systems (DSS)	Clinical staff may use systems such as scans, blood test data, information on the patient's history and information on drug doses and effects to decide how to treat the patient.

Expert systems	Some telephone 'triage' services (eg NHS Direct in the UK) gather information from the caller about the symptoms using a structured set of questions. The system will infer potential causes and will generate further questions leading to a preliminary diagnosis and decision on a course of action, such as calling paramedics, recommending pain killers, etc.
Knowledge work systems (KWS)	Clinical staff will complete records and reports on office automated systems. They may keep up to date with their areas with on-line journals. Some specialists use teleconferencing and image sharing workflow systems to discuss cases or to provide expert diagnoses to remote hospitals.
Office automation systems (OAS)	The patient appointment system will be automated and all correspondence typed. The hospital menus will be prepared in a graphics package as will occasional signage.
Transaction processing systems (TPS)	The pharmacy will order and dispense inventory through its TPS.

Worked example: Expert system for loan applications

Financial institutions use expert systems to process straightforward **loan applications**. The user enters certain key facts into the system such as the loan applicant's name and most recent addresses, their income and monthly outgoings, and details of other loans. The system will then:

- **Check the facts** given against its database to see whether the applicant has a good credit record
- **Perform calculations** to see whether the applicant can afford to repay the loan
- **Match up other criteria**, such as whether the security offered for the loan or the purpose for which the loan is wanted is acceptable, and to what extent the loan applicant fits the lender's profile of a good risk (based on the lender's previous experience)

A decision is then suggested, based on the results of this processing. This is why it is often possible to get a loan or arrange insurance **over the telephone**, whereas in the past it would have been necessary to go and speak to a bank manager or send details to an actuary and then wait for him or her to come to a decision.

Business applications of expert systems:

- **Legal** or tax advice
- **Forecasting** of economic or financial developments, or of market and customer behaviour
- **Surveillance**, for example of the number of customers entering a supermarket, to decide what shelves need restocking and when more checkouts need to be opened, or of machines in a factory, to determine when they need maintenance
- **Diagnostic systems**, to identify causes of problems, for example in production control in a factory, or in healthcare
- **Project management**
- **Education** and **training**, diagnosing a student's or worker's weaknesses and providing or recommending extra instruction as appropriate

Conditions when expert systems are most useful:

- The problem is **reasonably well-defined**
- The expert can define some **rules** by which the problem can be solved
- The problem cannot be solved by **conventional** transaction processing or data handling
- The **expert could be released** to more difficult problems. Experts are often highly paid, meaning the value of even small time savings is likely to be significant
- The **investment** in an expert system is **cost-justified**

Interactive question 3: Expert systems [Difficulty level: Intermediate]

Explain why businesses use expert systems for decision-making tasks which humans are naturally better able to perform than computers.

See **Answer** at the end of the chapter.

5.5.1 The internet

Definitions

Internet: a global network connecting millions of computers via telecoms links that allow them to send and receive information. It provides opportunities for a business to organise and automate tasks which would previously have required more costly interaction between the business and its contacts.

World wide web: the multimedia element of the internet which provides facilities such as full-colour, graphics and sound.

Websites: information points within the network created by members such as businesses for searchers to visit and benefit by the provision of information and/or by entering into a transaction.

5.5.2 Intranets and extranets

Businesses are increasingly using intranets and extranets to disseminate information.

- An **intranet** is like a mini version of the internet. People in the business use networked computers to access information held on a server. The user interface is a browser similar to those used on the internet. The intranet offers access to information on a wide variety of topics, and often includes access to the internet.
- An **extranet** is an intranet that is accessible to **authorised outsiders**, using a valid username and password. The username will have access rights attached that determine which parts of the extranet can be viewed. Extranets are becoming a very popular means for businesses within an alliance (joint venture etc) to exchange information.

6 Information security

Section overview

- Information is a valuable commodity and therefore needs to be kept secure.
- Risks to data include human error, technical error, natural disasters, deliberate damage and industrial action
- Information security involves prevention, detection and deterrence of problems, plus recovery and correction procedures and threat avoidance.
- A secure information system is only available when needed and maintains confidentiality. The information is authentic and has integrity. Changes must be authorised. It is designed so that users will not have to reject the information on the basis that it is faulty in any way (ACIANA – see later).
- Information security is ensured by means of physical access, security and integrity controls.

6.1 Why is information security important?

If you own **something that you value** – you **look after it**. **Information** is valuable and it deserves similar care.

Definition

Security (in information management): the **protection of data** from accidental or deliberate threats which might cause unauthorised modification, disclosure or destruction of data, and the **protection of the information system** from the degradation or non-availability of services (Lam: *Security of computer based information systems*).

The **risks to data** are as follows:

- Human error
- Entering incorrect transactions
- Failing to correct errors
- Processing the wrong files
- Technical error such as malfunctioning hardware or software
- Natural disasters such as fire, flooding, explosion, impact, lightning
- Deliberate actions such as fraud
- Commercial espionage
- Malicious damage
- Industrial action

Many of these are the physical risks that we saw in Chapter 5; risk management and controls are key issues in ensuring the security of information systems.

6.2 Ensuring the security of information

Aspects of security include the following:

- **Prevention**. It is in practice impossible to prevent all threats cost-effectively, but prevention is better than cure
- **Detection**. Detection techniques are often combined with prevention techniques: a log can be maintained of unauthorised attempts to gain access to a computer system
- **Deterrence**. As an example, computer misuse by personnel can be made grounds for disciplinary action
- **Recovery procedures**. If the threat occurs, its consequences can be contained (for example, checkpoint programs)
- **Correction procedures**. These ensure the vulnerability is dealt with (for example, by instituting stricter controls)
- **Threat avoidance**. This might mean changing the design of the system

6.2.1 Qualities of a secure information system: ACIANA

Availability	Information can always be accessed.
Confidentiality	Information cannot be accessed by anyone who does not have the right to see it.
Integrity	Data is the same as in its sources and has not been accidentally or deliberately reduced, altered, destroyed or disclosed.
Authenticity	Data and information are taken from *bona fide* sources.
Non-repudiation	Information is not open to being rejected by its intended users on the grounds of faults in the system.
Authorisation	Changes in the system can only be made by persons who are accountable for them.

6.2.2 Physical access controls

- **Personnel**, including receptionists and, outside working hours, security guards can help control human access
- **Door locks** can be used where frequency of use is low. (This is not practicable if the door is in frequent use.)
- Locks can be combined with:
  - A **keypad system**, requiring a code to be entered
  - A **card entry system**, requiring a card to be 'swiped'
- Intruder **alarms**
- **Laptops, tablets, smartphones** and **other devices** with access to the system should be kept secure
- Staff should be allocated an individual **personal identification number**, or PIN, which identifies him or her to the building

6.2.3 Security controls in the system

These help to prevent:

- Human error
  - Entering incorrect transactions
  - Failing to correct errors
  - Processing the wrong files
- Technical error such as malfunctioning hardware or software
- Deliberate actions such as fraud
- Commercial espionage
- Malicious damage

6.2.4 Integrity controls in the system

Data will maintain its **integrity** if it is **complete** and **not corrupted**.

- The original **input** of the data must be controlled in such a way as to ensure that the results are complete and correct. **Input controls** should ensure the **accuracy, completeness and validity** of input
  - **Data verification** involves ensuring data entered matches source documents
  - **Data validation** involves ensuring that data entered is not incomplete or unreasonable. Various checks include:
    - **Check digits**. A digit calculated by the program and added to the code being checked to validate it
    - **Control totals**. For example, a batch total totalling the entries in the batch
    - **Hash totals**. A system generated total used to check processing has been performed as intended
    - **Range checks**. Used to check the value entered against a sensible range, eg ledger account number must be between 5,000 and 9,999
    - **Limit checks**. Similar to a range check, but usually based on an upper limit, eg must be less than 999,999.99
- Any **processing and storage** of data must maintain the completeness and correctness of the data captured. **Processing controls** should ensure the **accuracy and completeness of processing**. Programs should be subject to **development controls** and to rigorous **testing**. Periodic running of **test data** is also recommended

- Reports or other **output** should be set up so that they, too, are complete and correct. **Output controls** could include:
  - Investigation and follow-up of **error reports** and **exception reports** produced by the system
  - **Batch controls** to ensure all items are processed and returned
  - Controls over distribution/copying of output
  - Labelling of storage media

The system should have a **back-up** and **archive** strategy, including:

- Regular back-up of data (at least daily)
- Archive plans
- A **disaster recovery** plan including off-site storage

Users of the system should be given a **password**. While unauthorised persons may circumvent physical access controls, a **logical access system** can use passwords to prevent access to data and program files, by measures such as:

- Identification of the user
- Authentication of user identity
- Checks on user authority

Personnel selection is important. Key people with access to the system should be carefully **recruited**. There should also be:

- Job rotation and enforced vacations
- Systems logs
- Review and supervision

For other staff, **segregation of duties** is a core security requirement. This involves division of responsibilities into separate roles:

- Data capture and data entry
- Computer operations
- Systems analysis and programming

Finally, there should be an adequate **audit trail**, so there is some means of identifying individual records and the input and output documents associated with the processing of any individual transaction.

7 Users of financial information and their information needs

Section overview

- Different stakeholders use financial information for different purposes, and require different amounts and types of information for these purposes.
- Financial information is useful when it supports decision-making by users, and allows them to hold managers to account.
- Financial information should have the fundamental qualitative characteristics of relevance and faithful representation and the enhancing qualitative characteristics of comparability, verifiability, timeliness and understandability.

7.1 What is financial information used for?

The *Conceptual Framework for Financial Reporting* (also known as the *IFRS Framework*), published by the International Accounting Standards Board (IASB) in September 2010, is focused on published financial statements in particular rather than financial information in general, but it usefully points out that nearly all users use financial information to **make decisions**, such as those to:

- Decide when to **buy, hold or sell an equity investment or a debt instrument**
- Decide whether to replace or reappoint the business's managers by assessing the **stewardship** or accountability of management

- Decide whether there is sufficient **security** to advance a loan to the business
- Decide on the ability of the entity to pay and provide other **benefits to its employees**
- Determine **distributable profits and dividends**

7.2 Who uses financial information?

The *IFRS Framework* identifies the following primary users of financial information and their specific information needs.

Primary users	Need financial information to:
Present and potential investors (shareholders)	• Make decisions about buying, selling or holding equity, therefore need information on: – Risk and return of investment – Ability of company to pay dividends
Lenders and other payables	• Make decisions about buying, selling or holding debt instruments and providing or settling loans or other forms of credit • Assess whether loans will be repaid, and related interest will be paid, when due

Other users and their financial information needs are as follows:

Other users	Need financial information to:
Employees	• Assess their employer's stability and profitability • Assess their employer's ability to provide remuneration, employment opportunities and retirement and other benefits
Customers	• Assess whether business will continue in existence – important where customers have a long-term involvement with, or are dependent on, the business, eg where they are supply chain partners
Suppliers and other business partners	• Assess the likelihood of being paid when due
Governments and its agencies, including regulators	• Assess allocation of resources and, therefore, activities of businesses • Assist in regulating activities • Assess taxation income • Provide a basis for national statistics • Help direct policy on, for instance, health and safety and equal opportunities issues
The public and community representatives	• Assess trends and recent developments in the business's prosperity and its activities – important where the business makes a substantial contribution to a local economy, eg by providing employment and using local suppliers

7.3 When is financial information useful?

Financial information is useful to users when it:

- Helps them to make **decisions**, and
- Shows the results of management's **stewardship** of the resources entrusted to them

For financial information to meet these two objectives it must be prepared on the basis of two **underlying assumptions**:

- The **accrual basis of accounting**: the effects of transactions and other events are recognised when they occur (not as they are realised in cash), and they are recorded and reported in the financial statements of the periods to which they relate
- The business is a **going concern** and will continue in operation for the foreseeable future

7.4 Information for making decisions and making managers accountable

When users make decisions they need financial information to evaluate:

- The ability of a business to generate cash so as to
  - Pay employees and suppliers
  - Meet interest payments
  - Repay loans and
  - Pay dividends
- The timing and certainty of cash flows

The *IFRS Framework* points out that primary users therefore need information about the entity's **'economic phenomena'**:

- the resources of the entity,
- claims against the entity, and
- the effects of transactions and other events and conditions that change those resources and claims

Information on these phenomena also helps the user to evaluate how efficiently and effectively the entity's management and governing board have discharged their responsibilities to use the entity's resources.

In order to evaluate whether the business can generate sufficient cash on time the user needs information on the business's:

- Financial position (its statement of financial position)
- Financial performance (its income statement) and
- Changes in financial position (its statement of cash flows)

These are contained in the business's **financial statements**.

7.4.1 Information on financial position

Factors affecting the business's financial position:	Information on this factor is useful for predicting:
The economic resources it controls	The business's ability to generate cash in the future
Its financial structure	• Future borrowing needs • How future profits and cash flows will be distributed among stakeholders • The business's likely success in raising new equity
Its liquidity	Whether cash will be available in the near future after taking account of current financial commitments

Factors affecting the business's financial position:	Information on this factor is useful for predicting:
Its solvency	The availability of cash in the longer term to meet financial commitments as they fall due
Its adaptability	Its capacity to adapt to changes in the environment in which it operates

7.4.2 Information on financial performance

Information on the business's profitability, especially variability in profits over time, helps the user to predict or assess:

- Potential changes in the economic resources the business is likely to control in the future
- The business's capacity to generate cash flows from its existing resource base
- How effectively the business might employ additional resources

7.4.3 Information on changes in financial position

Information on the business's past cash flows helps the user to predict or assess its investing, financing and operating activities during the reporting period. This helps the user to assess:

- How able the business is at generating cash
- How well the business uses cash that it has generated

7.5 Qualitative characteristics of financial statements

The *IFRS Framework* states that if financial information is to be useful, it must be **relevant** and **faithfully represent** what it purports to represent. It also states that the usefulness of financial information is enhanced if it is **comparable, verifiable, timely** and **understandable**.

Definitions

Fundamental qualitative characteristics: The attributes that are fundamental in making information provided in financial statements useful to users (*IFRS Framework*):

- Relevance
- Faithful representation

Enhancing qualitative characteristics: The attributes that enhance the fundamental usefulness of information provided in financial statements to users (*IFRS Framework*):

- Understandability
- Comparability
- Verifiability
- Timeliness

7.5.1 Fundamental qualitative characteristic: relevance

The *IFRS Framework* states that **relevant financial information** is capable of making a difference in the decisions made by users if it has predictive value, confirmatory value or both.

- It has **predictive value** if it can be used as an input to processes employed by users to predict future outcomes. Financial information need not be a prediction or forecast to have predictive value, as it can be in some other form and be employed by users in making their own predictions.

- It has **confirmatory value** if it provides feedback about (confirms or changes) previous evaluations

In other words, information is relevant to users when it influences their decisions because they can thereby:

- Evaluate past, present or future events, or
- Correct or confirm past evaluations

Relevance is affected by:

- The **nature** of certain items: some pieces of information are highly relevant whatever their monetary value, such as the acquisition of a new business with significantly increased risks

- The **materiality** of certain items. The *IFRS Framework* states that materiality is an entity-specific aspect of relevance based on the nature or magnitude, or both, of the items to which the information relates in the context of an individual entity's financial report. In other words, a piece of information is material if omitting it or misstating it could influence decisions that users make on the basis of financial information about a specific reporting entity.

7.5.2 Fundamental qualitative characteristic: faithful representation

To be useful, financial information must **faithfully represent** the entity's economic phenomena (as defined in the *IFRS Framework)* in words and numbers. To be a faithful representation it must therefore be:

- **complete,** including all **necessary descriptions and explanations**

- **neutral** (ie **without bias** in the selection or presentation of information) and

- **free from error (with no errors or omissions** in the description of the phenomena, and with no errors in the process used to produce the reported information)

7.5.3 Enhancing qualitative characteristic: understandability

Information should be clear and concise if it is to be readily understandable. Users are assumed to have a reasonable knowledge of economic and business affairs and to be willing to be reasonably diligent in the way they study financial information. Relevant information should not be excluded from financial statements merely because it is hard to understand.

7.5.4 Enhancing qualitative characteristic: comparability

Measurement and display of the financial effect of like transactions and other events must be carried out in a consistent way:

- Throughout the business
- Over time
- Across different businesses

7.5.5 Enhancing qualitative characteristic: verifiability

The *IFRS Framework* states that verifiability means different knowledgeable and independent observers could reach consensus, although not necessarily complete agreement, that a particular depiction is a faithful representation using either direct or indirect methods. Information about the future cannot be verified as such, but a statement of underlying assumptions about any such information will help verifiability.

7.5.6 Enhancing qualitative characteristic: timeliness

The *IFRS Framework* states that timeliness means having information available to decision-makers in time to be capable of influencing their decisions. Generally, the older the information is the less useful it is. However, some information may continue to be timely long after the end of a reporting period because, for example, some users may need to identify and assess trends.

7.6 The cost constraint on useful financial reporting

The *IFRS Framework* acknowledges that there is a cost constraint on the financial information that can be provided. The benefits derived from information for all users should justify the cost of providing it.

8 Limitations of financial information in meeting users' needs

Section overview

- Financial information may be of limited usefulness because its presentation is conventionalised, it is backward-looking and it omits non-financial information.

The *IFRS Framework* acknowledges that, as far as they go, general purpose financial statements are of most use to investors, lenders and other payables. Their use for other interested parties, especially regulators, may be more limited. In fact the usefulness of financial information is limited in general by a number of factors.

8.1 Conventionalised representation

Financial information, particularly financial statements, are usually highly **standardised** in terms of their overall format and presentation although businesses are very diverse in their nature. This may limit the usefulness of the information.

Financial statements are highly **aggregated** in that information on a great many transactions and balances is combined into a few figures in the financial statements, which can often make it difficult for the reader to evaluate the components of the business.

8.2 Backward-looking

Financial statements cover a period that has already ended; they are inherently historical and backward-looking, whereas most users of financial information base their decisions on **expectations about the future**. Financial statements contribute towards this by helping to identify trends and by confirming the accuracy of previous expectations, but they cannot realistically provide the complete information set required for all decisions by all users.

8.3 Omission of non-financial information

By their nature, financial statements contain information that is financial, not non-financial such as:

- **Narrative** description of **major operations**
- Discussion of business **risks** and **opportunities**
- Narrative analysis of the business's **performance and prospects**
- **Management policies** and how the business is **governed** and **controlled**

Instead these are normally covered in the Chairman's Statement and the Directors' Report, published alongside the financial statements.

8.4 Other sources of information

There are other sources of information available to at least some users of the basic financial statements.

- In owner-managed businesses, the owners have access to internal **management information** because they are the management. This information is, potentially, available on a continuous real-time basis and will include:
  - Future plans for the business
  - Budgets or forecasts
  - Management accounts, including, for example, divisional analysis
- **Banks** will often gain additional access to business information under the terms of loan agreements
- **Potential investors**, if they are planning to take a major stake or even a controlling interest, will negotiate additional access to information

- **Suppliers** may be able to obtain reports on the business's credit standing via **credit reference agencies** such as Experian. These are also used by **lenders**
- **Some** information, such as **brochures** and **publicity material** (eg press releases), is available to **all**
- **Brokers' reports** on major companies are available fairly widely
- **Press reports** and other **media coverage** (especially on the **internet**) is available to **all.**

9 The effects of poor financial information

Section overview

- Poor financial information undermines the integrity of financial markets and fails to serve the public interest.

Financial information **is poor** if it does not:

- Meet the **needs of users**
- Display the **qualitative characteristics** set out above

The **effect of poor financial information** is:

- To undermine the **integrity of financial markets** and **raise the cost of capital** for the economy as a whole.
- To fail to serve the **public interest**

Both these areas are fundamental to the work of the professional accountant, which we shall cover in Chapter 9 of this Study Manual, and also to the working of the financial system, which we shall look at in Chapters 8 and 11.

Summary and Self-test

Summary

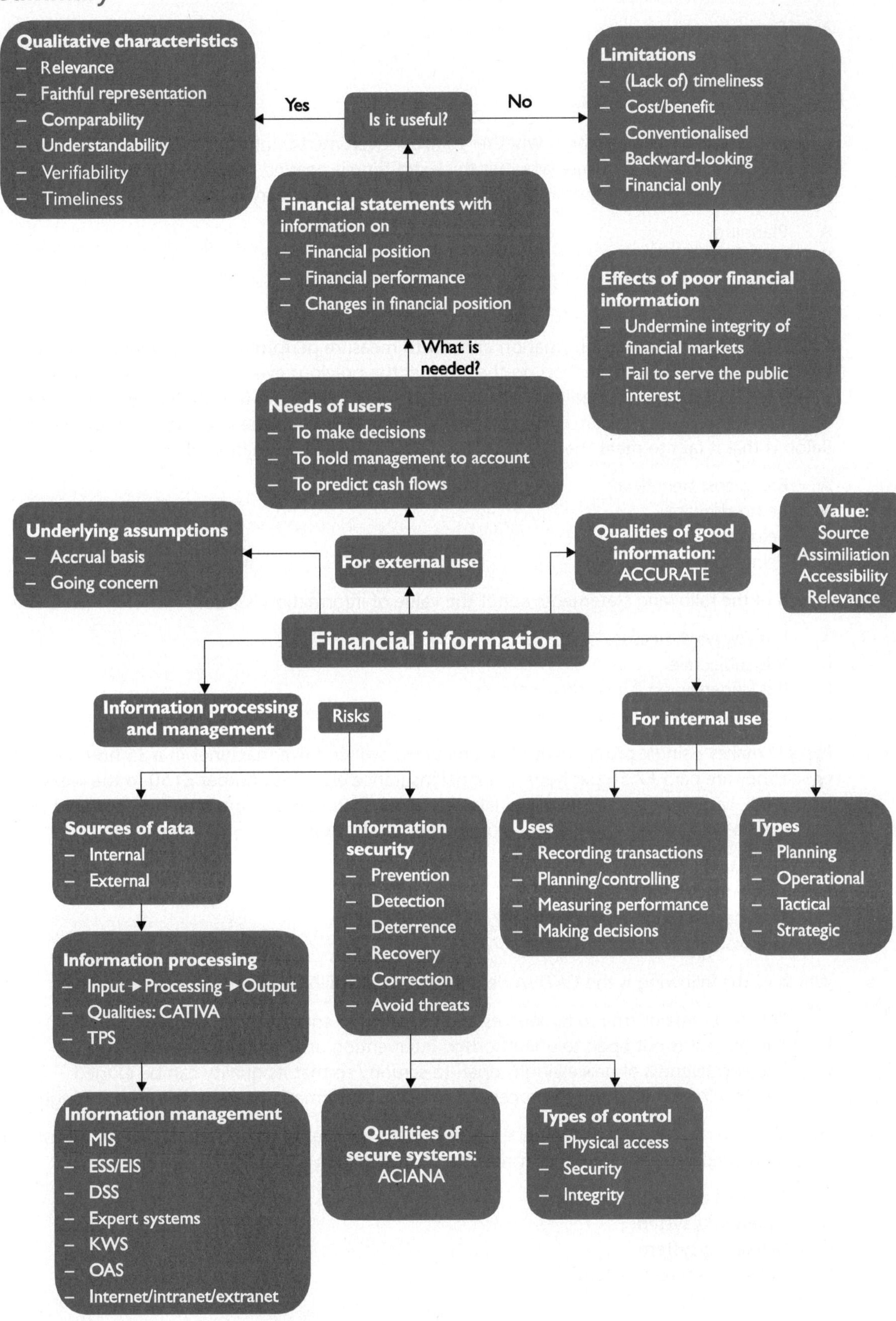
Qualitative characteristics
– Relevance
– Faithful representation
– Comparability
– Understandability
– Verifiability
– Timeliness
Yes
Is it useful?
No
Limitations
– (Lack of) timeliness
– Cost/benefit
– Conventionalised
– Backward-looking
– Financial only
Financial statements with information on
– Financial position
– Financial performance
– Changes in financial position
Effects of poor financial information
– Undermine integrity of financial markets
– Fail to serve the public interest
What is needed?
Needs of users
– To make decisions
– To hold management to account
– To predict cash flows
Underlying assumptions
– Accrual basis
– Going concern
For external use
Qualities of good information: ACCURATE
Value: Source Assimiliation Accessibility Relevance
Financial information
Information processing and management
Risks
For internal use
Sources of data
– Internal
– External
Information security
– Prevention
– Detection
– Deterrence
– Recovery
– Correction
– Avoid threats
Uses
– Recording transactions
– Planning/controlling
– Measuring performance
– Making decisions
Types
– Planning
– Operational
– Tactical
– Strategic
Information processing
– Input ➔ Processing ➔ Output
– Qualities: CATIVA
– TPS
Information management
– MIS
– ESS/EIS
– DSS
– Expert systems
– KWS
– OAS
– Internet/intranet/extranet
Qualities of secure systems: ACIANA
Types of control
– Physical access
– Security
– Integrity

Self-test

Answer the following questions.

1 Womble plc's managers are quick to address immediate problems as they arise in operations on the basis of financial information they receive. The company's trial balance always agrees. Monthly variance reports however consistently show that the operation is failing to meet its targets. It would appear that Womble plc's financial information fails to provide managers information for

A Decision making
B Recording transactions
C Planning and control
D Measuring performance

2 Ian has to make a decision about whether to allow overtime tonight to Gonzalez, a customer service adviser, but he is unsure whether this extra time is needed between 7pm and 9pm on a Wednesday. The type of information he needs to answer this query is

A Planning
B Operational
C Tactical
D Strategic

3 Ralph has presented some information on how to measure performance to a panel of managers at Jab plc. He found this information on the internet the previous evening as a PowerPoint file and has presented it to the panel unedited. Within five minutes they found it to be highly informative and targeted at the issues they are concerned with. The drawback to the information as presented by Ralph is that it fails to meet the ACCURATE criteria for good information of

A Being cost beneficial
B Being relevant
C Being easy to use
D Being authoritative

4 Which of the following statements about the value of information is true?

A It is always a measure of its scarcity
B It is subjective
C It is undermined if it is too accessible
D It is independent of its source

5 Pap plc makes a single product with five operatives working five machines in a 35 hour week, for which they are paid £7.50 per hour. National insurance etc adds another £150 to the weekly labour bill. Last week the gross cost of labour was £1,950. In which internal source should the managers of Pap plc refer to identify why the bill was this size?

A The payroll
B The ledger accounts
C The machine logs
D The workers

6 Which of the following is the CATIVA definition of verifiability of information processing?

A The data remains true to its sources and contains no errors
B The process is not open to unauthorised intervention or amendment
C The effectiveness of processing is open to scrutiny so that its quality can be judged
D The trail from data through processing to output information can be followed through

7 Hob plc needs to ensure that the prices it sets for the services of its consultants are rigorously and accurately prepared. To effect this, it needs a pricing system as part of its

A Financial accounting system
B Operations system
C Marketing system
D Human resources system

8 Cranfield, a highway engineer, inputs some data about the stage of completeness of the road-building project he is working on into his laptop each night, and by the morning the system has produced a report telling him which tasks will need completing that day and how many labourers will be required. This is an example of

A An expert system
B A management information system
C A transaction processing system
D A human resources system

9 Data verification is a form of

A Physical access control
B Output control
C Integrity control
D Security control

10 Which of the following groups is **not** a primary user of a company's financial statements?

A The government
B Shareholders
C Potential investors
D Lenders

11 The fact that financial statements should be free from bias is a facet of which of the following qualitative characteristics of financial information?

A Relevance
B Faithful representation
C Comparability
D Understandability

Now, go back to the Learning Objectives in the Introduction. If you are satisfied you have achieved these objectives, please tick them off.

Answers to Interactive questions

Answer to Interactive question 1

The most frequent problem encountered by managers is that the information is **not targeted** at the user, that is the information system has not been designed with users and their needs in mind. Information that is not actually **relevant** to the decisions they make is often included. Management information is frequently not **easy to use**, and it is late ie **not timely**.

Answer to Interactive question 2

The information already exists anyway, as it is used for a number of different purposes. It might be impossible to predict how often it will be used, and hence the economic benefits to be derived from it.

The enquiry software and MIS which are used to process these requests have also been purchased, so its cost is largely fixed. The cost of each individual enquiry is effectively zero.

Answer to Interactive question 3

The primary reason has to do with the relative costs. A 'human' expert is likely to be more expensive either to employ or to use on a consultancy basis.

Secondly, enshrining an expert's accumulated wisdom in a computer system means that this wisdom can be accessed by more people. The delivery of complicated services to customers, and decisions whether or not to extend credit and so forth, can be made by less experienced members of staff. If a manufacturing company has a complicated mixture of plant and machinery, then the repair engineer may accumulate a lot of knowledge over a period of time about the way it behaves: if a problem occurs the engineer will be able to make a reasoned guess as to where the likely cause is to be found. If this accumulated expert information is made available to less experienced staff, it means that some of the learning curve is avoided.

An expert system is advantageous because it saves time, like all computer systems (in theory at least) but it is particularly useful as it possesses both knowledge and limited reasoning ability.

Answers to Self-test

1 C The trial balance balancing suggests that the TPS is effective, and managers can make well-informed decisions when they have to. The company knows it is missing targets so it is measuring performance, so its failures must be due to lack of information to plan and then control operations

2 B By its short-term nature the information could not be planning or strategic; the fact that this is a day-to-day issue means it is not tactical

3 D Clearly the users have found the information easy to use and relevant, and the fact that Ralph spent very little time in generating it makes it cost-beneficial

4 B The value of information is in the eye of the beholder, ie there is no objective valuation of it. It is not always valued in terms of its scarcity (A) as even information that is available to all can be very valuable. Information is undermined if it is not accessible enough (C), and its value is very much dependent on its source (D)

5 A The first place to look is the payroll, which will show whether the variance comes from the pay rate, the number of workers paid, or the national insurance etc. The other sources will provide further information to back up the evidence in the payroll

6 D A describes accuracy; B describes inalterability; C describes assessability

7 C

8 A

9 C

10 A

11 B

CHAPTER 7

The business's finance function

Introduction

Examination context

Topic List

1 What does the finance function do?

2 The structure of the finance function

3 Managing the finance function

4 Providing information for management

5 Measuring performance

6 Establishing financial control processes

Summary and Self-test

Answers to Self-test

Introduction

Learning objectives

Tick off

- Specify the extent to which financial information:
  - Provides for accountability of management to shareholders and other stakeholders ☐
  - Reflects business performance ☐
  - Is useful to users in making decisions ☐
  - Meets the information needs of national, social and economic contexts (eg national statistical information) ☐
- Specify how accounting and finance functions support businesses in pursuit of their objectives ☐
- Specify how a strategic plan is converted into fully integrated business and operational plans ☐
- Identify the main considerations in establishing and maintaining accounting and financial reporting functions and financial control processes ☐
- Specify why the management of a business require information about performance measurement including non-routine areas such as in supporting an entity's sustainability management ☐
- Identify the accountant's role in preparing and presenting information for the management of a business ☐

Specific syllabus references are: 1g; 3a, b, c, e, f.

Syllabus links

The topic of what the finance function does and how and why it does it are developed as well in Accounting, Assurance and Management Information at Certificate level, in Financial Accounting and Reporting and Financial Management at Professional level, and in the Advanced level.

Examination context

Questions on the finance function could easily appear in the exam.

Questions are likely to be set in multiple choice format and in a scenario context. Knowledge-type questions are also likely, set on particular principles or definitions.

1 What does the finance function do?

Section overview

- The finance function looks after the business's money. Its tasks are: recording transactions, management accounting, financial reporting and treasury management.
- The finance function supports the business's pursuit of its strategic objectives by providing information to measure performance and support decision making, and by ensuring the business has sufficient funds for its activities.

In Chapter 2 we saw that the four main functions of a business are marketing, operations/production, human resources and finance. This reflects the model of the business as taking three basic types of resource – materials, labour and money – to produce goods and services which generate profit. It is a major part of the finance function's role to look after the business's **money**.

1.1 The tasks of the finance function

The finance function is involved in four specific, but often interrelated, tasks.

Definitions

Recording financial transactions: Ensuring that the business has an accurate record of its revenue, expenses, assets, liabilities and capital.

Management accounting: Providing information to assist managers and other internal users in their decision-making, performance measurement, planning and control activities.

Financial reporting: Providing information about a business to external users that is useful to them in making decisions and for assessing the stewardship of the business's management.

Treasury management: Managing the funds of a business, namely cash and other working capital items, plus long-term investments, short-term and long-term debt, and equity finance.

The separate parts of the finance function carry out the following tasks:

- **Recording financial transactions**:
  - Recording financial transactions (credit sales, credit purchases, and cash receipts and payments) in the books of original entry
  - Entering summaries of transactions in the permanent records (nominal, receivables and payables ledgers) from the books of original entry
  - Ensuring that resources are properly controlled (stewardship)
- **Management accounting**:
  - Preparing financial information for internal users (internal reporting for planning and control to those charged with management and with governance)
  - Identifying or determining the unit cost of the goods and/or services produced by the business, including classification into fixed and variable costs, or direct and indirect costs (cost accounting)
  - Planning ahead by preparing forecasts and budgets
  - Assisting management decision-making (cost-volume-profit (CVP) analysis, including breakeven and limiting factor analysis)
  - Preparing performance measures and identifying reasons for good and bad performance, including variance analysis

- Analysing capital investment decisions
- Determining sales and transfer prices

- **Financial reporting**:
  - Preparing financial information including financial statements for external users (external reporting) to enhance good corporate governance (see Chapters 11 and 12)
  - Tax reporting to HM Revenue and Customs (HMRC)
  - Regulatory reporting
- **Treasury management**:
  - Preparing and monitoring cash budgets
  - Managing surpluses and deficits in cash balances
  - Managing working capital from day to day so as to optimise cash flow, including inventory, receivables and payables management
  - Analysing short-term and long-term financing decisions
  - Managing investments
  - Managing foreign exchange
  - Managing financial risk
  - Raising long-term finance (debt and equity) (see Chapter 8)

1.2 How does the finance function support the pursuit of business objectives?

Although this a question which can produce a huge variety of answers depending on the business's situation, in general the finance function supports the business in achieving its objectives by:

- Undertaking **transaction processing** and ensuring there are sufficient **financial control processes** in the system
- Providing information to **support decisions** and **measure performance** (financial reporting and management accounting)
- Ensuring there is **finance and cash available** for the business's activities (treasury management)

2 The structure of the finance function

Section overview

- Many businesses centralise some if not all of the finance function's tasks.
- All aspects of the finance function's tasks depend on the efficient and effective initial recording of financial transactions.

How the finance function is organised depends on the size of the business and its overall organisational structure. In many businesses, even very large ones, some if not all of the finance function's tasks are **centralised**. This is particularly helpful with respect to overall management of cash and to external reporting, but it is not so helpful with respect to making sure that local operational managers get all the information and support they need (internal reporting). Total centralisation is even more problematic when the business operates in global markets, where exchange rates and time differences make the structure unwieldy.

A typical finance function which performs all the tasks set out above would be structured as in Figure 7.1. Note that the data and information provided by those responsible for recording financial transactions feed into each of the other three sections.

Against some items we have noted where you will encounter detailed coverage elsewhere in the ICAEW syllabus. We refer to:

ACC *Accounting; Financial Accounting and Reporting*
MI *Management Information*
FM *Financial Management*
TAX *Principles of Taxation; Tax Compliance*

In this chapter we provide an overview of the work of the finance function and how it supports achievement of the business's objectives.

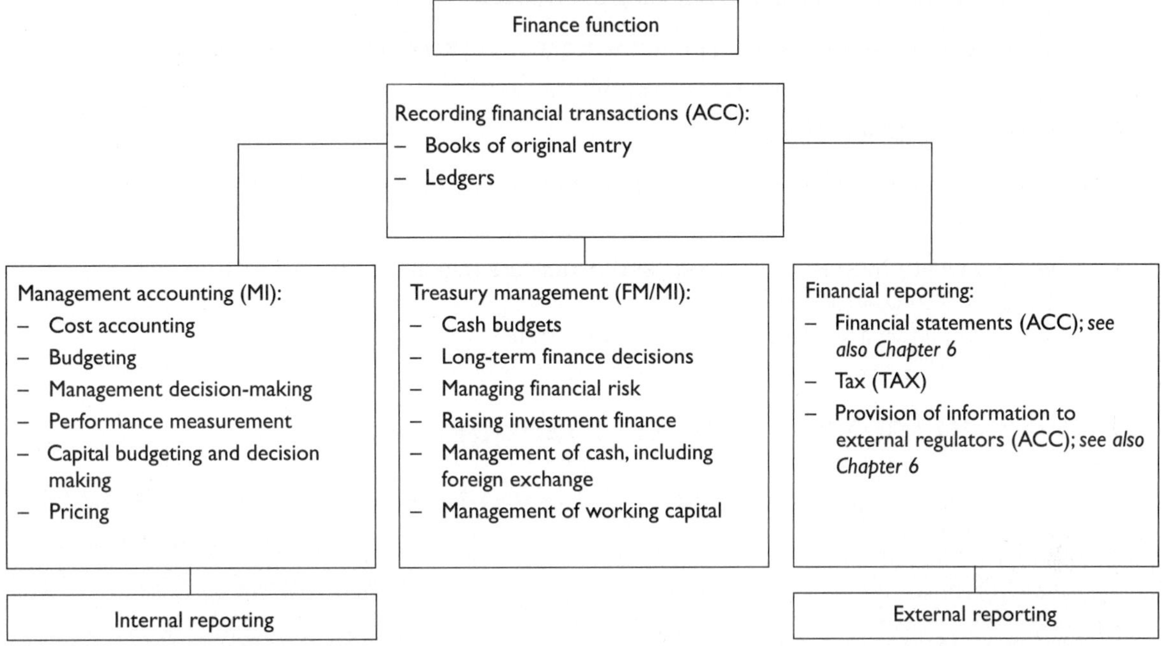

Figure 7.1: The finance function

3 Managing the finance function

Section overview

- As with any other of the business's functions, the finance function needs to be effectively organised and led, with its performance properly planned and controlled.

The optimum structure for any particular business's finance function will be affected by all the factors considered in Chapter 3, in particular:

- its **business structure** (sole trader, partnership, company)
- its **organisational structure**, size and geographical dispersion, including the degree of centralisation required
- its **markets**
- its history and **ownership**
- its **culture** (human relations, open systems, internal process or rational goal)

Within the finance function its managers are responsible for ensuring that the function is properly managed and achieves its objectives. The way in which they do this is to perform the tasks of management that we saw in Chapter 2.

3.1 Planning and control

The overall direction of the finance function's work needs to be planned and controlled, including:

- **Forecasting** what is needed (the processing that needs to be done, and the reports and finance that need to be available)
- Evaluating available **resources**, such as qualified staff and robust information systems
- Developing **objectives, plans and targets**
- Implementing the plan and **measuring performance**
- Using **feedback** from measuring performance to make necessary amendments to the plan

3.2 Organising and leading

Time and effort in the finance function need to be organised so that its objectives and targets are met, including:

- Defining what processes, technology and people are required
- Allocating and co-ordinating work
- Generating effort and commitment in finance staff

4 Providing information for management

Section overview

- The finance function provides information to assist managers with making decisions, with planning and with control and performance measurement.
- Not all costs are relevant for decision-making, which itself falls into two categories: decisions about allocating resources in the short to medium term, and decisions about long-term investment.
- When making decisions about allocating resources in the short to medium term, managers may need information generated by: cost-volume-profit (CVP) analysis (breakeven analysis; contribution analysis; limiting factor analysis); pricing analysis.
- When making decisions for long-term investments, managers need information based on: capital budgeting; capital investment appraisal.
- Information in the form of forecasts and budgets is central to managers' linked tasks of planning and control.

The managers of a business have to plan and control the resources used. To carry out this task effectively they must be provided with sufficiently accurate and detailed information to assist in:

- Establishing **asset valuations** (for example, for inventory)
- **Planning** (for example, providing forecast revenues and costs at different activity levels)
- **Control** (for example, providing actual and budgeted results for comparison purposes)
- **Decision-making** (for example, providing information about actual unit costs for the period for making decisions about pricing)

4.1 Costs for decision making

One of the key roles of the information produced by accountants is to assist managers in decision making.

A decision involving resources generally means deciding whether or not to incur some new costs, or raised levels of cost, in order to generate new or raised revenues. The accountant needs to be clear about the various ways in which we can look at costs so that information only on relevant costs is provided.

- Costs that have yet to be incurred by the business are termed **future costs**. We can contrast them with the costs of resources that have already been acquired, or **sunk costs**.
- Costs that may be saved by not adopting a particular course of action are termed **avoidable costs**. We can contrast these with **unavoidable costs**, which cannot be saved whether the particular course of action is taken or not.
- In many decisions the issue is whether to increase output from the existing level. It is useful here to concentrate on the *difference* in total costs between the new and existing levels (the **differential** or **incremental cost**), rather than just on the total costs at the two levels of output. The idea of differential cost leads onto that of **marginal cost**, namely the additional cost of one extra unit of output.
- A final cost to consider is the value of the best alternative course of action that is not chosen, or the **opportunity cost** of the resources. It is what best could have been done with those resources; it represents opportunities forgone.

Only future costs that will be changed by the decision made now are relevant costs for the decision-making process. Costs that will remain unchanged whatever decision is made are **irrelevant costs** for decision making.

Management decisions fall into two categories according to whether they are about the **allocation of resources** in the **short to medium term** (normally taken to be less than one year), or about **investment** in the long term (normally taken to be after one or more years). We shall look at each of these in turn.

4.2 Making resource decisions in the short to medium term

When making resource allocation decisions for the next week, month or even year we can assume in simple terms that managers want to **spend as little as possible to earn the most amount of revenue**: they want to **maximise revenue** and **minimise variable costs** so that the **contribution to fixed costs** is as large as possible.

What we have outlined here are the linked concepts of **marginal costing** and **contribution**.

Definitions

Marginal costing: Including only variable costs in unit cost when making decisions or valuing inventory (the **marginal cost** of a unit of inventory excludes fixed costs or its 'share' of overheads).

Contribution: Unit selling price less marginal cost.

Information on marginal cost and contribution are used to help answer many of the **resource allocation questions** that arise, such as:

- How many units must we sell of a new product to cover the fixed costs we will incur?
- Which of two new products should we choose to go ahead with?
- If we reduce our selling price and sell more units, what will be the effect on profit?
- We've got increased fixed costs – how many additional units do we need to sell?
- Our variable costs are going up – what should we do?
- We have limited amounts of resource – what is the best use we can make of them?

To help managers identify the answers to these questions the accountant provides information using a range of analytical techniques, with which you should be familiar from your *Management Information* studies:

Analytical technique	Comment	Output of the analysis
Cost-volume-profit (CVP) analysis	All the questions listed above relate to the relationship between changes in activity or output (**volume**) and changes in total revenue, **cost** (variable and fixed) and therefore **profit. Sales volume** is extremely difficult to forecast, while **output volume** is usually dependent on sales but needs to be planned. In the short term, some inputs can be increased, such as materials, but some – such as the capacity of machinery – cannot. It takes investment in the purchase of long-term assets to increase capacity.	Establishing what will happen if a specified level of activity fluctuates, based on the relationship between volume and sales revenue, costs and profit in the short term (one year or less), when the output of the business is restricted to what is available from its current operating capacity.
Breakeven analysis	An application of CVP analysis that supports decisions as to **whether to go ahead** with a new product, and on what scale.	Establishing the breakeven point – the level of production and sales at which, after deducting both fixed and variable costs from sales revenue, neither a profit nor a loss will occur.
Contribution analysis	This is a form of **sensitivity analysis,** which means that the business is aware of how sensitive its planned outcome is to changes in any of the variables (input prices or quantities, level of fixed costs) it has used in its calculations.	Calculating what would happen if the amount of contribution per unit or total fixed costs changed
Limiting factor analysis	This helps if the decision to be made involves a choice between, say, making either one product or another because the business has limited amounts of a certain factor of production, such as material or labour, available.	Establishing how much contribution each product makes per unit of the **limiting factor** (or **scarce resource**), then choosing the product which makes the **most contribution per unit of the limiting factor**.

A key decision that managers need to make is the **price** at which products or services are to be sold. The management accounting section of the finance function has great involvement in setting prices, especially in relation to costs and corporate objectives. The techniques listed here, and others, can help the accountant in providing information to managers who are making pricing decisions.

We shall come back to pricing in Chapter 13 when we look at the economic theory behind **demand, supply and price.**

4.3 Making investment decisions for the long term

The second category of management decision supported by the accountant is about **investment in the long term**, say to **increase capacity** following difficult decisions made in the short term because resources were limited.

There are two basic issues at stake:

- Does the business have enough long-term funds to make a long-term investment (**capital budgeting**)?
- Is the long-term investment worthwhile (**capital investment appraisal**)?

4.3.1 Capital budgeting

The accountant can prepare a capital budget, setting out what funds will be available and how they will be used over a time period of, say, two years.

Capital inflows will be funds from:

- Retained earnings (annual net profits less dividends)
- Share issues
- New loans or debentures
- Sales of non-current assets

Capital outflows will be in respect of:

- Purchases of non-current assets including investments
- Repayment of loans
- Redemption of debentures

We shall look at raising finance in Chapter 8.

4.3.2 Capital investment appraisal

If the business identifies a possible capital investment opportunity, the accountant needs to help evaluate or appraise the project to make a decision as to whether to go ahead with it.

The techniques that are most often used are as follows:

- **Payback method**: the business expects the capital outlay to be 'paid back' within a certain period of time so the accountant analyses the point in the future at which payback occurs. This favours investments which generate cash in the shorter term, so that there is less risk to the overall level of funding in the business.
- **Accounting rate of return (ARR)**: the business expects the investment to make a minimum level of return over its lifetime, so using accounting principles the accountant makes this calculation.
- **Net present value (NPV) and internal rate of return (IRR)**: the business expects the investment to achieve a certain value or make a certain level of return over its life, taking into account the fact that cash flows will arise over time and these are affected by the 'time value of money' (that is the value of a cash flow at an identified time in the future is measured in terms of cash held now). In order to make these decisions the accountant needs to use **discounted cash flow (DCF)**. This is a very important investment appraisal technique which you will see in a great deal more detail as you progress in your studies.

A business which has as its primary objective the maximisation of shareholders' wealth will choose investments which **maximise the present value of its future cash flows**.

4.4 Forecasting

A key element of the work of the accountant is to look into the future to try to answer these two questions:

- **What is going to happen?** Forecasts for the future are needed on the basis of known amounts, and estimates for areas of uncertainty
- **What are we planning to do?** Budgets are needed to assist in planning and control

Forecasting involves predicting what will happen in the future given what we already know about the present. It is particularly important regarding:

- Sales volumes
- Costs
- Economic factors (interest and exchange rates)
- Other environmental factors such as regulation, technological developments and taste

Information from external sources is very important when forecasting. Various mathematical techniques can help to make forecasts more sophisticated and more reliable, and these help to make the forecast realistic and up-to-date.

4.5 Budgets and budgeting

We saw in Chapter 4 that the strategic planning process results in the business making plans that eventually become detailed budgets for each area of operations.

Definition

Budget: A plan expressed in monetary terms.

4.5.1 Budgetary process

The preparation and use of budgets are processes that must be effectively managed by the accounting function. The key point is that budgets should not just be 'one-off' documents that are prepared and then placed in a file to gather dust; the process should be a continuous one. It is in fact a '**budget cycle**'.

• Establish objectives	Strategic planning – see Chapter 4
• Identify potential strategies	
• Evaluate options and select course of action	
• Prepare plans and standards	
↓	↓
• Prepare budgets for implementing the plan	Budgeting
• Implement the long-term plan via budgets	
• Measure actual outcomes and respond to deviations	

4.5.2 Preparing budgets

Budgets are usually prepared over a period of time such as one year, broken down monthly. There is usually a departmental budget for each separate function or operation in the business, such as for:

- **Sales** (volume and value): sales are often the **principal budget factor** for the business as a whole, since it is the volume of sales which determines the level of activity in each of the business's functions
- **Production/operations** (volume and value): resources are allocated to achieve the sales budget, and plans are made for how much the resources cost, how effectively they are used and how much inventory is to be kept
- **Expenses** (value): support activities such as logistics and human resources also need expenditure budgets

To prepare a set of departmental budgets and amalgamate them into the business's **master budget** the following steps must be followed:

- Decide on course of action and communicate to people responsible for preparing budgets
- Determine the factor that limits output (the principal budget factor, which is usually sales volume)
- Prepare budgets for the principal budget factor
- Prepare drafts of other budgets
- Negotiate budgets with managers
- Co-ordinate and review all budgets
- Accept budgets
- Review budgets over time (see below)

A **cash budget** should also be prepared to ensure that sufficient cash is available at all times to meet the level of operations outlined in the various departmental budgets.

4.5.3 Types of budgeting

Most businesses use a system of **incremental budgeting**. This means that they take the experiences they have had of direct costs and support activities in the past year and use these as the base for preparing the next year's budget, adjusting it for changes or increments (such as to inflation, product mix, volumes and prices) that are expected to occur in the new budget period.

Worked example: Incremental budgeting

Incro Ltd included an allowance for overheads in its 20X1 budget of £20,000. Inflation in 20X2 is expected to be 3%, so the overheads budget for 20X2 is set as £20,600.

This example is for illustration only. In the exam you will not be faced with questions on budgeting that require you to make calculations.

The major problem with incremental budgeting is that 'the costs of non-unit level activities become effectively fixed, so past inefficiencies and waste inherent in the current way of doing things is perpetuated' (Drury, *Management Accounting for Business Decisions*).

To address these problems with the incremental approach the business can implement **zero-based budgeting** (ZBB), which:

'requires that all activities are justified and prioritised before decisions are taken relating to the amount of resources allocated to each activity' (Drury, *Management Accounting for Business Decisions*).

4.5.4 Keeping budgets relevant to users

- **Flexible budgeting** involves adjusting the budget for a period to reflect actual levels of activity in that period. If, for instance, volume was budgeted in January at 100 units but in fact 200 units were produced and sold, a flexible budget system allows the management accountant to adjust all aspects of January's budget so it relates to the new, higher volume. This 'flexed' budget can then be compared with actual results via **variance analysis**, to see how far actual performance was in line with what would have been expected.
- A **rolling budget** system means that, as each month goes by, the budgets for the months ahead are reviewed and, if necessary, revised so that they remain relevant for the remainder of the budget period.

4.5.5 Purposes of budgets

Budgets are thus crucial in helping managers to **plan** and **control** the business's performance.

Purposes of budgets	Comments
Guiding managers on how to achieve objectives	Without a detailed plan the achievement of the business's principal objective will be left up to chance
Helping to compel planning	The process of preparing, monitoring and amending budgets is a rigorous one
Allocating resources	Every business has finite resources, at least in the short term, and the process of preparing budgets helps to identify what resources are limited and how best to use those
Setting targets and allocating responsibility	The budget identifies what is expected of each area of the business and therefore of each manager
Helping to co-ordinate activities	Budgets set out a plan for which different resources – materials, people and capacity – need to be co-ordinated

Purposes of budgets	Comments
Communicating plans	Numbers in a budget state plans very succinctly, assuming that the people to whom it is being communicated have been trained to understand what they denote in operational terms
Enabling control	Budgets that are kept relevant allow regular, accurate and timely comparison of actual performance against the budget, so that problems can be identified and control action taken
Helping to motivate employees	Managers and other employees are reassured that there is a plan in place, and are keen to see it achieved Many businesses link achievement of the budget with pay, in the form of bonuses or commission Specific reasons for failure to meet targets can be identified, so managers can focus on particular areas for improvement
Helping to evaluate performance	Assuming that the budget was realistic to begin with and was properly communicated, it can be used to assess how well the enterprise and its managers performed

4.6 Strategic management accounting

The traditional focus of management accounting has been to provide information for use internally by managers. This is not to say, however, that accountants are not concerned with information gathered outside the business itself.

Definition

Strategic management accounting: Providing and analysing financial information on the business's product markets and competitors' costs and cost structures, and monitoring the business's strategies and those of its competitors in these markets over a number of periods.

Strategic management accounting therefore extends the internal focus of traditional management accounting to include external information about:

- **Competitors**
- The business's **strategic position**
- How to gain **competitive advantage** by decreasing costs and/or enhancing the differentiation of the business's products

5 Measuring performance

Section overview

- Performance measures may be qualitative, or they may be financial or non-financial quantitative measures.
- They are calculated to assess the business's profitability, activity and productivity, in particular:
  - Resource use: effectiveness, economy and efficiency
  - Critical success factors (CSFs) using key performance indicators (KPIs)
  - Sustainability management: social, environmental and economic issues
- Performance measures should be focused on the user and what they need them for.
- Comparability (with budgets, trends, other parts of the business and other businesses), often using benchmarking, is a key issue for performance measurement.
- Problems with performance measures are due to information and comparison problems.
- The balanced scorecard combines measures relating to: financial performance, customers, innovation and learning, and business processes.

The planning and control system model (Figure 1.2 in Chapter 1) showed us that actual performance follows on from setting operational objectives and developing plans and standards; what is achieved is then compared with the plan so that control action may be taken to deal with any deviations. Provided this planning and control model is followed effectively the organisation's objective should be achieved.

It is on measuring performance and making the comparison that a great deal of the work of the accountant is focused. Each business will have different ways of measuring its performance and will place greater emphasis on certain factors over others.

5.1 Types of performance measure

- **Qualitative measures** are subjective and judgemental, and are not expressed in numerical terms (we do not consider these further here)
- **Quantitative measures** are objective and based on data which must be reliable; they are expressed in numerical terms and can be separated into:
  - **financial measures** (based on data as to sales, profit etc)
  - **non-financial measures** (based on data as to number of items produced or phone calls answered etc)

Both types of measure can be incorporated into a business-wide set or **balanced scorecard** of measures for use by senior managers and directors, as we shall see later in this chapter.

5.2 Measuring profitability, activity and productivity

In general, there are three **points of reference for measurement** in a business.

- **Profitability**

  Profit has two components: **cost and revenue**. All parts of a business and all activities within it incur costs, and so their success needs to be judged in relation to cost (these will be called **cost centres**). Only some parts of a business receive revenue, and their success should be judged in terms of both cost and revenue (as **profit centres**).

- **Activity**

  All parts of a business are also engaged in activities (activities cause costs). Activity measures could include the following.

  - Number of orders received from customers, a measure of the effectiveness of marketing
  - Number of machine breakdowns attended to by the repairs and maintenance department.

Each of these items could be measured in terms of **physical numbers**, **monetary value**, or **time spent**.

- **Productivity**

  This is the quantity of the service or product produced in relation to the resources put in, for example so many items processed per hour or per employee. It defines how efficiently resources are being used.

The **dividing line between productivity and activity is thin**, because every activity could be said to have some 'product' (if not it can be measured in terms of lost units of product or service).

5.2.1 Measuring profitability

Profit consists of **revenue** less the business's **costs.** It is measured initially in £s in **absolute** terms, for instance 'net profit of £18,000'. More meaningfully it is then measured in **relative** terms, usually relative to revenue ('net margin of 18% on revenue of £100,000') and capital ('return is 1.8% on capital of £1million').

If the desired level of profit is not achieved, the owner will **close the business** and try something else. Exactly the same idea applies to large companies financed by shares: if shareholders do not receive what they perceive to be an adequate return on their investment they will **take their money elsewhere**.

This concept of profit is important to the business's managers. If profit is to be a business's primary objective, it must be specified in **quantified terms**, that is a specific target rate of profit must be set. Effectively, this rate can only be determined by examining the **opportunity cost** of investing in the business: this is given by the **rate of profit available on alternative investments** with similar characteristics, particularly **risk**. This is then the **minimum** rate of return acceptable to the shareholders.

5.2.2 Measuring resource use: effectiveness, economy and efficiency

A business uses a great many different types of resource in going about its operations so as to achieve its objectives. As well as **materials**, **labour** and **finance** (as we saw in Figure 1.1 in Chapter 1), there are also:

- **Physical assets** (buildings, machinery etc)
- **Competences** (what the business is good at doing)
- **Intangible assets** (customer goodwill, corporate image, brands)
- The way in which the **business is structured**, and
- The **knowledge** that is available to the business.

Efficient use of **resources** is concerned with the **economy** with which resources are used, and the **effectiveness** of their use in achieving the objectives of the business.

- **Economy** is reduction or containment of cost; this can be measured against targets.
- **Effectiveness** is the measure of achievement and is assessed by reference to objectives, such as whether planning and control mechanisms work, and whether the target profit has been attained.
- **Efficiency** means being effective at minimum cost or controlling costs without losing operational effectiveness. **Efficiency** is therefore a **combination of effectiveness and economy.**

The accountant needs to supply managers with measurements of the business's performance so that an assessment can be made as to whether objectives of strategic business units (SBUs), or indeed the whole business are being met, and if so how:

- **Productively**: what is output relative to what is input?
- **Effectively**: how far are targets and objectives achieved?
- **Efficiently**: what is the gain that the business has achieved?

Many businesses emphasise the importance of developing resources, capabilities and competencies that will improve efficiency in the future, and so develop and measure **critical success factors** and **key performance indicators** to show whether performance has been good in key areas.

5.2.3 Measuring critical success factors (CSFs)

CSFs (which we saw in Chapter 5) differ from one business to another; in some areas of business keeping the right price level for the consumer may be key, whereas in others it may be quality, or delivery, and so on. CSFs concern not only the resources of the business but also the competitive environment in which it operates.

5.2.4 Identifying key performance indicators (KPIs)

Once a business has identified its CSFs and the things it must be good at to succeed (its **core competences**) it must identify **key performance indicators (KPIs)** in relation to them. Achievement of these KPIs at a certain level or target mean the business should be able to outperform its rivals.

Worked example: CSFs, core competences, KPIs and targets

An internet retailer identifies that its critical success factor (CSF) is delivering goods to mainland UK consumers within 36 hours of an order being placed over the internet. One of the core competences associated with that CSF is having sufficient capacity and reliability in its IT systems. A key performance indicator (KPI) to be measured for this is the level of downtime in its IT systems per month. If the business can achieve its target downtime of only, say, 2% per month then it may be satisfied that it is on the way to achieving its CSF.

One way of deciding on which KPIs to measure and what targets to set for them is to use **benchmarking**, defined as follows.

Definition

Benchmarking: The establishment, through data gathering, of targets and comparators, through whose use relative levels of performance (and particularly areas of underperformance) can be identified. By the adoption of identified **best practices** it is hoped that performance will improve. (CIMA)

5.2.5 Measuring sustainability management

Accountants are increasingly involved in providing information for performance measurement on a range of non-routine matters outside the traditional area of profitability/return. An important area is performance measurement of the business's sustainability management.

In Chapter 1 we looked briefly at the important issues of sustainability and corporate responsibility (CR), and saw that the key aspect is the use of resources (tangible and intangible) over the long term. The headings under which sustainability and CR can perhaps be most usefully measured are those of what is known as the **triple bottom line**, As well as traditional financial performance reporting frameworks, accountants can measure social and environmental performance in addition as follows:

Issues	Examples of areas to be measured
Social	Health and safety, workers' rights (in the business itself and its supply chain), pay and benefits, diversity and equality, impacts of product use, responsible marketing, data protection and privacy, community investment, and eradication of bribery, fraud and money laundering
Environmental	Climate change, pollution, emissions levels, waste, use of natural resources, impacts of product use, compliance with environmental legislation, air quality
Economic	Economic stability and growth, job provision, local economic development, healthy competition, compliance with governance structures, transparency, long-term viability of businesses, investment in innovation/NPD

A **strategic approach to sustainability management** put forward by the organisation Sustainability at Work is a five step programme that incorporates performance measurement:

- Identify the business's **key sustainability issues** and the factors (or 'drivers') that affect them – using the headings above (social, environmental and economic) is a good place to start
- Develop a strategy to **implement good practice** with respect to each material issue
- Establish **governance and accountability** by determining 'who does what?' to deliver the strategy for each material issue
- Set **targets** and an **action plan**, and decide where the business wants to be in regard to each issue in 'x' number of years
- **Measure performance in each of the three areas** in terms of both **processes** (the things the business said it would do to integrate sustainability into its activities) and **outcomes.** Trends should be identified and compared with targets and objectives, to help determine further action.
- **Report** on and evaluate the processes used

The sustainability reporting guidelines issued by the **Global Reporting Initiative** (GRI) are the best known example of a global, voluntary code for corporate responsibility and sustainability reporting. A GRI based report typically includes economic, social and environmental performance information, and sets out the organisation's direct and indirect impacts. Examples of GRI core performance indicators include:

Economic	Environmental	Social
Wages, pensions, other employee benefits	Energy material	Diversity, employee health and safety
Income from customers and supplier payment	Water use	Child labour
Taxes paid, subsidies and grants received	Greenhouse gas emissions	Bribery and corruption
Geographic analysis of key markets	Effluents and waste	Community relations
Return on capital employed	Waste reduction Fines and penalties	Labour practices Social security payments Employees pay levels

(*Source: GRI 2006*)

5.3 Using information on performance measurement

The performance measures that are calculated and reported are used by three groups:

- **Managers**, to make **control and planning** decisions
- **Directors**, to assess whether corporate **governance** is effective
- **External users**, to make **decisions**

A performance measure is only useful if it is given meaning in relation to something else: users need **comparability** against various yardsticks.

- **Budgets, targets or standards**
- **Trends over time** (comparing last year with this year, say). An upward trend in the number of rejects from a production process, say, would indicate a problem that needs investigating. The effects of inflation need to be recognised if financial measures are being compared over time
- **The results of other parts of the business.** Large manufacturing businesses may compare the results of their various production departments, supermarket chains will compare the results of their individual stores, while a college may compare pass rates in different departments
- **The results of other businesses.** Trade associations or regulators may provide details of key measures based on averages for the industry. Increasingly, businesses have access to benchmarking measures

As with all comparisons, it is vital that the performance measurement process compares **'like with like'**. There is little to be gained in comparing the results of a small supermarket in a high street with a huge one in an out-of-town shopping complex, for instance.

Performance measures **do not provide answers** but help to focus attention on important areas, thereby minimising the chance of failing to identify a significant trend or weakness. In other words, performance measures enable you to **ask informed questions**.

5.4 Limitations of financial measures

Using financial measures is not foolproof. There are many problems in trying to identify trends and make comparisons. Below are just a few.

- **Information problems**
  - The base information may be out of date, so timeliness of information leads to problems of interpretation.
  - Historical cost information may not be the most appropriate information for the decision for which it is being used.
  - For external users, information often comes from published financial statements which generally comprise summarised information; more detailed information may be needed.
  - Analysis of financial measures only identifies symptoms, not causes, and thus is of limited use on its own.
- **Comparison problems: trends**
  - Effects of price changes make comparisons difficult unless adjustments are made.
  - Impacts of changes in technology affect the value of assets, the likely return and future markets.
  - A changing environment affects the results reflected in the accounting information.
  - Changes in accounting policies can affect the reported results.
  - There can be problems in establishing a normal base year to compare other years with.
- **Comparison problems: different businesses.** Analysing measures for different businesses and comparing them can be difficult because of:
  - Selection of industry norms and the usefulness of norms based on averages
  - Different firms having different financial and business risk profiles, and the impact of this on analysis
  - Different firms using different accounting policies
  - Impacts of the size of the business and its comparators on risk, structure and returns
  - Impacts of different environments on results, e.g. different countries or home-based versus multinational firms

5.5 The balanced scorecard

A business of any size whose strategic objective is the maximisation of profit to build shareholder wealth will soon lose profits and therefore capital value if it fails to manage its key resources of capacity, labour, materials and cash productively, effectively and efficiently. On the other hand, its strategic objective would probably not be undermined if it used 5% more paper clips than it had budgeted for.

The **balanced scorecard** combines traditional financial performance measures with measures of other key areas: operational and staff performance, and customer satisfaction. The scorecard was developed by Robert Kaplan and David Norton, and it produces a set of measures that allows top managers to focus on factors that are significant in achieving long-term control and direction of the business, and hence profitability in the long term.

Definition

Balanced scorecard: An integrated set of performance measures linked to the achievement of strategic objectives.

The balanced scorecard looks at the business from four important perspectives and answers four basic questions when establishing the business's vision of itself and its future strategy.

Perspective	Question
Customer Examples of measures: satisfaction ratings, retention rates, returns rates	How do customers see us?
Internal business processes (ways of doing something) Examples of measures: product quality, failure rates	What must we excel at?
Innovation and learning Examples of measures: employee retention rates, time to market for new products	How can we continue to improve and create value?
Financial Examples of measures: gross margin, net margin, return on capital employed, gearing, interest cover	How do we look to our shareholders?

VISION AND STRATEGY

6 Establishing financial control processes

Section overview

- In the finance function there need to be effective financial controls. These depend on an effective control environment, risk assessment, control activities, effective information and communication, and good monitoring.

6.1 Why are financial control processes needed?

The central **importance** of the finance function and the **risks** it faces mean that specific financial control processes need to be implemented by its managers, in order to address risks faced by the business's money and other financial assets. Financial control is a form of internal control.

6.2 What is internal control?

Definition

Internal control: A process, effected by an entity's board of directors, management and other personnel, designed to provide reasonable assurance regarding the achievement of objectives in the following categories:

- Effectiveness and efficiency of operations
- Reliability of financial reporting
- Compliance with applicable laws and regulations

(COSO Committee of Sponsoring Organisations of the US Treadway Commission)

From this definition we can see that internal control:

- Is a **process**: it is a means to an end, not an end in itself
- Is effected by **people**, not merely by policy manuals and forms
- Can be expected to provide only **reasonable assurance,** not absolute assurance, to an entity's management and board that operations are effective and efficient, financial reporting is reliable and laws and regulations are being complied with
- Is geared to the achievement of **objectives** in one or more separate but overlapping categories

Internal controls are covered fully in the *Assurance* syllabus.

6.3 Effective internal control

According to COSO, internal control consists of five interrelated components which together provide an effective framework for describing and analysing the internal control system implemented in a business:

- control environment
- risk management
- control activities
- information and communication
- monitoring

6.3.1 Control environment

The control environment sets the tone of a business and the control consciousness of its people. It provides discipline and structure. Control environment factors include:

- The integrity, business ethics and operating style of management
- How far authority is delegated
- The processes for managing and developing people in the business

6.3.2 Risk management

We saw in Chapter 5 that every business faces a variety of risks from external and internal sources, and that these must be adequately managed via assessment, measurement and control activities to address those that threaten achievement of the business's objectives.

6.3.3 Control activities

Definition

Control activities: The policies and procedures that help ensure management directives are carried out. They may take the form of physical, financial, system or management controls.

Control activities occur throughout the business, at all levels and in all functions – not just the finance function. They include:

- Approval
- Authorisation
- Verification
- Reconciliation
- Review of operating performance
- Security of assets and
- Segregation of duties

Segregation (or separation) of duties is important where power could be abused if only one person was responsible for a transaction or asset from beginning to end. An example would be the purchase of a non-current asset such as a car. If only one person had the power to:

- Authorise its purchase
- Record the amount payable and/or pay the bill and
- Have custody of the car

then there is nothing stopping that person from buying the most expensive car possible then absconding with it.

6.3.4 Information and communication

Information systems produce reports, including operational, financial and compliance-related information, that make it possible to run and control the business. In a broader sense, effective communication must ensure information flows down, across and up the business. Effective communication with external parties, such as customers, suppliers, regulators and shareholders, is also important for control.

6.3.5 Monitoring

Internal control systems need to be monitored to assess the quality of the system's performance over time. This is accomplished through ongoing monitoring activities or separate evaluations. Deficiencies in internal control that are detected through these monitoring activities should be reported to more senior managers. Corrective action should be taken to ensure continuous improvement of the system.

6.4 Financial control processes

In Chapter 12 we shall look at the UK Corporate Governance Code, which contains a main principle (C2) that the board should maintain sound risk management and internal control systems.

It states that internal controls include financial, operational and compliance controls.

Summary and Self-test

Summary

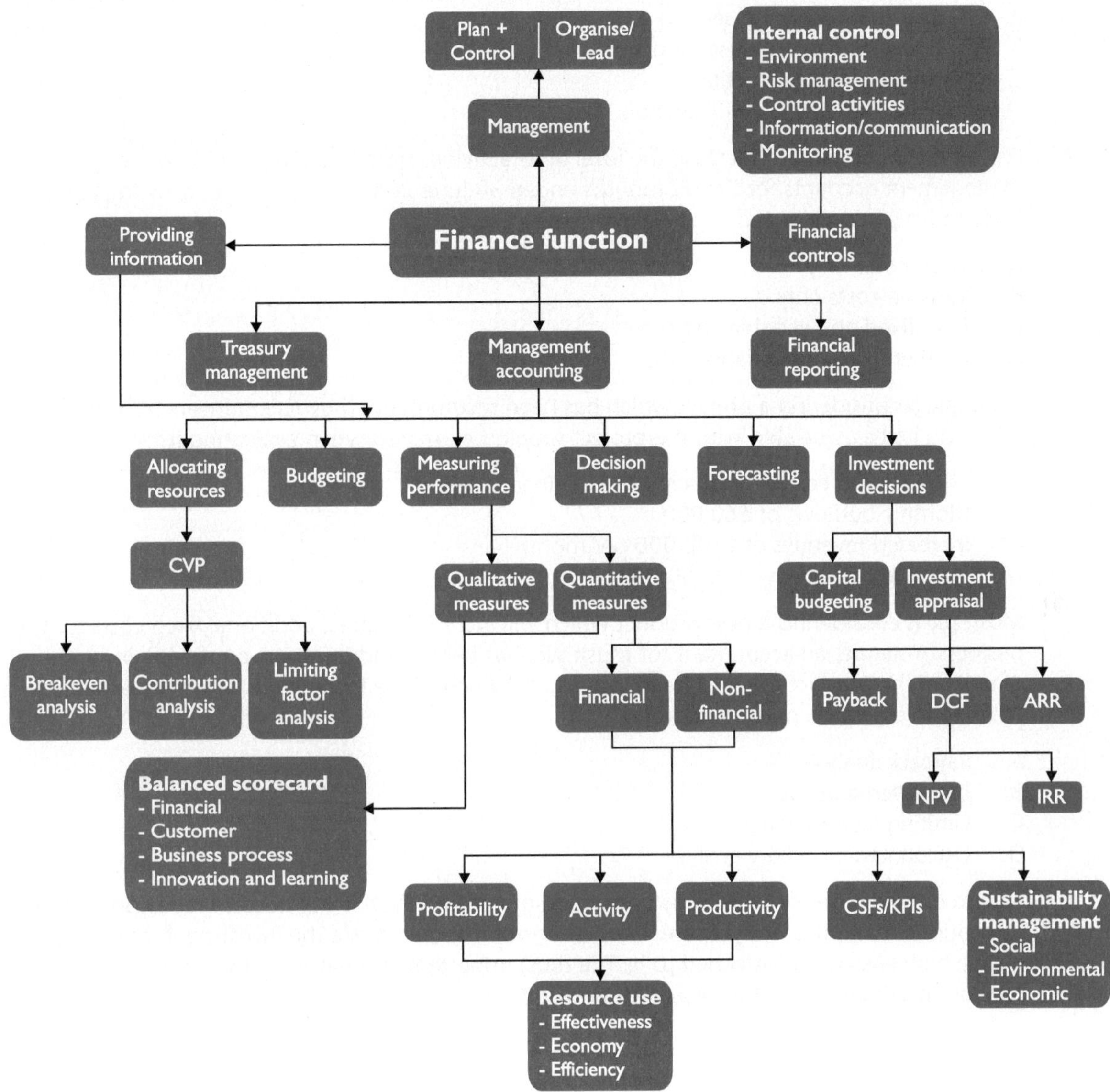

CHAPTER 7

Self-test

Answer the following questions.

1 Linus is an accountant for Magna plc, which is considering a substantial new project. Linus has been asked to assist in determining whether it should be financed by retained earnings, equity, loans or a mix of all sources. It would appear that Linus is employed by Magna plc's finance function's

A Transaction recording section
B Treasury management section
C Financial reporting section
D Management accounting section

2 Primus plc is planning to increase the level of its activities from 1 January 20X8. In the management accounts for the six months ended 30 June 20X7, which of the following costs are likely to have been affected by the expansion?

A Fixed costs only
B Variable costs only
C Both fixed and variable costs
D Neither fixed nor variable costs

3 Hobo plc is considering a project which has been recommended by its engineers. Which of the following items associated with the project should be ignored when evaluating it?

A The £10,000 cost of producing the engineers' report
B Monthly outflows of £60,000
C Increased revenues of £100,000 per month
D The investment now of £200,000

4 Mush plc is considering a new product which will incur substantial additional fixed costs for the business. Yolande, an accountant for Mush plc, has been asked to report on the minimum number of units of the product that will need to be sold. Which of the following is Mush plc expecting Yolande to use when making her report?

A Payback analysis
B Breakeven analysis
C Limiting factor analysis
D Discounted cash flow analysis

5 Quantock plc is considering a substantial investment for which it will need to raise considerable quantities of cash. It is not yet sure whether or not it should make the investment, as it appears to have a high level of risk attached to it. The most important technique that Quantock should use in relation to this investment at this point is

A Cash budgeting
B Discounted cash flow
C Capital budgeting
D Payback

6 Briar plc's managers have been asked to produce budgets for their departments. Raji has submitted a budget for the next year based on this year's actual performance plus an allowance for inflation of 3%, less an allowance for performance improvement of 2%. The method used by Raji is

A Zero-based budgeting
B Flexible budgeting
C Rolling budgets
D Incremental budgeting

7 Moody plc is reviewing its internal control system. Its control activities should be directed at controlling

A Threats to its operations
B Its operations
C Threats to achievement of its objectives
D Achievement of its objectives

8 In the balanced scorecard, measures of how quickly and fully employee suggestions are implemented would be included in

A Financial perspective measures
B Customer perspective measures
C Internal business process perspective measures
D Innovation and learning perspective measures

Now, go back to the Learning Objectives in the Introduction. If you are satisfied you have achieved these objectives, please tick them off.

Answers to Self-test

1 B

2 D As at 30 June 20X7 the expansion is still six months away, so no costs will yet have been affected

3 A The cost of the engineers' report is a sunk cost and so should not be considered when evaluating whether this project should be pursued

4 B

5 B Cash budgeting (A) is primarily concerned with working capital. The company is not really concerned with capital budgeting (C) currently because it already knows it will need to raise cash. It will need to prioritise DCF over payback because of the element of risk in the project

6 D Although Raji has made allowances for future changes (inflation and performance improvement), he is still basically using increments in past experience as the basis for his budget

7 C

8 D

CHAPTER 8

Business and personal finance

Introduction

Learning objectives

Tick off

- Identify the characteristics, terms and conditions and role of alternative short, medium and long term sources of finance available to different businesses ☐
- Identify the processes by which businesses raise equity capital and other long-term finance ☐
- Identify appropriate methods of financing exports, including bills of exchange, letters of credit and export credit insurance ☐
- Specify the relationship between a business and its bankers and other providers of financial products ☐
- Specify the general objectives of personal financial management ☐
- Identify the principles of personal financial management and the personal financial management process ☐

Specific syllabus references are: 3g, h, i, j, k, l.

Syllabus links

The implications of a financing decision will be seen in Financial Management, Financial Accounting and Reporting, Business Planning: Taxation, and Audit and Assurance at Professional level. It will be explored further at Advanced level.

Examination context

Questions on sources of finance and on personal financial management could easily appear in the exam.

Questions are likely to be set in multiple choice format and in a scenario context. Knowledge-type questions are also likely, set on particular principles or definitions.

1 Risk v return

Section overview

- Risk and return go hand in hand, and businesses need to bear in mind the risk-return trade-off of investors.
- A business is financed by a mix of equity (higher risk/higher return) and debt (lower risk/lower return)

A business is financed:

- by **equity** (from its **owners** in return for **dividends**), or
- by **debt** (from **lenders** in return for **interest**), or
- by a combination of equity and debt.

There are many forms of these two types of capital, but what distinguishes them is their different levels of **risk**.

- **Debt holders** face **lower risk** but **lower returns:**
  - they receive interest before equity holders receive any dividends, and
  - debt is often secured by fixed or floating charges, and
  - in the event of company failure, debt holders rank higher than equity holders to receive their capital back, but
  - the 'price' they pay is a lower rate of return on their capital
- **Equity holders** face **higher risk** but can enjoy **higher returns:** they suffer the downside of any loss but any profits after (interest and tax) go to the equity holders, not the debt holders.

Risk and return go hand in hand. Therefore in structuring its finances, a company must have regard to the **risk-return trade-off** desired by potential investors.

2 Balancing short-term and long-term finance

Section overview

- Every business has immediate, short-term, medium-term and long-term needs for finance, and each one faces risk in the way it finances itself.
- Businesses may be aggressive, average or defensive in their financing policies.
- Businesses have four motives for holding cash: transactions, finance, precautionary and investment motives.
- Short term surpluses of cash should be invested; short term shortages of cash need to be financed.

A key decision for any business is how it is going to finance both its operations now and its plans for the future. Its need for finance ranges from the very immediate short term to the very long term:

- **Immediate** needs: to pay **wages** and **petty expenses**
- **Short term** needs: to pay for goods/services bought on credit **(payables)**
- **Medium term** needs: to pay for an **increase in inventory and receivables** as the business grows, and to pay tax on profits earned
- **Long term** needs: to pay for **non-current assets** required in the long term such as machinery, vehicles and buildings.

Wages, payables, receivables and inventory all form part of the business's **working capital**, which is made up of current assets less current liabilities. While the management of working capital is covered in your *Management Information* syllabus at Certificate level, the fact that it produces the need for finance over different terms means we need to consider it briefly here too.

2.1 Financing current assets

Levels of inventory plus receivables less payables fluctuate but for most businesses a proportion of current assets will effectively be **permanent**. The methods of financing this level are best seen diagrammatically in Figure 8.1.

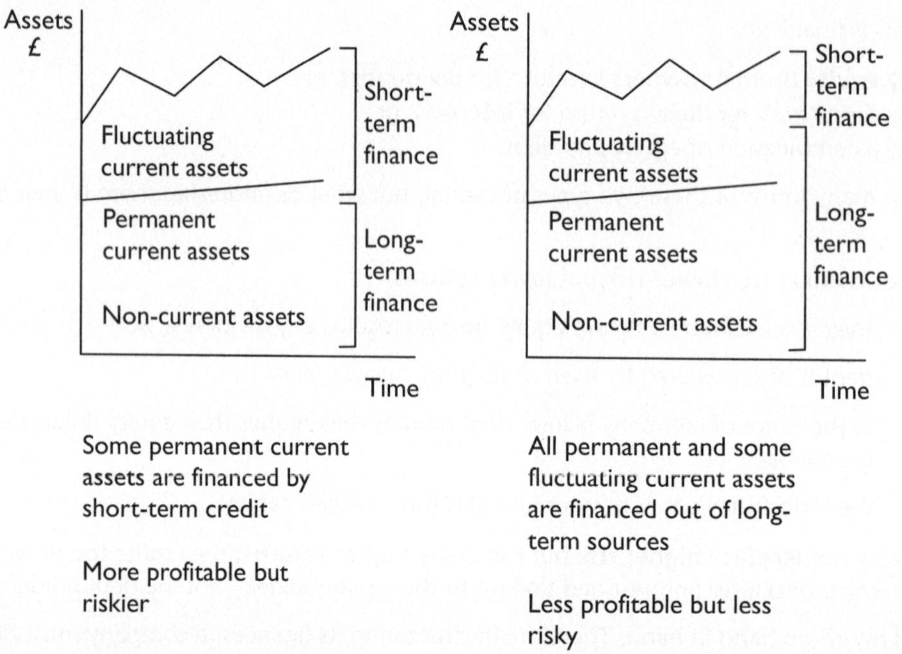

Some permanent current assets are financed by short-term credit

More profitable but riskier

All permanent and some fluctuating current assets are financed out of long-term sources

Less profitable but less risky

Figure 8.1: Financing working capital investment

The options set out in Figure 8.1 are only two of many possible approaches. For example, the use of short-term credit could be extended to finance a proportion of the non-current assets or, alternatively, all of the business's finance requirements could be provided by long-term finance.

The choice is a matter for managerial judgement of the trade-off between the relative **cheapness** of short-term finance versus its **risks**.

2.2 The cost of short-term finance

Short-term finance is usually **cheaper** than long-term finance due to the risks taken by lenders. For example, if a bank were considering two loan applications, one for one year and the other for 20 years, all other things being equal it would demand a higher interest rate on the 20-year loan. This is because it feels more exposed to **risk** on long-term loans, as more could possibly go wrong over a period of 20 years than over a period of one year. Long-term finance includes equity finance which is particularly expensive: because of the **risk they suffer shareholders expect high returns**, and dividends are not tax deductible.

Occasionally this situation can be reversed. Sometimes short-term interest rates will be higher than long-term rates, as when the market expects interest rates to fall in the long run. But if finance has been borrowed long-term, early repayment may not be possible or, if allowed, early repayment penalties may be experienced. **The flexibility of short-term finance may, therefore, reduce its overall cost.**

Finally, short-term finance also includes items such as the credit period offered by suppliers (trade payables); it can therefore have a low average cost since interest is charged by banks on overdrafts but not by ordinary suppliers unless an agreed credit period has been exceeded

2.3 The risks to borrowers of short-term finance

The price paid for the reduced cost of short-term finance is an increase in risk suffered by borrowers.

- **Renewal risk**
  Being short-term it has to be continually renegotiated as the various facilities expire. Either because of economic conditions (eg a credit squeeze) or because of the financial situation of the business, such renewal may be difficult to obtain.
- **Interest rate risk**
  If the business is constantly having to renew its funding arrangements, it will be at the mercy of fluctuations in short-term interest rates.

2.4 Making the decision between short-term and long-term finance

No single ideal financing package can be recommended as it all depends upon the **risk appetite** and the **perceived risk/return trade-off** of each individual business.

Businesses may be categorised as having **aggressive, average** or **defensive** positions in this area

- An **aggressive company** has **more short-term credit** than equity; it may return a **higher profit** but at the cost of **greater risk.**
- An **average company matches its maturities** so it has **less risk** than in the aggressive company but **less return** as well:
  - permanent current assets are financed by long-term debt
  - fluctuating current assets are financed by short-term credit..
- A **defensive company** sacrifices profitability for liquidity by having **little short-term credit**, which finances only some of the fluctuating current assets. This is a **low-risk, low return** company.

The financing choice must be made by the management of the individual business, bearing in mind the **willingness of suppliers of finance to lend** and the **risk of its industrial sector**.

CHAPTER 8

2.5 Holding cash or running out of cash

To manage its cash position successfully (the function of treasury management, which we saw in Chapter 7 is one of the key roles of the business's finance function) the business must **trade off the cost of holding cash against the cost of running out of cash.**

- The **cost of holding cash**, either as a cash float or in a current account, is the **opportunity cost** of what else could be done with the money. Cash is an idle asset and earns little or no return. If the finance was put to work elsewhere (ie invested) it could generate profits.
- The **costs of running out of cash** vary depending upon the circumstances of the business. Cash shortages result in the business not being able to pay its payables on time, and this could have many implications. Examples include:
  - **Loss of settlement discounts** from trade suppliers
  - Loss of **supplier goodwill,** eg refusal of further credit, higher prices, poor delivery
  - Poor **industrial relations** if wage payments are delayed
  - Payables petitioning for **winding-up** the business

Although the above costs may be difficult to quantify the business must at all times ensure that it has **sufficient liquidity**, in the form of cash balances or overdraft/loan facilities, to maintain its **solvency**.

2.5.1 Influences on the level of cash balances

There are a number of motives underlying how much a business would wish to hold as cash:

- **Transactions motive** – to meet current day-to-day financial obligations, eg payroll, the purchase of raw materials, etc
- **Finance motive** – to cover major items such as the repayment of loans and the purchase of non-current assets

- **Precautionary motive** – to give a cushion against unplanned expenditure, rather like buffer inventory
- **Investment motive** – to take advantage of market opportunities

We shall look at sources of short-term finance later in this chapter.

2.6 Investing surplus cash in the short term

If a business identifies a **short-term surplus of cash** it should aim to invest it to earn a return. If the surplus is of a **longer-term** nature it should be invested in longer-term projects to increase shareholder wealth, or returned to shareholders as dividends.

Surplus finance can be invested in various financial products in the **money markets,** which we shall come back to shortly. Most businesses will be looking for a **variety of investments** in order to **spread the risks** involved, and to ensure **flexibility**.

3 The banking system

Section overview

- Financial intermediation means that banks 'stand in the middle' and match up people with excess cash and those who have a deficit of cash
- The banking system comprises primary and secondary banks. Banks are heavily regulated.
- Primary banks depend on the clearing system and other money transmission systems for ensuring that money paid in at one bank can be drawn out at another.
- The bank/customer relationship is legally quite complex, involving four contractual relationships (receivable/payable, bailor/bailee, principal/agent and mortgagor/mortgagee) and a fiduciary relationship.

If a business is to raise additional short or long-term finance or to invest surplus cash, then this will be done either through a **bank** or within the **money or capital markets**.

3.1 Financial intermediation

Banks take deposits from customers and then use that money to lend money to other customers. This process is known as **financial intermediation**. The banks act effectively as middlemen providing finance for those that want loans from the deposits made by savers.

Benefits of financial intermediation:

- Small amounts deposited by savers can be combined to provide larger loan packages to businesses
- Short-term savings can be transferred into long-term loans
- Search costs are reduced as companies seeking loan finance can approach a bank directly rather than finding individuals to lend to them
- Risk is reduced as an individual's savings are not tied up with one individual borrower directly.

3.2 Banks

- **Primary banks** are those which operate the **money transmission service** or **clearing system** in the economy. They operate cheque accounts and deal with cheque clearing, though increasingly money transmission by and to account holders is effected by a variety of automated payments via internet banking, and cheque usage is consequently falling rapidly. They are sometimes also known as the **commercial, retail or clearing banks.**
- **Secondary banks** are made up of a wide range of merchant banks and other banks. They do not take part in the clearing system.

Banks as a key part of the financial system are heavily regulated in the UK. They are affected by the activities of the **Bank of England**, which has two main roles in the UK: carrying out monetary policy and ensuring financial stability.

3.2.1 Monetary policy

The **Bank of England** is banker to the banks, lending money to the banking sector through its financial market operations at the **base rate** set by its **Monetary Policy Committee** (MPC). The MPC decides on the base rate in order to meet a target for overall inflation in the economy set each year by the Chancellor of the Exchequer. The aim of this is **monetary stability**, which we shall see more about in Chapter 13.

The base rate is not necessarily the interest rate at which banks lend and borrow money among themselves (the most well-known of these rates is the London Inter Bank Offer Rate, or LIBOR), nor is it the rate at which customers receive interest on their deposits or pay interest on their advances. There are a great many other factors affecting these rates, but the base rate is nevertheless important as it is the rate which is often used as a comparator for the performance of organisations and their projects.

3.2.2 Financial stability

As well as monetary stability, the Bank of England also seeks to ensure the **financial stability** and resilience of the UK's financial system as a whole. A key way in which it does this is via its **Financial Policy Committee (FPC)**, which takes action to remove or reduce systemic risks in the UK financial system as a whole. An example of a systemic risk of this nature is reliance of banks and building societies on wholesale money markets, the stalling of which was a key factor in the financial crisis that hit the system from 2007. The FPC has a secondary objective to support the economic policy of the Government.

Following the financial crisis, the Financial Services Act 2012 broke up the previous regulator of operators in the financial industry, the Financial Services Authority (FSA), and created instead a **'twin peaks' regulatory regime,** half of which is operated by the Bank of England. The twin peaks regime operates via two separate bodies as follows.

- The **Prudential Regulation Authority (PRA)** is part of the Bank of England and is responsible for the prudential regulation and supervision of banks, building societies, credit unions, insurers and major investment firms. It is forward-looking, seeking to spot problems in individual firms before they can create instability for the system as a whole. The PRA has two statutory objectives:
  - to promote the safety and soundness of firms, by focusing primarily on the harm that firms can cause to the stability of the UK financial system, and
  - to secure, in relation to insurers, an appropriate degree of protection for policyholders.
- The **Financial Conduct Authority (FCA)** is an independent body responsible for:
  - promoting effective competition,
  - ensuring that relevant markets function well, and
  - regulating the conduct of all financial services firms, which includes acting to prevent market abuse and ensuring that consumers get a fair deal from financial firms.

The FCA also operates the prudential regulation and supervision of financial services firms which are not supervised by the PRA, such as asset managers and independent financial advisers.

3.2.3 The clearing system and other forms of money transmission

The interval between when amounts are paid into a primary bank and when they can be drawn upon depends on the **clearing mechanism** and other services used.

- **General clearing** (mainly of cheques, though internet transfers outside of the Faster Payments system can still take the same amount of time!) – this covers items of any size but there is a three to four day delay before amounts are cleared (ie can be drawn upon).
- **Electronic Funds Transfer (EFT)** – this refers to any *computer-based* system used to perform *financial transactions* electronically. Although the term is used for a number of different concepts it

is most commonly associated with cardholder-initiated transactions in shops, where a cardholder makes use of a debit card or credit card in an **electronic funds transfer at point of sale (EFTPOS)**

- **Banks Automated Clearing System (BACS)** – this is an EFT system that deals with salaries, standing orders and direct debits. The account of the payer is debited on the same day as the account of the recipient is credited.
- **Clearing House Automated Payment System (CHAPS)** – this organisation provides two key services:
  - CHAPS: an electronic bank-to-bank same-day value payment system made within the UK in sterling.
  - 'Faster Payments': a same-day clearing system of amounts from £1 up to £100,000 for some customers of some retail banks using either the phone or the internet to make the instruction.
- **Society for Worldwide Interbank Financial Telecommunication (SWIFT)** – this is the worldwide *financial messaging network* which exchanges messages between *banks* and other *financial institutions* so that a similar service to CHAPS is possible for international transfers of money.

3.3 The bank/customer contractual relationships

When money is paid into a bank by an individual or business and an account is opened then that individual or business becomes a **customer** of the bank.

The **legal relationship** between the bank and its customer is actually quite complex. There are potentially four **main contractual relationships** between the bank and the customer.

3.3.1 Receivable/payable relationship

When the customer deposits money the bank owes money (it is the customer's receivable) and the customer is a **payable** of the bank. If the customer's account is overdrawn however the bank is owed money (it is a payable of the customer) and the customer is the bank's **receivable**.

This relationship is essentially a **contract** between the bank and the customer.

- The bank borrows the customer's deposits and undertakes to repay them
- The bank must receive cheques for the customer's account
- The bank will only cease to do business with the customer with reasonable notice
- The bank is not liable to pay the customer until the latter demands payment
- The customer must exercise reasonable care when writing cheques

3.3.2 Bailor/bailee relationship

This element of the relationship concerns the bank accepting the customer's property for storage in its **safe deposit**. The bank as bailee undertakes to take reasonable care to safeguard the property against loss or damage and also to re-deliver it only to the customer (the bailor) or someone authorised by the customer.

3.3.3 Principal/agent relationship

An **agent** is someone who acts on behalf of another party, the **principal**. Within banking the principal/agent relationship exists where, for example, the customer pays a crossed cheque into the bank. The receiving bank acts as an agent of the customer, as principal, when it presents the cheque for payment to the paying bank, and then pays the proceeds into the customer's account.

3.3.4 Mortgagor/mortgagee relationship

If the bank asks the customer to secure a loan with a charge over its assets then the relationship between the two is that of **mortgagor** (the customer) and **mortgagee** (the bank). If the customer does not repay the loan then the bank has the right to sell the assets and use the proceeds to pay off the loan. We will see more about mortgages later in this chapter, in the sections on personal financial management.

3.4 The bank/customer fiduciary relationship

The bank and the customer also have a **fiduciary relationship** which means that the bank as the party with more relative power is expected to act with **good faith** in its relationship with the customer.

3.4.1 The bank's duties to the customer

- It must **honour a customer's cheques** provided they are correctly made out, there is no legal reason for not honouring them and the customer has enough money or sufficient overdraft limit to cover the amount of the cheque
- The bank must **credit cash/cheques** that are paid in to the customer's account
- If the customer makes a written request for repayment of money in its account, for example by writing a cheque, the bank must **repay the amount on demand**
- The bank must **comply with the customer's instructions** given by direct debit mandate or standing order
- The bank must provide **a statement** showing the transactions on the account within a reasonable period and provide details of the balance on the customer's account
- The bank must respect the **confidentiality** of the customer's affairs unless the bank is required by law, public duty or its own interest to disclose details or where the customer gives his consent for such disclosure
- The bank must tell the customer if there has been an attempt to **forge the customer's signature** on a cheque
- The bank should use **care and skill** in its actions
- The bank must provide **reasonable notice** if it is to close a customer's account.

3.4.2 The customer's duties to the bank

- To **draw up cheques carefully** so that fraud is not facilitated
- To tell the bank of any **known forgeries**

Note that there is **no specific legal duty on a customer to check their bank statements**.

3.4.3 The rights of the bank

- To charge **reasonable bank charges** and commissions over and above interest
- To **use the customer's money** in any way provided that it is legal and morally acceptable
- To be **repaid overdrawn balances on demand** (although banks rarely enforce this)
- To be **indemnified against possible losses** when acting on the customer's behalf.

4 The money markets

Section overview

- The money markets offer opportunities for investing surplus finance using Treasury bills, deposits, certificates of deposit, Gilts, bonds and commercial paper.

Definitions

The **money markets** is a term that covers a vast array of markets buying and selling different forms of money or marketable securities. The money markets are a wholesale market that provides financial institutions with a means of borrowing and investing to deal with short-term fluctuations in their own assets and liabilities.

Marketable securities are short-term highly liquid investments that are readily convertible into cash. Companies might use them to invest short-term surplus finance (see above).

The main traders in the money markets are **banks**, the government (through the **Bank of England**) and **local authorities**, plus brokers and other intermediaries.

4.1 Money market financial instruments

There are a variety of different financial instruments that are traded in the money markets. The main types are:

- **Treasury bills** issued by the Debt Management Office of HM Treasury, which have a minimum investment for members of the public of £500,000+, run for one to six months and are highly secure and liquid, but offer low returns. They can be converted into cash by selling them in the discount market
- **Deposits** – money in the bank accounts of banks and other financial intermediaries, which offer investment periods ranging from overnight to five years. They are available from banks, local authorities and building societies with yields exceeding that of Treasury bills
- **Certificates of deposit (CDs)** – issued mainly by commercial banks, a certificate for deposit endures for a fixed term of between one month and five years at a fixed rate of interest, and can be sold earlier than maturity in the CD market.
- **Gilts** issued by the Debt Management Office, which are longer-term government debt that offer a large range of maturities (five to 50 years) and rates based on money market rates
- **Bonds**, which are debentures and loans of companies quoted on the Stock Exchange; rates fluctuate with general interest rates and there is good liquidity.
- **Commercial paper** – IOUs issued by large companies which can be either held to maturity or sold to third parties before maturity

The **inter-bank market** is a market for very short-term borrowing, often overnight, between banks. It is used to smooth fluctuations in the banks' receipts and payments. The main interest rate charged in this market is the **London Inter-Bank Offered Rate (LIBOR)**. The individual banks then use this rate in order to determine the interest rate that they will offer to their customers.

5 The capital market for business finance

Section overview

- The capital market for businesses comprises: national stock markets, the retail and wholesale banks, bond markets, leasing, debt factoring and international markets
- A company can raise capital in the capital markets by issuing marketable securities:
  - Equity, or ordinary share capital
  - Preference shares
  - Loan stocks or debentures

Capital markets provide **a source of funds for businesses** (mostly companies) and an **exit route for investors**.

Definition

Capital market: the national and international market in which a business may obtain the finance it needs for its short-term and long-term plans.

There is no single capital market: there are many ways in which businesses can access finance.

National stock markets	For companies in the UK this includes the London Stock Exchange and the Alternative Investment Market (AIM). They act as: • **primary markets** ie a source of new finance via new share issues, and as • **secondary markets** for securities such as shares that are already in issue.
The banking system	This can be split between the **retail market** (for individuals/small businesses) and the **wholesale market** (for large companies).
Bond markets	Generally these are for very large organisations to raise typically very large amounts of money.
Leasing	This is a very important source of business finance for a whole variety of entities.
Debt factoring	This is normally used by smaller businesses to help finance their working capital requirements.
International markets	Typically available to larger companies, these allow finance to be raised in different currencies, typically in very large amounts.

Raising new long-term business finance invariably involves issuing **securities** in the form of **shares** (equity) or **bonds** (debt).

Definitions

Equity represents the **ordinary shares** in the business. Equity shareholders are the owners of the business and through their voting rights exercise ultimate control.

Preference shares form part of the risk-bearing ownership of the business but, since they are entitled to their dividends before ordinary shareholders, they carry less risk. As their return is usually a fixed maximum dividend, they are similar in many ways to debt.

Loan stocks and **debentures** are typically fixed interest rate borrowings with a set repayment date. Most are secured on specific assets or assets in general such that lenders are protected (in repayment terms) above unsecured payables in a liquidation.

6 Sources of equity finance

Section overview

- Retained earnings (profits earned over time but not immediately paid out to owners) are the main source of long-term finance for most businesses
- Rights issues of shares: the law protects shareholders by requiring that any new issues are first offered to the existing shareholders
- New issues of marketable securities may be done via:
  - Placings: the most common form of issue for companies first coming to market
  - Offer for sale: used by large companies raising large amounts in a high profile (but expensive) manner
  - Direct offer (offer for subscription: rarely used – involves a company issuing shares directly to investors)

- Pricing of new issues is difficult but getting the issue underwritten, or using an offer for sale by tender, can help
- Going public by obtaining a full listing has advantages and disadvantages.

There are broadly three methods of raising equity:

Method	Real world use
Retaining earnings (profits), rather than paying them out as dividends	By far and away the most important source of equity
Rights issues of new shares to existing shareholders	The next most important source
New issues of shares to the public: an issue of new shares to new shareholders	The least important source of new equity in practice

6.1 Retained earnings

The profits earned by a business can either be paid out to owners in the form of dividends or reinvested in the business. Shareholders will still expect a **return on the funds re-invested in the business**, ie they will expect the funds to be invested in projects which increase their wealth.

Retained earnings represent a very **easy and important source of finance**, particularly for young growing businesses where there may be a continual need for finance but where it is impractical to keep raising it using rights/new issues and debt.

6.2 Rights issues of shares

Definition

A **rights issue** is an issue of new shares for cash to existing shareholders in proportion to their existing holdings.

Legally a rights issue must be made before a new issue to the public. Existing shareholders have rights of first refusal (**pre-emption rights**) on the new shares and can, by taking them up, maintain their existing percentage holding in the company. However shareholders can, and often do, waive these rights by selling them to others.

6.2.1 Factors to be considered when making rights issues

- **Issue costs** – these have been estimated at around 4% on £2m raised but, as many of the costs are fixed, the percentage falls as the sum raised increases
- **Shareholder reactions** – shareholders may react badly to companies continually making rights issues as they are forced either to take up their rights or sell them. They may therefore sell their shares, driving down the market price
- **Control** – unless large numbers of existing shareholders sell their rights to new shareholders there should be little impact in terms of control of the business by existing shareholders
- **Unlisted companies** – often find rights issues difficult to use, as shareholders who do not have sufficient funds to take up their rights may not be able to sell them if the shares are not listed. This could mean that the company is forced either to use retained earnings or to raise loans.

6.3 New issues of shares

These may take the form of **placings, offers for sale** or **direct offers (offers for subscription)**.

6.3.1 Placings

Placings are the most common method of issuing shares when a company first comes onto the market. They work as follows:

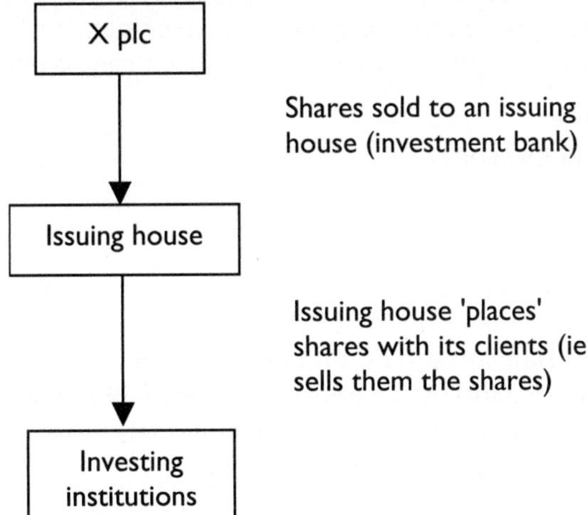

The investor base in a placing is made up of institutional investors, contacted by the issuing house. The general public does not tend to have access to the shares when *first* offered, although they can be involved in any subsequent trading in the shares.

- **Benefit**: lower transaction costs (eg advertising, administration) than public offers.
- **Drawback**: by only offering to a narrow pool of institutional investors, the spread of shareholders is more limited, which reduces the efficiency of the market in the shares (we shall come back to the efficient markets hypothesis later in this chapter).

6.3.2 Public offers

There are two methods of making a public offer

- Offer for sale
- Direct offer (offer for subscription)

In practice the **offer for sale is far more common**; in either method the issue is likely to be underwritten (see below). There is no restriction on the amount of capital raised by public offer. They are best illustrated diagrammatically:

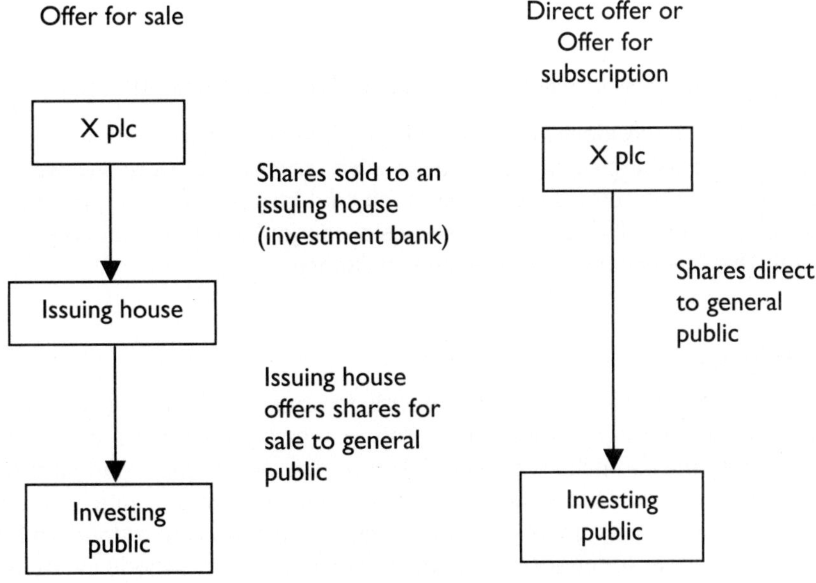

Both methods use very similar procedures. These include advertising, eg in newspapers, following the legal requirements, and Stock Exchange regulations in terms of the large volumes of information which must be provided (listing particulars, prospectus etc). Great expense is incurred in providing this information, as it requires the involvement of lawyers, accountants and other advisors.

6.3.3 Pricing of new issues

A company does not want to set the issue price too high, causing the issue to fail, or too low, as this will result in more new shares being issued than is necessary, which detracts from the wealth of existing shareholders. There are two ways in which the pricing problem can be addressed by:

- **Underwriting** the issue
- Using an **offer for sale by tender**.

Definitions

Underwriting is the process whereby, in exchange for a fixed fee (usually 1–2% of the total finance to be raised), an institution or group of institutions will undertake to purchase any securities not subscribed for by the public. **The main disadvantage of underwriting is its cost**, which depends on the characteristics of the company issuing the security and the state of the market. The cost is payable even if the underwriter is not called upon to take up any securities. Effectively, underwriting is an insurance policy that guarantees that the required capital will be raised.

Offer for sale by tender: The investing public is invited to tender (offer) for shares at the price it is willing to pay. A **minimum price**, however, is set by the issuing company and tenders must be at or above the minimum.

The procedure for an **offer for sale by tender** is as follows:

1 Receive all tenders

2 Set the actual issue price (a single price), either at:

- The **highest price at which the entire issue is sold**, all tenders at or above this price being allotted in full, or
- A **lower price**, with tenders at or above this lower price receiving only a proportion of the shares tendered for. This prevents the concentration of shares in the hands of one party.

As the shares are issued at **only one price** and not at several, investors who made tenders at high prices will usually pay less than the amount tendered.

6.4 Preference shares

Preference shares usually carry **no voting rights** and have **no right to share in excess profits**.

- **Benefits**: They can be attractive if a company is looking to raise new capital but wants to avoid additional debt and does not want to dilute the ordinary shareholders' influence.
- **Drawbacks**: While the dividend on ordinary equity shares will vary from one period to the next, preference shares offer a fixed rate of dividend each year. This is not guaranteed and if the company has insufficient profits the dividend may not be paid. However, most preference shares are 'cumulative' so that all arrears in preference dividends have to be paid before equity dividends can be paid. They are expensive to issue and to finance.

6.5 Going public

At some stage a successful large company may decide to obtain a full listing ('go public' or 'float') on the Main Market of the London Stock Exchange. This may be a premium listing or a standard listing. With a premium listing the company is expected to meet the UK's highest standards of regulation and corporate governance, and as a consequence may enjoy a lower cost of capital through greater transparency and through building investor confidence. Companies with a standard listing have a slightly lower requirement as to regulation and governance, and may include overseas companies with a

UK listing. Smaller companies may use lower level markets such as the Alternative Investment Market (AIM).

Advantages

- Gives access to a large source of finance
- Improves the marketability of shares, which should increase the value of the company
- Improves the standing of the company, as it will be under more scrutiny once listed, so raising more finance may then be easier

Disadvantages/problems

- Cost: costs run into hundreds of thousands of pounds even for modest issues
- Dilution of control (at least 25% of the company has to be in public hands)
- Need to have traded for three years
- Having to answer to other investors – often professional institutional investors
- Greater scrutiny of the affairs of the company and the actions of the directors
- Listing might not be successful unless the business is worth at least £50m (often referred to as market sentiment)
- Possibility of being taken over
- Extra costs of control and reporting systems to meet the increased demands on the company. A listing agreement commits directors to certain levels of compliance, of reporting to shareholders and of corporate governance (we shall see more about this in Chapter 12).

The process for obtaining a full listing on the Stock Exchange involves a number of specialist advisors.

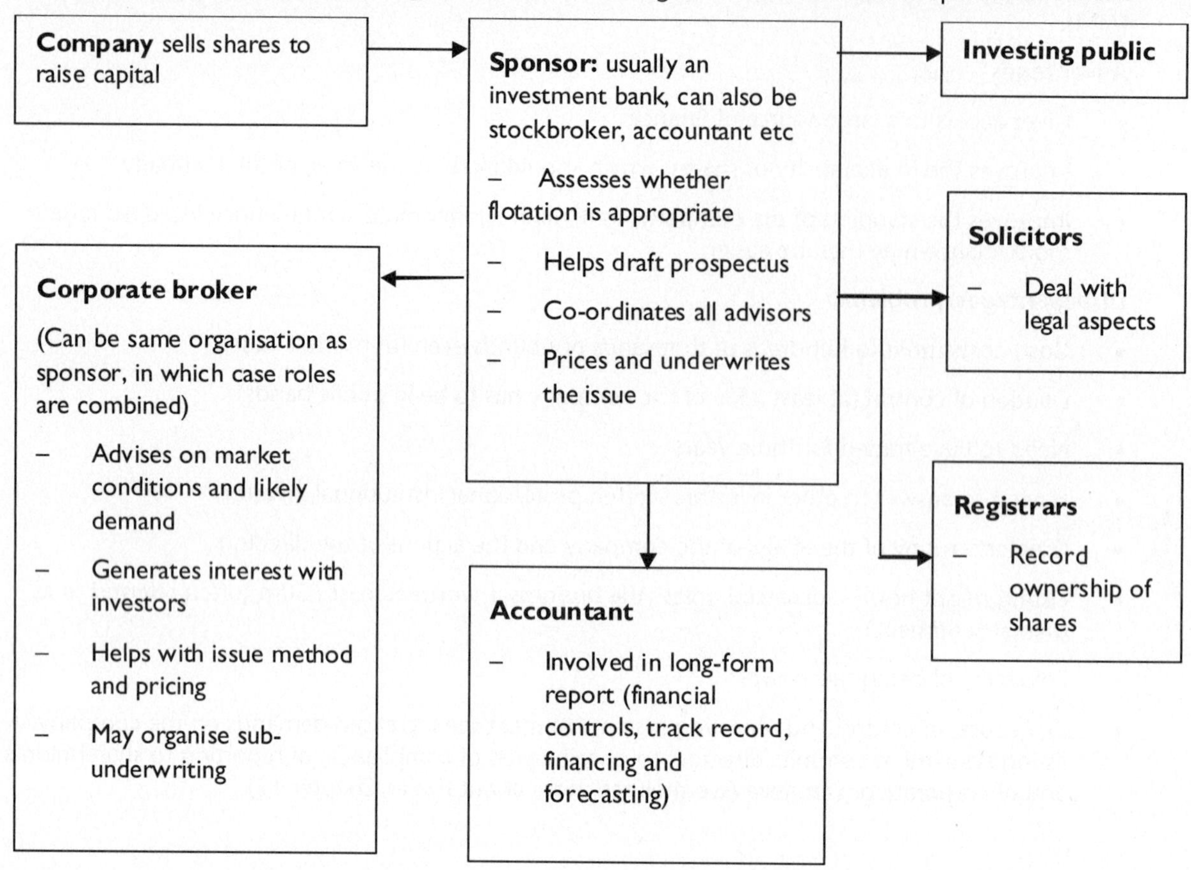

7 Sources of debt finance

Section overview

- Overdraft – short-term finance from a bank.
- Debt factoring – use of debt factors helps manage the risks of offering credit.
- Term loans – traditional finance from the banking sector.
- Loan stock – financial instruments detailing interest, repayment, redemption date and ownership.
- Leasing – a major source of funding for capital expenditure.
- Other forms of debt – relevant to a variety of organisations depending on the context.

7.1 Overdraft

Definition

Overdraft: An overdraft is a short-term loan of variable amount up to a limit from a bank, typically repayable on demand. Interest is charged on a day-to-day basis at a variable rate.

Overdrafts are used by businesses to meet their **short-term cash deficits**. They are **inappropriate as part of a company's long-term capital base** because they are normally **repayable on demand**. This means that the bank offering the overdraft is not committed to making that money available on an ongoing basis, as would be the case with say a term loan (see section below).

In spite of this, many companies take the risky step of having a **permanent overdraft** ie they use it as a long-term source of finance.

7.1.1 Advantages of an overdraft

- **Flexibility:** an overdraft can be used and repaid as desired, giving the borrower
- **Cost:** overall interest cost can be lower than a term loan, as interest is only paid when overdrawn

7.1.2 Disadvantages of an overdraft

- **Risk**: as it is repayable on demand it is not strictly suitable as a long-term source of capital, since banks can – and do – demand immediate repayment
- **Cost:** if the account is permanently in overdraft, the overall interest cost is higher than with a term loan as the interest rate is generally higher
- **Control**: the bank may require security on assets of the business

7.2 Debt factoring

Definition

Debt factoring: the business receives loan finance and insurance – known as non-recourse factoring – so that, in the event that a customer does not pay, the business does not have to repay the loan

The services typically offered by a debt factor include:

Financing the credit taken by customers	Offering credit to customers creates cash flow problems, which can be particularly acute for small businesses. Debt factors help by giving the business a loan of, say, 80% of the amount due from customers. When they pay at the end of their credit period, the business repays the loan from the debt factor, together with any interest and fees.
Insuring receivables	Offering credit to customers invariably carries a cost in the form of irrecoverable debts. Debt factors can assess the risk of whether customers will pay and offer insurance, in return for a premium.
Managing the running of the receivables ledger	The debt factor can carry out all aspects of running a receivables ledger eg invoicing, credit control, debt collection etc. For small businesses keen to keep their overheads down it can make sense to outsource this function to a specialist, efficient agency.

CHAPTER 8

7.3 Term loans

Definition

A **term loan** is a loan – typically but not always from a bank – where the repayment date (its termination) is set at the time of borrowing and, unlike overdrafts, they are not repayable on demand, unless the borrower defaults on repayment.

- **Interest rates** on term loans can be fixed or variable. The variable (or 'floating') rate is usually set at a certain % above base rate or LIBOR. Variable rates avoid the problem of the business being locked into a high fixed rate loan but they make cash flow planning difficult. A fixed rate loan could, of course, lock the business into a low interest rate but these are not always available
- **Arrangement fees** are usually payable on term loans, but these are small compared with issue costs for loan stocks on the Stock Exchange
- **Security**: term loans are usually secured against assets or, in smaller companies, by directors' personal guarantees
- **Flexibility**: repayment schedules are flexible and interest 'holidays' of typically up to two years can be negotiated to allow new ventures to become established before cash has to be used to repay a loan.

7.4 Loan stock

Definition

Loan stock: debt capital in the form of securities issued by companies, the government and local authorities. These are also referred to as **bonds** or **debentures**.

The holder of loan stock has much more **assurance** about what cash they will receive and when, which is attractive compared to the uncertainty faced by a shareholder.

Loan stock is both an **investment for the lender** and **borrowing for the company**, so its terms are drafted according to what the parties want.

Coupon (interest) rate	• The annual interest is the coupon rate x the nominal value of the stock eg on £100,000 nominal of 10% loan stock the annual coupon is £10,000 • Can be fixed rate (usually referred to as **bonds**), or variable rate (usually referred to as **floating rate notes**). • The coupon can sometimes be set at zero, in which circumstance the yield to investors is generated by the difference between what they buy the bond for and the redemption value. This generates a capital gain rather than income.
Redemption value	• A £100,000 loan can be repaid at par (with £100,000) or at a premium (say, £105,000) or discount (say £95,000) to the par value. In receiving £105,000 investors will find the stock more attractive and so be happier to accept a lower or zero coupon rate, which eases the company's cash flow.
Redemption date	• Loan stocks are normally medium- to long-term. Some bonds are undated (perpetual or irredeemable). • If the holder needs the capital back on undated bonds, they must sell the loan stock.
Recipient	• With UK domestic bonds issued on the London Stock Exchange, the bond holder's name is recorded on a register, as with shares. • Some bonds eg eurobonds, are 'bearer' bonds. The holder of the bond – whoever that is – will receive the payments due.

7.5 Leasing

Leasing is a particularly important source of finance and is now a common means of financing for vehicles, office and production equipment, etc.

Definition

A **finance lease** is a lease that transfers substantially all the risks and rewards of ownership of an asset from the lessor (the finance company or bank) to the lessee (the business). An **operating lease** is any other lease.

Finance lease	Operating lease
This is essentially **long-term debt finance**: a purchase of the asset by the lessee, financed by a loan from the lessor.	This is essentially the **short-term rental** of an asset.
One lease exists for the whole or major part of the asset's useful life.	The lease period is less than the asset's useful life.
Either ownership passes to the lessee at the end of the term, or any secondary lease period is at a very low rent.	Ownership remains with the lessor.
The lessor does not usually deal directly in this type of asset eg banks leasing airliners.	The lessor usually carries on a trade in this type of asset eg building contractors leasing equipment to builders.
The lessee takes on the risks or rewards of ownership eg bears the risk of downtime.	The lessor is normally responsible for repairs and maintenance.
The lease agreement cannot be cancelled or early cancellation charges mean the lessee effectively has a liability for all payments.	The lease can sometimes be cancelled at short notice.

7.6 Other forms of debt

7.6.1 Money markets

As well as using the money markets to invest surplus cash, a large business could also access them for borrowing large amounts on a **short-term** basis, ie less than a year. Transactions are typically £500,000 or more and are at comparatively **low rates of interest**.

7.6.2 Securitisation (asset-backed borrowing)

Asset-backed securitisation is a device used by banks and very large companies with highly reliable earnings streams. It involves the pooling of relatively small, homogeneous and illiquid financial assets – such as long-term loans to individuals secured by mortgages over their homes – into liquid assets which are sold to other institutions. The long-term assets – the right to receive future interest and capital payments – are replaced with cash, improving liquidity.

7.6.3 Public sector grants and loans

Both the UK government and the European Union make grants and loans to businesses at no or low cost. They are given to encourage training, research and development, investment in equipment and so on, and are often specific to particular areas in the UK.

8 Financing a growing business

Section overview

- Problems – growing businesses have particular characteristics that manifest themselves as problems in raising finance.
- Solutions – there are a diversity of sources of finance that have arisen to meet the particular issues facing growing businesses, including business angels, venture capital (VC), and the Alternative Investment Market (AIM)

Interactive question 1: Problems of small businesses [Difficulty level: Intermediate]

What are the likely characteristics of small but growing businesses that create financing problems?

See **Answer** at the end of this chapter.

Small businesses are unlisted so it is more difficult for equity investors to buy and sell shares. Small businesses therefore usually rely on retained earnings, rights issues, term loans from banks and leasing. If a business wishes to grow these sources of finance might prove insufficient, but the business may not be ready for a listing on the Londond Stock Exchange. There may be a **funding gap**, which may be met in various ways.

8.1 Business angels

Wealthy individuals investing £10,000 or more in start-up, early stage or expanding businesses. They tend to invest at an earlier stage than most formal venture capitalists (see below). In other respects they are similar in terms of investment, returns required and so on.

8.2 Venture capital (VC)

Definition

Venture capital is the provision of risk-bearing capital, usually in the form of a participation in equity, to companies with high growth potential.

A company which has potential, but with little assurance that the potential can be fulfilled, is **high risk** so providers of venture capital will expect **high returns** (eg 25%–40% per annum). In addition, the VC will often (though not always) request a presence on the board of the company. Venture capital can be distinguished from other forms of equity finance because:

- it is more **participatory** (they usually expect 20%–49.9% of the shares of a company, large enough to allow the venture capitalists to exert some control over the running of the business, but not so large that they become majority shareholders)
- it is provided with regard more for the **long term** than the short term, although the actual involvement by the VC is unlikely to extend beyond the **medium term**
- the investor provides **advice** and is able to **influence management**, but does not take on the running of the business themselves
- much of the return from providing the capital is in the form of **capital gains** after three to five years rather than steadily from the beginning, since by their nature companies needing venture capital will not be able to pay cash dividends in the early years
- a key issue is the VC's **exit route**, ie how the VC can liquidate the investment. This can be by:
  - a trade sale – the VC's shares, or indeed the whole company, is sold to another company
  - flotation
  - buy-back of shares on re-financing

8.3 Alternative Investment Market (AIM)

The AIM has **less stringent regulations** than the Main Market of the London Stock Exchange and is designed to provide an alternative source of capital for companies that are unwilling to join the Main Market but that have a substantial value (most have a value of at least £1m, though there is no minimum market capitalisation requirement for joining AIM). Entry documentation is made as simple as possible so there are **lower entry costs** but the **annual cost of listing** on the AIM is still at least £25,000.

Interactive question 2: Financing a business through its growth phase

[Difficulty level: Intermediate]

Ian's Sandwich Empire

Ian starts up on his own selling sandwiches from home, and the business develops into a national one over time. Given the characteristics at each stage, suggest possible sources of finance.

Stage	Characteristics	Possible sources of finance
Start-up	Very small scale. Make at home. Deliver by car to local customers (offices, trading estates etc).	
Growth to £100,000 revenue pa	Need small premises and a van.	
(Organic) growth to £500,000 revenue pa	Need new larger premises with refrigeration and refrigerated vans.	
Growth to £2 million revenue pa by acquisition	Established a brand/name/reputation and wants to expand regionally.	
Growth to £5 million revenue pa	Want to use brand/name/reputation more widely – sell ready-made sandwiches to local independent retail outlets and local branches of national retail chains (using their brand) on credit.	
Growth to £50 million revenue pa	Expand to national scale, by combination of organic growth and acquisition.	

See **Answer** at the end of this chapter.

9 Financing exports

Section overview

- Overseas trade raises additional trading risks, which include physical, credit, trade and liquidity risks.
- Credit (irrecoverable debt) risks can be reduced in a variety of ways, including the use of bills of exchange, letters of credit and export credit guarantees.

9.1 Trading risks

Both importers and exporters will face risks which are greater than those faced by domestic traders as a consequence of **political risk** and **cultural risk** as well as the increased distances and times involved.

Types of trading risk include:

- **Physical risk** – the risk of goods being lost or stolen in transit, or the documents accompanying the goods going astray
- **Credit risk** – the possibility of payment default by the customer. This is discussed further below

- **Trade risk** – the risk of the customer refusing to accept the goods on delivery (due to substandard/inappropriate goods), or the cancellation of the order in transit
- **Liquidity risk** – the inability to finance the credit given to customers

Such risks may be reduced with the help of **banks, insurance companies, credit reference agencies** and the **government's export credit agency,** UK Export Finance (the trading name of the Export Credits Guarantee Department (ECGD)).

Other ways to reduce these risks include **risk transfer**. For example a business shipping parcels overseas may agree a contract obliging the courier to pay for losses in excess of its statutory liability.

9.2 Reducing credit risk

Methods of minimising credit or irrecoverable debt risks are broadly similar to those for domestic trade: the company should **vet the creditworthiness of each customer,** and **grant credit terms accordingly**. There are further methods however in particular relation to foreign trade.

9.2.1 Bills of exchange

A bill of exchange is a document that is drawn up by the exporter (seller) and sent to the overseas buyer's bank, which **accepts the obligation to pay the bill by signing it**. Payment is therefore guaranteed by the buyer's bank, which means that the seller can then sell or 'discount' the bill to a third party in return for cash now. Thus the procedure both **mitigates the risk of irrecoverable debts** and can also **provide liquidity**.

9.2.2 Letters of credit

Letters of credit provide a method of payment in international trade which gives the exporter a risk-free method of obtaining payment. The arrangement must be made between the exporter, the buyer and participating banks **before the export sale takes place.**

- The **exporter receives immediate payment** of the amount due to him, less the discount, instead of having to wait for payment until the end of the credit period allowed to the buyer
- The buyer is able to get a **period of credit** before having to pay for the imports.

Documentary credits are **slow to arrange**, and **administratively cumbersome**; however, they are usually essential where the **risk of non-payment is high**, or when dealing for the first time with an **unknown buyer**.

The **procedures** are as follows where there is a UK exporter and a foreign buyer, say in Brazil (obviously it could work equally well for a Brazilian seller and a UK importer).

- The parties first of all agree a contract for the sale of the goods, which provides for payment through a letter of credit.
- The **buyer** then requests a bank in Brazil to issue a **letter of credit** in favour of the exporter. This bank is known as the **issuing bank.**
- The issuing bank, by issuing its letter of credit, **guarantees payment** to the exporter. Banks are involved in the credits, not in the underlying contracts.
- The issuing bank asks a bank in the UK to **advise the credit** to the exporter.
- The **advising bank** in the UK agrees to **handle the credit** on terms arranged with the issuing bank in Brazil.

9.2.3 Export credit insurance

Definition

Export credit insurance is insurance against the risk of non-payment by foreign customers for export debts.

Some **private companies** provide credit insurance for short-term export credit business, and the UK government's **Export Credits Guarantee Department (ECGD)** (known as UK Export Finance) provides long-term guarantees to banks on behalf of exporters.

Export credit insurance is not essential if exporters are reasonably confident that all their customers are trustworthy, but it helps cover some of the **special risks involved in exporting**.

- **Time**: If an export customer defaults on payment, the task of pursuing the case through the courts will be lengthy, and it might be a long time before payment is eventually obtained.
- **Variety**: export credit insurance covers non-payment for a variety of risks (described below), not just the buyer's failure to pay on time.

The guarantee contained in short-term export credit protects against non-payment by an overseas customer as a consequence of: the creditworthiness of the foreign buyer (**buyer risks**) and also the economic and political risks in the overseas country (**country risks**). Particular aspects of these two risk types are as follows:

Buyer risks	Country risks
Insolvency of the buyer	A **general moratorium** on debts to overseas suppliers which might be decreed by the government of the buyer's country
The **buyer's failure to pay** within six months of the due date, in cases where the buyer has accepted the goods sent to him by the exporter	**Political events**, **economic difficulties**, legislative measures or administrative measures arising outside the UK which prevent or delay payments under the contract
The **buyer's failure** to **accept the goods** sent to him (*provided* non-acceptance of the goods has not been caused or excused by the exporter's own actions, and the insurer decides it would serve no useful purpose for the exporter to take up or pursue legal proceedings against the buyer)	A **'shortfall' in revenue** to the exporter caused by **foreign exchange losses** when the exporter has to accept payment in a local currency for a debt which should be paid in sterling

10 Personal financial management

Section overview

- Key stages in the personal financial management (financial capability) process:
  - Establish individual objectives
  - Establish individual attitude to risk
  - Establish individual circumstances: stage in life cycle, age and commitments; risk profile; degree of control/budgeting
  - Identify and take appropriate action
- Sources of borrowing for individuals: secured (mortgages); unsecured (overdraft, credit card, personal loans, hire purchase)
- Savings and investments cover short-term and long-term needs.
- Key risks for individual investors: capital loss, falling short of target, lower interest rates than anticipated, inflation
- Insurance products represent the 'sharing' aspect of risk management so that individuals and their families are better protected from unexpected adverse events
- Personal financial management extends to retirement planning and estate planning

Personal financial management or **financial capability** is a broad concept, encompassing an individual person's knowledge and skills to understand their own financial circumstances, along with the motivation to take action. Financially capable consumers plan ahead, find and use information, know when to seek advice and can understand and act on this advice, leading to greater prosperity.

Definition

Financial capability: an individual being able to manage money, keeping track of their finances, plan ahead, choose financial products and stay informed about financial matters.

If a person were to sit down and develop a strategy for their own personal financial management – rather as a business does – the key issues they would address are as follows:

- What are my financial and other **objectives**?
- What is my **attitude to risk**?
- What are my current **individual circumstances**?
- What is my current **income and expenditure**?
- What immediate **action** do I need to take?
  - Borrowing
  - Investment and saving
  - Protection
  - Retirement planning
  - Estate planning

We shall look at each of these issues now.

10.1 Individual objectives and attitude to risk

At any particular point in time any individual is likely to have a number of **objectives**, for which some financial provision may be required. Examples of such **objectives in the short to medium term** include:

- Saving for a deposit on a house
- Paying for a child's university education
- Retraining
- Covering the cost of caring for small children
- Replacing a car
- Clearing credit card and other unsecured debt

Achievement of these **short to medium term objectives may be seen as essential by the individual,** but the same individual might have other **longer term objectives** in mind as well:

- Starting a business
- Going on a 'dream' holiday
- Buying a vintage car
- Owning a second home
- Retiring early

These **longer term objectives may be seen as less essential to the individual**; they are something the person accepts that they will have to do without if returns are not sufficient.

The effect of the relative difference in immediate importance of objectives to the individual therefore is that:

- **less risk** is desirable in the achievement of **short to medium term or high priority objectives,** even though this means **lower returns** will be expected
- **more risk** is acceptable in relation to achievement of the **longer term or lower priority objectives**, in the hope that this will create **higher returns** and so increase the chance of the objectives being achieved

Every individual is different, and the ways in which people rank their objectives and their **risk attitude** in relation to different objectives vary. For one person, having enough money to spend on a comfortable home may take a higher priority than having the finance to travel widely. Another person may treat travelling as a higher priority than spending on a home.

10.2 Individual circumstances

There are various **life stages**, and people have **differing financial needs** and **differing risk profiles**.

10.2.1 Life cycle, age and commitments

Individual circumstances may differ widely, but some aspects of common **life stages** encountered in different **approximate** typical **age groups** are described below.

- **Minors (under 18)**. A person under 18 may have very little in the way of financial management to do. They are likely to be dependent on one or two parents and nobody is going to suffer financially if they run out of money. A parent or grandparent who wants to give the minor a 'head start' is able to open a stakeholder pension for a child of any age, but the most important consideration at this age is **education** and having a **plan for a good career**.
- **Single and working (18 to 30).** A person in their early to mid-twenties may not yet have any dependants but may be financially independent of their parents even if they are still living at home. They may be renting a flat or possibly even **buying a home**. They are unlikely to have accumulated much capital as they may just spend everything they earn. They are more likely to be **employed** than self-employed. **Retirement planning** is worth starting in this age band: the effect of compounding of returns means that investment in retirement savings from a relatively early age can pay off.
- **Couple working but no dependants (20 to 30).** No longer dependent on parents, they will be earning and either renting or **buying a home**. This is the time when a couple will be **building up their income** at the fastest possible rate before the expenses of looking after children begin.
- **One or both of a couple working, with dependants (25 to 40).** The vital issue is to **maximise income** so that dependants can be supported, but **expenditure** (on childcare etc) is likely to use up most or all of income.
- **Couple with older children (35 to 50).** This is the point when the **expenditure** is probably at its highest. University costs increase the burden. The couple may again have two incomes and possibly even have a **higher net income** despite the higher level of expenses.
- **After children: 'empty nesters' (45 to 60).** When children have left home, their parents have their **highest net income** as a result of lower expenses relating to children. This is the key time for **saving** and **investment.**
- **Retired (60 or 65 plus).** Significantly **lower income** than when working is offset by **savings** that have been built up. The individual has more free time, which they may or may not wish to devote to managing their finances and ensuring that grandchildren are well provided for.

10.2.2 An individual's risk profile

Every individual has their own views, aspirations and attitudes. **Attitudes to risk** vary widely, and this particularly affects **savings and investment choices**. Some individuals will be reluctant to take on any significant risk of loss of their capital, while others are prepared to 'gamble' to a degree with their savings.

Attitudes to risk vary according to the different **objectives of the investor**. An investor may have a core amount of money as ready cash (effectively with **no risk)** that they wish to keep as an emergency fund, while they may be prepared to take greater risks with other money they hold.

10.2.3 Personal budgeting

Just like a business, an individual should make sure they **budget** for their personal finances. Constructing a simple **spreadsheet** is an easy way to set out such a budget and make sure that nothing gets forgotten. People who know how they spend their money will generally have better control over their personal finances than those who do not budget.

Every individual is different but the following categories for a budget are typical:

Income	Outgoings
Gross earnings from job or self-employment	Tax
Pensions from former employers or personal pension	Mortgage, rent, home maintenance
	Council tax
State pension	Utility bills
Child benefit, tax credits and other state benefits	Food, drink and personal care
Interest from savings accounts	Clothing and footwear
Income from investments (shares, unit trusts etc)	Household goods
	Travel (car, train etc)
	Holidays
	Social life

10.3 Taking action

Having established one's objectives and attitude to risk, and having worked out one's budget, the consumer should proceed as follows:

- If outgoings exceed income, there is an income shortfall: cut back on spending to keep it within income. For example, if there are borrowings, there may be ways of re-arranging these so that the overall interest burden is lower. A further advance might be sought on a mortgage, at relatively low cost, to replace higher-cost credit card, personal loan or other borrowings. In this type of case, the costs of re-arranging loans should be considered.
- If income exceeds outgoings, you could put your **surplus income towards achieving your financial objectives.**

Budgeting can also be an excellent aid to planning possible **changes in an individual's circumstances.** For example:

- What will be the impact on a family's finances if a child is sent to a fee-paying school for their two final years of schooling? A budget covering the years concerned will help to show whether this can be financed from income, or whether loans may be required or investments may need to be sold.
- What will be the effect of a salary earner switching to part-time working? Expenditure may be affected as well as income: travel-to-work costs may be lower, although there could be additional costs if the person is planning to take up new interests as part of the change in lifestyle.

We shall now look briefly at the areas in which action is possibly needed by an individual who has taken control of their personal financial management.

10.4 Borrowing

We saw earlier in this chapter how the financial system plays a role in channelling money from those who have a **surplus** to invest to those who wish or need to **borrow.** We also looked at **how businesses borrow.**

In this section we shall see that the key distinction when it comes to individual borrowing is whether the borrowing is **secured** on assets (typically the individuals' home) or **unsecured.**

10.4.1 Secured borrowing: mortgages

For most people, home purchase is the largest type of transaction they will enter into in the course of their lives. Most home buyers are not able to finance the purchase of a home from their own capital resources and so will usually seek a **loan** from a bank, building society or other lender to finance the purchase.

Definition

A mortgage is a loan given on the **security** of a property. The borrower (the mortgagor) 'mortgages' the property: that is, the borrower creates a legal **charge** over the property to the lender (the mortgagee), as security for the loan.

The process is usually as follows:

- The purchaser pays a proportion of the purchase price of a property – the **deposit** – and the balance is provided as a **loan** by the mortgage lender.
- The **interest rate** on the loan may be fixed (for at least part of the mortgage's term) or variable, often in relation to base rate (a 'tracker' mortgage). Because the loan is secured, the **risk for the lender is lower** and so the **interest rate on mortgages is typically lower than for unsecured borrowing.**
- The loan is normally repayable not later than the end of a **fixed term** (usually 25 years) which is agreed at the inception of the loan.
- The borrower gives the lender **legal rights over the property** for the duration of the loan. While the loan is outstanding, the property remains the lender's **security** that the loan will be repaid. The borrower cannot sell the property without repaying the mortgage, and if they do not make the required repayments on the loan ('default'), after going through appropriate steps **the lender can gain the right to take possession of the property**, sell it, recover the amount of the loan (assuming the sale price is higher than the loan) and pay the balance after costs to the borrower.
- The loan is finally **repaid** according to the terms of the mortgage, so the legal rights over the property revert back to the owner at the end of the mortgage term.

There are two main **types of mortgage**.

- **Capital and interest** (also called a **repayment mortgage**)
- **Interest only mortgage**, which is normally combined with a **repayment vehicle** (such as an endowment policy) which will repay the capital at maturity.

10.4.2 Unsecured borrowing

Borrowing that is not secured on property comes in various forms. Given the lack of security, the **risk for the lender is greater so the cost to the borrower is higher** than for mortgages.

- **Current account overdraft:** as for a business, an individual bank or building society customer will pay variable rate interest, typically on a daily basis, on the amount by which they overdraw their current account. If the customer exceeds authorised overdraft limits, a higher interest rate may be charged, and the bank may try to impose further charges because the account conditions have been breached.
- **Credit card borrowing**: the account will have an authorised credit limit and interest (usually at a variable rate) is charged on the balance on the account, normally after an initial interest free period depending on the credit card statement date. If the full balance is paid off each month, no interest is charged.
- **Personal loans:** the individual borrows a specific sum at a fixed rate and makes regular payments of capital and interest over the loan's term (usually two to five years). Payments early in the loan's term therefore consist mainly of interest, while later payments include a greater proportion of capital repayment.
- **Hire purchase:** this is similar to a **finance lease** taken out by a business, so the customer does not own the item being purchased (for example, a car) until all the payments have been made.

10.5 Investment and saving

Savings and investment needs can be divided into **short- and long-term needs.**

- The **short-term need** may be for a car or a holiday, for which an obvious type of **savings** vehicle will be a **deposit account**, such as a bank or building society account.
- **Longer-term needs** could include **investing** for retirement or providing capital for children as they reach adulthood. These can include a huge variety of investment vehicles, including equities, bonds, investment and unit trusts, commodities such as gold, and property.

An important consideration is **ease of access**. This will influence whether money is:

- **saved** - easy, short-term vehicles which are highly liquid at lower risk and lower return, including an emergency fund which may be needed at very short notice, so it should not be tied up in accounts that do not permit easy withdrawals or
- **invested** - more complex, long-term access which are much less liquid and at (possibly) higher risk and higher return.

Risk is very important in relation to savings and investments. The **risks** faced by an individual investor can be categorised as follows.

- **Capital risk** is the risk of losing part or all of the capital invested.
- **Shortfall risk** applies when there is a financial target, and this is the risk that the chosen investments will fail to meet the target amount.
- **Interest risk** is a term we can apply to interest-bearing investments and describes the risk that interest received will be lower than it might have been.
- **Inflation risk** describes the risk that rising prices will reduce the purchasing power of what is invested.

An individual with a relatively large amount of money to invest should aim for a **diversified investment portfolio** made up of different **asset classes**, mixing lower-risk **deposits** or **bond** investments with higher-risk **property** and **equity** investments.

You will cover more about diversifying risk, plus the tax aspects of investments, in your Professional level studies.

10.6 Protection

Life always involves **risk** of various kinds and a key part of personal financial management involves **risk management.** In Chapter 5 we saw that meant a combination of:

- **Avoidance**: not doing the risky activity,
- **Reduction**: doing the activity, but using whatever means are available to ensure that the probability of the event occurring and the impact if it does are as small as possible,
- **Sharing**: taking out **insurance** against the risk involved in the activity, and then
- **Acceptance**: of the remaining risk

Insurance therefore is a means of sharing the risk that we are not prepared just to accept, so that the individual has adequate protection against the occurrence of risks.

- The need to comply with **regulation** requires an individual to have some types of insurance, such as **motor insurance** and **employers' liability insurance**
- Other external requirements necessitate some types of insurance, such as a mortgagor requiring the mortgagee to obtain **buildings insurance**
- The need to **protect oneself** in the event of harm leads people to take out insurance against **sickness, injury, long-term disability redundancy** and **theft of possessions**
- The need to **protect one's dependants** leads people to take out **life insurance**

10.7 Retirement planning

Longer life expectancies and lower birth rates than in the past have all contributed to the relative ageing of our population. There are more people who are over retirement age than in the past. Planning for retirement, when people need money to meet expenses, but no longer have their full working income, is an important issue at the level of national policy as well as for the individual.

The issues to be considered are:

- Planned **age** of retirement
- **Income expectations** for retirement
- Whether there are expected to be **dependants**, such as a spouse, children or grandchildren, during retirement
- What **assets** will be available at retirement, including businesses, property, investments, savings and pension funds
- What provision from the **state** can be expected, such as the state pension

10.8 Estate planning

Someone's **estate** is the wealth they leave when they die. **Estate planning** is therefore concerned with:

- how that wealth is passed on to beneficiaries, who may typically be children or grandchildren. The sensible option being to make a **will** so that who gets what is clear – this is a specialist area
- how far the estate's liability for **inheritance tax** (due on death) can be minimised – this topic is covered at the Professional level.

Summary and Self-test

Summary

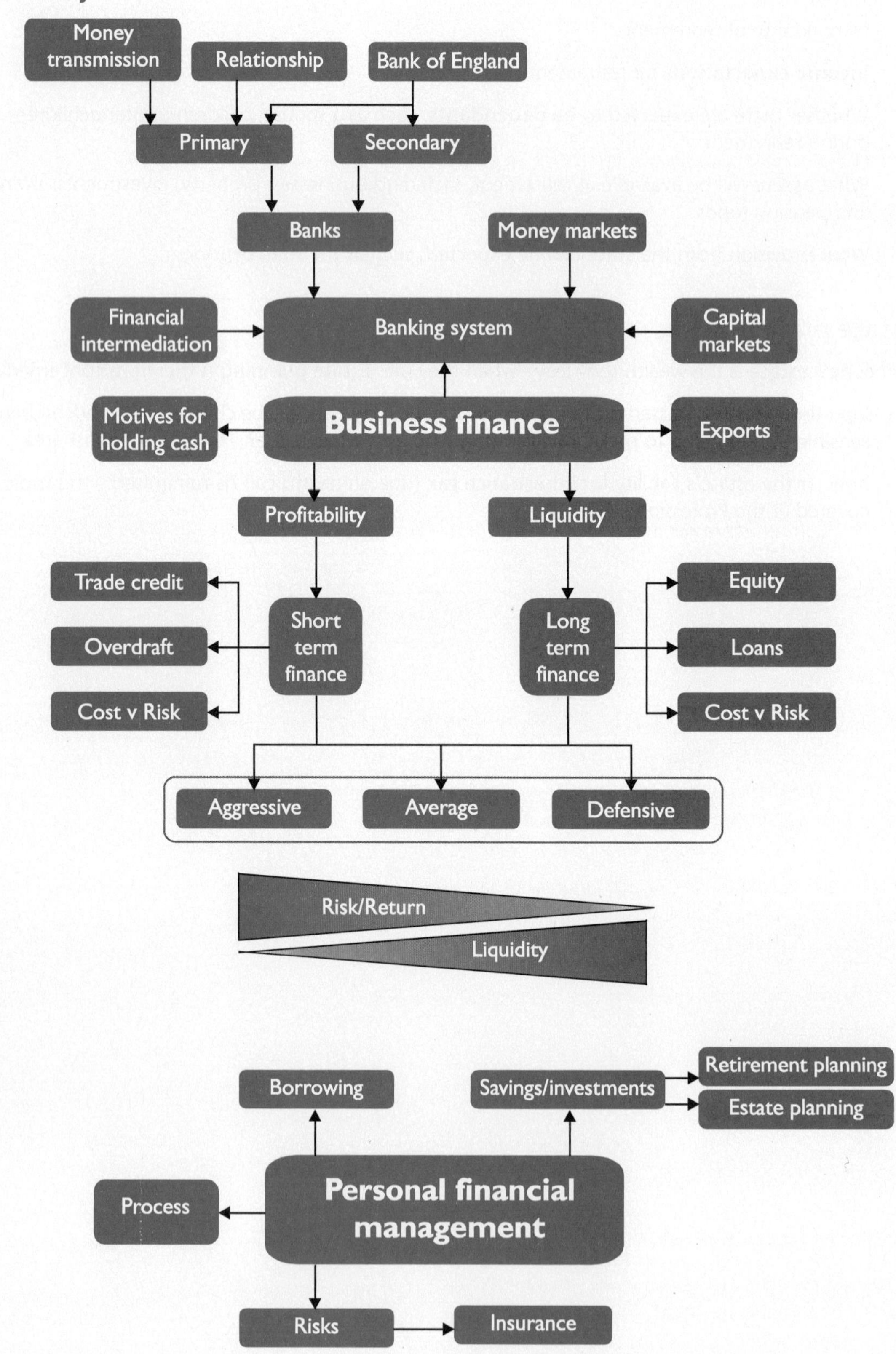

Self-test

Answer the following questions.

1 Capital markets in the UK are split into

A The London Stock Exchange and the Bank of England
B Stock markets and bond markets
C Primary and secondary markets
D Securities markets and banks

2 Which of the following are financial intermediaries?

A Retail banks
B Merchant banks
C Building societies
D Insurance companies
E Pension funds

3 Which of the following is NOT an alternative name for a primary bank?

A Retail bank
B Commercial bank
C Merchant bank
D Clearing bank

4 A bank's loan to a customer is secured by a charge on the customer's house. Who is the mortgagor and who is the mortgagee?

5 What is a fiduciary relationship?

6 List three rights and three duties of a banker.

7 A .... is a loan for a fixed amount for a specified period.

8 With a finance lease, who is responsible for upkeep of the asset?

A The lessor
B The lessee

9 Which of the following sources of finance to companies is the most widely used in practice?

A Bank borrowings
B Rights issues
C New share issues
D Retained earnings

10 Debentures are more similar to equity than preference shares.

A True
B False

11 Holders of loan stock are long-term receivables of the company.

A True
B False

12 Why should a non-current asset NOT be financed by current liabilities?

Now, go back to the Learning Objectives in the Introduction. If you are satisfied you have achieved these objectives, please tick them off.

Answers to Interactive questions

Answer to Interactive question 1

Financing problems of small businesses	
Management	A lack of knowledge about the possible sources of finance available, and a potential lack of financial acumen, may compound the inherent problems facing a small business
History	Businesses in their early stages of development are small. Such businesses lack any convincing trading history upon which potential investors can rely, making them unattractive investments
Size	A small business will lack assets to offer as security. It will also have less diversity of products and markets to spread risk, and the small scale of business will not generate reliable cash flows, all of which preclude investment finance

Answer to Interactive question 2

Stage	Characteristics	Possible sources of funds
Start-up	Very small scale. Make at home. Deliver by car to local customers (offices, trading estates etc).	Savings or second mortgage on home. Borrow from family and friends (no security or past record, so bank reluctant to lend).
Growth to £100,000 revenue pa	Need small premises and a van.	Borrowing from bank to purchase premises (secured by premises and personal guarantees) or lease premises. Possibly grant, but unlikely as not innovating, employing people in an area of high unemployment (eg former coalfield) or manufacturing.
(Organic) growth to £500,000 revenue pa	Need new larger premises with refrigeration and refrigerated vans.	Borrowings from bank secured by premises or lease. Become a limited company (Ltd) and bring in new shareholders/money. Possibly grant, as it may be possible to site the new premises in an area offering grants to create employment.
Growth to £2 million revenue pa by acquisition	Established a brand/name/reputation and wants to expand regionally.	(Secured) bank borrowings remain. Acquisition is higher risk; main possibilities: • Issue more shares. • Venture capital or business angels (although they tend to prefer bigger deals than this). • Loans (at higher interest than bank, acknowledging the higher risk and lack of security).

Stage	Characteristics	Possible sources of funds
Growth to £5 million revenue pa	Want to use brand/name/reputation more widely – sell ready-made sandwiches to local independent retail outlets and local branches of national retail chains (using their brand) on credit.	Main sources likely to be: • Continuing bank borrowings (secured). • Venture capital or business angels. (Now at a viable size for this) • Loans/debentures. • Invoice discounting (now they have receivables and they are reputable).
Growth to £50 million revenue pa	Expand to national scale, by combination of organic growth and acquisition.	Convert to plc and float on Stock Exchange (AIM or Main Market).

CHAPTER 8

Answers to Self-test

1	C	Securities markets comprise stock markets and bond markets; together with banks they operate in the primary capital market (ie as a source of funds for business), but they also act as the secondary market which ensures that holders of securities can sell and buy securities so as to manage their wealth
2		All of them.
3	C	A merchant bank is a secondary bank
4		The customer is the mortgagor and the bank is the mortgagee.
5		A relationship based on trust in which the superior party must act in good faith.
6		Examples of rights include: to levy reasonable charges and commissions; to use customer's money in a legal and morally acceptable way; and to be repaid overdrawn balances on demand. Examples of duties include: to honour customers' cheques; to receive customers' funds; to comply with customers' instructions; and to provide statements in a reasonable time.
7		A term loan is a loan for a fixed amount for a specified period.
8	B	The lessee.
9	D	Retained earnings
10	B	False. Debentures are a form of loan stock and are more similar to preference shares as there is usually a fixed rate of interest
11	B	False. They are long-term PAYABLES of the company.
12		When the loan becomes repayable, the company cannot be certain that it will have generated enough profits to repay the loan.

CHAPTER 9

The professional accountant

Introduction

Examination context

Topic List

1 Introduction to the accountancy profession
2 The importance of the accountancy profession
3 Professional responsibility
4 Technical competence
5 The work of the accountancy profession
6 Professional principles
7 Accounting principles
8 Accounting standards
9 Roles of the professional accountant
10 Limits of the professional accountant's responsibilities

Summary and Self-test

Technical reference

Answers to Interactive questions

Answers to Self-test

Introduction

Learning objectives

Tick off

- Identify the importance to the public interest of high quality, accurate financial reporting and assurance ☐
- Specify the rationale for key parts of the accountancy profession's work ☐
- Specify the links between technical competence and professional responsibility ☐
- Specify the rationale for accounting principles, accounting standards, sound business management and the public interest ☐

Specific syllabus references are: 4a, b.

Syllabus links

The topic of professionalism in accounting underlies many areas of the Certificate, Professional and Advanced syllabuses.

Examination context

Questions on the professional accountant will almost certainly appear in your exam.

Questions are likely to be set in multiple choice format and in a scenario context, though knowledge-type questions are also likely on particular definitions and principles.

1 Introduction to the accountancy profession

Section overview

- A professional has skill, technical competence and professional values.
- The accountancy profession is concerned with assurance and financial reporting so that people may make resource allocation decisions.

The **accountancy profession** started to take shape as an organised group of professionals in the early to mid-nineteenth century. Initially it grew as a result of the commercial and legal activities involved in personal bankruptcy, and the insolvency and winding up of limited companies, but from quite early on the profession began to incorporate many of the features that are familiar today. **The Institute of Chartered Accountants in England and Wales** was formed in 1880 by Royal Charter; the earliest accountancy societies can be traced back to Scotland in 1853.

For the purpose of this chapter the term '**professional accountant**' is limited in meaning to a member of the ICAEW.

Definitions

Professional: A person who 'professes' to have skill resulting from a coherent course of study and training based on professional values, and who continues to develop and enhance those skills by experience and continuing professional education.

Accountancy: the profession of accounting which comprises measurement, preparation, validation, disclosure, auditing of and provision of assurance and advisory services on financial information.
Accountancy profession: The profession concerned with the measurement, disclosure or provision of assurance about financial information that helps managers, investors, tax authorities and other decision makers make resource allocation decisions.

Thus at the heart of the accounting profession are:

- Financial reporting, and
- Assurance

Definitions

Financial reporting: The provision of financial information about an entity to external users that is useful to them in making decisions and for assessing the stewardship of the entity's management.

Assurance: The expression of an opinion or conclusion by a professional accountant in public practice which is designed to enhance the confidence of intended users.

Interactive question 1: Accountancy profession [Difficulty level: Intermediate]

Think back to when you first decided that you wished to follow a career as a professional chartered accountant. What were your motives? What were the reactions of your friends and family? Would they have been different if you had chosen a career in general management under a large company's Management Trainee Scheme? If so, where did the differences lie? What did the term 'profession' mean to you then, and what does it mean now?

See **Answer** at the end of this chapter.

2 The importance of the accountancy profession

Section overview

- The accountancy profession is concerned with supporting the effective working of capital markets and the public interest.
- Because accountancy is technically complex, the public interest is best served by having access to professionals on whom they can rely.
- Public confidence in accountants is driven by their integrity (professional responsibility) and expertise (technical competence).

The work of the accountancy profession is most important and relevant to supporting:

- The effective working of capital markets, and
- The public interest.

2.1 The effective working of capital markets

The accountancy profession is actively involved in ensuring that organisations (both private and public sector) have access to **sufficient finance**. We have covered sources of finance in Chapter 8.

The capital markets can only operate effectively where there is accurate and open information which can be used by investors and other providers of finance to make decisions, as we saw in Chapter 6. If there is **inadequate information**, or if information is available to some people and not others (**asymmetric information**), then some or all investors are at a disadvantage. They will not make optimum decisions and will not make the returns that they seek. Ultimately confidence in the capital markets will erode, and the source of new capital for business would dry up.

If financial statements demonstrate the **qualitative characteristics** that we saw in Chapter 6, they are more likely to be relied upon by investors. **Hence it is in ensuring that there is high quality, accurate financial reporting and assurance that the professional accountant supports the effective working of capital markets for the benefit of businesses.**

We shall be seeing in Chapter 13 more about how (capital) **market failures** can undermine certain aspects of business.

2.2 The public interest

The public interest is in fact a fairly abstract notion. Who exactly is included in the term 'public', and how do we know what best serves their interest? However, a wording is used in the ICAEW Code of Ethics which we shall adopt here:

Definition

Public interest: the legitimate interests of clients, government, financial institutions, employers, employees, investors, the business and financial community and others who rely upon the objectivity and integrity of the accounting profession (ICAEW Code of Ethics s100.1)

Working in the public interest means that professional accountants must keep up to date with the expectations of society in order to fulfill their role and build confidence in the profession. But how far should the public interest be served specifically by the accounting profession?

> 'Many of the areas in which professional accountants operate are **technically complex**. They provide advice on which others, such as shareholders in audited companies, may rely. It is therefore crucially important that the public should have confidence in [their] **integrity**.'
>
> *Regulation within the accounting profession in the UK: an ICAEW perspective*

It is **confidence** in the profession's **expertise** and **integrity** as demonstrated in high quality **financial reporting** and **assurance** that is most crucial:

> 'Public and investor confidence in financial reporting is achieved through the publication of consistently high quality reports that are informative, relevant and transparent and free of material misstatements, whether caused by errors, disclosure deficiencies, erroneous interpretations or intentional manipulation. Maintaining this confidence requires **expertise** and **integrity** across the profession.'

Review of Training and Education in the Accountancy Profession, Professional Oversight Board (POB) April 2005

This links **professional accountants in business** – the accountants who, as members of boards of directors or in exercise of the authority devolved by boards of directors, are responsible for preparing a company's financial statements – with **professional accountants in public practice** who, as auditors or as professionals on other assurance engagements, are responsible for reporting on these statements.

To be seen to have integrity as well as expertise, the professional accountant needs:

> 'A strong foundation in **professional values** and in the practical aspects of how these relate to the needs of users of accounts, including investors in capital markets... [S/he] should have a clear line of sight from **accounting principles** through **accounting standards** and other regulation to **high quality financial reporting and governance** and the **public interest**.'

Review of Training and Education in the Accountancy Profession, POB April 2005

A key issue is that an accountant's **ethical behaviour** serves to **protect the public interest**. The ICAEW Code of Ethics s100.1 makes it clear that a distinguishing mark of the accountancy profession is its acceptance of the **responsibility to act in the public interest**. It states that this involves:

> 'Acting in the public interest involves having regard to the legitimate interests of clients, government, financial institutions, employers, employees, investors, the business and financial community and others who rely upon the **objectivity** and **integrity** of the accounting profession to support the propriety and orderly functioning of commerce. This reliance imposes a public interest responsibility on the profession. Professional accountants should take into consideration the public interest and reasonable and informed public perception in deciding whether to accept or continue with an engagement or appointment, bearing in mind that the level of the public interest will be greater in larger entities and entities which are in the public eye.'

ICAEW Code of Ethics Section 100.1

A key consequence of working in the public interest is that **ICAEW members must report acts of misconduct** which, if they were to go unreported, could adversely affect the good name of the profession.

The ICAEW Code of Ethics is issued to all members and states five fundamental **professional principles or values** with which the professional accountant in public practice must comply in carrying out their work (100.5). The first two principles, **integrity** and **objectivity**, are highlighted above as being the qualities which underlie the reliance of the public on accountants.

This means that a professional accountant should show:

- Professional responsibility (integrity)
- Technical competence (expertise)

3 Professional responsibility

Section overview

- People who have less expertise must be able to trust accountants, who have more. The ICAEW Code of Ethics is a conceptual approach to professional ethics so that members of the ICAEW can ensure that they warrant that trust.
- To ensure integrity the ICAEW Code of Ethics has five fundamental principles and also sets out the types of threat to these principles that arise, and the sorts of safeguard that can protect against the threats.
- To maintain public confidence in its members' technical competence the ICAEW has a regulatory role that ensures: rigorous entry and education requirements; additional requirements for

accountants in public and some other types of practice; a requirement for PII for accountants in public practice.

- To ensure public confidence further, the Financial Reporting Council (FRC) operates an oversight mechanism over how the ICAEW self-regulates.

3.1 Trust and ethical behaviour

Many of the areas in which professional accountants operate are technically complex. Advice is provided on which others, such as shareholders in audited companies, may rely. It is therefore important that the public should have confidence in the integrity of professional accountants: they should be able to **trust** accountants, so professional accountants should **behave ethically**.

- An accountant's ethical behaviour serves to protect the **public interest**, as we have seen.
- Ethical issues may be a matter of **law and regulation** and accountants are expected to apply them.
- By upholding professional standards, the profession's **reputation and standing** are protected.
- Consequences of unethical behaviour include **disciplinary action** against the accountant by their employer, ICAEW or the FRC (which we shall cover later in this Study Manual) and **adverse effects** on jobs, financial viability and business efficacy of their organisation.
- Accountants employed in the public sector have a duty to **protect tax-payers' money**.

3.2 The ICAEW Code of Ethics: a conceptual framework

There are two theoretical approaches that can be followed by a governing body such as the ICAEW when developing a code of ethics for its members.

- **Compliance-based approach** (also known as **rules-based**): the governing body will attempt to anticipate every possible ethical situation and lay down specific rules for members to follow. As with law, members are expected to follow the rules and will be accountable if they breach them – effectively members are legally bound. It is often called a 'tick box' approach to ethics and is well established in the US.
- **Ethics-based approach** (also known as **framework-based**): principles are set out which describe the fundamental values and qualities that members should embody. There is no attempt to prescribe detailed rules but general guidelines are developed to give advice on how certain situations should be handled. This approach means members follow examples of good or best practice.

The ICAEW follows the ethics-based approach, having developed a Code of Ethics which is a **conceptual framework**. Professional accountants must comply with its five **fundamental principles** (integrity, objectivity, professional competence and due care, confidentiality and professional behaviour). 'Fundamental' in this context means the principles form the **bedrock of professional judgements, decisions, reasoning** and **practice**. ICAEW members must not only **know** them, but also **apply** them in their everyday work.

The Code identifies potential **threats** to the principles and some corresponding **safeguards**. This conceptual framework enables members to apply ethical standards consistently in a rapidly changing business environment. Because the balance of threats and safeguards must be considered in each case, there is no opportunity to 'get round' rules by sticking to the letter but not the spirit of the requirements.

We shall see a little later in this chapter how these principles were developed, what exactly they mean and how they help to ensure professional responsibility in practice.

3.3 Regulation of the accountancy profession

As well as requiring professional accountants in public practice to live by the fundamental professional principles, the accountancy profession has other methods by which public confidence is maintained in the professional responsibility of accountants. **Professional regulation by the ICAEW** itself entails:

Rigorous entry and education requirements	Together these help to ensure **technical competence**.
Specific additional requirements for professional accountants engaged in the reserved areas of audit, investment business and insolvency work	
Professional accountants in public practice to hold professional indemnity insurance (PII)	
Oversight regulation of the ICAEW's professional regulation of its members by the Financial Reporting Council (FRC)	We shall come back to these points in Chapter 10.
A rigorous complaints procedure involving the ICAEW and, ultimately, the FRC	

4 Technical competence

Section overview

- The ICAEW's entry and education requirements aim to ensure that accountants have the knowledge, understanding, skills, abilities, personal commitment and professional abilities required.
- There are further requirements regarding continuing membership, and regarding accountants in reserved areas of practice.

4.1 The ICAEW's entry and education requirements

The success of the accountancy profession in the UK has always been closely identified with its **commitment to training and education**. The principal requirements for initial admission to membership of the ICAEW are:

- Two passes at **A level** or the equivalent
- Completion of at least three years' **training** with an approved training organisation
- Completion of a course of **theoretical instruction**
- Passing the ICAEW's **professional examinations**
- Submission of a **certificate of suitability for membership** signed by the member responsible for training
- Payment of the **admission and subscription fees**

By undertaking prescribed training and education the student accountant is:

- Acquiring the **knowledge and understanding** that underlie what accountants do
- Developing the **skills and abilities** necessary to perform the tasks and roles undertaken by the professional accountant
- Building **personal commitment** and **professional principles**

Accounting training covers both **fundamental values** and **competencies** and increasing quantities of **technical knowledge** and **skills** in tax, financial reporting, governance and related assurance requirements. A balance is needed between knowing the underlying principles and rules that apply to all or most transactions and knowing detailed requirements related to specialised transactions. There is an increasingly strong argument that the ability to read, understand and apply principles and rules is more important in students and newly-qualified accountants than knowledge of detailed technical rules.

Most importantly students should be able to:

- Apply **basic accounting skills**
- Understand the **accounting principles** underlying financial reporting and assurance
- Understand what the **numbers** that come out of the reporting process are telling them

4.2 Continuing membership of ICAEW

To **continue in membership** all professional accountants must:

- Obey the Institute's **rules and regulations**
- Pay the **subscription fee** annually, and
- Undertake **continuing professional development (CPD)**: this involves certain levels of relevant reading and/or course attendance. The purpose of the CPD requirements is to maintain expertise in a professional environment and individual career, especially regarding levels of technical and ethical competence.

Members engaged in **public practice** must in addition:

- Hold a **Practising Certificate**: this is obtained by showing that the member has maintained appropriate levels of education and work experience
- Implement the **ICAEW Code of Ethics**
- Be covered by **professional indemnity insurance** (PII).

4.3 Reserved areas of practice

Most activities carried out by accountants are open to all. However, there are three activities, known as **reserved areas**, which legislation requires to be carried out by members of certain bodies which are 'recognised professional regulators':

- Statutory audit
- Investment business
- Insolvency

The purpose of the legislation is to ensure, in the public interest, that those practising in the reserved areas have the required level of **technical competence** and are subject to an appropriate **disciplinary regime**.

The Institute is a **recognised professional regulator** for each of the three reserved areas. Its Audit Regulations, DPB (investment business) Handbook and Insolvency Licensing Regulations are drawn up to meet the requirements of the legislation. They apply only to members or firms registered, authorised or licensed to carry out these activities.

The contents of each set of regulations cover:

- Eligibility
- Conduct (integrity, monitoring, enforcement of discipline, etc)
- Competence (eg continuing professional education)

We shall see more about the overall regulation of the profession in Chapter 10.

5 The work of the accountancy profession

Section overview

- Three aspects support high quality financial reporting and assurance: maintaining control and safeguarding assets; financial management; financial reporting.
- Underlying financial reporting are professional and accounting principles.

There are three basic aspects of the professional accountant's work which should be appreciated by any accountancy trainee:

- Maintaining control and safeguarding assets
- Financial management
- Financial reporting

We shall look at each of these in turn.

5.1 Maintaining control and safeguarding assets

Stakeholders in a business are concerned that the business's assets are kept safe, and that the managers of the business are acting in the stakeholders' (especially the shareholders') best interests. The professional accountant will therefore seek to ensure that:

1. The **recording of transactions** is complete, timely and accurate (as we have seen in earlier chapters).
2. The business's **internal controls** are sufficient.
3. The business's **audit committee** is properly constituted and has the information and resources that it needs to fulfil its objectives.
4. The business has **non-executive directors** who are adequately qualified and resourced so that they can fulfil their role.

Points 2 to 4 apply particularly to large listed companies. We shall come back to internal controls, and the roles of the audit committee and non-executive directors, when we look at **corporate governance** in Chapter 12.

5.2 Financial management

Definition

Financial management: The management of all the processes associated with the raising and use of financial resources in a business.

Financial management therefore incorporates aspects of many issues that we have seen in earlier chapters.

- Transactions recording
- Raising new finance
- Using existing funds in ways which support achievement of the business's objectives
- Planning and control systems
- Treasury management

High quality financial management supports good **corporate governance** as it **protects investors against the interests of managers**, who may be tempted to take unnecessary or unconsidered **risks** with the business's finances. We shall return to this key issue in Chapters 11 and 12.

5.3 Financial reporting

The transactions and activities of the business, as represented in its accounting records, must be reported to **external stakeholders**, including investors in capital markets. As we saw in Chapter 6, financial reporting involves reporting on the financial position of the entity at a particular point in time (the balance sheet), and its financial performance over a period of time (the income statement). It is a key plank in corporate governance, as we shall see in Chapters 11 and 12.

In seeking to ensure that there is **high quality financial reporting**, the professional accountant has two sets of principles which underlie everything he or she does:

- Professional principles
- Accounting principles

6 Professional principles

Section overview

- Professional principles, such as those in ICAEW Code of Ethics, guide the accountant in how to be seen to act in a professional manner in the course of professional work.
- The fundamental professional principles as set out in the ICAEW Code of Ethics are integrity, objectivity, professional competence and due care, confidentiality and professional behaviour.
- Threats to the fundamental principles arise from self-interest, self-review, advocacy, familiarity and intimidation.
- Safeguards against threats vary according to the circumstances but include: education, training and experience; continuing professional education; corporate governance regulations; professional standards; monitoring and disciplinary procedures; external review.

6.1 The IESBA Code of Ethics

The **International Federation of Accountants** (IFAC) is an international body representing all the major accountancy bodies across the world. Its mission is to develop the **high standards** of professional accountants and enhance the quality of services they provide.

To enable the development of high standards, IFAC's International Ethics Standards Board of Accountants (IESBA) established a **Code of Ethics** which aligned standards globally. The code has the aim of **identifying the responsibilities** that a person employed as an accountant takes on, in return for a traditionally well-paid career with high status. It identifies potential situations where pitfalls may exist and offers advice on how to deal with them. By doing this the code indicates a minimum level of conduct to which all accountants must adhere.

The IESBA Code of Ethics is split into three parts:

- **Part A General application of the Code** introduces the fundamental principles which are those of the ICAEW too (see below).
- **Part B Professional Accountants in Public Practice** provides guidance on applying the principles that is relevant to those who work in public practice, for example issues of professional appointment, conflicts of interest, second opinions, fees and other types of remuneration, marketing professional services, gifts and hospitality, custody of client assets, objectivity, and independence in both audit and review engagements and other assurance engagements.
- **Part C Professional Accountants in Business** provides guidance that is particularly relevant to those who work in commerce, such as potential conflicts, the preparation and reporting of information, acting with sufficient expertise, financial interests and inducements.

6.2 The ICAEW Code of Ethics

As a member of IFAC, the ICAEW Code of Ethics builds on IESBA's. Additionally, ICAEW has an overriding commitment to **protect the public interest** which requires members to act **ethically**. Another difference is that the ICAEW Code contains Part D for insolvency practitioners.

The conceptual framework in the ICAEW Code of Ethics is used by the professional accountant in practice to identify, evaluate and address any **threats** to their professionalism, and then to implement **safeguards**.

The ICAEW Code of Ethics is covered in detail in your *Assurance* syllabus. Here we shall use it as a guide to how a professional accountant should be seen to act in a **professionally responsible manner** in the course of professional work.

6.3 Integrity

Definition

Integrity: The principle of integrity imposes an obligation on all professional accountants to be straightforward and honest in all professional and business relationships. Integrity also implies fair dealing and truthfulness. It follows that a professional accountant's advice and work must be uncorrupted by self-interest and not be influenced by the interests of other parties.

(ICAEW Code of Ethics Section 110.1)

A professional accountant therefore behaves with **integrity** when he or she is:

- Straightforward
- Honest
- Fair
- Truthful

A professional accountant does **NOT** behave with integrity if he or she is:

- Corrupted by **self-interest**
- Corrupted by the **undue influence** of others
- Associated with information which is **false or misleading** (for instance if certain parts of it are omitted or obscured)
- Associated with information which is supplied **recklessly**

6.4 Objectivity

Definition

Objectivity: The principle of objectivity imposes an obligation on all professional accountants not to compromise their professional or business judgement because of bias, conflict of interest or the undue influence of others. Objectivity is the state of mind which has regard to all considerations relevant to the task in hand but no other.

(ICAEW Code of Ethics Section 120.1)

Being objective means:

- Being independent of mind
- Not allowing professional or business judgement to be overridden by:
  - **Bias** (allowing one's judgement to be clouded by preconceived or irrational arguments)
  - **Conflict of interest** (allowing one's judgement to be affected by the fact that allegiance is owed to both parties in a situation)
  - **Undue influence** of others (allowing one's judgement to be swayed by persons who wish to impose their ideas and interests)

6.5 Professional competence and due care

The principle of professional competence and due care imposes the following obligations on all professional accountants:

(a) To maintain professional knowledge and skill at the level required to ensure that clients or employers receive competent professional service; and

(b) To act diligently in accordance with applicable technical and professional standards when providing professional services

(ICAEW Code of Ethics Section 130.1)

When providing professional services 'professional competence and due care' therefore mean:

- Having appropriate professional **knowledge and skill**
- Having a continuing awareness and an understanding of relevant technical, professional and business developments
- Exercising **sound and independent judgement**
- Acting **diligently**, that is:
  - **Carefully**
  - **Thoroughly**
  - On a **timely** basis and
  - In accordance with the requirements of an assignment
- Acting in accordance with applicable **technical and professional standards**
- Distinguishing clearly between an **expression of opinion** and an **assertion of fact**

6.6 Confidentiality

The principle of confidentiality is not only to keep information confidential, but also to take all reasonable steps to preserve confidentiality. Whether information is confidential or not will depend on its nature. A safe and proper approach for professional accountants to adopt is to assume that all unpublished information about a client's or employer's affairs, however gained, is confidential. Some clients or employers may regard the mere fact of their relationship with a professional accountant as being confidential.

The principle of confidentiality imposes an obligation on all professional accountants to refrain from:

- Disclosing outside the firm or employing organisation confidential information acquired as a result of professional and business relationships without proper and specific authority or unless there is a legal or professional right or duty to disclose; and
- Using confidential information acquired as a result of professional and business relationships to their personal advantage or the advantage of third parties.

(ICAEW Code of Ethics Sections 140.0 and 140.1)

The professional accountant should assume that all unpublished information about a prospective, current or previous client's or employer's affairs, however gained, is **confidential**. Information should then:

- Be kept confidential (confidentiality should be actively preserved)
- Not be disclosed, even inadvertently such as in a social environment
- Not be used to obtain personal advantage

6.7 Professional behaviour

'A professional accountant should comply with relevant laws and regulations and should avoid any action that discredits the profession.'

(ICAEW Code of Ethics Section 150.1)

Behaving professionally means:

- Complying with relevant **laws and regulations**
- Avoiding any action that **discredits the profession** (the standard to be applied is that of a reasonable and informed third party with knowledge of all relevant information)
- Conducting oneself with
  - **Courtesy** and
  - **Consideration**

When marketing themselves and their work, professional accountants should:

- Be honest and truthful
- Avoid making exaggerated claims about:
  - What they can do
  - What qualifications and experience they possess
- Avoid making disparaging references to the work of others

Interactive question 2: Conceptual framework [Difficulty level: Exam standard]

Charis is a chartered accountant who acts on behalf of a charitable trust set up by her family, though she is not a beneficiary of the trust. Her elder sister is a powerful and articulate trustee and Charis has frequently followed her wishes in the past, contrary to those of her younger sister and mother who are also trustees. As a result of Charis' and her elder sister's actions a great deal of money has been diverted to the elder sister and the trust has become insolvent. Charis' conduct has been called into question. Which of the fundamental principles in the Code of Ethics have been contravened by Charis?

See **Answer** at the end of this chapter.

6.8 Threats to professional principles

Compliance with the professional principles may potentially be **threatened** by a broad range of circumstances. Threats generally fall into the following categories:

- **Self-interest threats**, which may occur as a result of dominance of the financial or other interests of the professional accountant or an immediate or close family member
- **Self-review threats**, which may occur when a previous judgement needs to be re-evaluated by the professional accountant responsible for that judgement
- **Advocacy threats**, which may occur when a professional accountant promotes a position or opinion to the point that subsequent objectivity may be compromised
- **Familiarity threats**, which may occur when, because of a close relationship, a professional accountant becomes too sympathetic to the interests of a particular group
- **Intimidation threats**, which may occur when a professional accountant is deterred from acting objectively by threats, actual or perceived

6.9 Safeguards against threats

Safeguards that may eliminate or reduce such threats to an acceptable level fall into two broad categories:

- Safeguards created by the profession, legislation or regulation
- Safeguards in the work environment

Safeguards created by the profession, legislation or regulation include, but are not restricted to:

- **Educational, training and experience requirements** for entry into the profession (as we have seen)
- **Continuing professional education** and development (CPD) requirements
- **Corporate governance** regulations (covered in Chapter 12)
- **Professional standards** (the conceptual framework)
- Professional or regulatory **monitoring and disciplinary procedures** (covered in Chapter 10)
- **External review** by a legally empowered third party of the reports, returns, communications or information produced by a professional accountant (covered in Chapter 10)

Certain safeguards may increase the likelihood of identifying or deterring unethical behaviour. Such safeguards may be created by the accounting profession, legislation, regulation or an employing organisation. They include, but are not restricted to:

- Effective, well-publicised **complaints systems** operated by the employing organisation, the profession or a regulator, which enable colleagues, employers and members of the public to draw attention to unprofessional or unethical behaviour
- An explicitly stated **duty to report breaches of ethical requirements**

We shall see more about this in Chapter 11.

The nature of the **safeguards to be applied in the workplace** will vary depending on the circumstances. In exercising professional judgement, a professional accountant should consider what a **reasonable and informed third party**, having knowledge of all relevant information, including the significance of the threat and the safeguards applied, would conclude to be unacceptable.

7 Accounting principles

Section overview

- Accounting principles inform professional judgements.
- Key accounting principles are: accruals, going concern, double entry, faithful representation (accuracy and completeness), the primacy of substance over form, materiality, neutrality, prudence, timeliness, cost/benefit, consistency and no offsetting.

7.1 What are accounting principles used for?

The professional accountant should always be aware that there are certain **accounting principles** that underlie accounting, financial reporting and assurance. If in doubt about how to report a transaction or event, the professional accountant should always come back to these principles to inform the professional judgement that needs to be made. They are covered in detail elsewhere at Professional stage, but we summarise them briefly here too.

7.2 Accrual basis

Transactions and other events are recognised when they occur, and not just when cash is received or paid. They are therefore recorded in the accounting records and financial statements of the periods to which they relate; for instance, revenue is matched with the expenditure incurred in earning it. Users are thereby informed both of past transactions and of future obligations to pay and receive cash.

7.3 Going concern

Financial statements are prepared on the basis that the business is a going concern. This assumes that, unless there is a clear intention or need for the business to liquidate or materially scale back its operations, it will continue in operation for the foreseeable future.

If a business is not a going concern, then realistically its value is limited to the resale or salvage value of its assets less its liabilities.

7.4 Double entry bookkeeping

The fact that every transaction has a **dual effect** when entered into the ledger accounts of a business is a prime control on the completeness of the accounting records. Even though most businesses use computer software to record transactions it is part of the role of the professional accountant to be able to identify, in terms of debits and credits, what entries should be recorded for each transaction. This application of this principle means that the professional accountant is best placed to identify and remedy errors.

7.5 Faithful representation: accuracy and completeness

For it to be a faithful representation of the business's transactions and other events, the information contained in financial statements or other outputs of the professional accountant should:

- Be free from error ie be **accurate**
- Be **complete** (within the bounds of materiality and cost), as incomplete information can be false or misleading

Information should therefore be as accurate as possible. At the transactions recording level this means that both sides of each transaction should be recorded with total accuracy.

7.6 Substance over form

To represent the business's transactions and other events faithfully, the professional accountant should take into account their **substance and economic reality** rather than just their legal form. For example, two lease agreements, of which one is a means of funding the acquisition of an asset while the other is simply allowing the entity use of the asset in the short-term are treated differently according to their economic reality rather than their legal form.

7.7 Materiality

Something may be of material importance to the relevance of financial information either by virtue of its **size** (in relation to the business) or its **nature**. Information is material if its omission or misstatement could influence users' decisions. This often means that material items should be presented separately and should not be aggregated with other items.

7.8 Neutrality

To be a faithful representation, information must be neutral, that is **free from bias**. Information is biased if it has been selected or presented so as to influence a decision or judgement in order to achieve a predetermined result or outcome.

7.9 Prudence

Where there are uncertainties that affect how far the information is a faithful representation of the business's transactions and other events the professional accountant should:

- **Disclose** the nature and extent of the uncertainty
- Exercise **prudence** or 'a degree of caution' when making judgements, so that income and assets are not overstated, and expenses and liabilities are not understated

7.10 Timeliness

There should not be undue delay in reporting information, but neither is it absolutely necessary to know about all aspects of a transaction or other event before it is reported.

- **Late reporting** undermines **relevance**
- **Reporting too early** undermines how far information can be a **faithful representation**

A balance must be achieved between early and late reporting based on satisfying the decision-making needs of users.

7.11 Cost versus benefit

The **benefit** derived from information should exceed the **cost** of providing it.

7.12 Consistency

Unless there are good reasons for the contrary, items in financial statements should be presented and classified in the same way from one period to the next.

7.13 Offsetting

Assets and liabilities, and income and expense, should not usually be set off against each other, with only net figures reported.

8 Accounting standards

Section overview

- Accounting standards identify proper accounting practice.
- Financial statements should comply with accounting standards.
- Listed companies must comply with International Accounting Standards and International Financial Reporting Standards.
- Some companies can choose whether to present financial statements using IFRSs or UK standards.

8.1 What is the purpose of accounting standards?

To demonstrate technical competence, the professional accountant needs to be aware of and apply **accounting standards** as well as accounting principles.

The basic purpose of accounting standards is to **identify proper accounting practice** for the benefit of preparers, auditors and users of financial statements. Accounting standards create a common understanding between users and preparers of financial statements on how particular items should be treated, so financial statements are expected to comply with applicable accounting standards other than in rare, exceptional cases.

8.2 Types of accounting standard

There are two types of accounting standard that affect the professional accountant in the UK:

- **International standards**, namely International Accounting Standards (IASs) and International Financial Reporting Standards (IFRSs), produced by the International Accounting Standards Board (IASB)
- **UK standards**, namely Statements of Standard Accounting Practice (SSAPs) and Financial Reporting Standards (FRSs), produced by the UK's own Accounting Standards Board (ASB)

Differences between the ASB's and the IASB's standards exist, but these have become progressively less important.

9 Roles of the professional accountant

Section overview

- Professional accountants work in public practice or outside it, in business management.
- Some areas of public practice are reserved, so that additional regulations apply to those working in them. These are audit, investment business and insolvency.

A professional accountant who is technically competent and professionally responsible can perform a wide **variety of roles**.

Traditionally professional accountants have tended to:

- Work in **public practice** with an accountancy firm, or
- Be employed by a private or public sector organisation to help in its **management**

In recent times there have been more opportunities to specialise within these two general fields.

9.1 The professional accountant in public practice

A professional accountant in public practice is in a firm providing professional services that require accountancy or related skills, including:

- Accounting
- Auditing and assurance (reserved area)
- Taxation
- Management consulting
- Investment business (reserved area)
- Insolvency (reserved area)
- Financial management
- Corporate finance
- Information and communications technology
- Forensic accounting

Firms vary in size from the sole practitioner to one of the 'Big Four' multinational accountancy firms:

- PricewaterhouseCoopers
- Deloitte
- Ernst & Young
- KPMG

These firms are associations of the partnerships in each country rather than having the classical structure of parent company and subsidiaries, but each has an international 'umbrella' organisation for co-ordination.

As we saw above, there are three reserved areas in public practice: statutory audit, investment business and insolvency. There is more regulation involved in working in these areas. We shall look here at auditing in particular.

9.1.1 Qualification for appointment as external (statutory) auditor

Definition

Audit: An expression of an opinion as to whether an entity's financial statements have been prepared, in all material respects, in accordance with an applicable financial reporting framework, and thereby give a 'true and fair view'. *Auditing Practices Board* (APB)

Alternatively an audit is a review of an entity's financial statements resulting in the publication of an independent opinion on whether those financial statements are relevant, accurate, complete, and fairly presented.

The Companies Act 2006 sets out the rules as to who is eligible for appointment by a company as its external auditor (now formally called its statutory auditor). The appointee must be **independent** and:

- May be a sole practitioner, a partnership or a corporate body
- Must be a member of a recognised supervisory body, such as the ICAEW, and
- Must be eligible for appointment under the rules of that body by virtue of holding an appropriate qualification (which does not necessarily have to be obtained in the UK)

The Companies Act 2006 also sets out who is **NOT** eligible to act as statutory auditor:

- Any person who does not meet the eligibility criteria above, or who no longer meets them
- An officer or employee of the company or its parent or subsidiary
- A partner or employee of such a person, or a partnership in which the person is a partner
- Certain persons 'connected' to the company, as defined by the Secretary of State

Although the Companies Act 2006 does not prevent a shareholder, receivable, payable or officer/employee's close relative from being an auditor of a particular company, regulations set out by the accountancy and audit profession do prevent this.

9.2 The professional accountant in business

A professional accountant in business is one who is employed or engaged, in an executive or non-executive capacity, in such areas as:

- Commerce
- Industry
- Service
- The public sector
- Education
- The not-for-profit sector
- Regulatory or professional bodies

9.2.1 Roles and responsibilities of the professional accountant in business

In business a professional accountant could be engaged in a wide variety of roles and responsibilities, some of which need not involve use of their technical competence at all. Usually however a professional accountant would be involved mainly in the finance function, in some capacity.

Quite often, especially in smaller businesses, a professional accountant may become involved in areas which are outside their sphere of technical competence, including making decisions on matters concerning:

- Law
- Administration
- Insurance
- Pensions
- Property
- Personnel
- Procurement, and
- IT

This is perfectly acceptable to some degree, but the professional accountant should remember that professional principles require him or her to act with **professional competence and due care** so they should:

- Be open about acting outside their own professional knowledge and skill if this is the case, but still
- Exercise sound and independent judgement, and
- Act diligently

In fact many of these areas are ones in which other professionals would normally be involved. It is important therefore for the professional accountant to know the limits to their professional responsibilities.

10 Limits of the professional accountant's responsibilities

Section overview

- While the professional accountant is often engaged in many different areas of business management, there are limits to their professional competence which means they must know when to call in further expertise, such as from lawyers, actuaries, surveyors and HR specialists.

10.1 How far do the professional accountant's responsibilities go?

Legal matters are normally dealt with by **qualified solicitors** or **barristers** in an advisory or representative capacity. Many companies employ in-house legal teams, staffed with professional lawyers. The professional accountant should be careful not to stray too far into legal matters, beyond those in which they are technically competent to some degree (such as company, business and employment law).

Certain **administrative matters** often fall directly into the role of the professional accountant, such as the tasks performed by a **company secretary**:

- Share registrations
- Calling meetings
- Drafting resolutions for meetings
- Submitting the annual return to the Registrar of Companies.

Under the Companies Act 2006, a company secretary of a listed company should be a member of one of a list of qualifying bodies (ICAEW, ICAS, ICAI, ACCA, ICSA, CIMA, CIPFA) or a solicitor, barrister or advocate.

The company secretary of a company is often a professional accountant but in a very large or complex organisation it is normal to have a qualified **chartered secretary** appointed to this role, especially as the company secretary plays a significant role in ensuring good corporate governance (see Chapter 12).

Taking out and claiming against **insurance** policies often falls into the role of the professional accountant in business. Again professional principles can be very helpful in this role, but beyond a certain level of complexity **insurance specialists** and **actuaries** should be used.

The services of **actuaries** and other specialists should also be engaged when the company is faced with issues concerning its **pension fund**.

The acquisition, refurbishment or disposal of **property** often involves the professional accountant in valuation, negotiation, tax and legal aspects. In most circumstances however other professionals will also be involved, such as **estate agents, valuers, architects** and **lawyers**.

Since people are paid by the payroll function in the accounting and finance department, many companies have historically also made the whole of **personnel** the responsibility of the professional accountant. Given the complexity of laws and regulations surrounding human resources, and the central strategic role it plays in a business's success, this is an area where an **HR professional** should really be engaged in an organisation of any size.

For similar reasons – that is, because suppliers are paid by the accounting and finance department – **procurement** is also often included in the professional accountant's role. As supply chain management is central to achieving strategic objectives, so again above a certain size and complexity it is advisable for most companies to use **procurement professionals** in this role.

The acquisition and effective use of **IT** is an important part of the professional accountant's role when it is related to transactions recording and all the other aspects of the accounting and finance function's work. **Specialist advice** should also be sought however.

Summary and Self-test

Summary

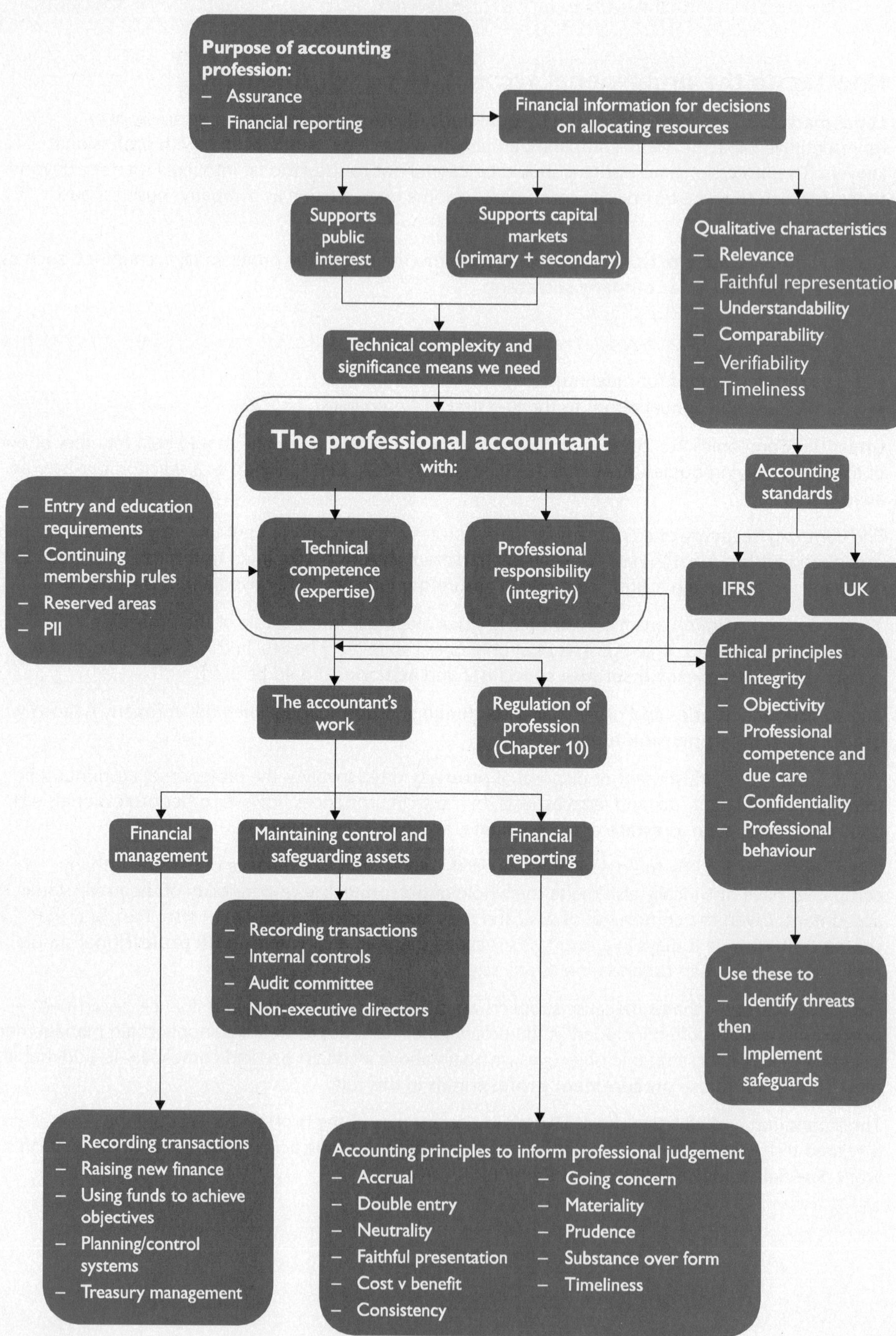

Purpose of accounting profession:
– Assurance
– Financial reporting
Financial information for decisions on allocating resources
Supports public interest
Supports capital markets (primary + secondary)
Qualitative characteristics
– Relevance
– Faithful representation
– Understandability
– Comparability
– Verifiability
– Timeliness
Technical complexity and significance means we need
The professional accountant with:
Accounting standards
IFRS
UK
– Entry and education requirements
– Continuing membership rules
– Reserved areas
– PII
Technical competence (expertise)
Professional responsibility (integrity)
Ethical principles
– Integrity
– Objectivity
– Professional competence and due care
– Confidentiality
– Professional behaviour
The accountant's work
Regulation of profession (Chapter 10)
Financial management
Maintaining control and safeguarding assets
Financial reporting
– Recording transactions
– Internal controls
– Audit committee
– Non-executive directors
Use these to
– Identify threats
then
– Implement safeguards
– Recording transactions
– Raising new finance
– Using funds to achieve objectives
– Planning/control systems
– Treasury management
Accounting principles to inform professional judgement
– Accrual
– Double entry
– Neutrality
– Faithful presentation
– Cost v benefit
– Consistency
– Going concern
– Materiality
– Prudence
– Substance over form
– Timeliness

ICAEW

Self-test

Answer the following questions.

1 The public must have confidence in the integrity of professional accountants because

A The reputation of the profession depends on it
B They provide advice on technically complex areas on which others rely
C This will encourage more people to enter the profession
D This will encourage more people to seek the services of a professional accountant

2 Which are the **two** fundamental principles in the ICAEW Code of Ethics that underlie the reliance of the public on accountants?

A Integrity
B Objectivity
C Professional competence and due care
D Confidentiality
E Professional behaviour

3 What is the minimum period of training with an approved training organisation which is required for student members of the ICAEW?

A Two years
B Two and a half years
C Three years
D Three and a half years

4 Which of the following requirements applies to a member who is in public practice over and above a member who is not?

A Obey the ICAEW's rules and regulations
B Undertake CPD
C Pay the annual subscription fee
D Maintain PII

5 For members of the ICAEW audit, investment business and insolvency are

A Recognised areas
B Reserved areas
C Regulated areas
D Registered areas

6 Distinguishing clearly between an expression of opinion and an assertion of fact is part of the professional accountant's fundamental principle of

A Professional competence and due care
B Professional behaviour
C Objectivity
D Integrity

7 When a professional accountant promotes a position to the point that their subsequent objectivity is compromised they have fallen prey to the threat of

A Self-interest
B Familiarity
C Intimidation
D Advocacy

8 Capitalising the cost of a non-current asset which is not owned but for which a monthly payment is made implements the accounting principle of

A Materiality
B Prudence
C Substance over form
D Faithful representation

9 Identify whether each of the following statements is true or false.

(a) The ICAEW Code of Ethics is based on the IESBA Code of Ethics.

A True
B False

(b) The approach taken by the ICAEW Code of Ethics is compliance-based.

C True
D False

Now, go back to the Learning Objectives in the Introduction. If you are satisfied you have achieved these objectives, please tick them off.

Technical reference

1 ICAEW Code of Ethics	**100.1, 110.1, 120.1, 130.1** **140.0, 140.1, 150.1**

Answers to Interactive questions

Answer to Interactive question 1

Many people want to be chartered accountants because it is a 'good career' rather than because they are intrinsically interested in assurance and financial reporting; these are interests that come later. But it is worth thinking through why you thought it would be a 'good career'. Certainly the rewards are worth it, but what about the hard work in qualifying, and the expectation that you will behave professionally at all times? The requirement for objective assessment in technical competence (exams etc) distinguishes the accountancy profession from most Management Trainee Schemes, plus the need to pay annual subscriptions and to keep up your technical expertise. Are professionals 'set apart' as a result of all this?

Answer to Interactive question 2

A great deal more about the history and the outcome of this situation needs to be identified, but on the evidence it would appear that Charis has succumbed to her sister's undue influence. Her objectivity has therefore been compromised; if corruption is proved then her integrity has also suffered. Not exercising sound and independent judgement contravenes professional competence and due care, and her actions have discredited the profession which means that she has not behaved professionally.

Answers to Self-test

1 B

2 A, B See Code of Ethics section 100.1

3 C

4 D

5 B

6 A

7 D

8 C

9 A, D The ICAEW Code of Ethics is based on the IESBA Code and as such is ethics-based or framework-based.

CHAPTER 10

Structure and regulation of the accountancy profession

Introduction

Learning objectives

Tick off

- Specify the rationale for key parts of the accountancy profession's work ☐
- Specify the key features of the structure of the accountancy profession ☐
- Specify the regulatory framework within which professional accountants work ☐

Specific syllabus references are: 4, b, c.

Syllabus links

The topic of professional regulation underlies many areas of the Professional and Advanced levels.

Examination context

Questions on the structure and regulation of the profession will almost certainly appear in your exam.

Questions are likely to be set in a multiple choice format and in a scenario context, though knowledge-type questions are also likely on particular definitions and principles.

1 The structure of the accountancy profession

Section overview

- Members of the UK's umbrella association of accountancy bodies, the CCAB, are the ICAEW, ICAS, ACCA, CIPFA and Chartered Accountants Ireland.
- The international global organisation for accountants is IFAC.
- Anyone can call themselves an accountant.

1.1 The Consultative Committee of Accountancy Bodies (CCAB)

The UK accountancy profession does not only comprise the ICAEW. The major accountancy professional bodies in the UK and Ireland joined together in 1974 to form the Consultative Committee of Accountancy Bodies (CCAB). CCAB currently has five members.

- The Institute of Chartered Accountants in England and Wales (ICAEW)
- The Institute of Chartered Accountants of Scotland (ICAS)
- The Institute of Chartered Accountants in Ireland (Chartered Accountants Ireland)
- The Association of Chartered Certified Accountants (ACCA)
- The Chartered Institute of Public Finance and Accountancy (CIPFA)

The Board of CCAB consists of five directors, who are senior members of the five member bodies.

CCAB provides a forum in which matters affecting the profession as a whole can be discussed and co-ordinated. It enables the profession to speak with a unified voice to government.

Together with the Chartered Institute of Management Accountants (CIMA) the ICAEW, ICAS and CIPFA sponsor the **Association of Accounting Technicians (AAT)**, whose members act as accounting technicians and often go on to membership of one of the sponsoring bodies.

1.2 International Federation of Accountants (IFAC)

IFAC is the global organisation for the accountancy profession. It has 172 member organisations and associates, including the ICAEW. IFAC members represent 2.5 million accountants worldwide, employed in public practice, industry and commerce, government and education in 129 countries and jurisdictions.

The aim of IFAC is to **protect the public interest** by encouraging high quality practices by the world's accountants. This includes **best practice guidance for professional accountants employed in business**, plus a **membership compliance programme**.

IFAC emphasises the importance of:

- **Strong international economies**
- Adherence to **high-quality professional standards** in the areas of audit, education, ethics and public sector financial reporting
- **Convergence** of professional standards
- Speaking out on **public interest and public policy issues** where the profession's expertise is most relevant

Through its IESBA Code of Ethics, which we saw in Chapter 9, IFAC encourages accountants worldwide to adhere to the **fundamental principles**.

1.3 Who can call themselves an accountant?

There is **no legal requirement for an accountant to be a paid-up member of any professional body at all**, let alone one of the CCAB or IFAC bodies. Unlike the Law Society, which can legally stop an unqualified 'solicitor' from practising, accountancy bodies have no such authority. The term **'accountant'** enjoys no special position in law. Anyone is free to advertise as an 'accountant' and offer the full range of accountancy services, except in the three reserved areas (statutory audit, investment business and insolvency) where statute demands specific levels of competence. Institute members are therefore open to competition from anyone, whether professionally qualified or not, who chooses to enter the market.

2 Regulation of professions

Section overview

- Professions are regulated so that the various aspects of the public interest are kept in balance.
- Regulation of professions can take the form of government or government agency regulation, self-regulation by the profession itself, or a combination.
- An oversight mechanism can be used to ensure that self-regulation works, and this is the approach taken to regulation of the UK accountancy profession.

2.1 Why regulation of professions is necessary

Regulation of professions (either self-regulation or external regulation, or a combination) is needed to provide the **public interest** with **protection and assurance** in situations where the issues are **too technically complex** for the public to be reasonably expected to look after their own interests. The activities of many professions typically fall into such a category.

Interactive question 1: Regulation [Difficulty level: Intermediate]

What do you think should be the aims of regulation of the accountancy profession?

See **Answer** at the end of this chapter.

Many of the aims of regulation result in **different priorities** for **different aspects** of the 'public interest'. Subjective judgements are needed to balance interests.

Regulation should **not**:

- **Protect vested interests** from competition
- Be for **personal gain** or to satisfy **prurient interest**
- Be **disproportionate to the benefit gained**, such as imposing huge and costly quantities of detailed restrictions in a heavy-handed and over-rigid manner
- **Distort competition** by imposing extra burdens on some, but not others

2.2 Methods of regulation

Regulation can be:

- By government directly via **legislation**
- By separate agencies established by government (**delegated legislation**)
- By the profession/industry itself (**self-regulation** – see below) or
- By a **combination** of methods

2.3 Self-regulation

Self-regulation in theory provides a common sense, flexible approach because there is **detailed knowledge** within the profession of the issues facing it. It should result in a more **efficient and effective outcome**.

Self-regulation only works if:

- The regime does not seem to act against the public interest
- Regulatory guidance and its importance are both understood and enforced
- Members of the profession 'buy in' to the process
- There is no unjustifiable self-protecting regulation

In fact, self-regulation works best when there is an **oversight mechanism** to ensure that the entire process is working.

2.3.1 The oversight mechanism

Society requires **proof of good intent and actions**. It is more ready to lay blame and to seek legal remedies ('litigiousness'). Any form of regulation therefore requires an oversight mechanism to ensure that it is achieving what it set out to achieve. In the case of self-regulation, it is particularly important that the oversight mechanism be **independent**, to counter accusations of self-interest.

An **effective oversight mechanism** requires:

- Sufficient **independence** from the profession being regulated and any other single stakeholder to ensure that its decisions are not compromised or perceived to be compromised by undue influence
- **Knowledge** of the profession being regulated
- Significant, but non-controlling, **input from the profession itself** to ensure that decisions:
  - Are workable
  - Will not achieve the opposite of what they intend and
  - Do not impose costs on society in excess of the benefits gained
- The ability to take a wide view to **balance the various stakeholder interests** that comprise the public interest, and to judge the regulator's attempts to do the same
- **Authority** to have decisions acted on across the whole profession, through legislation or voluntary agreement
- **Good communication**, to ensure that the public interest is seen to be served, without alienating the profession being regulated
- Sufficient **resources** to carry out effective examination of the regulatory arrangements

The **key participants** in an effective oversight mechanism are therefore likely to be:

- The **government** – the ultimate guardian of the public interest in a democracy
- **Regulators** operating in relevant sectors
- **Members of the profession**, to provide an informed insight based on professional experience and in-depth technical knowledge
- **Members of the public**, independent of the profession, with the character and intellectual ability to make sound judgements on complex issues

3 Regulation of the accountancy profession

Section overview

- The UK government is responsible for the statutory elements of the regulatory framework of the accountancy profession.
- The ICAEW is the primary regulator of its members, which is the form of self-regulation adopted in the UK. In respect of reserved areas it has additional regulatory duties.
- The FRC makes sure that self-regulation of the accountancy profession is effective. It has statutory powers in respect of auditing.

Following lengthy debate, the **regulatory regime for the accountancy profession** involves:

- The **government**
- **Self-regulation** by the accountancy profession
- An **oversight mechanism** by the FRC

3.1 The role of the government

The government is responsible for the **legislative elements** of the regulatory framework, though the FRC acts as adviser to the government on necessary legislative changes. The government **delegates certain statutory powers to the FRC**, but the government remains responsible via these powers and so has a continuing responsibility for the system's effectiveness.

3.2 Self-regulation by the accountancy profession

The professional accountancy bodies, including the ICAEW, have **primary regulatory responsibility for supervision of their members acting in their professional capacity** so as to maintain standards and the professional standing of accountancy.

In relation to **audit, investment business and insolvency** (reserved areas) certain professional accountancy bodies, including the ICAEW, act as **recognised professional regulators.** They must have the necessary arrangements in place to ensure that members and firms comply with the statutory requirements.

3.2.1 The role of the ICAEW

In relation to its membership the **ICAEW has direct responsibility** for:

- **Entry and education** requirements (as seen in Chapter 9)
- **Eligibility** to engage in **public practice** (as seen in Chapter 9)
- Eligibility for the performance of **reserved activities** under statutory powers delegated by the government (see Chapter 9)
- **Professional conduct requirements** (see Chapter 9)
- Dealing with **professional misconduct** by its members (see later in this chapter)

3.3 The FRC's oversight mechanism

The **Financial Reporting Council (FRC)** is the UK's independent regulator responsible for overseeing the regulatory activities of the professional accountancy bodies. This oversight is effected by its **Conduct Division's Professional Oversight team.**

The FRC has three main roles regarding the oversight of **audit and accountancy**:

- **Non-statutory oversight of the professional accountancy bodies** in the way they exercise their regulatory responsibilities in relation to their members beyond those who are statutory auditors

- **Statutory oversight of the regulation of statutory auditors** by the recognised supervisory and qualifying bodies, including ICAEW. This means the FRC is responsible for the recognition, supervision and de-recognition of those accountancy bodies responsible for supervising the work of statutory auditors or offering an audit qualification. As recognised supervisory bodies, they must have in place amongst other things effective arrangements for registration, monitoring and disciplining of auditors
- **Independent monitoring of the quality of the auditing function** by the Audit Quality Review team in relation to major public interest entities (listed companies plus some other entities that affect the public interest)

On **audit**, the **FRC has statutory powers** in relation to recognised supervisory bodies and recognised qualification bodies:

- It can recognise and derecognise them
- It can require information from them
- It can serve an enforcement order on them that they are failing to meet their statutory responsibilities
- It can fine them for failing to meet their statutory responsibilities

On **accountancy** the **FRC does not have statutory powers** but can investigate and make **recommendations** on:

- Education
- Training
- Continuing professional education and development
- Standards
- Ethical matters
- Professional conduct
- Professional discipline
- Registration
- Monitoring

In relation to the **FRC's recommendations** the ICAEW is committed to:

- **Considering** them carefully, and either
- **Implementing** them within a reasonable period, or
- **Giving reasons in writing for not doing so**

FRC is involved in regulation of the **actuarial profession** in a similar way to how it regulates the accountancy profession.

4 The Financial Reporting Council (FRC)

Section overview

- The FRC's goal is to support investment by ensuring high quality corporate reporting, auditing and corporate governance by setting standards, reviewing quality, regulating, overseeing self-regulation, and taking disciplinary action.
- The FRC has two divisions: the Conduct Division is responsible for professional oversight, professional discipline, corporate reporting review and audit quality review, and the Codes and Standards Division is responsible for codes and standards in relation to actuarial, accounting and reporting policy, audit and assurance, and corporate governance

4.1 What does the FRC do?

The FRC acts as the UK's independent regulator for corporate reporting and governance. Its goal is to foster a climate in which investment can flourish.

The FRC is engaged in:

- Setting **standards** for corporate governance (see Chapter 12), financial (corporate) reporting, and audit and assurance
- Monitoring and reviewing the **quality** of audit and financial reporting in large entities
- **Regulating the audit profession**
- **Overseeing self-regulation** in the accountancy, audit and actuarial professions (see above)
- Acting as the ultimate **disciplinary body** for the accountancy and actuarial professions

4.2 Structure of the FRC

The FRC has two divisions:

- The Conduct Division is responsible for professional oversight, professional discipline, corporate reporting review and audit quality review
- The Codes and Standards Division is responsible for codes and standards in relation to actuarial, accounting and reporting policy, audit and assurance, and corporate governance.

4.3 Conduct Division: professional oversight

As well as its functions in relation to audit and accountancy set out above, the Professional Oversight team also oversees the regulation of the **actuarial profession** by the professional actuarial bodies, and seeks to promote high quality actuarial work.

4.4 Conduct Division: professional discipline

FRC's Conduct Division operates an **independent** investigative and disciplinary body for both accountants and actuaries in the UK, previously known as the Accountancy and Actuarial Discipline Board (AADB). It is responsible for operating and administering an independent disciplinary scheme (the Accountancy Scheme) covering members of the CCAB bodies plus CIMA.

The Accountancy Scheme deals with cases which raise important issues affecting the **public interest** in the UK and which need to be investigated to determine whether or not there has been any **misconduct** by an accountant or accountancy firm.

We shall look at the work of the FRC in this respect in more detail later in this chapter.

4.5 Conduct Division: corporate reporting review

The FRC, via its **Financial Reporting Review Panel (FRRP)**:

- Makes **enquiries** into apparent departures from the requirements for financial statements of large companies established in the Companies Act 2006 and applicable accounting/financial reporting standards
- Can seek **voluntary remedial action**
- Can apply to the court for an **order for remedial action** (so far this is an action that has not had to be taken)

The FRC can ask directors to explain apparent departures from the requirements. If it is not satisfied by the directors' explanations it aims to persuade the directors to adopt a more appropriate accounting treatment. The '**remedial action**' sought can be:

- **Voluntary withdrawal** of financial statements and replacement with revised ones that correct the matters in error
- **Correction of the comparative figures** in the next set of annual financial statements

If the case concerns financial statements issued under the FCA Disclosure rules and Transparency rules, the Panel may report the company to the relevant regulatory body (see below).

4.6 Conduct Division: audit quality review

The FRC, via its **Audit Quality Review (AQR)** team (formerly known as the Audit Inspection Unit (AIU)), monitors the quality of the audits of listed and other major public interest entities and the policies and procedures supporting audit quality at the major audit firms in the UK. The objective of its work is to monitor and promote improvements in the quality of auditing of listed and other major public interest entities.

4.7 Codes and Standards Division: actuarial policy

The role of the FRC in relation to actuarial standards was previously undertaken by the Board for Actuarial Standards (BAS). The FRC seeks to establish and improve actuarial standards, primarily of a technical nature, to ensure that they are coherent, consistent and comprehensive and thereby to help promote high quality actuarial practice.

4.8 Codes and Standards Division: audit and assurance

The FRC:

- Develops **standards for auditing and assurance services** and their effective application
- Develops **ethical standards for auditors** relating to the independence, objectivity and integrity of auditors

You will look at the work of the FRC in relation to audit and assurance in more detail elsewhere in your Certificate and Professional level studies.

4.9 Codes and Standards Division: accounting and reporting policy

The FRC makes, amends and withdraws UK **accounting** and **financial reporting standards**. Previously this role was undertaken by the Accounting Standards Board (ASB).

4.10 Codes and Standards Division: corporate governance

The FRC maintains and updates two codes in relation to corporate governance: the UK Corporate Governance Code and the Stewardship Code. We shall be looking at these in detail in Chapters 11 and 12 of this Study Manual.

Interactive question 2: Audit inspection [Difficulty level: Intermediate]

Your firm has been informed that it can expect a visit from the FRC's Audit Quality Review team in the near future. What requirement will such a visit fulfil, and to what type of client will it relate?

See **Answer** at the end of this chapter.

5 Regulation of the financial services industry

Section overview

- Regulation of financial services affects the accountancy profession via the FCA's investment business rules (one of the ICAEW's reserved areas) and via the FCA's UK Listing Authority's rules, which require compliance with the main principles of the FRC's UK Corporate Governance Code 2012 for companies listed in the FTSE 350.
- Other regulators in the financial services industry are the Financial Ombudsman and the Pensions Regulator.

5.1 Regulation of financial services: effects on the accountancy profession

We saw in Chapter 8 that the financial services industry has a twin peaks regulatory regime, operated by the Bank of England's **Prudential Regulation Authority (PRA)** and the independent **Financial Conduct Authority (FCA).**

The only ways in which the **accountancy profession** is directly affected by financial services regulation are as follows:

- Regulations on **investment business** (one of the profession's 'reserved areas') are set out in the Designated Professional Body (DPB) Handbook that is agreed with the FCA and published by the ICAEW as a DPB for investment business under the Financial Services and Markets Act 2000.
- The FCA is the competent authority for listing so it comprises the **UK Listing Authority (UKLA)** for all companies whose securities are listed on public exchanges in the UK, whether with a premium listing or a standard listing. It is therefore the body which has given considerable force to the **FRC's UK Corporate Governance Code 2012.** Large companies with a premium listing in the FTSE 350 (the 350 largest companies listed by market capitalisation) must comply with the main principles of the Code, as we shall see in Chapter 12, in accordance with the **FCA Disclosure rules and Transparency rules.** The UKLA also issues the **Prospectus Rules**, with which companies must comply when issuing new securities.

5.2 Other financial regulators

Other financial regulators that may affect the work of the professional accountant include:

- The **Financial Ombudsman**, who settles disputes between providers of financial services and their customers.
- The **Pensions Regulator**, who regulates work-based pensions; personal pensions are currently regulated by the FSA.

6 Disciplinary procedures against accountants

Section overview

- Part of the ICAEW's approach to self-regulation is to ensure there is a clear and effective complaints and disciplinary procedure relating to members.
- The FRC's oversight role has required an additional independent level of disciplinary proceeding outside the profession's control, namely the FRC's Accountancy Scheme.
- The ICAEW's procedure involves three potential stages: conciliation, investigation and disciplinary proceedings.
- The FRC's Accountancy Scheme takes on cases via referral from an accountancy body, or by self-referral.
- As an independent disciplinary mechanism the FRC aims to be transparent, independent and fair.

6.1 Why are disciplinary procedures required?

In Chapter 9 we noted that regulation of its members by the ICAEW requires a rigorous complaints and disciplinary procedure involving the ICAEW itself. Oversight of self-regulation by the FRC necessitates an additional, independent disciplinary regime. Both types of procedure have been put in place to fulfill the regulatory need to **protect the public interest**.

6.2 ICAEW's complaints and disciplinary procedures: the Professional Standards Department (PSD)

The **Professional Standards Department** of the ICAEW is responsible for implementing the ICAEW's disciplinary procedures, including the handling of complaints against members (both individuals and firms).

6.2.1 What is a complaint and who can bring one?

Complaints are usually that a member or firm have breached the ICAEW's bye-laws by:

- **Breaching a regulation**
- **Departing from guidance**
- **Bringing discredit** on the ICAEW, the profession or themselves

Fee disputes are not covered by the procedures, but the Institute does offer a **fee arbitration service** on a voluntary basis.

Anyone can make a complaint: firms, clients, other accountants, the Department for Business, Innovation and Skills (BIS), other regulators, members of the public and even the ICAEW itself.

A complaint in relation to a very serious matter which is already in the public domain and which may affect the reputation of the accountancy profession may be referred straight to the **FRC's Accountancy Scheme** for investigation (see below).

6.2.2 What is the ICAEW complaints and disciplinary procedure?

The procedure for most complaints is as follows:

- **Conciliation**: When a client identifies a problem with a member or a firm, the first step is conciliation. This means trying to find a practical solution, such as giving an explanation or providing information to resolve the problem
- **Investigation** (if it has not been resolved through conciliation) by the **Investigation Committee (IC)**
- **Disciplinary proceedings** by the **Disciplinary Committee (DC)**

This procedure is summarised in Figure 10.2, which has been used by the PSD to explain the procedure to a complainant (throughout the chart, 'we' refers to the PSD).

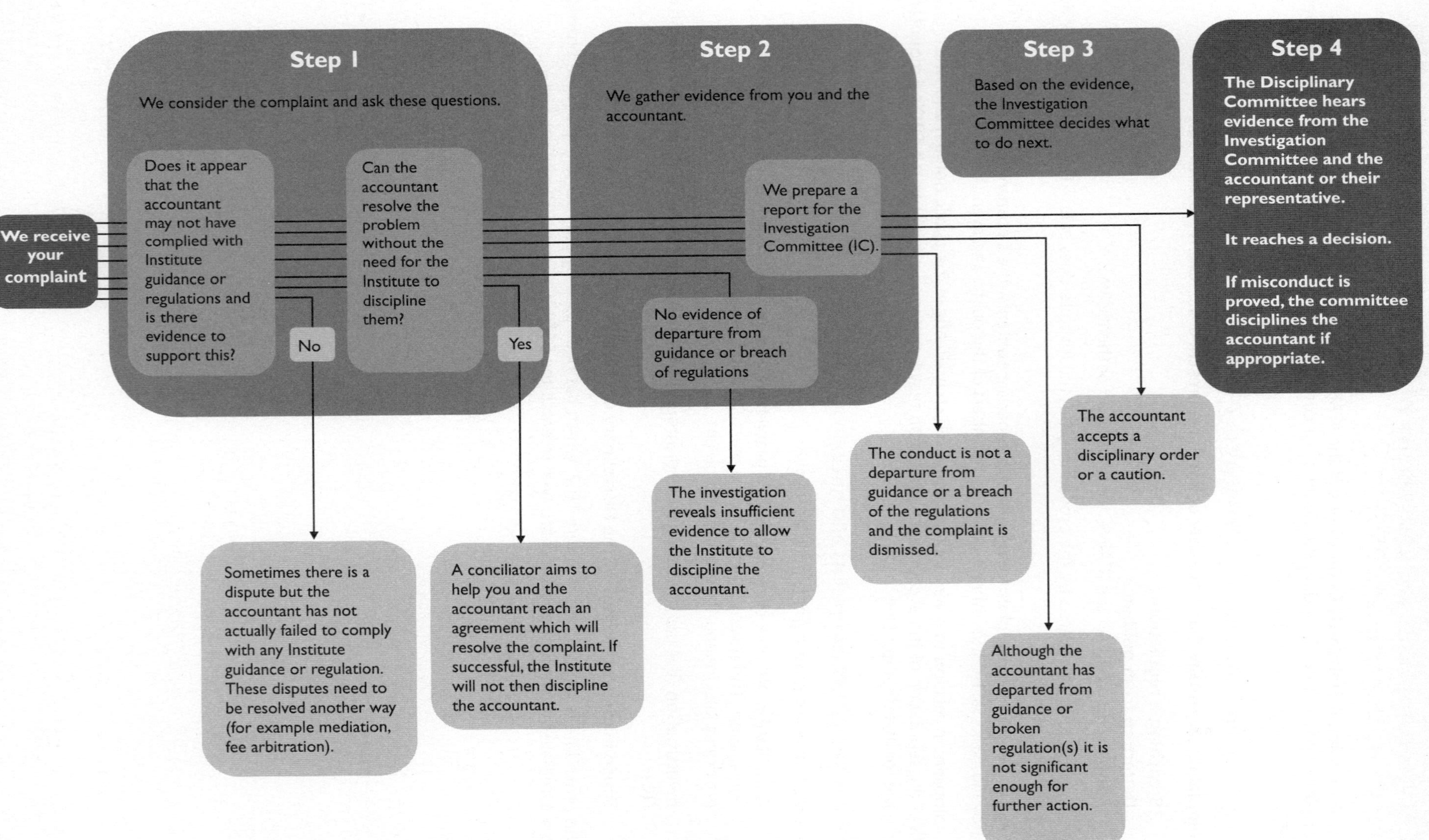

We receive your complaint
Step 1
We consider the complaint and ask these questions.
Does it appear that the accountant may not have complied with Institute guidance or regulations and is there evidence to support this?
No
Sometimes there is a dispute but the accountant has not actually failed to comply with any Institute guidance or regulation. These disputes need to be resolved another way (for example mediation, fee arbitration).
Can the accountant resolve the problem without the need for the Institute to discipline them?
Yes
A conciliator aims to help you and the accountant reach an agreement which will resolve the complaint. If successful, the Institute will not then discipline the accountant.
Step 2
We gather evidence from you and the accountant.
No evidence of departure from guidance or breach of regulations
The investigation reveals insufficient evidence to allow the Institute to discipline the accountant.
We prepare a report for the Investigation Committee (IC).
The conduct is not a departure from guidance or a breach of the regulations and the complaint is dismissed.
Step 3
Based on the evidence, the Investigation Committee decides what to do next.
Although the accountant has departed from guidance or broken regulation(s) it is not significant enough for further action.
The accountant accepts a disciplinary order or a caution.
Step 4
The Disciplinary Committee hears evidence from the Investigation Committee and the accountant or their representative.
It reaches a decision.
If misconduct is proved, the committee disciplines the accountant if appropriate.

Figure 10.2: the ICAEW's complaint and disciplinary procedures

6.2.3 The committees involved in dealing with complaints

If the member or firm appears to be in breach of regulations or has departed from guidance, the IC and DC, as well as the **Appeal Committee** (AC), may be involved.

If the member or firm appears to be in breach of the regulations relating to the reserved areas (insolvency, investment business or audit work), the following committees may also be involved:

- The Audit Registration Committee (ARC), which may withdraw a firm's audit registration
- The Investment Business Committee (IBC)
- The Insolvency Licensing Committee (ILC), which may withdraw an insolvency licence.

These committees see the results of disciplinary proceedings (such as action taken by the IC or DC), and can take action against the member or firm if this is appropriate.

Members and firms can appeal against a decision of the ARC, IBC or ILC to the Review Committee (RC). The RC appoints a panel of three people to conduct these reviews.

6.2.4 How are complaints investigated?

The ICAEW first writes to the person who has made the complaint (the **complainant**), then to the **member or firm** setting out full details of the complaint and **inviting their comments**. It is one of the ICAEW's rules that members must:

- Answer questions
- Provide any information the ICAEW asks for

If members do not reply to letters initially, the ICAEW can **require them to answer questions and produce books or papers**. If members fail to respond to the request, they will be in breach of a bye-law and can be disciplined for this.

Following the initial investigation, if it appears there is a **case to answer** (or if the complainant insists that the IC considers the case) it is reported to the IC. The IC consists of **at least 14 people**, of whom at least **25% are not chartered accountants**.

Complainants do not have the right to appear before the IC in person. Members also do not have the right to appear before the IC but, on rare occasions, the IC can require them to attend.

If the IC decides there is **no case to answer**, the matter is **closed**, unless the complainant asks for the case to be referred to the independent **Reviewer of Complaints** to review the IC's decision (or an earlier decision not to refer the complaint to the IC in the first place). The Reviewer of Complaints is an independent non-accountant appointed to see whether a complaint has been dealt with correctly.

If the **member or firm agrees the complaint is valid**, the IC can impose one of a range of penalties. It has the power to:

- Issue a **reprimand**
- **Fine** the member or their firm
- **Suspend** or **remove** a member's practising certificate

6.2.5 What happens if the IC finds that there is a case to answer?

If the IC finds that there is a case to answer and the member or firm have not agreed the complaint is valid, it has four options, as follows:

- **Take no further action**: it may still take the complaint into account if it finds there is a case to answer in a subsequent case. If the member or firm does not agree that there is a case to answer, they can ask the DC to consider the case

- **Offer an unpublicised caution**: there will be no publicity and no fine but the member or firm may have to pay a fixed sum of costs. Again, if they do not agree that there is a case to answer, they can ask the DC to consider the case

- **Offer a consent order**: there is a case to answer but the matter is not serious enough to exclude the member(s) from membership or suspend their practising certificate, so the IC offers a **consent order**. If the member or firm is prepared to accept the IC's decision, including financial penalties, the IC makes the order without referring the case to the DC. The order has exactly the same effect as an order of the DC and receives the same publicity.

- Make a **formal complaint to the Disciplinary Committee (DC)** if the member or firm does not accept the IC's decision, or if the IC thinks the case is so serious that it may lead to the member being excluded from membership.

6.2.6 What happens at a DC hearing?

In cases of misconduct referred by the IC the DC appoints a **tribunal of three people** – two chartered accountants and one person who is not an accountant – to hear the case.

- The IC presents the case and is usually represented by a **solicitor or barrister**

- A **Legal Assessor** gives the DC advice on law and procedure but is not involved in taking decisions. The Legal Assessor is an independent solicitor or barrister

- The member or firm can attend and be represented by a **barrister, solicitor or member of the ICAEW**

The DC can impose **penalties** including:

- **Reprimands**
- **Fines**
- **Taking away a member's practising certificate**
- **Excluding them from membership** of the ICAEW

If the DC dismisses the case, that is the end of the matter as far as the ICAEW is concerned. However, members do have the right to appeal to the **Appeal Committee** (AC) against a decision or order of the DC. They must do this in writing within 28 days of the DC's decision.

6.2.7 The Appeal Committee (AC)

The AC consists of five people: three chartered accountants, one non-accountant member and a chairman who holds a legal qualification.

- If an **appeal is successful**, the AC may ask the **ICAEW to pay costs**

- If an **appeal is unsuccessful** the AC may order **the member to pay any additional costs** the ICAEW has incurred as a result of having to present the case again to the AC

6.2.8 Publicity of the results of hearings

Details of IC **consent orders** and **orders of the DC and AC** are sent to the **national press** and to **accountancy publications**. If someone is excluded from membership or if their practising certificate is taken away, details are sent to the **press in their local area**. The names of third parties are not normally published.

Interactive question 3: Complaints **[Difficulty level: Exam standard]**

One of your clients is planning to complain to the ICAEW about work carried out by your firm and the prices it has charged. On what grounds may the client make a complaint to the ICAEW?

See **Answer** at the end of this chapter.

6.3 FRC's Accountancy Scheme

6.3.1 What does the FRC do?

The FRC runs the disciplinary Accountancy Scheme as the independent investigative and disciplinary body for accountants in the UK, covering members of:

- ICAEW
- ACCA
- CIMA
- CIPFA
- ICAS
- ICAI

The FRC deals with cases which raise or appear to **raise important issues affecting the public interest** in the UK, or which need to be investigated to determine whether or not there has been any misconduct by an accountant or accountancy firm. It regards issues of public interest as being those which give rise to **serious public concern or to damaged public confidence in the accountancy profession** in the UK.

The FRC's general running expenses in this respect are funded by the bodies covered by the Accountancy Scheme, but the cost of an FRC enquiry into individual cases is borne by the relevant accountancy bodies.

6.3.2 How are FRC disciplinary cases dealt with?

The FRC takes on cases in two different ways:

- **Referrals from an accountancy body**: complaints about accountants or accountancy firms are made to the accountancy body of which the accountant or the firm is a member. Matters which raise serious issues affecting the public interest may be referred to the FRC by the ICAEW
- **Self-referral**: the FRC may decide of its own accord to investigate a matter without it having been referred to it by one of the accountants' professional bodies

If the FRC decides to investigate a matter, the professional discipline team within the Conduct Division refers it to the FRC's Executive Counsel (a barrister). The Executive Counsel and the professional discipline team can conduct preliminary enquiries (with the relevant professional body's consent) to help make the decision to investigate, and are also responsible for conducting the full investigation. The Executive Counsel decides whether or not any accountant or accountancy firm should be subject to disciplinary proceedings. In making this decision, the Executive Counsel acts independently.

6.3.3 Powers of the Executive Counsel

The Executive Counsel can:

- Require the participating accountants' professional bodies to provide documents relevant to any particular matter
- Seek information and documents from accountants and accountancy firms
- Require accountants and accountancy firms to give evidence to a tribunal

Failures to comply with any such request are themselves grounds for disciplinary proceedings.

If disciplinary proceedings are to be commenced, the Executive Counsel files a complaint with the FRC's Conduct Committee, which then instructs a Convener to appoint a **Disciplinary Tribunal** (composed of either three or five suitably qualified people drawn from a Panel of Tribunal members maintained by the FRC) to decide on the complaint.

6.3.4 Role of the Disciplinary Tribunal

The Chairman is a lawyer. In a three-person Tribunal there is one lay person and one accountant; in a five-person Tribunal there are two lay persons and two accountants. This means a majority of the Tribunal is always formed of non-accountants. To ensure their independence, no member of a Tribunal can be an officer or employee of:

- Any of the accountants' professional bodies
- The FRC or any of its operating bodies

Tribunal hearings are normally **open to the public** except in exceptional circumstances where the Tribunal decides that this would not be in the interests of justice. The Tribunal sits and is presented with the evidence; witnesses may be called. A Tribunal hearing is less formal than court proceedings and it is not restricted as a court might be in accepting evidence. The accountant or firm which is the subject of the complaint is entitled to attend and be legally represented at the hearings, and will have a full opportunity to defend any complaints, present evidence and challenge any evidence against them.

- When a **complaint is upheld** the Tribunal can fine the accountant or firm and order them to pay all or part of the costs of the investigation and the hearing.
- When a **complaint is dismissed** the Tribunal can order the FRC to pay legal costs.

The Tribunal does NOT have the power to order compensation to be paid.

6.3.5 Appealing against a finding of the Disciplinary Tribunal

An accountant or accountancy firm can appeal against any finding against it to an **Appeal Tribunal**. A retired judge or a senior barrister first considers the appeal. If they give leave to appeal, it is heard by an Appeal Tribunal set up by the FRC in the same way and subject to the same criteria as the Disciplinary Tribunal which heard the original complaint.

6.3.6 Upholding transparency, independence and fairness

To be an effective part of the oversight of self-regulation, the FRC as the independent disciplinary organ is:

- **Transparent**: all decisions made by the FRC, the Executive Counsel, Disciplinary Tribunals and Appeal Tribunals are published unless it is not in the public interest to do so and subject to any legal constraints. The hearings of the Disciplinary Tribunals and Appeal Tribunals are normally open to the public.
- **Independent**: a majority of the FRC's members and its chairman are non-accountants. The tribunals comprise a majority of non-accountants. No officers or employees of any of the accountancy bodies, the FRC or any of its subsidiary bodies may be appointed to a tribunal.
- **Fair**: any accountant or firm under investigation or subject to disciplinary proceedings is able to be legally represented at all times during the investigation and at any hearings. They are told what complaints they face and are given access to all documentary evidence obtained by the Executive Counsel in the course of the investigation. They have the opportunity to comment on any preliminary views formed by the Executive Counsel before a decision to present a formal complaint is made. They are entitled to attend hearings, present evidence on their behalf and challenge any evidence against them, including cross-examining witnesses.

Summary and Self-test

Summary

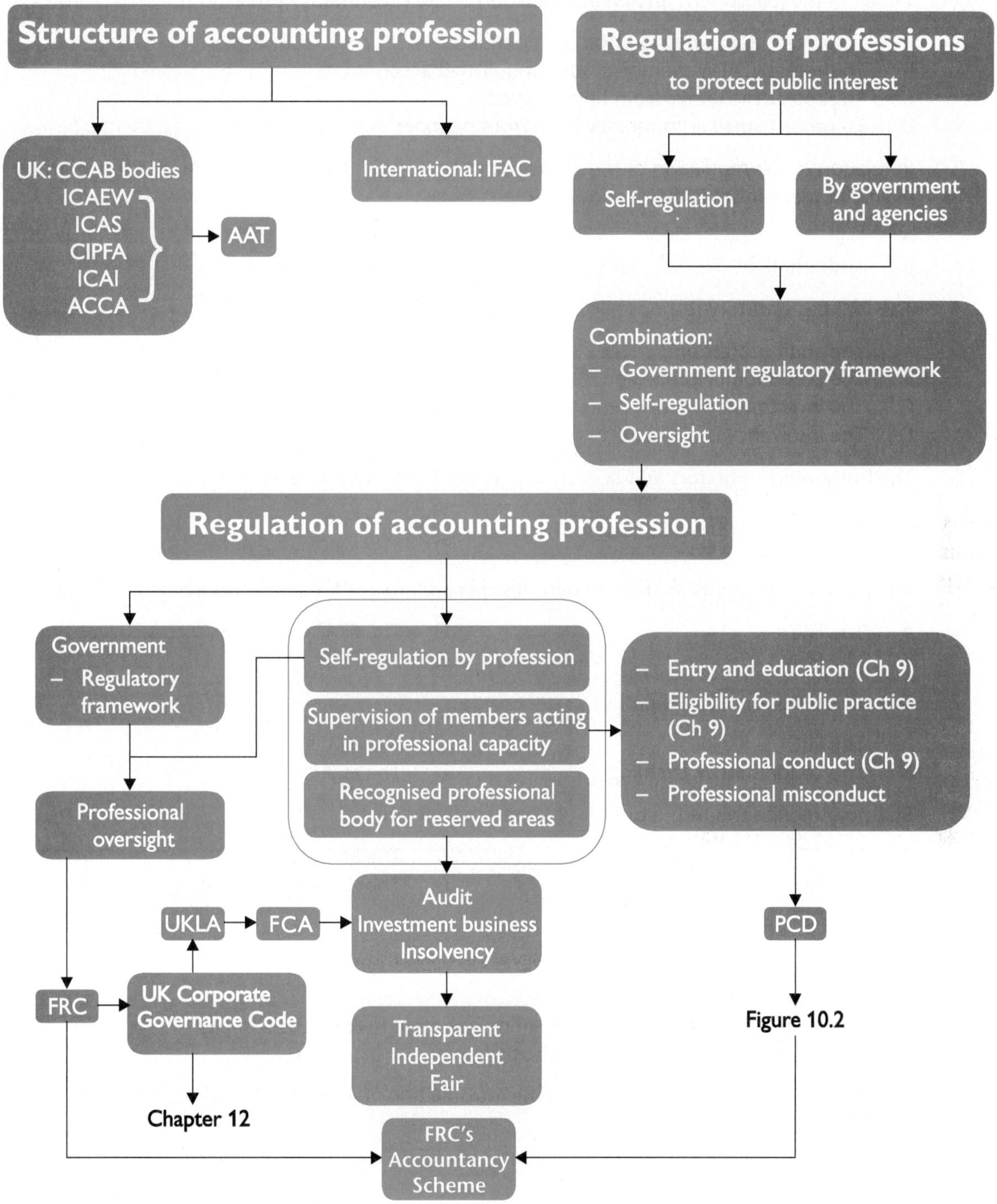

Structure of accounting profession

UK: CCAB bodies
ICAEW
ICAS
CIPFA
ICAI
ACCA
→ AAT

International: IFAC

Regulation of professions
to protect public interest

Self-regulation

By government and agencies

Combination:
- Government regulatory framework
- Self-regulation
- Oversight

Regulation of accounting profession

Government
- Regulatory framework

Professional oversight

Self-regulation by profession

Supervision of members acting in professional capacity

Recognised professional body for reserved areas

- Entry and education (Ch 9)
- Eligibility for public practice (Ch 9)
- Professional conduct (Ch 9)
- Professional misconduct

PCD

Figure 10.2

Audit
Investment business
Insolvency

UKLA → FCA

FRC → UK Corporate Governance Code

Chapter 12

Transparent
Independent
Fair

FRC's Accountancy Scheme

Self-test

Answer the following questions.

1 The forum for discussion of matters affecting all the accountancy bodies in the UK is called

A IFAC
B CCAB
C FRC
D FCA

2 Which of the following is an aim of regulation of the accountancy profession?

A To protect the profession from competition
B To protect ICAEW members from unqualified accountants
C To protect the public from being misled
D To protect small accountancy firms from big ones

3 In relation to self-regulation of the accountancy profession, the most important aspect of the oversight mechanism is that it should be seen to be

A Fair
B Authoritative
C Objective
D Independent

4 The FRC has statutory responsibility for monitoring the quality of

A The audit profession
B The accountancy profession
C The investment business profession
D The insolvency profession

5 The body which monitors and acts on departures from requirements for financial statements is

A The FCA
B The FRRP
C The FPA
D The MPC

6 The body which acts as an independent disciplinary process for the accountancy profession is

A The FRC
B The FCA
C The FPA
D The FRRP

7 The UK Listing Authority is part of

A The FRC
B The London Stock Exchange
C The ICAEW
D The FCA

8 Statutory monitoring of the quality of audit is effected by

A The FCA
B The FPA
C The FRC
D The ICAEW

9 If a member is offered a caution by ICAEW's Investigation Committee this means that

A There will be neither publicity, fines nor costs to pay
B There will be a fine but no publicity
C There will be neither publicity nor a fine but there may be costs to pay
D There will be publicity, a fine and costs to pay

Now, go back to the Learning Objectives in the Introduction. If you are satisfied you have achieved these objectives, please tick them off.

Answers to Interactive questions

Answer to Interactive question 1

Regulation should:

- **Protect the public** from being misled, or from suffering from abuse of power through knowledge or monopoly
- In a market economy, **facilitate competition** and **reduce barriers to trade**
- In the case of professions, ensure that **technical, educational and ethical standards** are maintained at a level the public has a right to expect
- Be **flexible** enough to ensure the right result in each of the infinite variety of circumstances that occur in practice, as we have seen in the principles-based framework approach to accounting
- Take account of reasonable and informed opinion to ensure that **justice is reasonably seen to be done**
- **Enforce** the standards required firmly but fairly to ensure that the general support of those subject to the regulation is retained, but that transgressors are effectively dealt with
- Be **transparent** in its setting and enforcement to maintain confidence that the public interest is being safeguarded

Answer to Interactive question 2

The Audit Quality Review team of the FRC's Conduct Division fulfils the FRC's statutory function of monitoring the quality of the audit profession. The audit client to which the visit relates must be an economically significant entity, so it is either listed or of other major public interest.

Answer to Interactive question 3

Complaints may be on the grounds that the firm is in breach of an ICAEW regulation, has departed from guidance or has brought the ICAEW into disrepute. The ICAEW does not deal with disputes over fees, though it does offer a fee arbitration service.

Answers to Self-test

1	B	
2	C	
3	D	All these qualities are important, but independence is of the greatest importance if the mechanism is not to be seen as pursuing the self-interest of the profession
4	A	
5	B	
6	A	
7	D	
8	C	
9	C	

CHAPTER 11

Governance, corporate responsibility, sustainability and ethics

Introduction

Learning objectives

Tick off

- State the reasons why governance is needed ☐
- Identify the role that governance plays in the management of a business ☐
- Identify the key stakeholders and their governance needs for a particular business ☐
- Specify how differences in national and business cultures affect corporate governance ☐
- Specify the nature of ethics, business ethics, sustainability and corporate responsibility ☐
- Specify the policies and procedures a business should implement in order to promote an ethical culture ☐

Specific syllabus references are: 5a, b, d, g, h.

Syllabus links

Governance is developed further as a topic in Audit and Assurance and Financial Accounting and Reporting at the Professional level, and at the Advanced level. Ethics are a continuing theme in all papers. Sustainability and corporate responsibility are studied further in Business Strategy.

Examination context

Questions on governance, corporate responsibility, sustainability and ethics are almost certain to appear in your exam.

Questions are likely to be set in multiple choice format in a scenario context, though knowledge-type questions are also likely on particular definitions and principles.

1 What is governance?

Section overview

- Governance is the system by which an organisation is directed and controlled so that its objectives are achieved in an acceptable and sustainable manner.
- Agency theory states that managers and directors act as shareholders' agents when managing the company.
- Managers and directors should reflect the interests of shareholders, not their own interests. Historically they were able to pursue their own interests because they had better information than shareholders, and were not held accountable to them.

Management is essentially a very practical matter: 'getting things done'. It should not be confused with a term that is frequently used interchangeably with management, which is **governance**.

The **UK Corporate Governance Code 2012** helpfully sets out the '**underlying principles of all good governance**':

- Accountability
- Transparency
- Probity (honesty)
- Focus on the sustainable success of an entity over the longer term

Governance incorporates concepts of ethics, risk management and stakeholder protection, extending way beyond management alone. Governance is not the same thing as managing a business and running business operations. It is concerned with exercising **overall control**, to ensure that the objectives of the company are achieved in an acceptable and sustainable manner. If a business is properly led, directed and controlled then it should be able to get things done properly and should be sustainable in the long term.

Interactive question 1: Corporate governance [Difficulty level: Intermediate]

You have probably heard a great deal about 'good corporate governance' in the press and maybe in the office too. What do you think it means? Why is it an important issue?

See **Answer** at the end of this chapter.

1.1 Why is governance an important issue?

Governance has become a very major business issue in recent years – especially since the financial crisis since 2007 – because, simply put, in getting things done a business's managers very often lose sight of:

- Whom they are seeking to benefit, and
- The fact they should not harm others

This is often referred to as the **agency problem**.

1.2 Agency problem: shareholders and management

Managers of a company are there to ensure that the interests of the shareholders, who in large companies are not usually also the managers, are looked after. Managers therefore effectively act as the '**agents**' of the shareholders when managing the company, though not in the full legal sense. This means that:

- **ownership and control are separated**, and
- **conflicts** arise between the interests of those in control of the company and those who own it.

These issues are known together as **agency theory** or stewardship theory, as described by the Organisation for Economic Co-operation and Development (OECD).

'Put simply, the interests of those who have effective control over a firm can differ from the interests of those who supply the firm with external finance. The problem, commonly referred to as a principal-agent problem, grows out of the separation of ownership and control and of corporate outsiders and insiders. In the absence of the protections that good governance supplies, asymmetries of information and difficulties of monitoring mean that capital providers who lack control over the corporation will find it risky and costly to protect themselves from the opportunistic behaviour of managers and controlling shareholders.'

OECD, *Principles of Corporate Governance*

Historically, when managers ran a company in a way that suited their own interests, without due regard to the interests of the shareholders, they often got away with it because:

- They had better **information** than the shareholders about what was going on
- They were not sufficiently **accountable** for their stewardship, decisions and actions

1.2.1 The importance of information

Shareholders make **decisions** to invest in the company's shares, and/or to hold onto the shares, largely on the basis of information supplied by managers in the company's name. The value of a shareholder's investment can therefore be at risk from receiving inadequate information to judge what is happening.

1.2.2 The need for accountability

Shareholders also rely on managers to **account to them for their stewardship of the company's resources**. Through a combination of withholding information, failing to report to shareholders as required (basically, hiding information) and making decisions that are in their own rather than the company's interests, managers and company directors have historically been able to avoid true accountability to shareholders.

2 What is corporate governance?

Section overview

- Corporate governance is the set of relationships between a company's management, board, shareholders and other stakeholders that provides the structure through which the company's objectives are set, attained and monitored. It specifies the distribution of rights and responsibilities between stakeholders, and establishes rules and procedures for making decisions about the company's affairs.
- Three perspectives on corporate governance all emphasise shareholders but the public policy and stakeholder perspectives place more emphasis on non-shareholders, and on the need to balance the interests of all stakeholders.

Definitions

Corporate governance: 'A set of relationships between a company's management, its board, its shareholders and other stakeholders...that provides the structure through which the objectives of the company are set ...attained...and monitored'.

OECD, *Principles of Corporate Governance*

Corporate governance: 'the system by which companies are directed and controlled. Boards of directors are responsible for the governance of their companies. The shareholders' role in governance is to appoint the directors and the auditors and to satisfy themselves that an appropriate governance structure is in place. The responsibilities of the board include setting the company's strategic aims, providing the leadership to put them into effect, supervising the management of the business and reporting to shareholders on their stewardship. The board's actions are subject to laws, regulations and the shareholders in general meeting'.

Cadbury Committee *Code on Corporate Governance*

2.1 What are the objectives of corporate governance?

There are four broad perspectives on what the **objectives** of corporate governance should be.

2.1.1 The public policy perspective on corporate governance

Some would argue that the aim of corporate governance is to ensure that the company meets:

- The objectives of its **shareholders, plus**
- The interests of other individuals and groups with a direct '**stake**' in the company, **plus**
- The interests of the **public at large**

In other words, there is a public policy perspective to corporate governance, as well as a corporate perspective.

'From a public policy perspective, corporate governance is about **nurturing enterprise** while ensuring **accountability** in the exercise of power and patronage by firms. The role of public policy is to provide firms with the incentives and discipline to minimise the divergence between private and social returns and to protect the interests of stakeholders.'

OECD, *Principles of Corporate Governance*

2.1.2 The stakeholder perspective on corporate governance

Taking a more narrow 'stakeholder view', corporate governance means a **balance between economic and social goals and between individual and communal goals**. The framework of corporate governance should therefore:

- Encourage the **efficient use of resources** through efficient investment
- Require **accountability** from the company's senior management (its board of directors) to shareholders for the way it has managed and taken care of those resources
- Aim to **align the interests of shareholders and companies with those of other stakeholders**

2.1.3 The corporate perspective on corporate governance

We normally think of the aim of a company as being to maximise the wealth of the shareholders, provided it conforms to the rules of society (its laws and customs). This means that a company's senior management should balance the interests of shareholders with those of other stakeholders in order to **achieve long-term sustained value for shareholders.**

2.1.4 The stewardship perspective on corporate governance

Probably the most narrow view of corporate governance is to take the approach that the law requires directors to **act in the best interests of the company** when acting as 'stewards' of the company's resources. This is called the stewardship approach or perspective, and is related most directly to solving the agency problem outlined above.

2.2 A definition of corporate governance

Whether a corporate, public policy or stakeholder perspective is taken, rather than the OECD's definition set out above, we could use the following:

Definition

Corporate governance: A structured system for the direction and control of a company that:

- Specifies the distribution of rights and responsibilities between stakeholders, such as the shareholders, the board of directors and management.
- Has established rules and procedures for making decisions about the company's affairs.

The UK Corporate Governance Code 2012 defines corporate governance in terms of its purpose, and takes a stewardship perspective on this.

Definition

Corporate governance: 'The purpose of corporate governance is to facilitate effective, entrepreneurial and prudent management that can deliver the long-term success of the company...[it] is therefore about what the board of a company does and how it sets the values of the company, and is to be distinguished from the day to day operational management of the company by full-time executives'

FRC, *UK Corporate Governance Code 2010*

3 Stakeholders' governance needs

Section overview

- Governance extends beyond management to take explicit account of stakeholders.
- Stakeholders' interests can often be in conflict, and it is not enough simply to let the most powerful (the shareholders) 'win'.
- Stakeholders need the company's corporate governance to ensure that: their interests and expectations will be reflected in the company's objectives; the scope for conflict of interests is reduced; the company follows good practice in corporate governance and business ethics.

3.1 What are stakeholders' governance needs?

In Chapter 1 we saw the stakes, interests and expectations of each category of stakeholder in a company, and in Chapter 4 we saw how companies can 'map' these points as an aid in determining what the company's objectives should be. We need now to look at both **conflicts** between stakeholders' interests and their **governance needs**.

3.2 Conflicts between stakeholders' interests

No company can exactly meet all the expectations of all its stakeholders all of the time. There is often a **conflict of interests** between different stakeholder groups, with each group wanting different things, in order to achieve incompatible objectives. In most cases the company will set itself a strategy that at least attempts to balance these conflicting interests whilst acknowledging that the interests of shareholders are dominant.

Occasionally however there will be a **serious conflict of interests**.

3.2.1 What are the symptoms of a serious conflict of interests?

There is no standard way in which a serious conflict of interest becomes apparent. It may become evident by:

- **Financial collapse without warning**, as in the case of US energy corporation Enron in 2002
- Directors trying to **disguise the true financial performance of the company** from shareholders by 'dressing up' the published financial statements so shareholders cannot judge properly the condition of their investment
- Disputes over **directors' remuneration** such as huge salaries, bonuses, pension schemes, share options, golden hellos and golden goodbyes and other benefits and, in general, directors' rewards that do not vary according to the company's performance and the benefits obtained for the shareholders
- Decisions taken by a board of directors to satisfy their own wish for power and rewards rather than to boost the interests of shareholders, such as recommendations on shareholders accepting certain **takeover bids and offers**

3.3 Stakeholders' governance needs

- For their interests and expectations to be reflected in the company's **objectives**
- For the **scope for conflicts to be reduced**
- For the company to adhere to **good practice in corporate governance**
- For the company to adhere to **good business ethics**

4 Symptoms of poor corporate governance

Section overview

- There is a range of symptoms that, alone or together, may indicate poor corporate governance in an organisation.

The following symptoms can indicate that there is poor corporate governance:

- **Domination of the board** by a single individual or group, with other board members merely acting as a rubber stamp
- **No involvement by the board**: meeting irregularly, failing to consider systematically the organisation's activities and risks, or basing decisions on inadequate information
- **Inadequate control function**, for instance no internal audit, or a lack of adequate technical knowledge in key roles, or a rapid turnover of staff involved in accounting or control
- Lack of **supervision** of employees
- Lack of independent scrutiny by **external or internal auditors**
- Lack of **contact with shareholders**
- Emphasis on **short-term profitability**, leading to concealment of problems or errors, or manipulation of financial statements to achieve desired results
- **Misleading financial statements and information**

Worked example: Poor corporate governance

Techpoint plc is a medium sized public company that produces a range of components used in the manufacture of computers. The board of directors consists of Chairman Max Mallory, Chief Executive Richard Mallory, and Finance Director Linda Mallory, all of whom are siblings. There are five other unrelated executive directors. All directors receive bonuses based on sales. The company's sales are made by individual salesmen and women each of whom has the authority to enter on the company's behalf into contracts unlimited in value without the need to refer to a superior or consult with other departments. It is this flexibility that has enabled the company to be very profitable in past years. However, a number of bad contracts in the current year have meant that the Finance Director has re-classed them as 'costs' to maintain healthy sales and to protect the directors' bonuses.

What are the corporate governance issues at Techpoint plc?

Solution

The main corporate governance issues are:

(a) **Domination by a small group**: all the key directors are related which gives them power over the other executives.

(b) **Short-term view**: directors' bonuses are based on short-term sales and caused the manipulation of accounts to achieve them.

(c) **Lack of supervision**: the sales force can tie the company into large loss-making contracts without any checks. There is no authorisation or communication with other departments which means the company may take on contracts that it cannot fulfil. The company has been hit hard with bad contracts in the current year.

5 What is meant by 'good practice' in corporate governance?

Section overview

- Good practice in corporate governance is concerned with: risk management; ethical and sustainable behaviour; transparency; integrity; accountability; reducing the potential for conflict; reconciling the interests of shareholders and directors.
- Key elements in corporate governance: the board (executive and non-executive directors, and committees); senior management; shareholders; external auditors; internal auditors.

Good practice in corporate governance is concerned with:

- **Risk** management and reduction
- **Ethical and sustainable pursuit of the business's strategy** in a way which safeguards against misuse of resources, physical or intellectual and which aims at ensuring **success over the long term**
- **Openness** and **transparency**: disclosure of information
- **Integrity** and **probity**: applying the **spirit of the law** as well as its letter, and being **honest** in all dealings
- **Accountability**: monitoring and judging directors' performance based on the returns that the company has achieved under their stewardship
- **Reducing the potential for conflict**
- **Reconciling** the **interests** of shareholders and directors as far as possible

The five **key elements of good corporate governance** are as follows:

- **The Board of Directors**
  - **Executive directors** of a very high standard in terms of their decision-making and of the culture that they create in the company
  - **Non-executive directors** who are independent of the executives yet who accept that they have collective responsibility with the rest of the board for corporate governance
  - **Committees of the board of directors as a whole** that are properly constituted and have the power and resources to make the decisions delegated to them by the main board.
- **Senior management** of high quality and able to:
  - Put into effect the decisions of the board
  - 'Whistle-blow' on the activities of the company should the need arise
- **Shareholders** who are proactive at meetings and generally ensure that the board is acting in their best interests and within the spirit of good corporate governance
- **External auditors** working on behalf of the shareholders totally independently of the directors when reaching a conclusion as to whether the company's financial statements show a true and fair view
- **Internal auditors** who are independent of the directors as far as possible, reporting to the Audit Committee of the board or to some other committee dominated by non-executives

6 The effect of types of financial system on governance

Section overview

- The type of financial system in an economy affects the type of corporate governance that prevails.
- There are two broad types of financial system: bank-based and market-based. Which one operates in a particular economy depends on: household preference re saving; degree of financial intermediation; balance of debt and equity in business finance
- Which system is in place depends on: whether there is instability associated with financial markets; how far government intervenes in and regulates the system; how effective markets as opposed to intermediaries are at allocating resources; how far markets are limited by market imperfections, such as transaction costs, insider dealing and asymmetric information.
- Bank-based financial systems are seen in Japan, France and Germany. In these systems, bank lending is the most important source of business finance, after retained earnings (though not in Japan), and banks and businesses are highly integrated.
- Market-based financial systems are seen in the UK and the US, with markets being more important than banks for long-term finance. This means that the dominant force in external finance for businesses is represented by institutional shareholders.
- The increasing influence of institutional shareholders means that there is increasing pressure on companies: to conduct themselves well; to respond to the requirements of active or 'engaged' institutional shareholders; to provide good information via financial reporting.

In Chapter 8 we looked at the **UK financial system** and its role in business finance. We now need to determine why the type of financial system overall influences so profoundly the approach taken to corporate governance.

6.1 Types of financial system

There are two broad types of financial system:

- Bank-based systems
- Market-based systems

Whether a system favours **banks** or the **markets** is determined by how the factors we saw in Chapter 8 are balanced, namely:

- How **households** prefer to hold their assets
- The degree of dominance of the system by financial intermediaries and therefore by **indirect investment** as opposed to **direct investment**
- How businesses are financed, that is the **balance of retained earnings, debt and equity**

In turn, many of these preferences in a system are determined by its attitude to some of the problems inherent in any system that is designed to ensure the flow of funds from savers to borrowers:

- **Instability** associated with financial markets
- The degree of **government intervention** in and regulation of the system (government activity has become increasingly discredited)
- How effective markets as opposed to intermediaries are at **allocating resources** (in economic terms, markets are perceived as being better at this)
- How far markets are limited by **market imperfections**, such as:
  - **Transaction costs**
  - **Insider trading**, and
  - **Asymmetric information**

We shall cover market imperfections in Chapters 13 and 14 of this Study Manual.

6.2 Bank-based financial systems

Continental European systems, especially those of **France** and **Germany**, have traditionally been bank-based systems, as has the **Japanese** financial system. While there are significant differences between them, we can characterise a bank-based financial system as follows:

- Households prefer to bear **little risk** and so allocate more of their financial assets to cash and cash equivalents ie deposits with banks
- Households have **less access to investments in physical assets** such as housing ie less choice
- Where households do invest in securities, this is primarily done via **intermediaries** such as pension and mutual funds, so **institutional shareholders** are influential
- There is comparatively **more government regulation**, often as a result of historic financial catastrophes
- **Banks are highly concentrated and integrated** in terms of providing both banking (deposit-taking) and non-banking (insurance, etc) services
- **Bank lending** is the most important source of business finance, after retained earnings (though not in Japan)
- **Banks and businesses are highly integrated**: banks have a long-term relationship with the businesses they lend to, usually cemented by the bank:
  - Holding equity in the business as well as debt
  - Having equity held by the business (a 'cross-holding')
  - Having access to detailed management information so there is less risk that their lending will be jeopardised by undesirable activities
  - Being involved in the business's strategic decisions, often by having seats on the board
  - Becoming actively involved if there are financial problems
- **Markets are volatile and speculative** because companies are dependent on bank finance and thus have high gearing

Together these factors mean that the dominant force in external finance for businesses is represented by **banks**. However, most bank-based systems are becoming increasingly market oriented, with less regulation and a higher profile for financial markets.

Interactive question 2: Risk [Difficulty level: Exam standard]

In the UK households hold proportionately more of their assets in the form of equity than in Japan. What does this say about UK households' attitude to risk?

See **Answer** at the end of this chapter.

6.3 Market-based financial systems

The **US** and **UK** systems have traditionally been market-based systems. While there are significant differences between them, we can characterise a market-based financial system as follows:

- Households **bear more risk** and so hold proportionately more equity and proportionately fewer deposits with banks
- Households have **greater access to investments in physical assets** such as housing ie more choice
- High levels of **indirect investment via intermediaries** such as pension and mutual funds mean that **institutional shareholders** have a great deal of influence
- **Markets** are more important than banks for long-term finance, though retained earnings remain the most important source of funds
- They are **comparatively unregulated**

- **Banks are more fragmented** with less integration of banking and non-banking services (though this has changed to a large degree)
- **Banks have less close relationships with the businesses they lend to,** not holding equity and not being involved in decision-making

Together these factors mean that the dominant force in external finance for businesses is represented by **institutional shareholders**.

6.4 Financial intermediation and the importance of information

In both types of system financial intermediation is of increasing importance, because intermediation is seen as the way to overcome market imperfections, especially that of **asymmetric information**. While lending banks in bank-based systems have access to information about companies that is not shared with investors in the financial markets, so too have institutional shareholders in market-based systems historically been kept better-informed than the general public about the affairs of the business in which the intermediary holds debt and equity.

The increasing influence of **institutional shareholders** means that there is increasing pressure on companies:

- To conduct themselves well (**good corporate governance**)
- To respond to the requirements of **institutional shareholders**
- To provide good **financial information** via **financial reporting**

7 Governance structures

Section overview

- A governance structure is the set of legal or regulatory methods that has been put in place to ensure good corporate governance. It may comprise both direct regulation and non-statutory codes of practice.
- The OECD's principles on corporate governance are: promotion of transparent and efficient financial markets; protection of shareholders' rights; equitable treatment of shareholders; recognition of the rights of shareholders; timely and accurate disclosure of information; an effective board.
- A board of directors may be unitary or have a dual (management and supervisory) structure.
- The UK's governance structure emphasises shareholders, especially institutional shareholders: insurance companies, pension funds, investment trusts and their investment managers.
- The UK's governance structure incorporates: statute (the Companies Act 2006); a code of practice (the FRC's UK Corporate Governance Code 2012); and the UKLA rules (for listed companies).

7.1 What is a governance structure?

Definition

Governance structure: The set of legal or regulatory methods put in place in order to ensure effective corporate governance.

There are two basic governance structures:

- Statutes
- Codes of practice

Different countries use different combinations of statutes and codes of practice, depending in part on whether they have **principles-based** or a **shareholder-led approach** to governance structures.

7.2 Principles-based approach to governance structures

In most countries the approach to governance structure is determined initially by the desire to adhere to certain **principles of good corporate governance**, as set out in the OECD's *Principles of Corporate Governance* (revised in 2004). These Principles 'focus on governance problems that result from the separation of ownership and control' and are intended to assist:

> 'Governments in their efforts to evaluate and improve the legal, constitutional and regulatory framework of corporate governance...and to provide guidance and suggestions for stock exchanges, investors and companies.'
>
> *Preamble to Principles of Corporate Governance*, OECD

The OECD Principles are that the corporate governance framework (the governance structure) should:

1. Promote **transparent and efficient financial markets**, be consistent with the **rule of law** and clearly articulate the **division of responsibilities** among different supervisory, regulatory and enforcement authorities.
2. Protect and facilitate **shareholders' rights**, including the following basic rights:
   - To have secure methods of **ownership registration**
   - To **convey and transfer shares**
   - To obtain relevant and material **information** on the company on a timely and regular basis
   - To participate in and vote at **general meetings**, including the right to ask questions of the board
   - To elect and remove **members of the board**
   - To share in the company's **profits**
   - To participate and be involved in **fundamental company changes** such as amendments to the company's constitution
3. Ensure the **equitable treatment of all shareholders**, including minority and foreign shareholders. All shareholders should have the opportunity to obtain effective redress for violation of their rights:
   - All shareholders in the same class should be treated equally
   - Insider trading should be prohibited
   - Directors and key managers should disclose whether they have an interest in material transactions entered into by the company
4. Recognise the **rights of stakeholders** established by law or through mutual agreements, and encourage active co-operation between companies and stakeholders in creating wealth, jobs, and the sustainability of financially sound entities.
5. Ensure that **timely and accurate disclosure** is made on all material matters, including the company's:
   - Financial position and performance
   - Ownership
   - Objectives
   - Board remuneration policy
   - Related party transactions
   - Foreseeable risk factors
6. Ensure the strategic guidance of the company by **the board**, the effective monitoring of management by the board, and the board's accountability.

Principle 5 enshrines in particular:

- The need for and status of the **external audit**, and
- The need for an effective approach to the **provision of analysis or advice** by analysts, brokers, rating agencies and others, that is:
  - Relevant to decisions by investors
  - Free from material conflicts of interest that might compromise the integrity of their analysis or advice

7.3 Shareholder-led approach to governance structures

In the UK and the US in particular, greater emphasis has been placed on the role of **shareholders** in governance structures. This is because they are market-based financial systems where institutional shareholders have very high levels of investment in the shares of leading companies.

'**Institutional shareholders**' is a broad term for organisations which invest money on behalf of other people (their beneficiaries). In the UK they comprise:

- Insurance companies
- Pension funds
- Investment trusts
- Investment managers who act as agents of the above bodies, eg unit trusts

Good corporate governance is greatly assisted when institutional shareholders have an agenda for dialogue with boards of directors and follow that up so they can secure their own interests and those of their beneficiaries. Where this is the case, as in the UK and the US, determining the appropriate governance structure is said to be a '**shareholder-led process**' rather than a principles-based one.

We shall see the effect of the UK's emphasis on institutional shareholders when we look at the UK Corporate Governance Code 2012 in Chapter 12 .

7.4 Possible structures for the board of directors

There are two types of structure for the board of directors as a whole.

- A **unitary board** is responsible for both management of the business and reporting to the shareholders, via the financial statements and shareholder meetings. This is the basic system under UK statute
- A **dual or supervisory board** structure, as is seen in Germany for instance, with roles split between:
  - The **management board**, with responsibility to manage the company using similar powers to the unitary board, and
  - The **supervisory board**: an independent separate board elected by the shareholders and the employees, often comprising a series of committees with delegated powers. In Germany for instance the supervisory board has powers to:
    - Appoint and remove members of the management board
    - Request information from members of the management board
    - Receive formal reports on policy, financial performance, the state of the company's affairs and exceptional occurrences
    - Approve or not approve the income statement, balance sheet and dividends declared
    - Inspect books and records
    - Perform independent reviews
    - Convene shareholder meetings

7.5 The governance structure of the UK

In the UK **company law** sets out a great many of the rules on corporate governance, especially with regard to:

- The **board of directors** (a unitary board is required)
- **Directors' powers and duties**
- The **relationship of the company with directors**, such as loans to directors and the interests of directors in company contracts
- Accountability for stewardship and financial reporting via the **financial statements**
- Rules on **meetings and resolutions**

Statutory provisions on corporate governance are outside the scope of the *Business and Finance* syllabus.

In addition to these statutory rules, large companies (both UK and overseas companies) that have a premium listing in the Main Market of the London Stock Exchange and a market capitalisation which brings them within the FTSE 350 index of listed companies are **regulated** by the FCA's UKLA (which we saw in Chapter 10). They must:

- **Comply** with the **main principles** of the FRC's UK Corporate Governance Code 2012 contained in the UKLA Listing Rules (see Chapter 12), and either
- **Comply** with the supporting **provisions** of the Code, or
- **Explain** why they have not so complied.

Finally, with reference back to the Cadbury Committee definition of the context of the UK Corporate Governance Code 2012, remember that the board is subject to the **shareholders in general meeting** as well as to **laws** and **regulations.**

We saw above that companies should display **integrity** and **probity**, and also that one of the key governance needs of stakeholders is for the company to adhere to good **business ethics.** We shall look at these points, and the related idea of an **ethical culture** in a company now, and then return to the UK Corporate Governance Code 2012 in Chapter 12.

8 Ethics, business ethics and an ethical culture

Section overview

- Ethics tell us how to behave.
- Acceptable business values may include: integrity, objectivity, accountability, openness, honesty, truth, transparency, fairness, responsibility and trust.
- Business values should be seen throughout the company's culture, and should be actively promoted by the board.
- Business ethics are the moral standards that society expects of businesses.
- An ethical culture can be promoted by: ethical leadership from the board; codes of ethics or business conduct; supporting policies and procedures.
- An ethical profile produced by means of an ethical audit measures the consistency of a company's values base.
- Sustainability and corporate responsibility can be promoted by adopting international standards and codes of conduct, and an environmental management system.

8.1 What are ethics?

Definition

Ethics: A system of behaviour which is deemed acceptable in the society or context under consideration. Ethics tell us 'how to behave'.

8.2 What is an ethical culture?

Definition

Ethical culture: A business culture where the basic values and beliefs in a company encourage people within the company to behave in line with acceptable business ethics.

Every company has different sets of **beliefs and values**, which together make up its culture, as we saw in Chapter 2. What particular business values underlie an ethical culture?

Some of the **Nolan principles** established by the Committee for Standards in Public Life are a useful starting point for **business values** in a company as a whole:

- Integrity
- Objectivity
- Accountability
- Openness
- Honesty

In *Setting the tone: ethical business leadership* by Philippa Foster Back (published by the Institute of Business Ethics) the author lists further business values:

- Truth
- Transparency
- Fairness
- Responsibility
- Trust

The importance of business values in a company's culture is that they underpin both policy and behaviour throughout the company, from top to bottom.

Along with the business values listed above are **statutory requirements** of all companies:

- Equality for all
- No discrimination on any grounds
- Freedom of information

Values are promoted in the company by the **board of directors** which should be committed to:

- **Openness and transparency** in decisions and use of resources
- Promoting **good relationships** wherever possible
- **High standards in their own personal behaviour**, especially preparing adequately for and attending meetings, and being involved in decision making

Stakeholders, including customers, employees, investors, government and regulators, place great pressure on companies about their values and their business ethics.

8.3 What are business ethics?

Definition

Business ethics: The ways in which a company behaves in a society which has certain expectations of how a decent company should behave. They represent the moral standards that are expected.

Acceptable business ethics may comprise as a minimum:

- Paying staff **decent wages** and pensions
- Providing **good working conditions** for staff
- **Paying suppliers** in line with agreed terms
- **Sourcing supplies** carefully (Fairtrade etc)
- Using sustainable or **renewable resources**
- Being **open and honest** with customers

The important point to note however is that **society's expectations**, which can and do change, mould business ethics. Expectations have an effect at three levels:

- At the overall level of 'what is the **role of business in society**?'
- At the level of a **specific company**, and what it can do to manifest business ethics
- At the level of **individuals** within the company

The term **social responsibility** is often used in this context.

Definition

Social responsibility: How far a company exceeds the minimum obligations it owes to stakeholders and society by virtue of regulations and corporate governance. In particular, it is concerned with the company's obligations to those stakeholders which are unprotected by contractual or business relationships with the company, namely local communities, consumers in general and pressure groups.

In a survey in 2012 by the Institute of Business Ethics, members of the public were asked what issues of company behaviour most needed addressing. The results, in descending order of importance, are a useful list of what society asks of business at a particular point in time:

- Executive pay
- Corporate tax avoidance
- Discrimination in treatment of people
- Bribery and corruption
- Employees being able to speak out about company wrongdoing ('whistle-blowing' – see below)
- Fair and open pricing of products and services
- Environmental responsibility
- Harassment and bullying in the workplace
- Openness with information
- Sweatshop labour
- Advertising and marketing practices
- Human rights
- Work-home balance for employees
- Safety and security in the workplace
- Treatment of suppliers

Interactive question 3: Ethical pressures [Difficulty level: Intermediate]

In what areas of a business would you say there were the greatest pressures not to behave ethically, and from what source does this pressure come?

See **Answer** at the end of this chapter.

8.4 How can an ethical culture be promoted?

An ethical culture can be promoted by a combination of:

- **Ethical leadership** from the board of directors
- **Codes of ethics or business conduct**
- **Policies and procedures** to support ethical behaviour

8.4.1 Ethical leadership from the board of directors

Most of the scandals which created so much interest in corporate governance and business ethics since the first years of this century centred on the fact that the company involved was being led by unethical directors. The degree of their unethical behaviour may range from criminal dishonesty (such as Bernie Ebbers at WorldCom) to a simple failure to accept responsibility (such as Fred Goodwin at RBS). Such behaviour undermines **trust**.

The board should provide **ethical leadership** to the company: it should lead by example. Philippa Foster Back identifies the following attributes and behaviours of ethical leaders:

Attributes	Behaviours
Openness	Be open minded and willing to learn, and encourage others to learn.
Courage	Be determined and direct; actively stamp out poor behaviour.
Ability to listen	Be aware of what is going on and know that doing the right thing is the right thing to do.
Honesty	Be considerate and cautious in managing expectations.
Fair mindedness	Be independent and willing to challenge the *status quo.*

8.4.2 Codes of ethics or business conduct

There is no general ethical code such as the UK Corporate Governance Code 2012 to which companies can subscribe when it comes to business ethics and conduct. Instead each company should draw up a written code of ethics or statement of business conduct which is suited to its own unique situation, values and culture. In a survey in 2012 in the UK and the US, CIMA found that 80% of organisations surveyed provided a code of ethics to guide employees about ethical standards in their work, up from 72% in 2008.

Definition

Code of ethics: A formalisation of moral principles or values, responsibilities and obligations.

Organisations have several reasons for introducing ethical codes.

- **Communication**: ethical codes communicate the standard of behaviour expected of employees.
- **Consistency of conduct**: with the message effectively communicated, the behaviour of employees can be standardised or made consistent across all its operations and locations. Customers, suppliers and other stakeholders will receive similar treatment wherever they are.
- **Risk reduction**: standardised behaviour reduces the risk of unethical actions as employees who are unethical will 'stand out' and can be dealt with. This reduces the risk of a few employees irrevocably damaging the reputation of the organisation and the trust people have in it.
- **Compliance with UK corporate governance rules**: the Cadbury Committee Report on corporate governance in 1992 first recommended that businesses draw up codes of conduct and publish them internally and externally, so all employees know what is expected of them.

The **functions of a code of ethics** are:

- To tell the world at large what the company is striving to achieve in terms of ethical conduct
- To communicate a guide for the company as a whole to follow in its dealings with third parties
- To provide guidance for individuals within the company as to how to act
- To describe what the company aims to do in the event that an employee highlights unethical behaviour and abuse within the company

A company should have three **objectives for a code of ethics** in mind:

- To improve **behaviour**
- To build the company's **reputation** and the trust of stakeholders in the company
- To improve **performance** and build **value**

A code of ethics should ideally inform directors and everyone else in the company that **ethical behaviour** is expected of them. This may mean:

- Performing their duties and undertaking their responsibilities honestly, objectively and with diligence
- Loyalty
- Not acting in a way which will discredit the company
- Avoiding a situation where they have a conflict of duty between the company's interests and their own
- Not accepting inducements or bribes which will affect their judgement
- Keeping information confidential and not using it for personal gain
- Maintaining high standards of dignity, morality and competence
- Respecting human rights (of suppliers, workers and the public)
- Being environmentally aware (in many forms, depending on the industry)
- Making ethical investments
- Fighting corruption
- Whistle-blowing to a regulator or other external body where appropriate (see below)

8.4.3 Whistle-blowing

Employees who make the decision to '**blow the whistle**' are driven to do so by their own moral values and their need to 'do the right thing', but they will normally only do so once they have tried but failed to get the problems addressed internally. This is where an effective code of ethics could make all the difference; if there were true backing in the company for ethics then problems would get sorted out before the whistle was blown externally.

The Public Interest Disclosure Act seeks to ensure that workers who feel the need to 'speak out' externally against unethical, illegal or dangerous practices in their own company are protected without fear, in particular, of losing their jobs and reputations.

8.4.4 Policies and procedures to support ethical behaviour

- Active leadership by managers
- Consultation and communication procedures so everyone is aware of the code of ethics
- Piloting of the code in draft form so that people have an input to its content
- Review of the code so that it retains its position at the heart of how the company actually does business
- Training
- Speak-up lines/helplines for internal whistle-blowing
- Performance appraisals incorporating values
- Remuneration policies not cutting across values
- Disciplinary policies enforcing values

- Monitoring of how ethical behaviour is taking place
- Audit and assurance regarding values
- Reporting regularly
- Complaints systems that help employees to draw attention to unethical behaviour
- An explicitly stated duty to report breaches of specific ethical requirements

8.4.5 Ethical audit

In order to ensure that the code of ethics and its supporting policies and procedures are operating effectively, and to improve accountability and transparency towards stakeholders, many companies now conduct **ethical audits**.

Definition

Ethical audit: A process which measures the internal and external consistency of a company's values base.

International Society of Business, Economics and Ethics

The ethical audit produces an **ethical profile,** which brings together all of the factors affecting a company's reputation by examining the way in which it does business. At a given point in time, this ethical profile:

- Clarifies the actual values to which the company operates
- Provides a baseline by which to measure future improvement
- Points the way towards meeting any societal expectations which are not currently being met
- Gives stakeholders the opportunity to clarify their expectations of the company's behaviour
- Identifies specific problem areas within the company
- Identifies the issues which motivate employees
- Identifies general areas of vulnerability, particularly related to lack of openness

8.5 ICAEW members and business ethics

We studied the ICAEW Code of Ethics in Chapter 9 of this Study Manual. Note that there is no requirement on ICAEW's members in business to implement the Code for the business itself, nor to implement policies and procedures such as a unique code of ethics for the business, or an ethical audit. However, members in business are encouraged by the ICAEW to promote an ethical culture as far as possible, and of course must apply the Code in relation to their own conduct.

8.6 Promoting sustainability and corporate responsibility

Businesses adopt international standards and codes of conduct for many reasons, including;

- to meet **legal compliance requirements**
- to build **trust and credibility**
- to gain **external verification and certification**
- to gain or restore **stakeholder confidence**
- to improve management systems through the use of **standards and processes**

Environmental management systems (EMS) consist of procedures for compliance with a number of stated environmental policy objectives and targets, and therefore they assist the business in promoting sustainability and corporate responsibility. As well as documenting system procedures and instructions they also help to ensure internal communication for implementation of agreed actions. An EMS requires a supporting audit programme.

The internationally recognised **ISO 14001 Environmental Management Standard** is not itself a measurement system, but companies with ISO 14001 in place may evaluate environmental performance against a stated environmental policy, objectives, targets and other performance criteria with an explicit commitment towards continuous improvement. Adopting ISO 14001 helps a company to develop comprehensive, quantitative measures of environmental performance as well as purely qualitative descriptions of related company practices.

Summary and Self-test

Summary (1/2)

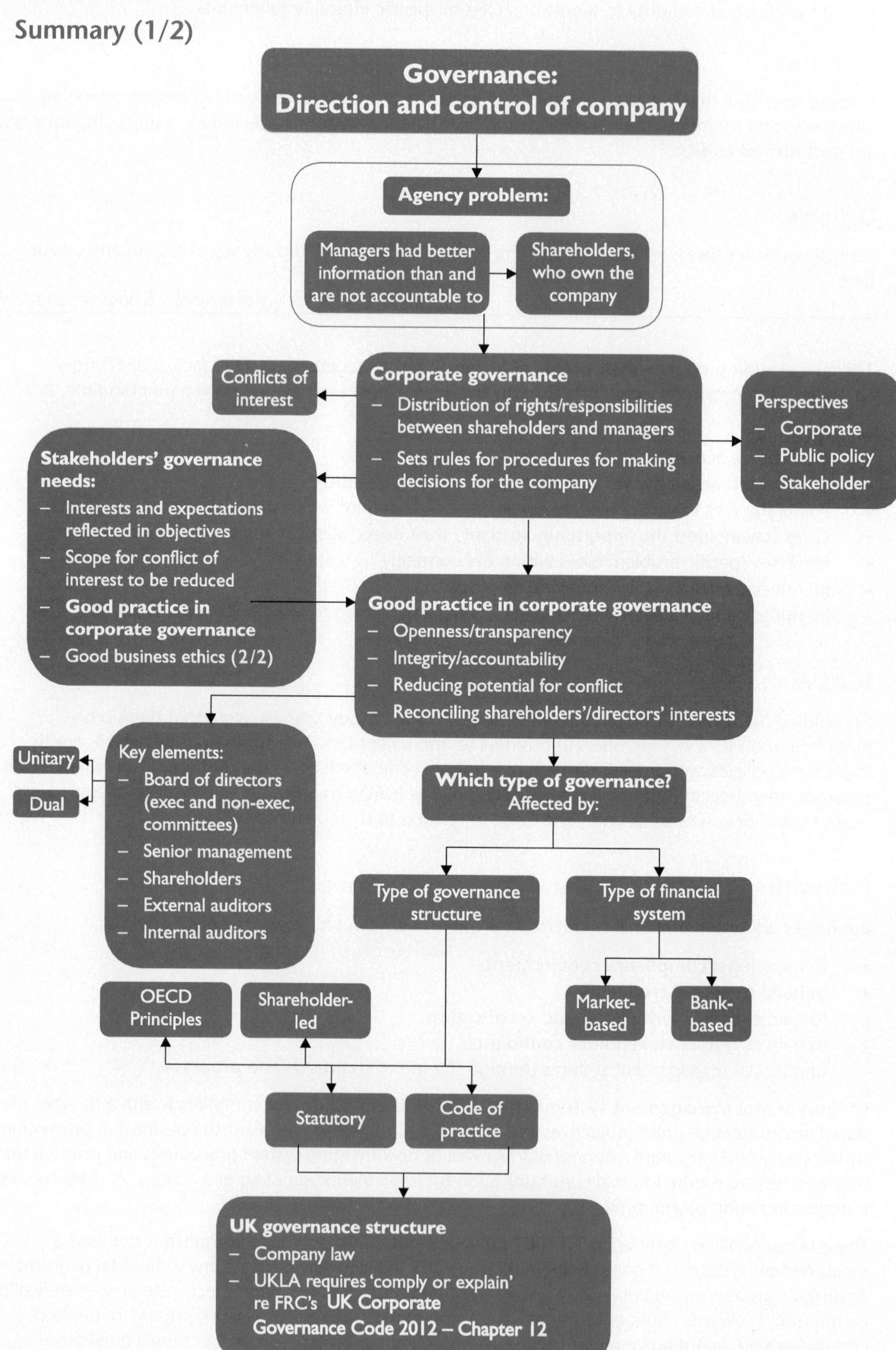

Governance:
Direction and control of company
Agency problem:
Managers had better information than and are not accountable to
Shareholders, who own the company
Corporate governance
– Distribution of rights/responsibilities between shareholders and managers
– Sets rules for procedures for making decisions for the company
Conflicts of interest
Perspectives
– Corporate
– Public policy
– Stakeholder
Stakeholders' governance needs:
– Interests and expectations reflected in objectives
– Scope for conflict of interest to be reduced
– Good practice in corporate governance
– Good business ethics (2/2)
Good practice in corporate governance
– Openness/transparency
– Integrity/accountability
– Reducing potential for conflict
– Reconciling shareholders'/directors' interests
Unitary
Dual
Key elements:
– Board of directors (exec and non-exec, committees)
– Senior management
– Shareholders
– External auditors
– Internal auditors
Which type of governance? Affected by:
Type of governance structure
Type of financial system
Market-based
Bank-based
OECD Principles
Shareholder-led
Statutory
Code of practice
UK governance structure
– Company law
– UKLA requires 'comply or explain' re FRC's UK Corporate Governance Code 2012 – Chapter 12

Summary (2/2)

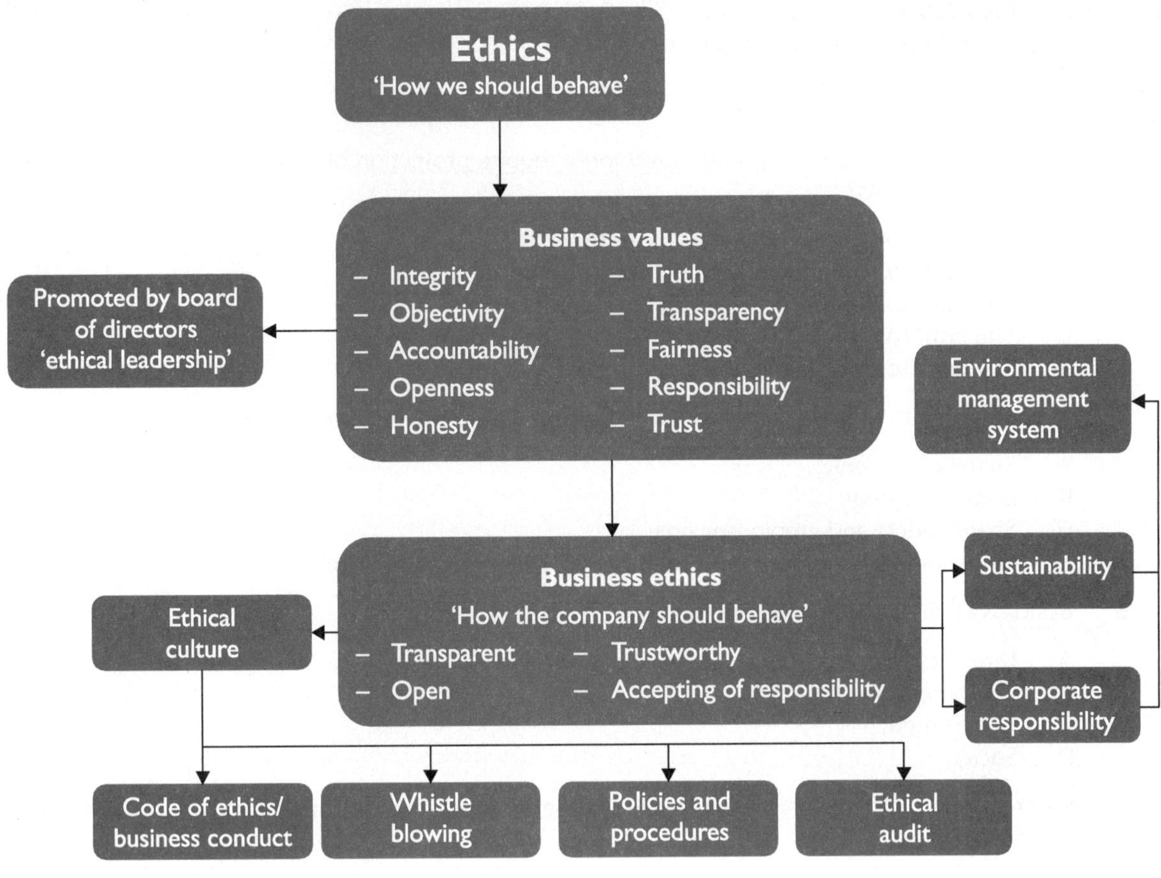

Self-test

Answer the following questions.

1 The agency problem concerns the misalignment in interests and conflicts of interest between

- A Banks and financial markets
- B Regulators and professional bodies
- C Government and industry
- D Directors and shareholders

2 In a company with weak corporate governance managers may be able primarily to pursue their own rather than the company's interests because, in relation to shareholders

- A They have more information and high levels of accountability
- B They have less information and high levels of accountability
- C They have more information and low levels of accountability
- D They have less information and low levels of accountability

3 In comparison with the corporate and the public policy perspectives on corporate governance, the stakeholder perspective places least emphasis on

- A Accountability
- B Alignment of interests of shareholders and other stakeholders
- C Good information
- D Efficient use of resources

4 Good practice in corporate governance requires that openness and transparency should be supported by

- A Reducing the potential for conflicts of interest
- B Disclosure of information
- C Reconciling the interests of shareholders and directors
- D Judging performance of directors on the basis of return on investment

5 In the Japanese financial system the biggest source of finance for businesses is

A Bank loans
B Loans from private individuals
C Retained earnings
D The capital markets

6 The OECD's *Principles of Corporate Governance* require protection of which **two** of the following shareholders' rights?

A The right to quarterly general meetings
B The right to real-time information on the company
C The right to a share in the company's profits
D The right to inspect the company's books of account
E The right to remove members of the board

7 In countries with a dual board structure, the supervisory board is elected by

A Shareholders only
B Employees only
C Shareholders and employees only
D Shareholders, employees and members of the management board

8 Business ethics are primarily moulded by the expectations of

A Directors
B Customers
C Government
D Society

9 Workers who blow the whistle externally on unethical practices in their own company are protected by

A The Data Protection Act
B The Public Interest Disclosure Act
C The Freedom of Information Act
D The Companies Act

Now, go back to the Learning Objectives in the Introduction. If you are satisfied you have achieved these objectives, please tick them off.

Technical reference

1 Governance Principles of corporate governance 2004 (OECD)

Answers to Interactive questions

Answer to Interactive question 1

Good corporate governance is more than good management and effective leadership: it is about directing and controlling a company so that it meets the objectives that have been agreed with stakeholders, particularly shareholders, and so that it meets the needs of users and the markets for information, accountability and good behaviour. This should ensure that the company has a sustainable future in the long term.

Answer to Interactive question 2

Equity is a more risky form of investment than cash and cash equivalents so it would appear that UK households are less risk averse than Japanese ones.

Answer to Interactive question 3

The pressure not to behave ethically in business mainly derives from the need to gain commercial advantage in a fiercely competitive world. Areas where unethical behaviour often occurs are:

- Procurement – bribe taking, exploitation of suppliers
- Excessive client and supplier entertainment
- Inflated directors' expenses
- Engaging in conflicts of interests
- Disclosing or using confidential information

Answers to Self-test

1 D

2 C

3 C

4 B

5 A

6 C, E

7 C

8 D

9 B

CHAPTER 12

Corporate governance

Introduction

Learning objectives

Tick off

- Identify and show the distinction between the roles and responsibilities of those charged with corporate governance and those charged with management, including the basics of the UK Corporate Governance Code ☐
- Identify the roles and responsibilities of the members of the executive board, any supervisory board, the audit committee and others charged with governance, internal audit and external audit ☐
- Identify the roles and responsibilities of those responsible within a business for internal audit and for the external audit relationship ☐

Specific syllabus references are: 5c, e, f.

Syllabus links

Corporate governance is developed further in Audit and Assurance at the Professional level, and at the Advanced level.

Examination context

Questions on corporate governance are certain to appear in your exam.

Questions are likely to be set in multiple choice format in a scenario context, though knowledge-type questions are also likely on particular definitions and principles.

1 The UK Corporate Governance Code

Section overview

- The FRC promotes good corporate governance via the UK Corporate Governance Code and related guidance, and by encouraging shareholder engagement via the Stewardship Code.
- Irrespective of the UK Corporate Governance Code, all companies must treat shareholders equally.
- The disclosure statement for the Code requires a FTSE 350 company to state that it applies its main principles, and then either to state that it complies with the Code's supporting principles and provisions, or to explain why it does not so comply.
- The Code contains principles for companies and institutional shareholders to apply.
- The corporate governance principles for companies concern: leadership; effectiveness; accountability; remuneration; relations with shareholders.
- The engagement principles for institutional shareholders concern: dialogue with companies; evaluating governance disclosures; voting.

The Corporate Governance Committee of the **FRC** is responsible in the UK for promoting high standards of corporate governance. It aims to do so by:

- Maintaining an effective UK **Corporate Governance Code** and promoting its widespread application
- Ensuring that **related guidance**, such as that on internal control, is current and relevant
- Encouraging **shareholder engagement** via the **Stewardship Code**

We shall look at each of these points in this chapter.

1.1 What is the UK Corporate Governance Code?

The **UK Corporate Governance Code** is a **code of practice** embodying a **shareholder-led approach to corporate governance.** It includes requirements of shareholders as well as of companies themselves. It began life in 1992 as the Cadbury Committee Report on the *Financial aspects of corporate governance*, and has been developed and enhanced in the decades since then.

It is important to recognise that **compliance with the UK Corporate Governance Code is not a legal requirement**. However, the FCA Disclosure Rules and Transparency Rules implemented by the UKLA require all **companies listed in the FTSE 350** to **apply the Code's main Principles** and to **include in their annual reports a statement of compliance with the supporting principles and provisions of the Code** or **an explanation of non-compliance**. Other companies are encouraged to follow the Code as an example of '**best practice**'. Companies may experience pressure from their stakeholders if they do not adopt it.

The principles of the Code are designed **to help boards discharge their duties in the best interests of their companies** by:

- Encouraging all involved in a company to **accept their legal obligations**. This includes the board of directors (including non-executive directors), auditors and shareholders
- Encouraging the **scrutiny of corporate stewardship** (the Stewardship Code for institutional investors, which we shall see later in this chapter, helps to support this)
- Imposing certain **checks and controls on executive directors** but without restricting the commercial enterprise aspect of business

The UK approach starts from the position that good governance is a tool that can improve the board's ability to manage the company effectively as well as provide accountability to shareholders.

1.2 The UK Corporate Governance Code

The UK Corporate Governance Code was updated by the Corporate Governance Committee of the FRC in September 2012; it is based on the previous corporate governance code (known as the Combined Code) which was last published in 2008. The FCA Disclosure Rules and Transparency Rules for companies with a premium listing of equity shares in the UK, whether they are incorporated in the UK or elsewhere, incorporate the UK Corporate Governance Code for reporting years beginning on or after 1 October 2012.

The 2010 revision was made in light of the global financial crisis that started in 2007, and puts into effect two principal conclusions of the FRC's review of the Code prompted by the crisis:

- Much more attention needed to be paid to following the **spirit of the Code** as well as its letter
- The **impact of shareholders in monitoring the Code could and should be enhanced** by better interaction between the boards of listed companies and their shareholders. To this end, the FRC has assumed responsibility for a **Stewardship Code** to provide guidance on good practice for investors

The Preface to the Corporate Governance Code published in June 2010 contained the following warnings:

'Nearly two decades of constructive usage have enhanced the prestige of the Code. Indeed, it seems that there is almost a belief that complying with the Code in itself constitutes good governance. The Code, however, is of necessity limited to being a guide only in general terms to principles, structure and processes. It cannot guarantee effective board behaviour because the range of situations in which it is applicable is much too great for it to attempt to mandate behaviour more specifically than it does. Boards therefore have a lot of room within the framework of the Code to decide for themselves how they should act.

'To follow the spirit of the Code to good effect, boards must think deeply, thoroughly and on a continuing basis, about their overall tasks and the implications of these for the roles of their individual members. Absolutely key in this endeavour are the leadership of the chairman of a board, the support given to and by the CEO, and the frankness and openness of mind with which issues are discussed and tackled by all directors.

'The challenge should not be underrated. To run a corporate board successfully is extremely demanding. Constraints on time and knowledge combine with the need to maintain mutual respect and openness between a cast of strong, able and busy directors dealing with each other across the different demands of executive and non-executive roles. To achieve good governance requires continuing and high quality effort.'

The 2012 revision of the Code seeks to enhance further the principles of transparency, diversity and fairness that underlie it. The role and accountability of the audit committee have been enhanced, and FTSE 350 companies are required to put the external audit contract out to tender at least every 10 years.

1.3 Compliance with the UK Corporate Governance Code

Nothing in the UK Corporate Governance Code overrides the general statutory requirement on companies to **treat shareholders equally** with respect to access to information.

While large listed companies with a premium listing on the London Stock Exchange (primarily those listed in the FTSE 100 and the FTSE 350 indices) must comply with the main principles of the UK Corporate Governance Code, **departure from compliance with certain supporting principles and provisions may be justified** in particular circumstances. The company must review all provisions of the UK Corporate Governance Code carefully and give a considered explanation if it departs from any of them. However, shareholders are encouraged *not* to consider departures as necessarily being breaches of the UK Corporate Governance Code.

Smaller listed companies outside the FTSE 350, and externally managed investment companies which have a different board structure, can be more flexible about how they apply the UK Corporate Governance Code.

1.3.1 Disclosure statement: comply or explain

Under the FCA Disclosure Rules and Transparency Rules listed companies in the FTSE 350 must make a disclosure statement about the UK Corporate Governance Code:

- Reporting on how the company **applies the main principles** in the UK Corporate Governance Code, then either
- Confirming that it **complies** with the UK Corporate Governance Code's **supporting principles and provisions** or, where it does **not**
- **Explaining** why it does not comply

The 'comply or explain' section of the UK Corporate Governance Code recognises that:

'an alternative to following a provision may be justified in particular circumstances if good governance can be achieved by other means. A condition of doing so is that the reasons for it should be explained clearly and carefully to shareholders, who may wish to discuss the position with the company and whose voting intentions may be influenced as a result. In providing an explanation, the company should aim to illustrate how its actual practices are both consistent with the principle to which the particular provision relates and contribute to good governance and promote delivery of business objectives. It should set out the background, provide a clear rationale for the action it is taking, and describe any mitigating actions taken to address any additional risk and maintain conformity with the relevant principle. Where deviation from a particular provision is intended to be limited in time, the explanation should indicate when the company expects to conform with the provision.

'In their responses to explanations, shareholders should pay due regard to companies' individual circumstances and bear in mind, in particular, the size and complexity of the company and the nature of the risks and challenges it faces. Whilst shareholders have every right to challenge companies' explanations if they are unconvincing, they should not be evaluated in a mechanistic way and departures from the Code should not be automatically treated as breaches. Shareholders should be careful to respond to the statements from companies in a manner that supports the ''comply or explain'' process and bearing in mind the purpose of good corporate governance. They should put their views to the company and both parties should be prepared to discuss the position.'

2 The detailed content of the UK Corporate Governance Code

The UK Corporate Governance Code is set out as a series of **main principles,** some of which have **supporting principles** and all of which have **provisions**. It contains five main sections:

- Leadership
- Effectiveness
- Accountability
- Remuneration
- Relations with shareholders

2.1 Leadership: the role of the board (main principle A1)

Every company should be headed by an **effective board** which is **collectively responsible** for the long-term success of the company.

2.1.1 Supporting principles for the role of the board

The board's role is to provide **entrepreneurial leadership** of the company within a framework of prudent and effective controls which enables risk to be assessed and managed. The board should:

- Set the company's **strategic aims**.
- Ensure that the **necessary financial and human resources** are in place for the company to meet its objectives.
- **Review management performance.**
- Set the company's **values and standards** and ensure that its **obligations** to its shareholders and others are understood and met.

- **All directors** – both executives and non-executives – must act in what they consider to be the best interests of the company, consistent with their statutory duties (these are set out in ss 170-177 Companies Act 2006 and are not examinable in *Business and Finance*).

2.1.2 Provisions supporting the role of the board

- The board should **meet sufficiently regularly** to discharge its duties effectively, with a formal schedule of matters specifically reserved for its decision.
- The **annual report** should include a statement of how the board operates, including a high level statement of which types of decision are taken by the board and which are delegated to management.
- The annual report should identify the board's **Chairman**, the **Deputy Chairman** (where there is one), the **Chief Executive**, the **senior independent (non-executive) director** and the **chairmen and members of the board committees** (including the nomination, audit and remuneration committees). It should also set out the number of meetings of the board and its committees and individual attendance by directors.
- The company should arrange appropriate **insurance cover** in respect of **legal action against its directors.**

Interactive question 1: Board effectiveness **[Difficulty level: Intermediate]**

What should the board do in order to provide entrepreneurial leadership for its company?

See **Answer** at the end of this chapter.

2.2 Leadership: division of responsibilities (main principle A2)

There should be a clear **division of responsibilities** at the head of the company between the **running of the board** and the executive responsibility for the **running of the company's business.** No one individual should have **unfettered powers of decision.**

2.2.1 Provision supporting the division of responsibilities

The roles of the Chairman and Chief Executive should **not be exercised by the same individual.** The division of responsibilities between the Chairman and Chief Executive should be clearly established, set out in writing and agreed by the board.

2.3 Leadership: the Chairman (main principle A3)

The chairman is responsible for leadership of the board and ensuring its effectiveness in all aspects of its role.

2.3.1 Supporting principle for the Chairman

The Chairman:

- Is responsible for setting the board's **agenda** and ensuring that adequate **time** is available for discussion of all agenda items, in particular strategic issues.
- Should promote a **culture of openness and debate** by facilitating the effective contribution of non-executive directors in particular and ensuring **constructive relations** between executive and non-executive directors.
- Is responsible for ensuring that the **directors receive accurate, timely and clear information.**
- Should ensure **effective communication with shareholders.**

2.3.2 Provision supporting the Chairman

The Chairman should, on appointment, **meet the independence criteria** set out in section 2.5.2 below, though thereafter the test of independence is not appropriate in relation to the Chairman.

A Chief Executive should not go on to be Chairman of the same company. If, exceptionally, a board decides that a Chief Executive should become Chairman, the board should consult major shareholders in advance and should set out its reasons to shareholders at the time of the appointment and in the next annual report.

2.4 Leadership: non-executive directors (main principle A4)

As part of their role as members of a unitary board, non-executive directors should **constructively challenge and help develop proposals on strategy**.

2.4.1 Supporting principle for non-executive directors

Non-executive directors should:

- **Scrutinise the performance of management** in meeting agreed goals and objectives
- **Monitor the reporting of performance**
- Satisfy themselves on the **integrity of financial information** and that **financial controls** and systems of **risk management** are robust and defensible
- Be responsible for determining appropriate levels of **remuneration of executive directors**
- Have prime roles in **appointing, and where necessary removing, executive directors**, and in **succession planning**

2.4.2 Provisions supporting the non-executive directors

The board should appoint one of the independent non-executive directors to be the **senior independent director**:

- To provide a **sounding board for the chairman** and
- To serve as an **intermediary for the other directors** when necessary.

The **senior independent director** should be available to shareholders if they have concerns which contact through the normal channels of Chairman, Chief Executive or other executive directors have failed to resolve, or for which such contact is inappropriate.

The **Chairman should hold meetings with the non-executive directors without the executives present**. Led by the senior independent director, the non-executive directors should meet without the Chairman present at least annually to **appraise the Chairman's performance** and on such other occasions as deemed appropriate.

Where directors have concerns which cannot be resolved about the running of the company or a proposed action, they should ensure that their concerns are recorded in the **board minutes**.

On resignation, a non-executive director should provide a **written statement** to the Chairman, for circulation to the board, if they have any such concerns.

2.5 Effectiveness: the composition of the board (main principle B1)

The board and its committees should have the **appropriate balance of skills, experience, independence** and **knowledge** of the company to enable them to discharge their respective duties and responsibilities effectively.

2.5.1 Principles supporting the composition of the board

The board should be **big enough** that the requirements of the business can be met, and that changes to the board's composition can be managed without undue disruption. The board should **not be so large** as to be unwieldy.

The board should include an appropriate combination of **executive and non-executive directors** (and in particular **independent non-executive directors**) such that no individual or small group of individuals can dominate the board's decision taking.

Committee membership must be refreshed and undue reliance should not be placed on particular individuals. This should be taken into account in deciding chairmanship and membership of committees.

Only the committee chairman and members are entitled to be present at meetings of the nomination, audit or remuneration committees, though others may attend at the invitation of the committee.

2.5.2 Provisions supporting the composition of the board

The board should identify in the annual report each **non-executive director** (including the Chairman of the board) it considers to be **independent**. The board should determine whether the director is **independent in character and judgement** and whether there are relationships or circumstances which are likely to affect, or could appear to affect, the director's judgement. The board should state its reasons if it determines that a director is independent notwithstanding the existence of relationships or circumstances which may appear relevant.

A director **may** be determined as being **not independent** if they:

- Have been an **employee** of the company within the last **five years**.
- Have, or have had within the last **three years**, a **material business relationship** with the company either directly, or as a partner, shareholder, director or senior employee of a body that has such a relationship with the company.
- Have received or receives additional **remuneration** from the company apart from the director's fee, participates in the company's **share option** or a **performance-related pay scheme**, or is a member of the company's **pension scheme**.
- Have close **family ties** with any of the company's advisors, directors or senior employees.
- Hold **cross directorships** or have significant links with other directors through involvement in other companies or bodies.
- **Represent a significant shareholder.**
- Have served on the board for more than **nine years** from the date of their first election.

At least **50% of the board**, excluding the Chairman, should comprise **independent non-executive directors**. A smaller company (below the FTSE 350 threshold throughout the year immediately prior to the reporting year) should have at least **two** independent non-executive directors.

2.6 Effectiveness: appointments to the board (main principle B2)

There should be a formal, rigorous and transparent procedure for the **appointment of new directors** to the board.

2.6.1 Principles supporting board appointments

The search for board candidates and their appointment to the board should be made:

- **On merit** and
- Against **objective criteria** and
- With due regards to the **benefits of diversity** on the board, including gender.

Essentially this involves a **nomination committee** making a recommendation to the board as a whole, which then makes the appointment to the board. This appointment must then be voted on by the shareholders at the next annual general meeting (AGM).

The board should satisfy itself that plans are in place for orderly **succession of appointments** to the board and to senior management, so as to **maintain an appropriate balance of skills and experience** within the company and on the board and to ensure progressive refreshing of the board.

2.6.2 Provisions supporting board appointments: the nomination committee

- There should be a **nomination committee** which should lead the process for board appointments and make recommendations to the board.

- **Over 50%** of members of the **nomination committee** should be **independent non-executive directors.**
- The board Chairman or an independent non-executive director should **chair the nomination committee**, but the board Chairman should not chair the nomination committee when it is dealing with the appointment of a successor to the Chairmanship.
- The nomination committee should make available its **terms of reference**, explaining its role and the authority delegated to it by the board. This can be done via an appropriate website.
- The nomination committee should evaluate the **balance of skills, knowledge, independence and experience on the board** and, in the light of this evaluation, prepare a description of the role and capabilities required for a particular appointment.
- Non-executive directors should be appointed for **specified terms** subject to re-election and to statutory provisions relating to the removal of a director. **Any term beyond six years for a non-executive director should be subject to particularly rigorous review**, and should take into account the need for progressive refreshing of the board.
- A separate section of the annual report should describe the work of the nomination committee, including the process it has used in relation to board appointments. This section should include a description of the board's policy on **diversity**, including gender, any measurable objectives that it has set for implementing the policy, and progress on achieving the objectives.
- An explanation should be given if neither an external search consultancy nor open advertising has been used in the appointment of a Chairman or a non-executive director. Where an external search consultancy has been used, it should be identified in the report and a statement should be made as to whether it has any other connection with the company.

2.7 Effectiveness: commitment (main principle B3)

All directors should be able to allocate **sufficient time** to the company to discharge their responsibilities effectively.

2.7.1 Provisions supporting commitment

- For the **appointment of the board Chairman**, the nomination committee should prepare a job specification, including an assessment of the time commitment expected, recognising the need for availability in the event of crises.
- A Chairman's other **significant commitments** should be disclosed to the board before appointment and included in the annual report. Changes to such commitments should be reported to the board as they arise, and included in the next annual report. An individual may chair more than one FTSE 100 company.
- The **terms and conditions of appointment of non-executive directors** should be made available for inspection at the registered office and at the annual general meeting (AGM).
- The letter of appointment for non-executive directors should set out the expected **time commitment.** Non-executive directors should undertake that they will have sufficient time to meet what is expected of them.
- Non-executive directors should disclose their **other significant commitments** to the board before appointment, with a broad indication of the time involved, and the board should be informed of subsequent changes.
- The board should not agree to a **full-time executive director** taking on more than one non-executive directorship in a FTSE 100 company nor the Chairmanship of such a company.

2.8 Effectiveness: development (main principle B4)

All directors should receive **induction** on joining the board and should regularly **update and refresh** their skills and knowledge.

2.8.1 Principles supporting development

The board Chairman should ensure that the **directors continually update their skills** and the knowledge and familiarity with the company required to fulfil their role both on the board and the board committees. The company should provide the necessary resources for developing and updating its directors' knowledge and capabilities.

To function effectively, all directors need appropriate knowledge of the company and access to its operations and staff.

2.8.2 Provisions supporting development

- The Chairman should ensure that new directors receive a **full, formal and tailored induction on joining the board**. As part of this, directors should avail themselves of opportunities to meet **major shareholders.**
- The Chairman should regularly review and agree with each director their **training and development needs.**

2.9 Effectiveness: information and support (main principle B5)

The board should be supplied in a **timely** manner with **information in a form and of a quality** appropriate to enable it to discharge its duties.

2.9.1 Principles supporting information and support

The Chairman is responsible for ensuring that the directors receive **accurate, timely and clear information**. Management has an obligation to provide such information but **directors should seek clarification or amplification where necessary.**

Under the direction of the Chairman, the **company secretary's** responsibilities include ensuring good information flows within the board and its committees and between senior management and non-executive directors, as well as facilitating induction and assisting with professional development as required. The company secretary should also be responsible for advising the board through the Chairman on all **governance matters.**

2.9.2 Provisions supporting information and support

- The board should ensure that directors, especially non-executive directors, have access to **independent professional advice** at the company's expense where they judge it necessary to discharge their responsibilities as directors.
- **Committees** should be provided with **sufficient resources** to undertake their duties.
- All directors should have access to the advice and services of the **company secretary**, who is responsible to the board for ensuring that board procedures are complied with.
- Both the **appointment and removal of the company secretary** should be a matter for the board as a whole.

Interactive question 2: Chairman's responsibilities **[Difficulty level: Intermediate]**

What are the Chairman's responsibilities relating to ensuring a well-informed, well-developed board?

See **Answer** at the end of this chapter.

2.10 Effectiveness: evaluation (main principle B6)

The board should undertake a formal and rigorous annual **evaluation of its own performance** and that of its **committees** and individual **directors.**

2.10.1 Principles for evaluation

The Chairman should **act on the results of the performance evaluation** by recognising the strengths and addressing the weaknesses of the board. Where appropriate the Chairman should propose that **new members** be appointed to the board, or should seek the **resignation of directors**.

Individual evaluation should aim to show whether each director continues to contribute effectively and to demonstrate commitment to the role (including commitment of **time** for board and committee meetings and any other duties).

Evaluation of the board should consider the **balance** of skills, experience, independence and knowledge of the company on the board, its **diversity**, including gender, **how the board works together as a unit**, and other factors relevant to its effectiveness.

2.10.2 Provisions for evaluation

- The board should state in the **annual report** how performance evaluation of the board, its committees and its individual directors has been conducted
- Evaluation of the board of FTSE 350 companies should be externally facilitated at least every three years. The external facilitator should be identified in the annual report and a statement should be made available as to whether they have any other connection with the company.
- The **non-executive** directors, led by the senior independent director, should be responsible for performance evaluation of the Chairman taking into account the views of executive directors

2.11 Effectiveness: re-election (main principle B7)

All directors should be submitted for **re-election** at **regular intervals**, subject to continued satisfactory performance.

2.11.1 Provisions for re-election

All **directors of FTSE 350 companies** should be subject to **annual election** by shareholders

With regards to the directors of other companies:

- Directors should be subject to election by shareholders at the **first AGM** after their appointment and re-election thereafter at intervals of **no more than three years**. (Note that with the advent of the Companies Act 2006 private companies no longer need to have an AGM, so where such companies are voluntarily applying the Code this provision, and any others related to the AGM, will not apply.)
- Non-executive directors who have served longer than nine years should be subject to annual re-election

The names of directors submitted for election or re-election should be accompanied by sufficient **biographical details** and any other relevant information to enable shareholders to take an informed decision on their election.

Accompanying a resolution to **elect a non-executive director** should be papers from the board setting out why they believe an individual should be elected. The Chairman should confirm to shareholders when proposing re-election that, following formal performance evaluation, the individual's **performance** continues to be effective and to demonstrate commitment to the role.

2.12 Accountability: financial and business reporting (main principle C1)

The board should present a **fair, balanced and understandable assessment of the company's position and prospects.**

2.12.1 Principles supporting financial and business reporting

The board's responsibility to present a fair, balanced and understandable assessment extends to:

- **Interim reports**
- **Other price-sensitive public reports**
- Reports to **regulators**
- The statutory **financial statements**

The board should establish arrangements that will enable it to ensure that the information presented is fair, balanced and understandable.

2.12.2 Provisions supporting financial and business reporting:

- The directors should explain in the annual report:
  - their responsibility for preparing the annual report and accounts and state that they consider the report and accounts, taken as a whole, is fair, balanced and understandable and provides the information necessary for shareholders to assess the company's performance, business model and strategy.
  - the basis on which the company generates or preserves value over the longer term (the business model) and the strategy for delivering the objectives of the company
- There should be a statement by the auditor about their reporting responsibilities
- The directors should report in annual and half-yearly financial statements that the business is a **going concern**, with supporting assumptions or qualifications as necessary

Interactive question 3: Preparation of financial statements **[Difficulty level: Intermediate]**

As well as the annual report and accounts, how far does the board's responsibility to provide balanced and understandable financial and business reporting extend?

See **Answer** at the end of this chapter.

2.13 Accountability: risk management and internal control (main principle C2)

The board is responsible for determining the nature and extent of the significant risks it is willing to take in achieving its strategic objectives. The board should maintain **sound risk management and internal control systems.**

2.13.1 Provision supporting risk management and internal control

The board should, at least annually, conduct a **review of the effectiveness of the company's risk management and internal control systems** and should report to shareholders that they have done so. The review should cover all material controls, including **financial, operational and compliance controls.**

Ways of applying this principle are contained in the Turnbull Guidance, which we shall look at shortly.

2.14 Accountability: audit committee and auditors (main principle C3)

The board should establish formal and transparent arrangements for considering how they should **apply the corporate reporting and risk management and internal control principles** and for maintaining an appropriate relationship with the company's **auditors.**

2.14.1 Provisions supporting the audit committee and auditors

- The board should establish an **audit committee** of at least **three** or, in the case of smaller companies, **two independent non-executive directors**. In smaller companies the Chairman may be a member of, but not chair, the committee in addition to the independent non-executive directors, provided he or she was considered independent on appointment as Chairman.
- At least one member of the audit committee should have **recent and relevant financial experience.**
- Roles and responsibilities of the audit committee should be set out in written terms of reference and should include:
  - monitoring the **integrity of the financial statements** of the company, and any formal announcements relating to the company's financial performance, reviewing significant financial reporting judgements contained in them

- reviewing the company's **internal financial controls** and, unless expressly addressed by a separate board risk committee composed of independent directors, or by the board itself, to review the company's internal control and risk management systems
- monitoring and reviewing the **effectiveness of the company's internal audit function**
- making recommendations to the board and thereby to shareholders for their approval in general meeting regarding the **appointment, re-appointment and removal of the external auditor** and to approve the **remuneration and terms of engagement of the external auditor**
- reviewing and monitoring the external auditor's **independence and objectivity** and the effectiveness of the audit process, taking into consideration relevant UK professional and regulatory requirements
- developing and implementing policy on the engagement of the external auditor to supply **non-audit services**, taking into account relevant ethical guidance regarding the provision of non-audit services by the external audit firm, and to report this to the board, identifying any matters in respect of which it considers that action or improvement is needed and making recommendations as to the steps to be taken
- reporting to the board on how it has discharged its responsibilities

- The audit committee's terms of reference, including its role and the authority delegated to it by the board, should be made available (via a website if desired).
- Where requested by the board, the audit committee should provide advice on whether the annual report and accounts, taken as a whole, is fair, balanced and understandable and provides the information necessary for shareholders to assess the company's performance, business model and strategy.
- **Whistle-blowing**: the audit committee should review arrangements by which staff of the company may, in confidence, raise concerns about possible improprieties in matters of financial reporting or other matters. Arrangements should be in place for the proportionate and independent investigation of such matters and for appropriate follow-up action.
- The audit committee should monitor and review the effectiveness of the **internal audit** activities. Where there is no internal audit function, the audit committee should consider annually whether there is a need for an internal audit function and make a recommendation to the board, and the reasons for the absence of such a function should be explained in the relevant section of the annual report.
- The audit committee should have primary responsibility for making a recommendation on the appointment, re-appointment and removal of **external auditors**. FTSE 350 companies should put the external audit contract out to tender at least every ten years.If the board does not accept the audit committee's recommendation, it should include in the annual report, and in any papers recommending appointment or re-appointment, a statement from the audit committee explaining the recommendation and should set out reasons why the board has taken a different position.
- A separate section of the annual report should describe the work of the committee in discharging its responsibilities. The report should include:
  - the significant issues that it considered in relation to the financial statements, and how these issues were addressed;
  - an explanation of how it has assessed the effectiveness of the external audit process and the approach taken to the appointment or reappointment of the external auditor, and information on the length of tenure of the current audit firm and when a tender was last conducted;
  - and, if the external auditor provides non-audit services, an explanation of how auditor objectivity and independence is safeguarded.

Ways of applying this principle and these provisions are contained in the FRC Guidance on Audit Committees, which is outside the scope of this Study Manual.

2.15 Remuneration: level and components of remuneration (main principle D1)

Levels of remuneration should be sufficient to **attract, retain and motivate directors** of the quality required to run the company successfully, but a company should avoid paying more than is necessary for this purpose. A significant proportion of executive directors' remuneration should be structured so as to **link rewards to corporate and individual performance.**

2.15.1 Principle supporting the level and components of remuneration

The **performance-related elements** of **executive directors'** remuneration should be **stretching** and designed to promote the **long-term success of the company**.

The **remuneration committee** should judge where to position their company relative to other companies, but they should use such comparisons with caution. They must avoid **an upward ratchet of remuneration levels with no corresponding improvement in performance**. They should also be sensitive to pay and employment conditions elsewhere in the company, especially when determining annual salary increases.

2.15.2 Provisions supporting the level and components of remuneration

- In designing schemes of performance-related remuneration for executive directors, the remuneration committee should follow the guidance provided in Schedule A of the Code. The full details of this are not examinable in *Business and Finance*, though you should know the following outline:
  - Performance conditions for annual bonuses should be relevant, stretching and designed to promote the long-term success of the company
  - Shares granted under share option schemes etc should not vest in or be exercisable by the director in less than three years
  - Any new proposed long-term incentive scheme should be approved by shareholders, and the total potentially available rewards of all schemes should not be excessive
  - Payouts etc should be subject to challenging performance criteria linked to the company's objectives, and should be compatible with risk policies and systems
  - Consideration should be given to mechanisms for clawing back some performance-related remuneration in exceptional circumstances of misstatement or misconduct
  - Only basic salary should generally be pensionable
- Levels of remuneration for **non-executive directors** should:
  - Reflect the time commitment and responsibilities of the role
  - Not include share options or other performance-related elements (as these can undermine independence) unless shareholder approval is sought in advance and any shares acquired by exercise of the options are held until at least one year after the non-executive director leaves the board. Holding of share options could be relevant to the determination of a non-executive director's (lack of) independence
- Where an executive director is released to serve as a non-executive director elsewhere, the **remuneration report** should include a statement as to whether or not the director will retain such earnings and, if so, what the remuneration is
- The remuneration committee should carefully consider what **compensation commitments** (including pension contributions and all other elements) their directors' terms of appointment would entail in the event of early termination. The aim should be to avoid rewarding poor performance. They should take a robust line on reducing compensation to reflect departing directors' obligations to mitigate loss
- Notice or contract periods should be set at **one year or less**. If it is necessary to offer longer notice or contract periods to new directors recruited from outside, such periods should reduce to one year or less after the initial period

2.16 Remuneration: procedure (main principle D2)

There should be a formal and transparent procedure for developing **policy on executive remuneration** and for fixing the remuneration packages of individual directors. **No director should be involved in deciding his or her own remuneration.**

2.16.1 Principles supporting procedure

The **remuneration committee** should:

- Consult the Chairman and/or Chief Executive about their proposals relating to the remuneration of other executive directors
- Be responsible for appointing any consultants in respect of executive director remuneration

Where executive directors or senior management are involved in advising or supporting the remuneration committee, care should be taken to recognise and avoid **conflicts of interest**.

The board Chairman should ensure that the company maintains contact as required with its **principal shareholders** about remuneration in the same way as for other matters.

2.16.2 Provisions supporting procedure

- The board should **establish a remuneration committee** of **at least three, or in the case of smaller companies two, independent non-executive directors**.
- **The board Chairman may be a member of, but not chair**, the remuneration committee if they were considered independent on appointment as Chairman.
- The remuneration committee should make available its **terms of reference**, on a website if desired, explaining its role and the authority delegated to it by the board.
- Where remuneration consultants are appointed, they should be identified in the annual report and a statement made as to whether they have any other connection with the company.
- The remuneration committee should have delegated responsibility for **setting remuneration for all executive directors and the Chairman,** including pension rights and any compensation payments.
- The committee should also recommend and monitor the level and structure of remuneration for **senior management**. The definition of 'senior management' for this purpose should be determined by the board but should normally include the first layer of management below board level.
- The board itself or, where required by the company's Articles, the shareholders should **determine the remuneration of the non-executive directors** within the limits set in the Articles. Where permitted by the Articles, the board may however delegate this responsibility to a committee, which might include the Chief Executive.
- **Shareholders** should be invited specifically to approve all new **long-term incentive schemes** and significant changes to existing schemes.

2.17 Relations with shareholders: dialogue with shareholders (main principle E1)

There should be a **dialogue with shareholders** based on the **mutual understanding of objectives**. The board as a whole has responsibility for ensuring that a satisfactory dialogue with shareholders takes place. Nothing should override the general requirements of law to **treat shareholders equally with regard to access to information**.

2.17.1 Principles supporting dialogue with shareholders

Most shareholder contact is with the Chief Executive and Finance Director, but the board Chairman should ensure that all directors are made aware of their major shareholders' **issues and concerns.**

The board should keep in touch with shareholder opinion in whatever ways are most practical and efficient.

2.17.2 Provisions supporting dialogue with shareholders

- The board Chairman should ensure that the **views of shareholders** are communicated to the board as a whole.
- The Chairman should **discuss governance and strategy** with major shareholders.
- **Non-executive directors** should be offered the opportunity to attend scheduled meetings with major shareholders and should expect to attend meetings if requested by major shareholders.
- The **senior independent director** should attend sufficient meetings with a range of major shareholders to listen to their views in order to help develop a balanced understanding of the issues and concerns of major shareholders.
- The board should state in the **annual report** the steps they have taken to ensure that the members of the board and, in particular, the non-executive directors, develop an understanding of the views of major shareholders about the company, for example through direct face-to-face contact, analysts' or brokers' briefings and surveys of shareholder opinion.

2.18 Relations with shareholders: constructive use of the AGM (main principle E2)

The board should use the AGM to **communicate with investors** and to **encourage their participation.**

2.18.1 Provisions supporting the use of the AGM

- At any general meeting, the company should propose **a separate resolution on each substantially separate issue**, and should in particular propose a resolution at the AGM relating to the **report and accounts.**
- For each resolution, **proxy appointment forms** should provide shareholders with the option to direct their proxy to vote either for or against the resolution or to withhold their vote.
- The proxy form and any announcement of the results of a vote should make it clear that a **'vote withheld'** is not a vote in law and will not be counted in the calculation of the proportion of the votes for and against the resolution.
- The company should ensure that all **valid proxy appointments** received for general meetings are properly recorded and counted.
- For each resolution, after a vote has been taken, except where taken on a poll, the company should ensure that the following **information is given at the meeting and on the company's website**:
  - The number of shares in respect of which proxy appointments have been validly made
  - The number of votes for the resolution
  - The number of votes against the resolution
  - The number of shares in respect of which the vote was directed to be withheld.
- The chairman should arrange for the **chairmen of the audit, remuneration and nomination committees** to be available to answer questions at the AGM, and for **all directors to attend.**
- The company should arrange for the Notice of the AGM and related papers to be sent to shareholders at least **20 working days** before the meeting.

3 Internal control

Section overview

- Internal control is a process designed to ensure reasonable assurance about whether the company has achieved its objectives, via effective and efficient operations, reliable financial reporting and compliance with applicable laws and regulations.
- The Turnbull Guidance on internal control emphasises that an internal control system should facilitate: operations; risk response; safeguarding of assets; management of liabilities; reporting; compliance.
- The board must make a statement on internal control in the annual report.

CHAPTER 12

3.1 What is internal control?

Definition

Internal control: A process designed to provide reasonable (not absolute) assurance regarding the achievement of objectives via:

- Effective and efficient operations
- Reliable financial reporting
- Compliance with applicable laws and regulations

3.2 The Turnbull Guidance on internal control

In order to maintain a sound system of internal control (principle C2) the UK Corporate Governance Code recommends following what is known as the Turnbull Guidance. The full title of this FRC document is *Internal control: revised guidance for directors* issued in October 2005.

Definition

Internal control system: A **system** encompassing the policies, processes, tasks, and behaviours in a company that allow it to:

- **Operate** effectively and efficiently
- Respond appropriately to **risks**
- **Safeguard assets** from inappropriate use, loss or fraud
- Ensure **liabilities** are identified and managed
- Ensure the quality of internal and external **reporting**
- Ensure **compliance** with applicable laws and regulations, and internal policies

FRC *Turnbull Guidance*

3.2.1 Who is responsible for internal control?

The Guidance makes it clear that the **board of directors** as a whole has responsibility for:

- **Policy-making** on an effective system of internal control in the company, covering financial, operational and compliance controls
- **Reviewing** the effectiveness of the internal control system in addressing the risks that the board has identified face the company (the review tasks can be delegated to board committees)
- **Reporting** on the internal control system to shareholders each year

Management is responsible for **implementation** of internal control, and for day-to-day **monitoring** of the system.

3.2.2 What constitutes a sound system of internal control?

In determining what constitutes a **sound system of internal control** for the company, the board's deliberations should take a **risk-based approach**, including:

- The **nature and extent** of the risks facing the company
- The extent and categories of risk which it regards as **acceptable**
- The **likelihood of the risks concerned materialising**
- The company's ability to **reduce the incidence and impact** on the business of risks that do materialise
- The **costs** of operating particular controls relative to the **benefit** thereby obtained in managing the related risks

A sound system of internal control **reduces but cannot eliminate the possibilities** of:

- Poor judgement in decision-making
- Human error
- Deliberate circumvention of control processes by employees and others
- Management overriding controls
- Occurrence of unforeseen circumstances

The **system of internal control** should:

- Be **embedded in the operations** of the company and form part of its **culture**
- Be capable of responding quickly to **evolving risks** to the business arising from factors within the company and to **changes in the business environment**
- Include procedures for **reporting any significant control failings** or weaknesses immediately to appropriate levels of management, together with details of **corrective action** being taken

3.2.3 Statement on internal control

In the board's narrative **statement on internal control** in the annual report it should disclose that:

- It acknowledges responsibility for the system of internal control and for reviewing its effectiveness
- The system is designed to manage rather than eliminate the risk of failure to meet business objectives
- The system can only provide reasonable, not absolute, assurance against material misstatement or loss
- An ongoing process is in place for identifying, evaluating and managing significant risks facing the company
- The process has been in place for the year under review and up to the date of the annual report and accounts
- The process is regularly reviewed by the board and is in accord with the Turnbull Guidance
- There is a process to deal with the internal control aspects of any significant problems disclosed in the annual report and accounts

4 Engaging institutional shareholders: the Stewardship Code

Section overview

- Institutional shareholders should engage with companies to help improve long-term returns to shareholders and the efficient exercise of governance responsibilities.

Definition

Shareholder engagement: procedures designed to ensure that shareholders derive value from their investments by **dealing effectively with concerns over under-performance.**

Stewardship: accountability of management for the resources entrusted to them as agents of the company's owners

---

The Walker Report on the financial crisis of 2008 highlighted the role played by the agency problem of directors being responsible for the resources of shareholders. As a result the FRC assumed responsibility for governance of investors, specifically large institutional investors such as insurance companies and pension funds. The Stewardship Code focuses on encouraging institutional investors to take a more rigorous approach to making sure that managers and directors act as reliable stewards of the company's resources.

The Code sets out principles of good practice on how institutional investors should engage with the companies in which they invest and encourage good stewardship. Engagement is purposeful dialogue with companies on those matters as well as on issues that are the immediate subject of votes at general meetings.

As with the UK Corporate Governance Code, the Stewardship Code is applied on a 'comply or explain' basis. This means that the investing institution's website should:

- describe how the principles of the Stewardship Code have been applied by the institution, and either
- disclose specific information listed under Principles 1, 5, 6 and 7; or
- explain if these elements of the Code have not been complied with.

4.1 Principles of the Stewardship Code

The Code states that institutional investors should:

1 publicly disclose their policy on how they will discharge their stewardship responsibilities

2 have a robust policy on managing conflicts of interest in relation to stewardship, and this policy should be publicly disclosed

3 monitor their investee companies

4 establish clear guidelines on when and how they will escalate their activities as a method of protecting and enhancing shareholder value

5 be willing to act collectively with other investors where appropriate

6 have a clear policy on voting and disclosure of voting activity

7 report periodically on their stewardship and voting activities.

5 The role of external audit

Section overview

- The external (statutory) audit reports on whether the financial statements present a true and fair view of the company's financial performance and position.
- For listed companies, it also reports on the remuneration report and the company's compliance with the UK Corporate Governance Code.

5.1 What is an external audit?

The financial statements of larger companies are subject to **external audit** ('statutory audit' in the Companies Act 2006) each year by an auditor carrying out an independent and objective investigation, unless they are exempted.

The **purpose of the external audit** is to issue an **opinion** in an audit report whether the financial statements produced by the directors give a **'true and fair view'** of the **financial performance** of the company during the reporting period and of its **financial position** as at the end of the period.

Auditors of **listed companies** also have to report on:

- The **directors' remuneration report**
- The **company's compliance with the UK Corporate Governance Code**

To act as an external auditor a body corporate, partnership or individual must be a member of a recognised supervisory body, such as the ICAEW. They must also hold an appropriate qualification, which may include approved non-UK qualifications.

External auditors are appointed by a shareholder vote, following recommendations by the board and audit committee.

5.2 What does the audit opinion mean?

Shareholders often believe the external auditor's opinion means that the financial statements of the company are 'correct'. If the published financial statements are subsequently found to be incorrect, perhaps due to a fraud, shareholders then blame the auditor for:

- Failing to spot the problem
- Lacking objectivity
- Failing to challenge the views of the company's management about accounting policies and the accounting treatment of certain items

In fact, although the external audit must be conducted to professional standards, the external auditor is **not** responsible for detecting fraud and error. The **responsibility for preventing and detecting fraud and error** lies with:

- **Directors**, who are required by the UK Corporate Governance Code and the Turnbull Guidance to satisfy themselves that the systems of internal control and risk management are working effectively
- **Management**, who implement and monitor the system of internal control determined by the directors

5.3 What is the external audit's role in corporate governance?

The role of the external audit is a key issue in corporate governance, but in relation to corporate governance as a system the external auditor simply reports an independent and expert opinion on how the company is complying with the UK Corporate Governance Code. The responsibility to do something about it remains with the directors and shareholders.

6 The role of internal audit

Section overview

- Internal audit reports on the company's internal controls and risk management system.
- The audit committee monitors the role and performance of internal audit, including appointing its head and ensuring it has sufficient resources.

Definition

Internal audit: A semi-independent part of the company which monitors the effective operation of its internal control and risk management systems. Internal audit is itself a key element of the company's system of internal control.

CHAPTER 12

The independence of Internal auditors should be preserved so they can carry out the following tasks based on detailed reviews of areas of the company:

- Assessing how **risks are identified, analysed and managed**
- Advising management on embedding **risk management processes** into business activities
- Advising management on **improving internal controls**
- Ensuring that **assets are being safeguarded**
- Ensuring that **operations** are conducted effectively, efficiently and economically in accordance with the company's policies
- Ensuring that **laws and regulations** are complied with
- Ensuring that **records and reports** are reliable and accurate
- Helping management **to detect or deter fraud**
- Helping management **to identify savings and opportunities**

We saw above that internal audit plays a role in ensuring good corporate governance, along with the board, management, shareholders and external audit. Its remit extends beyond that of external audit however, as it covers **operational controls** and **non-financial compliance issues**.

The UK Corporate Governance Code recommends that the board's **audit committee** should monitor and review the effectiveness of the internal audit function. This includes:

- **Appointing the head of internal audit**
- Ensuring the function has **sufficient resources** eg staff, access to management, and a framework of professional standards

Ideally internal auditors should be able to **confer privately with the audit committee**, without the presence of management, and should have **direct access to any member of the board**.

Summary and Self-test

Summary

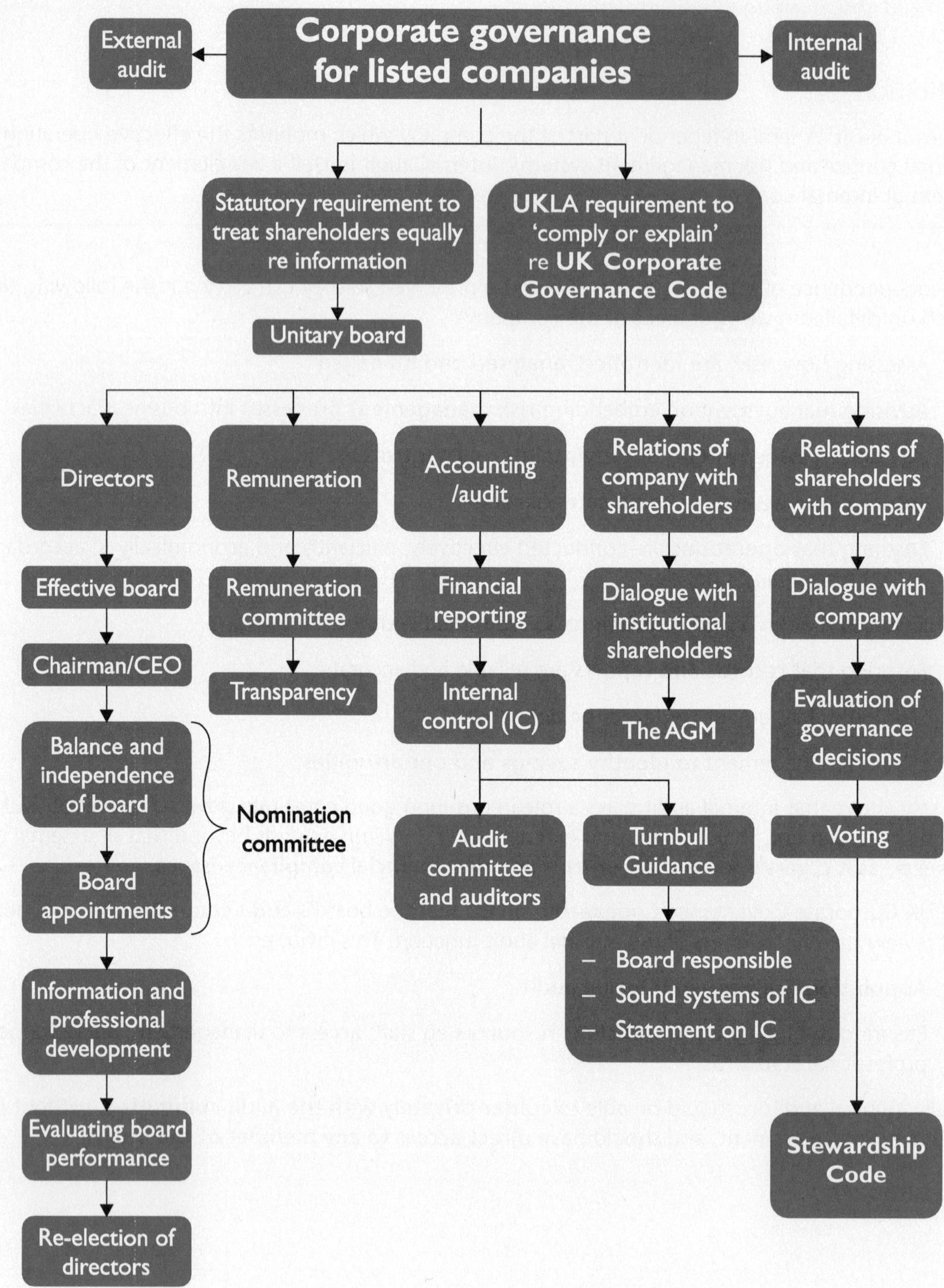

Self-test

Answer the following questions.

1 Non-executive directors have a prime role in

A Setting the company's strategic aims
B Providing entrepreneurial leadership
C Constructively challenging proposals on strategy
D Determining remuneration levels for non-executive directors

2 Trent plc's Chief Executive Terence Darby has been appointed by the Board as its next Chairman. The company has consulted major shareholders about this. It should set out its reasons for the appointment to all shareholders

A At the time of appointment
B At the time of appointment and in the next annual report
C In the next annual report
D At the time of appointment and in the next three annual reports

3 When non-executive directors exceptionally receive share options as part of their remuneration, and as approved by shareholders, these can only be exercised after the non-executive leaves the board and then only after:

A One year
B Two years
C Three years
D Five years

4 Biz plc is currently listed on the FTSE 350 but its operations are likely to reduce in size over the next year so that it will no longer qualify as a FTSE 350 company. Currently it has 12 board members, including the chairman. How many independent non-executive directors should Biz plc have now and in one year's time?

	Now	*One year's time*
A	5	2
B	5	5
C	6	2
D	6	6

5 The board's Chairman may chair the nomination committee when it is dealing with the appointment of a non-executive director. True or false?

6 The person who must advise the board via the Chairman on all corporate governance issues is

A The chairman of the audit committee
B The company secretary
C The external auditor
D The senior independent non-executive director

7 Annual re-election in FTSE 350 companies applies to

A All directors
B All executive directors only
C All executive directors and non-executives who have served nine years
D All non-executives who have served nine years

8 In relation to the remuneration committee of a FTSE 350 company, a board Chairman who was independent at the time of appointment

A May be one of the two members but may not chair the committee
B May be one of the three members but may not chair the committee
C May be one of the two members and may chair the committee
D May be one of the three members and may chair the committee

9 The audit committee should comprise

A Only independent non-executive directors, at least one of whom should have recent and relevant financial experience

B Both independent and non-independent non-executive directors

C A balance of non-executive and executive directors

D Both non-executive and executive directors, at least one of whom should have recent and relevant financial experience

10 Implementing policy for an effective system of internal control is the responsibility of

A Managers
B The Chairman
C The audit committee via the internal audit function
D The board of directors as a whole

Now, go back to the Learning Objectives in the Introduction. If you are satisfied you have achieved these objectives, please tick them off.

Technical reference

- UK Corporate Governance Code 2012 (FRC)
- Internal control: revised guidance for directors 2005 (FRC)
- Stewardship Code 2012 (FRC)

Answers to Interactive questions

Answer to Interactive question 1

It should set the company's strategic aims, ensure the company has the right resources to meet its objectives, review management's performance and set the company's values and standards so that its obligations to shareholders and others are understood and met.

Answer to Interactive question 2

The Chairman should ensure directors receive accurate, timely and clear information and that they continually update their skills, and their knowledge and familiarity with the company. The Chairman should direct the company secretary in relation to information flows, induction of directors and professional development. The Chairman should ensure there is proper induction for new directors.

Answer to Interactive question 3

It extends as well to interim reports, other price-sensitive public reports and reports to regulators.

Answers to Self-test

1	C	Principles supporting A4 of Corporate Governance Code
2	B	Provisions supporting A3 of Corporate Governance Code
3	A	Provisions supporting D1
4	C	Excluding the Chairman, Biz plc has 11 directors. A majority must be independent non-executives, which means there must currently be 6/11. Once it falls out of the FTSE 350, Biz plc only needs two independent non-executives (Provisions supporting B1)
5		True. The Chairman is only prevented from chairing the nomination committee when it is dealing with the appointment of the Chairman's successor (Provisions supporting B2)
6	B	Principles supporting B5
7	A	Provisions supporting B7
8	B	Provisions supporting D2
9	A	Provisions supporting C3
10	A	The board sets the policy, the management implements it

CHAPTER 13

The economic environment of business and finance

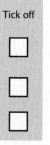

Introduction

Learning objectives

Tick off

- Specify the signalling, rewarding and allocating effects of the price mechanism on business (including the concept of price elasticity) ☐
- Specify the potential types of failure of the market mechanism and their effects on business ☐
- Identify the key macroeconomic factors that affect businesses ☐

Specific syllabus references are: 6a, b, c.

Syllabus links

The economic environment is studied further in Business Strategy and Financial Management at Professional level, and at the Advanced level.

Examination context

Questions on the economic environment will certainly come up in your exam.

Questions will be set in multiple choice format, in either a scenario context or as a test of knowledge of key principles.

1 Introduction to the economic environment

Section overview

- A business's economic environment comprises the macroeconomic environment (national and global influences) and its own microeconomic environment, especially how market forces affect it.

We saw in Chapter 4 how PESTEL analysis can help a business identify important factors in the environment in which it functions. In this chapter we shall focus on the **economic environment of business and finance**.

There are two economic environments that affect businesses:

- The **macroeconomic environment** in which all businesses have to operate, which incorporates:
  - **National influences**: the business cycle, government policies (eg fiscal and monetary policy), interest rates, exchange rates, inflation
  - **Global influences**: internationalisation of trade, influence of regional economic groups such as the EU, globalisation of markets
- The **microeconomic environment** of the particular business, which basically involves looking at how the market (or price) mechanism works

2 The macroeconomic environment

Section overview

- The macroeconomic environment comprises firstly the national economy (GDP, factors of production, growth) and also the global economy.
- The government acts as producer, purchaser, investor and transferor in the national economy.
- The consumer's role is to consume, the level of consumption being affected by: changes in the marginal propensity to consume and disposable income; changes in wealth distribution; government policy; new technology; interest rates; price expectations. Savers are affected in an equal but opposite way.
- Investment by businesses is key to the health of the national economy. This is affected by: interest rates; expectations and business confidence; consumer demand; opportunity cost; new technology.
- The main stages of the business/trade cycle are: boom, recession, depression and recovery.
- Most governments aim for stable prices, so inflation must be kept under control.
- Types of inflation: demand-pull and cost-push (fiscal and credit)
- Policies to influence aggregate demand: monetary(interest rates) and fiscal (taxation, borrowing and spending) policy
- Policies to influence aggregate supply: spending levels; privatisation; tax reductions; workforce amendments; deregulation/relaxing competition laws; free movement of capital

Businesses operate in the economy as a whole and changes in the macroeconomic environment can have major implications for them.

2.1 The national economy

The amount of **national output** by firms or government agencies which produce goods and services in the national economy is measured as its **gross domestic product** or **GDP**. To create GDP four **factors of production** are employed, each of which enjoys a **return**:

Factor of production	Return
Land	Rent
Labour	Wages
Capital	Interest
Entrepreneurship	Profit

GDP equals the amount of **expenditure** incurred by those who purchase the output:

- consumers (or **households**),
- the government and
- foreign buyers (the **overseas sector**)

The **level of national output** is important because it is a measure of the economic activity in a country:

- It is an **aggregate of personal incomes** – the bigger this is, the more income individual inhabitants will be earning on average (assuming a stable population).
- More income means more **spending** by consumers (households) on the output of firms, and more spending (ignoring the effects of price rises) means that a higher output of goods and services is required to be produced.
- **Growth** in GDP per head of population is an economic policy objective of most, if not all, governments. The growth potential of an economy will depend on the **amount of factors of production** available, and their **productivity**.

2.1.1 The role of the government in the national economy

The government has several functions within the national economy.

- It acts as the **producer** of certain goods and services instead of privately-owned firms, and the production of public administration services, education and health services, the police force, armed forces, fire services and public transport are all aspects of output. The government in this respect acts, like firms, as a producer and must also pay wages to its employees.
- It acts as the **purchaser** of final goods and services and adds to total consumption expenditure. National and local government obtain funds from the firms or households of the economy in the form of taxation and then use these funds to buy goods and services from other firms.
- It **invests** by purchasing capital goods, for example building roads, schools and hospitals.
- It makes **transfer payments** from one section of economy to another, for example by taxing working households and paying pensions, and by paying unemployment benefits and social security benefits.

2.1.2 The role of the consumer in the national economy

Definition

Disposable income: income available to individuals after payment of personal taxes. It may be consumed or saved.

Total spending or **consumption** by households is affected by six influences.

- **Changes in disposable income, and the marginal propensity to consume (MPC)**. Changes in disposable income are affected by matters such as pay rises and changes in tax rates. An increase in disposable income from a pay rise, or because of a reduction in tax rates, may simply increase consumption and have no effect on savings. If a household believes that saving is a good thing however it will save as much as possible of the increase, and spend as little of it as possible. How far an increase in disposable income is allocated to consumption rather than saving is known as the marginal propensity to consume (MPC).

In the economy as a whole, a general belief in the value of saving may mean that the MPC is low. The prestige attached to the possession of consumer goods may however overcome the admiration for saving, making the MPC high.

- **Changes in the distribution of wealth**. Some sections of the population will have a higher MPC than others so a redistribution of wealth might affect consumption. (A redistribution of wealth might be accomplished by taxing the rich and giving to the poor in the form of more government allowances.)
- **Government policy**. Government can influence consumption levels through taxation and/or public spending. For example, an increase in direct taxation will reduce disposable income and therefore will also reduce consumption.
- **The development of major new products**. When such developments happen, they can create a significant increase in spending by consumers who want to buy the goods or services.
- **Interest rates**. Changes in interest rates will influence the amount of income that households decide to **save**, and also the amount that they might elect to **borrow** for spending. High interest rates will make saving more attractive while low interest rates will reduce the **cost of credit** and will therefore increase borrowing and levels of consumption.
- **Price expectations**. Expectations of price increases may increase current consumption while expectations of price reductions may have the opposite effect.

2.1.3 The role of the saver in the national economy

Saving is the amount of income which is not consumed. Therefore, not surprisingly, the influences which affect savings are very similar to those that affect consumption – but in mirror image.

- **Income**. The level of income will be a key determinant in the level of savings. It is difficult to save when your income is very low!
- **Interest rates and the cost of credit**. If interest rates rise, saving becomes more attractive relative to consumption. Similarly, as the cost of credit rises, borrowing becomes less attractive meaning that as a result people will save more.
- **Long-term savings**. A large amount of household savings goes into long-term, contractual savings such as pension schemes. These savings may be less likely to vary with income than with demographics – for example, savings into pension schemes have risen alongside increases in life expectancy in developed countries.

2.1.4 The role of investment by businesses in the national economy

An **investment** involves the acquisition of more fixed capital (buildings, machinery, plant and equipment) or inventories of goods and so on. The total volume of investment in the economy, from the private sector or the public sector or both, depends on:

- The **interest rate** on capital (the price of money)
- **Expectations** about the future and business confidence, including expectations about future cash flows and profit flows arising from the investment
- The strength of **consumer demand** for goods
- The **opportunity cost** of investment
- The level of **new technology** to be invested in

If **interest rates are high** the effects are as follows (low interest rates have a mirror image effect):

- firms will demand a **higher return** when appraising investments and so some investments may not occur, thereby **restricting economic growth** (firms will be less willing to invest, but remember they cannot always cut their investment plans quickly and at short notice).
- individuals will be tempted to **consume less of their income and save more**, so that they will invest more of their savings – that is, to hold less cash and more interest-bearing investments.

New technology will be a **boost to investment**:

- If it **reduces the unit costs of production** via new methods of production (such as robotics) then new technology will **increase profitability**. Firms will invest in order to achieve lower costs and remain competitive.
- If it leads to **new types of good** then new technology will **stimulate demand**. Firms will invest to make the product and meet the consumer demand.

Private sector investment will come from retained profits, new issues of shares, or borrowing (as we saw in Chapter 8). However, in an economic recession (see below) profits might be low, and investors might lack confidence in a recovery, so that new share issues are impossible on a large scale.

Public sector investment might be financed by higher taxation, or by an increased deficit between government income and expenditure, that is, a higher **public sector net cash requirement (PSNCR)**, though this might force up interest rates in the capital markets and **crowd out private sector investment.**

2.2 The business/trade cycle

Definition

Business cycles/trade cycles: the continual sequence of rapid growth in GDP, followed by a slow-down in growth and then a fall. Growth then comes again, and when this has reached a peak, the cycle turns once more.

Four main phases of the business cycle can be distinguished.

- Recession (A)
- Depression (B)
- Recovery (C)
- Boom (D)

Recession tends to occur quickly, while recovery is typically a slower process. Figure 13.1 below can be used to help explain how this is so.

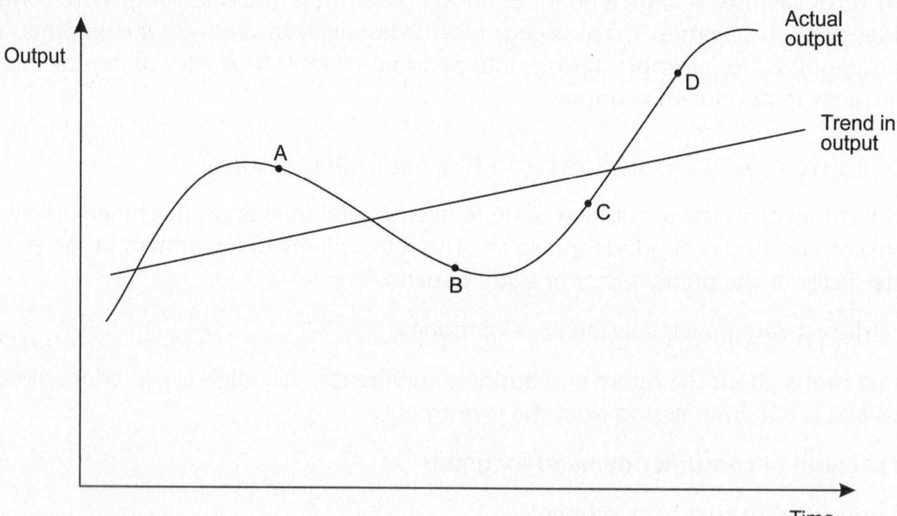

Figure 13.1 The business/trade cycle

2.2.1 Recession

At point **A** in Figure 13.1, the economy is **entering a recession**:

- consumer demand falls
- investment projects already undertaken begin to look unprofitable
- orders are cut
- inventory levels are reduced
- business failures occur as firms find themselves unable to sell their goods

- production and employment fall
- general price levels begin to fall
- business and consumer confidence diminish
- investment remains low
- the economic outlook appears to be poor

Recession can begin relatively quickly because of the speed with which the effects of declining demand will be felt by businesses suffering a loss in sales revenue. The knock-on effects of reducing inventory and cutting back on investment exacerbate the situation and add momentum to the recession.

2.2.2 Depression

Eventually, in the absence of any stimulus to demand, a period of full **depression** may set in and the economy will reach point **B**.

2.2.3 Recovery

At point **C** the economy has reached the **recovery** phase of the cycle. This can be slow to begin because of the effect of recession/depression on levels of confidence. Governments will try to limit the decline by boosting demand in the economy as a whole (we shall come back to this). Once begun, recovery is likely to quicken as confidence returns.

- Output, employment and income will all begin to rise.
- Business expectations will be more optimistic so new investment will be more readily undertaken.
- The rising level of demand can be met through increased production by bringing existing capacity into use and by hiring unemployed labour.
- The average price level will remain constant or begin to rise slowly.

Decisions to purchase new materials and machinery may lead to benefits in efficiency from new technology. This can enhance the relative rate of economic growth in the recovery phase once it is under way.

2.2.4 Boom

As recovery proceeds, the output level climbs above its trend path, reaching point **D**, in the **boom** phase of the cycle. During the boom:

- Capacity and labour will become fully utilised causing bottlenecks in some industries which are unable to meet increases in demand (no spare capacity, shortage of skilled labour or key material inputs).
- Further rises in demand will therefore be met by price rather than production increases
- Business will be profitable, with few firms facing losses.
- Expectations of the future may be very optimistic and the level of investment expenditure high.

2.2.5 Avoiding the 'boom and bust' cycle

Governments generally seek to stabilise the economic system, trying to avoid the distortions of a widely fluctuating cycle.

- In a **recession** they will try to **boost overall demand**
- In a **boom** they will try to keep **dampen overall demand** through raising taxation or interest rates, and by reducing public expenditure.

We will come back to these points when we look at fiscal and monetary policy.

2.3 Inflation

Definitions

Inflation: an increase in price levels generally, and a decline in the purchasing power of money.

Deflation: falling prices generally, which is normally associated with low rates of growth and recession.

2.3.1 Why is inflation a problem?

Most governments aim for **stable prices**. A high rate of price inflation is harmful and undesirable for the following reasons.

- **Redistribution of income and wealth**

  Inflation leads to a redistribution of income and wealth from suppliers to customers because outstanding amounts lose 'real' value with inflation. In addition those with fixed incomes, such as pensioners and the low-paid, fare worse than those with significant earning power, as the nominal amount of a fixed income stays the same but its purchasing power falls.

- **Balance of payments effects**

  If a country has a higher rate of inflation than its major trading partners, its exports will become relatively expensive and imports relatively cheap, although its exchange rate will usually alter to take account of this.

- **Price signalling and 'noise'**

  Prices act as signals to both consumers and producers, affecting both demand and supply respectively. Inflation, particularly at high rates, can undermine the ability of the price mechanism to influence the allocation of resources in an economy. Business confidence is undermined because planning and forecasting are less accurate. Inflation is often referred to as 'noise' in an economy for this reason.

- **Wage bargaining**

  Wage demands increase in times of high inflation. A wage/price spiral may take hold, which will reinforce the problem and valuable time is wasted negotiating new wage rates rather than producing new goods.

- **Consumer behaviour**

  People may stockpile goods fearing price increases later, which could create shortages for other people. Consumers will be more anxious to consume now rather than waiting until costs rise; this will raise consumption levels and possibly push prices up even further – a spiral that can contribute to hyper-inflation (extremely high rates of inflation).

2.3.2 Types of inflation

Definitions

Demand pull inflation: price rises resulting from a persistent excess of demand over supply in the economy as a whole. Supply cannot grow any further once 'full employment' of factors of production is reached.

Cost push inflation: price rises resulting from an increase in the costs of production of goods and services, eg of imported raw materials or from wage increases.

There are two main **causes of demand pull inflation**.

- **Fiscal**. An increase in government spending or a reduction in taxes will raise demand in the economy.
- **Credit**. If levels of credit extended to customers increase, perhaps because of a decrease in interest rates, expenditure is likely to rise. In this case, inflation is likely to be accompanied by customers increasing their debt burdens.

Once the rate of inflation has begun to increase, **expectational inflation** can occur. Regardless of whether the factors that have caused inflation are persistent or not, there will be a generally held view of what inflation is likely to be. To protect future income, wages and prices will therefore be raised in anticipation of the expected amount of future inflation. This can lead to the vicious circle of a **wage-price spiral**, in which inflation becomes a relatively permanent feature because of people's expectations that it will occur.

2.4 Government objectives and policies

To achieve economic growth and control inflation the **macroeconomic policies** used by the government are:

- influencing **overall demand** in the economy (**aggregate demand**) via:
  - **Monetary policy**: government policies on the money supply, the monetary system, interest rates, exchange rates and the availability of credit.
  - **Fiscal policy**: government policies on taxation, public borrowing and public spending.
- influencing **overall supply** in the economy (**aggregate supply**) via **supply-side policies**

CHAPTER 13

2.4.1 Monetary policy and aggregate demand

Interest rates – the price of money – are a target of monetary policy if it is considered that there is a direct relationship between interest rates and the level of expenditure in the economy, or between interest rates and the rate of inflation. In the UK, the objective of monetary policy has been principally to **reduce the rate of inflation to a sustainable low level**, though since 2008 interest rates have also been used to support consumer spending in order first to avoid and then to shorten the recession which followed the banking crisis.

Effects of a rise in interest rates

- The **price of borrowing** in the economy will **rise**.
  - If **companies** see the rise as relatively permanent, rates of return on investments will become less attractive and investment plans may be curtailed. **Spending will fall.** Corporate profits will fall as a result of higher interest payments. Companies will reduce inventory levels as the cost of having money tied up rises.
  - **Households** will reduce or postpone consumption in order to reduce borrowings, and should become less willing to borrow for house purchase. **Spending will fall.**

  (Although it is generally accepted that there is likely to be a connection between interest rates and investment (by companies) and consumer expenditure, **the connection is not a stable and predictable one**, and interest rate changes are only likely to affect the level of expenditure after a **considerable time lag**.)
- The **exchange rate for sterling will be higher** than it would otherwise be. This will keep the cost of exports higher and the cost of imports will be cheaper.
- There will be **capital inflows** as foreign investors will be attracted to sterling investments.
- The reductions in spending and investment will **reduce aggregate demand in the economy**.

2.4.2 Fiscal policy and aggregate demand

Definition

Fiscal policy: the government's policy on government spending, taxation and borrowing.

- **Spending**. The government spends money at national and local levels to provide goods and services, such as a health service, public education, a police force, roads, public buildings and so on, and to pay its administrative work force. It may also, perhaps, provide finance to encourage investment by private industry, for example by means of grants. **Increased government spending** increases the size of the economy, so expenditure and therefore GDP will rise.
- **Taxation**. Expenditure must be financed, and the government must have income. Most government income comes from **taxation**, but some income is obtained from **direct charges** to users of government services such as National Health Service charges. **Increased taxation** without increased government spending reduces the size of the economy. A government might deliberately raise taxation to reduce inflationary pressures.
- **Borrowing**. The government must borrow the amount by which its expenditure exceeds its income. In the UK government this is known as the **Public Sector Net Cash Requirement (PSNCR).** Where the government borrows from has an impact on the effectiveness of fiscal policy.

The government's **'fiscal stance'** may be **neutral, expansionary** or **contractionary,** according to its effect on national income.

- **Increased borrowing** and **spending** ⇨ **expansionary** fiscal stance.
- **Increased taxation** but **no increase in spending** (or **decreased borrowing** and **decreased spending)** ⇨ **contractionary** fiscal stance.
- **Increased taxation** and **spending** ⇨ **broadly neutral** fiscal stance (income diverted from one part of the economy to another).

2.4.3 Supply-side macroeconomic policies

Macroeconomic demand-side intervention by government using monetary and fiscal policy may be harmful:

- **Demand management interventions** are inflationary in the long run
- High taxes act as a **disincentive** to economic activity
- The possibility of politically motivated policy changes creates damaging **uncertainty** in the economy, discouraging long-term investment

The main **supply side macroeconomic policies** are:

- More **involvement of the private sector** in the provision of services
- **Reduction in taxes** in order to increase incentives to supply
- **Increasing flexibility** in the labour market by curbing the power of trade unions
- Improving **education and training** so the quality of labour and hence the economy's productive capacity are enhanced
- **Increasing competition** through deregulation and privatisation of utilities
- **Abolition of exchange controls** and allowing the free movement of capital

We shall now look at the business's **microeconomic environment**.

3 The market mechanism

Section overview

- In a market buyers and sellers exchange 'goods' via the market mechanism, which determines price according to the interaction of supply and demand.

Definition

Market mechanism: The interaction of demand and supply for a particular item.

3.1 What is a market?

The concept of a market in microeconomics goes beyond the idea of a single geographical place where people meet to buy and sell goods. It refers to the buyers and sellers of goods or services who influence its price. Markets can be worldwide, as in the case of oil, wheat, cotton and copper for example. Others are more localised, such as the housing market or the market for second-hand cars.

Definition

Market: A situation in which potential buyers and potential sellers (or 'suppliers') of an item (or 'good') come together for the purpose of exchange.

Markets for different goods are often inter-related. All goods compete for customers so that if more is spent in one market, there will be less to spend in other markets.

3.2 How is the market price of goods determined?

Price theory (or **demand theory** as it is sometimes referred to) is concerned with how market prices for goods are arrived at, through the **interaction** of **demand and supply**.

4 Demand

Section overview

- Demand quantifies how much of a good buyers would buy at a certain price level.
- The demand curve is usually downward sloping from left to right when price is measured on the y (vertical) axis and quantity is measured on the x (horizontal) axis. This means that a rise in price causes a fall in the quantity demanded.
- Within one demand curve only price determines the level of demand.
- Other determinants of demand will shift the demand curve left or right. These include: substitutes and complements; income levels (normal and inferior goods); fashion and expectations; advertising; income distribution.
- The level of demand can change quite rapidly in response to a change in a determinant.

4.1 What is meant by 'demand'?

Definition

Demand: The quantity of a good that potential purchasers would buy, or attempt to buy, if the price of the good were at a certain level.

If demand is satisfied, actual quantities bought equals demand. If some demand is unsatisfied, more would-be purchasers are trying to buy a good that is in insufficient supply.

4.2 The demand schedule and the demand curve

The relationship between demand for a good and the price of the good can be shown graphically as a **demand curve**. The demand curve is derived by estimating in a **demand schedule** how much of a good would be demanded at various hypothetical market prices.

Worked example: Demand schedule and demand curve

Suppose that the following *demand schedule* shows demand for biscuits by one household over a period of one month.

Price per kg	*Quantity demanded at this price*
£	kg
1	9²/₃
2	8
3	6¹/₄
4	4¹/₂
5	2²/₃
6	1

We can show this schedule graphically on a demand curve (Figure 13.1), with:

(a) Price on the y axis, and
(b) Quantity demanded on the x axis

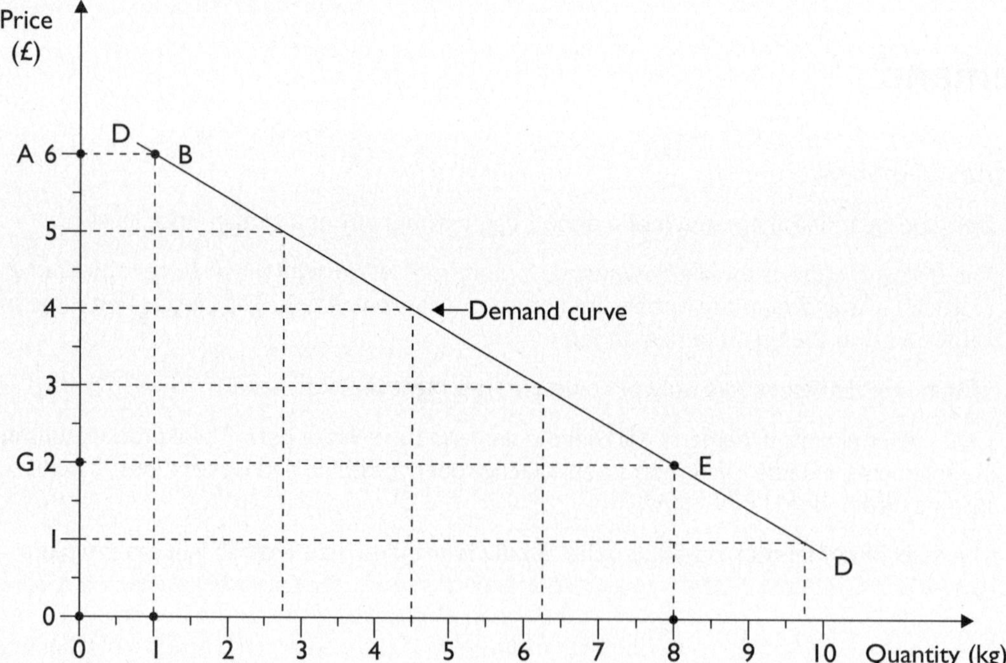

Figure 13.1: Demand for biscuits

Changes in demand caused by changes in price **only** are represented by movements **along the demand curve**, from one point on the curve to another. The price has changed, so the quantity demanded changes, but the demand curve itself stays in the same place.

A demand curve generally slopes down from left to right for the following reasons.

(a) For the individual consumer, a fall in the price of the good makes it relatively cheaper compared to other goods so expenditure will be shifted to the good whose price has fallen. It is the *relative price* of the good that is important. A fall in the relative price of a good increases demand for it.

(b) A fall in the good's price means that people with lower incomes will also be able to afford it or more of it. The overall size of the market for the good increases. The converse argument applies to an increase in prices; as a price goes up, consumers with lower incomes will no longer be able to afford the good, or will buy something else whose price is relatively cheaper, and the size of the market will shrink.

4.3 What factors determine demand?

Several factors influence the total market demand for a good. One of these factors is obviously its **price**, but there are other factors too since people buy not just one good with their money but a whole range of goods and services.

Within the control of the business (see Chapter 2):

- Price
- Marketing research
- Product research and development
- Advertising
- Sales promotion
- Training and organisation of sales force
- Effectiveness of distribution
- After-sales service
- Granting of credit to customers

Seven Ps
- **P**roduct
- **P**rice
- **P**romotion
- **P**lace
- **P**eople
- **P**rocesses
- **P**hysical evidence

Outside the control of the business

- Price of **substitute goods** (items to which the consumer will switch if the price changes)
- Price of **complementary goods** (items which the consumer buys as a result of buying the goods, such as blades for razors)
- Consumers' **income**
- **Fashion** and **expectations**

4.3.1 Price

In the case of most goods (with some exceptions, such as Giffen goods, which we will look at later), the higher the price, the lower will be the quantity demanded. It is common sense that at a higher price, a good does not give the same value for money as it would at a lower price, so people will not want to buy as much. This **dependence of demand on price applies to all goods and services**, from bread and salt to houses and satellites.

A demand curve shows how the quantity demanded will change in response to a change in price **provided that all other factors affecting demand are unchanged** – that is, provided that there is no change in the prices of other goods, tastes, expectations or the distribution of household income.

4.3.2 Other factors affecting demand

A different demand curve needs to be produced if there is a change in the other factors affecting demand. We call this a **shift of the demand curve**. If the change means that demand rises then the downward-sloping demand curve moves to the right; if demand falls then it moves to the left.

4.3.3 Inter-related goods: substitutes and complements

A change in the price of one good will not necessarily change demand for another good. For example, we would not expect an increase in the price of cocoa to affect the demand for cars. However, there are goods for which the market demand is inter-related, referred to as either **substitutes** or **complements**.

- **Substitute goods** are goods that are alternatives to each other, so that an increase in the demand for one is likely to cause a decrease in the demand for another. Switching demand from one good to another 'rival' good is **substitution**. Examples of substitute goods and services are:
  - Rival brands of the same commodity, like Coca-Cola and Pepsi
  - Tea and coffee
  - Bus rides and car rides
  - Some different forms of entertainment

  Substitution takes place when the price of one good rises or falls relative to the substitute good.
- **Complements** are goods that tend to be bought and used together, so that an increase in the demand for one is likely to cause an increase in the demand for the other. Examples of complements are:
  - Cups and saucers
  - Holidays and travel insurance
  - Cars and the components and raw materials that go into their manufacture

Interactive question 1: Substitute or complementary goods? **[Difficulty level: Easy]**

What might be the effect of an increase in the ownership of domestic freezers on the demand for perishable food products?

See **Answer** at the end of this chapter.

4.3.4 Income levels: normal and inferior goods

More income gives people more to spend, so they will want to buy more goods at existing prices. However, a rise in income will not increase market demand for all goods and services. The effect of a rise in income on demand for an individual good will depend on the nature of the good.

(a) A rise in income may increase demand for a particular good. This is what we might normally expect to happen, so they are called **normal goods**.

(b) Demand for another good may rise with income up to a certain point but then fall as income rises beyond that point. Goods whose demand eventually falls as income rises are called **inferior goods:** examples might include cheap brands of sausages or wine. The reason for falling demand is that as incomes rise, demand switches to superior products, for example gourmet sausages and champagne.

4.3.5 Income distribution

Market demand for a good is influenced by the way in which the national income is shared among people. In a country with many rich and many poor households and few middle income ones, we might expect a relatively large demand for luxury cars and yachts and also for bread and potatoes. In a country with many middle-income households, we might expect high demand for medium-sized cars and foreign holidays, and other 'middle income' goods.

Interactive question 2: Income distribution [Difficulty level: Intermediate]

What do you think might be the demand for swimming pools amongst a population of five households enjoying total annual income of £1m, if the distribution of income is either as under assumption 1 or as under assumption 2?

	Annual income	
	Assumption 1	*Assumption 2*
	£	£
Household 1	950,000	200,000
Household 2	12,000	200,000
Household 3	13,000	200,000
Household 4	13,000	200,000
Household 5	12,000	200,000
	1,000,000	1,000,000

See **Answer** at the end of this chapter.

4.3.6 Fashion and expectations

A change in **fashion** will alter the demand for a product. For example, when it became fashionable to drink wine with meals, expenditure on wine increased. In addition, there may be passing 'crazes', such as football strips during the World Cup.

If consumers expect that prices will rise, or that shortages will occur, they may attempt to stock up on the product, thereby creating excess demand in the short term which will increase prices. This can then lead to panic buying. Examples include fear of war or the effect of strikes. Similarly, if prices are expected to fall, purchasing might be postponed – a potential effect of deflation in the economy.

4.4 Shifts of the demand curve

When there is a change in one of these demand determinants other than price, the relationship between demand quantity and price will also change, and there will be a different price/quantity demand schedule and so a different demand curve. We refer to such a change as a **shift of the demand curve**.

Figure 13.2 depicts a demand curve shifting to the right, from D_0 to D_1. For example, at a single price, price P_1, demand for the good would rise from Q_0 to Q_1. This shift could be caused by any of the following:

- A rise in household income
- A rise in the price of substitutes
- A fall in the price of complements
- A positive change in tastes towards this good
- An expected rise in the price of the good

A fall in demand at each price level would be represented by a shift of the demand curve in the opposite direction: to the *left*. Such a shift may be caused by the opposite of the changes above.

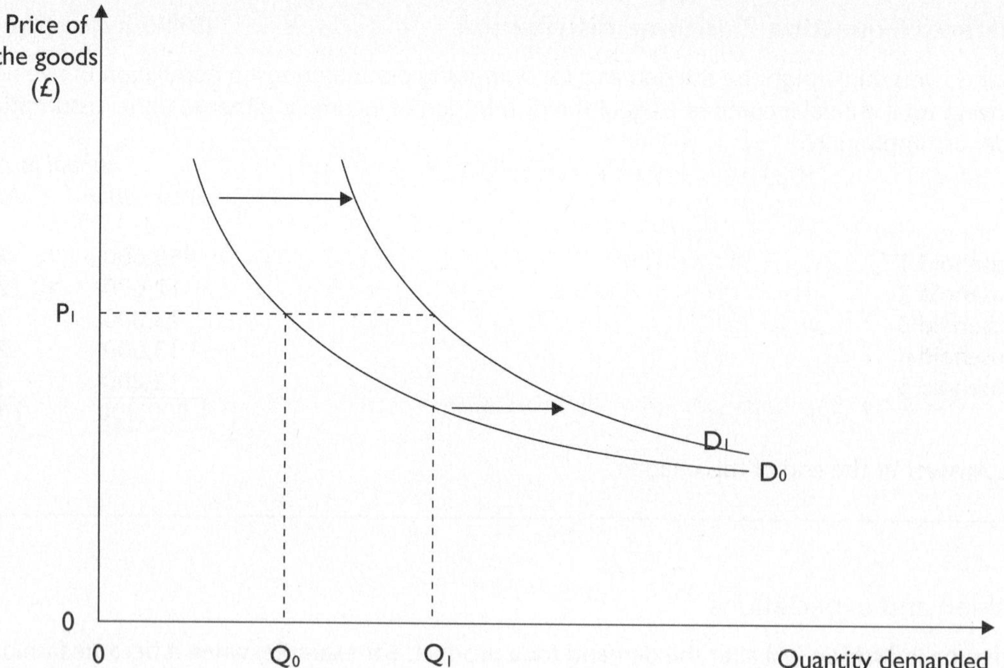

Figure 13.2: Outward shift of the demand curve

Remember that:

- **Movements along a demand curve** are caused by changes in the good's **price**
- **Shifts of the demand curve** are caused by changes in any of the **other factors** which affect demand for a good, other than its price

5 Supply

Section overview

- Supply quantifies how much of a good sellers will supply at a certain price level.
- The supply curve is usually upward sloping from left to right when price is measured on the y axis. This means that a rise in price causes a rise in the quantity supplied.
- Within one supply curve only price determines the level of supply.
- Other determinants of supply will shift the supply curve. These include: prices of other goods; prices of related goods; costs; changes in technology; other seasonal and random factors.
- For most goods and services, the level of supply changes less rapidly than demand in response to a change in a determinant.

5.1 What is meant by 'supply'?

Definition

Supply: The quantity of a good that existing suppliers or would-be suppliers would want to produce for the market at a given price.

The quantity of a good that can be supplied to a market varies up or down, as a result of either:

- Existing suppliers increasing or reducing their output **quantities**, or
- Suppliers stopping production altogether and leaving the market, or new suppliers entering the market and starting to produce the good.

If the quantity that suppliers want to produce at a given price exceeds the quantity that purchasers demand, there will be an **excess of supply**, with suppliers **competing** to win what demand there is. Over-supply and competition result in price-competitiveness and ultimately a **fall in price**.

5.2 The supply schedule and the supply curve

A **supply schedule** and **supply curve** are constructed in a similar manner to a demand curve (from a schedule of supply quantities at different prices) but show the quantity suppliers are willing to produce at different price levels. It is an upward sloping curve from left to right, because greater quantities will be supplied at higher prices.

Worked example: Supply schedule and supply curve

The supply schedule for product Y is as follows.

Price per unit	*Quantity that suppliers would supply at this price*
£	Units
100	10,000
150	20,000
300	30,000
500	40,000

The relationship between supply quantity and price is shown as a supply curve in Figure 13.3.

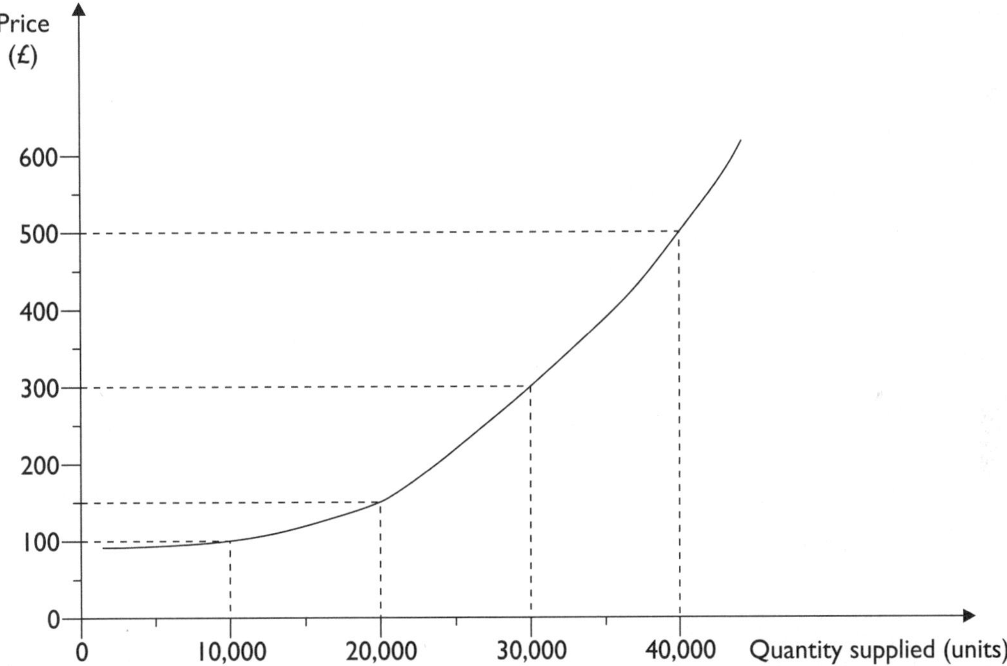

Figure 13.3: Supply curve

5.3 What factors influence supply?

- The **price** obtainable for the good
- The **prices of other goods**. An increase in the price of other goods would make the supply of a good whose price does not rise less attractive to suppliers, or they may want to switch to supplying something else
- The **price of related goods** in 'joint supply'. For instance, leather and beef are related goods which are produced jointly when cattle are slaughtered. If the price of beef rises, more will be supplied and there will be an accompanying increase in the supply of leather

- The **costs of making the good**, including raw materials costs, wages, etc. A rise in the price of one raw material will cause producers to shift away from supplying goods whose costs and profits are closely related to the price of that raw material, towards the supply of goods where the cost of that raw material is less significant
- **Changes in technology**. Technological developments which reduce costs of production (and increase productivity) will raise the quantity of supply of a good at a given price
- **Other factors**, such as changes in the weather in the case of agricultural goods, natural disasters or industrial disruption

The supply curve itself shows how the quantity supplied will change in response to a change in **price,** provided that all other conditions affecting supply remain unchanged. If supply conditions (the price of other goods, or costs of making the goods, or changes in technology) alter, a different supply curve must be drawn. In other words, a **change in price** will cause a **shift in supply along the supply curve.** A change in **other supply conditions** will cause **a shift of the supply curve itself.**

A shift of the supply curve as the result of a fall in costs, either in absolute terms or relative to the costs of other goods, is shown in Figure 13.4. If the market price of the good is P_1, suppliers will be willing to increase supply from Q_0 to Q_1 under the new supply conditions.

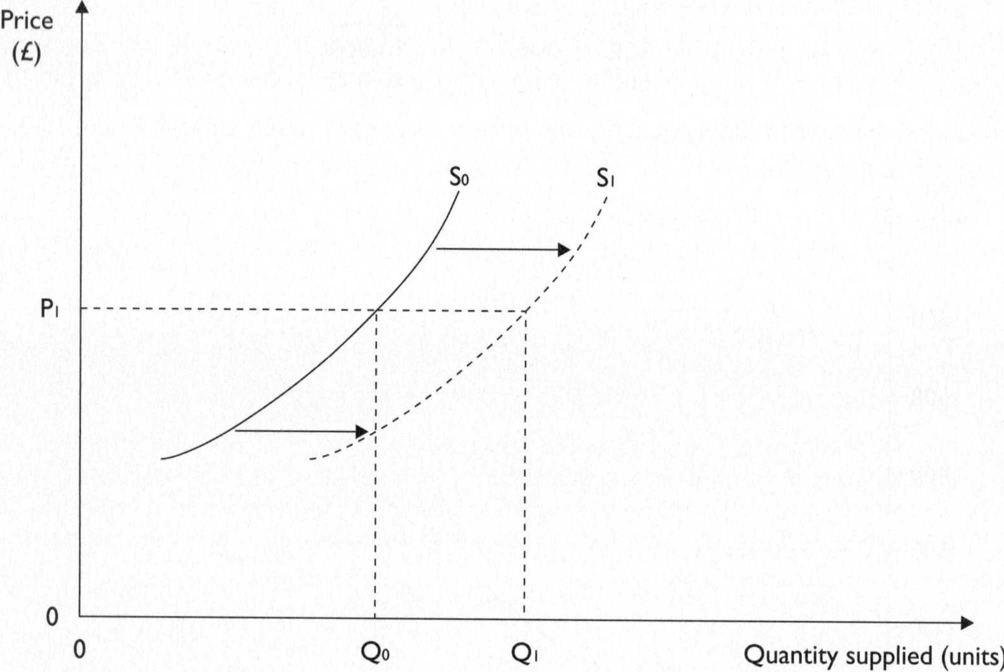

Figure 13.4: Outward shift of the supply curve

5.4 The effect of time on supply and demand

We need to distinguish between short-run and long-run responses of both supply and demand to changes in determinants. In the **short run** both supply and demand are relatively unresponsive to changes in price, as compared to the **long run**.

- **In the case of supply,** changes in the quantity of a good supplied often require the laying off or hiring of new workers, or the installation of new machinery. These changes, brought about by management decisions, take some time to implement
- **In the case of demand,** it takes time for consumers to adjust their buying patterns, although demand often responds more rapidly than supply to changes in price or other demand conditions

Response times vary between markets. In stock markets, for example, supply and demand for company shares respond very rapidly to price changes, whereas in markets for fuel oils or agrichemicals response times are much longer.

Interactive question 3: Market prices in financial markets [Difficulty level: Intermediate]

In a stock market the 'products' bought and sold include shares in companies. What can you say about the supply of and demand for these 'products', and how quickly does their price change in response to changes in supply and demand factors?

See **Answer** at the end of this chapter.

6 The equilibrium price

Section overview

- An efficient market brings supply and demand into equilibrium at the market price, which is where the supply and demand curves intersect.

6.1 Price signals and incentives

People who want goods only have a limited disposable income and they must decide what to buy with the money they have. The **prices** of the goods they want will affect their buying decisions (ignoring other factors).

Businesses' supply decisions will be influenced by both demand and supply considerations.

- Market demand conditions influence the **price** that a supplier will get for its output. Prices act as **signals** to suppliers, and changes in prices should stimulate a response from a supplier to change its production quantities.
- Supply is also influenced by production **costs** and profits. The objective of maximising profits provides the **incentive** for suppliers to respond to changes in price or cost by changing their production quantities.

Decisions by businesses about what industry to operate in and what markets to produce goods for will be influenced by the prices obtainable and the costs incurred. Although some businesses have been established in one industry for many years, others are continually opening up, closing down or switching to new industries and new markets. Over time, businesses in an industry might also increase or reduce the volume of goods they sell.

6.2 What is the equilibrium price?

The **market mechanism brings demand and supply into equilibrium.**

Definition

Equilibrium price: The price of a good at which the volume demanded by consumers and the volume businesses are willing to supply are the same.

This can be illustrated by drawing the market demand curve and the market supply curve on the same graph (Figure 13.5).

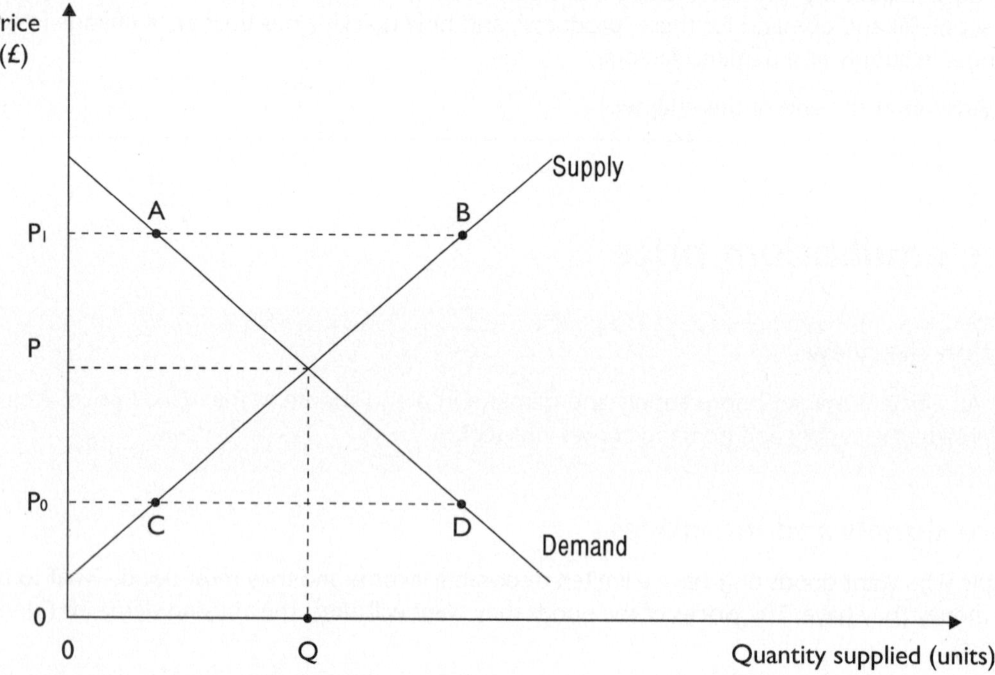

Figure 13.5: Market equilibrium or the equilibrium price

At price P_1 in Figure 13.5, suppliers want to produce more than is demanded at that price the amount of the over-supply being equal to the distance AB. The reaction of suppliers as unsold inventories accumulate would be:

- To cut down the current level of production (reduce supply) in order to clear unwanted inventories, and/or
- To reduce prices in order to encourage sales

The opposite will happen at price P_0, where there is an excess of demand over supply, equal to the distance CD. Output would increase and/or the price would rise.

At price P the amount that suppliers are willing to supply is equal to the amount that customers are willing to buy. There will be no unusual variation in inventory and, as long as nothing else changes, there will be no change in price. Consumers will be willing to spend a total of (P × Q) on buying Q units of the product, and suppliers will be willing to supply Q units to earn revenue of (P × Q). P is the **equilibrium price**.

The forces of supply and demand push a market to its equilibrium price and quantity.

- If there is no change in the determinant of supply or demand, the **equilibrium price** will rule the market and will remain stable.
- If the equilibrium price does not rule, the market is in **disequilibrium**, but supply and demand will push prices towards the equilibrium price.
- Shifts in the supply curve or demand curve because of determinants other than price will **change the equilibrium price and quantity**.

6.3 Adjustments to equilibrium

Equilibrium price, supply and demand must adjust following a shift of the demand or supply curve. There are four possibilities, therefore, which are illustrated by Figure 13.6.

(i) Increase in consumer incomes

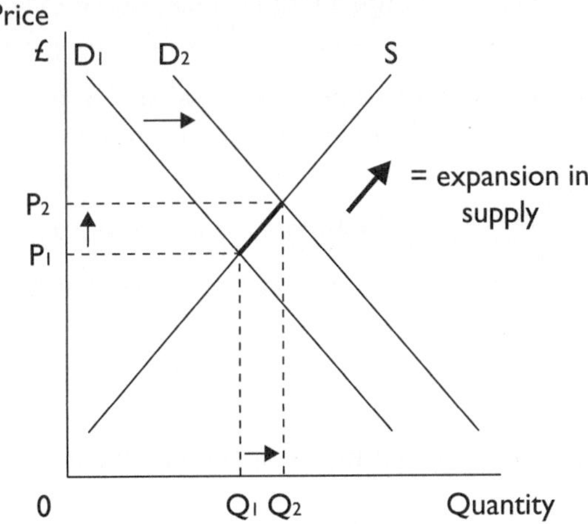

Prediction

- Rise in market price
- Rise in quantity supplied

(ii) Product becomes unfashionable

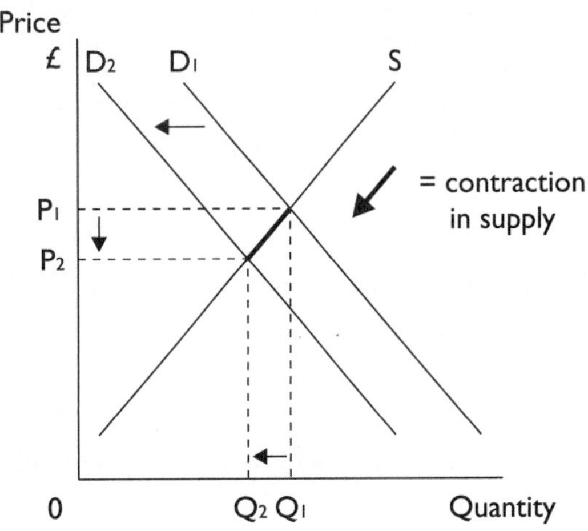

Prediction

- Fall in market price
- Fall in quantity supplied

(iii) Improvement in production technology

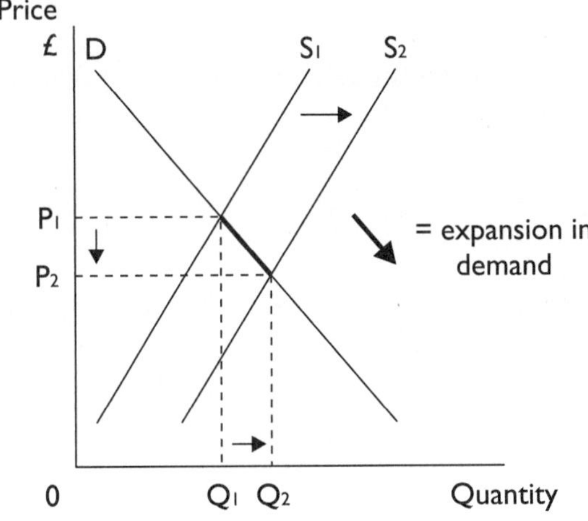

Prediction

- Fall in market price
- Rise in quantity supplied

(iv) Rise in factor costs

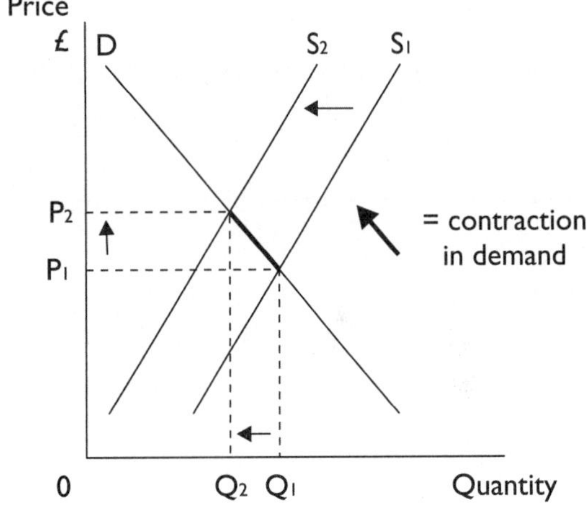

Prediction

- Rise in market price
- Fall in quantity supplied

Figure 13.6: Adjustments in equilibrium

Interactive question 4: Price determinants

[Difficulty level: Intermediate]

Explain, in detail, what conditions will determine price in:

(a) A retail fruit and vegetable market;
(b) An auction of antiques and paintings.

See **Answer** at the end of this chapter.

6.4 Price regulation

The regulation of prices by government provides an illustration of how demand and supply analysis can be applied. Government might introduce regulations either:

- To set a **maximum price** for a good, perhaps as part of an anti-inflationary economic policy (such as a prices and incomes policy) so that suppliers cannot charge a higher price even if they wanted to, or
- To set a **minimum price** for a good below which a supplier is not allowed to fall. For example, OPEC (the Organisation of Petroleum Exporting Countries) has in the past attempted to impose minimum prices for oil on the world markets.

The government may try to prevent prices of goods rising by establishing a maximum price.

- If this price is **higher than the equilibrium price**, its existence will have no effect at all on the operation of market forces,
- But if the maximum price is **lower than what the equilibrium price would be**, there will be an excess of demand over supply. The low price attracts customers, but deters suppliers so supply will fall unless there is scope for the market to exist outside government-sanctioned channels – a so-called 'black market'.

7 Elasticity

Section overview

- Price elasticity of demand (PED) measures how far demand for a good will change in response to a change in its price.
- The PED of a good is affected by: the availability of substitutes; time; pricing by competitors; whether it is a necessity or a luxury; what percentage of income is spent on it; whether it is habit-forming.
- Income elasticity of demand measures how far demand for a good will change in response to a change in income levels.
- Some goods are cross-elastic, so there is a relationship between a change in price for one good and a change in demand for the other.
- Price elasticity of supply measures how far supply of a good will change in response to a change in its price.

Definition

Elasticity: The extent of a change in demand and/or supply given a change in price.

7.1 Price elasticity of demand

If prices went up by 10% would the quantity demanded fall by 5%, 20%, 50% or what? **Price elasticity of demand (PED)** is a measure of the extent of change in demand for a good in response to a change in its price. It is measured as:

$$\text{PED} = \frac{\text{Change in quantity demanded, as a percentage of original demand}}{\text{Change in price, as a percentage of original price}}$$

Since demand usually increases when the price falls, and decreases when the price rises, elasticity usually has a negative value. It is usual to ignore the minus sign, therefore, but note that there are types of goods where elasticity is actually positive (we shall come back to this).

$$PED = \frac{\text{Proportional change in quantity}}{\text{Proportional change in price}}$$

$$= \left[\frac{Q_2 - Q_1}{Q_1}\right] \div \left[\frac{P_2 - P_1}{P_1}\right]$$

(Where P_1, Q_1 are the initial price and quantity; P_2, Q_2 are the subsequent price and quantity.)

PED less than 1 = inelastic demand
PED more than 1 = elastic demand
PED = 1 = unit elasticity

Worked example: Price elasticity of demand

The price of a good is £1.20 per unit and annual demand is 800,000 units. Market research indicates that an increase in price of 10 pence per unit will result in a fall in annual demand of 70,000 units.

Requirement

Calculate the elasticity of demand when the price is £1.20.

Solution

At a price of £1.20, annual demand is 800,000 units. For a price rise:

% change in quantity $\frac{70{,}000}{800{,}000} \times 100\% = 8.75\%$ (fall)

% change in price $\frac{10\text{p}}{120\text{p}} \times 100\% = 8.33\%$ (rise)

Price elasticity of demand at price £1.20 = $\frac{-8.75}{8.33} = -1.05$

Ignoring the minus sign, the price elasticity at this point is 1.05. Demand is *elastic* at this point, because the elasticity is greater than one.

Interactive question 5: Price elasticity of demand [Difficulty level: Exam standard]

Using the same details and assuming that the demand curve is a straight line, calculate the elasticity of demand when the price is £1.30.

See **Answer** at the end of this chapter.

7.2 Elastic and inelastic demand

The value of price elasticity of demand may be anything from zero to infinity. Demand is referred to as:

(a) **Inelastic** if the absolute value is less than 1, and
(b) **Elastic** if the absolute value is greater than 1.

Think about what this means.

- Where demand is **inelastic**, the quantity demanded changes by a **smaller percentage** than the percentage change in price
- Where demand is **elastic**, demand changes by a **larger percentage** than the percentage change in price

7.2.1 Special values of price elasticity of demand

There are three special values of price elasticity of demand: 0, 1 and infinity.

- **Demand is perfectly inelastic:** PED = 0. There is no change in quantity demanded, regardless of the change in price. This is the case where the demand curve is a **vertical straight line**.
- **Demand is perfectly elastic:** PED = ∞ (infinitely elastic). Consumers will want to buy an infinite amount, but only up to a particular price level. Any price increase above this level will reduce demand to zero. This is the case where the demand curve is a **horizontal straight line**.
- **Unit elasticity of demand:** PED = 1. The percentage change in quantity demanded is equal to the percentage change in price. **Demand changes proportionately to a price change.**

7.3 What is the significance of price elasticity of demand?

The price elasticity of demand is relevant to **total spending** on a good or service, which in turn is a matter of interest to **suppliers**, to whom sales revenue accrues, and **government**, which may receive a proportion of total expenditure in the form of taxation.

- When demand is **elastic**, an **increase** in price will result in a **fall in the quantity demanded** such that **total expenditure will fall.**
- Demand **inelasticity** above zero means an **increase** in price will still result in a **fall in quantity demanded,** but **total expenditure will rise.**
- With **unit elasticity**, expenditure will stay **constant** given a change in price.

Information on price elasticity of demand therefore indicates how consumers can be expected to respond to different prices, so the effect of different prices on total revenue and profits can be predicted.

Interactive question 6: Effect of PED on revenue [Difficulty level: Exam standard]

Product A currently sells for £5, and demand at this price is 1,700 units. If the price fell to £4.60, demand would increase to 2,000 units.

Product B currently sells for £8 and demand at this price is 9,500 units. If the price fell to £7.50, demand would increase to 10,000 units.

In each of these cases, calculate:

(a) The price elasticity of demand (PED) for the price changes given; and

(b) The effect on total revenue, if demand is met in full at both the old and the new prices, of the change in price.

See **Answer** at the end of this chapter.

7.3.1 Positive price elasticities of demand: Giffen goods and Veblen goods

When the price of a good rises, there may be a **substitution effect**: consumers will buy other goods instead because they are now relatively cheaper. But there will also be an **income effect** in that the rise in price will reduce consumers' real incomes, and will therefore affect their ability to buy goods and services. The 19th century economist Sir Robert Giffen observed that this income effect could be so great for certain basic goods (called **Giffen goods**) that the demand curve may be upward sloping. The price elasticity of demand in such a case would be positive.

Giffen observed that among the labouring classes of his day, consumption of bread rose when its price rose. This happened because the increase in price of this commodity, which made up a high proportion of individuals' consumption, had a significant effect on real incomes: people had to increase their consumption of bread because they could not afford other foods to supplement their diets.

The demand curve for a good might also slope upwards if it is bought **for purposes of ostentation,** so that having a higher price tag makes the good more desirable to consumers and thus increases demand. Such goods are sometimes called **Veblen goods**.

7.4 Factors influencing price elasticity of demand for a good

Factors that determine price elasticity of demand are similar to the factors – other than price – that affect the volume of demand. The PED is really a **measure of the strength of these other determinants of demand**.

7.4.1 Availability of substitutes

The **more substitutes** there are for a good, especially close substitutes, the **more elastic** will be the price elasticity of demand for the good. For example, in a supermarket, a rise in the price of one vegetable such as carrots is likely to result in a switch of customer demand to other vegetables, many vegetables being fairly close substitutes for each other. This factor is probably the most important influence on price elasticity of demand.

7.4.2 The time horizon

Over time, consumers' demand patterns are likely to change, and so if the price of a good is increased, the initial response might be very little change in demand (inelastic demand) but then as consumers **adjust their buying habits** in response to the price increase, demand might fall substantially. The time horizon influences elasticity largely because the longer the period of time which we consider, the greater the knowledge of substitution possibilities by consumers and the greater provision of substitutes by suppliers.

7.4.3 Competitors' pricing

If the response of competitors to a **price increase** by one business is to **keep their prices unchanged**, the supplier raising its prices is likely to face **elastic** demand for its goods at higher prices. If the response of competitors to a **reduction in price** by one supplier is to **match the price reduction** themselves, the supplier is likely to face **inelastic** demand at lower prices. This is a situation which probably faces many large suppliers with one or two major competitors.

7.4.4 Luxuries and necessities

Necessities tend to have a **more inelastic** demand curve, whereas **luxury** goods and services tend to be **more elastic**.

7.4.5 Percentage of income spent on a good

The **smaller** the percentage of an individual's income spent on purchasing the good, the **more inelastic** demand will be.

7.4.6 Habit-forming goods

Goods such as cigarettes and alcohol tend to be **inelastic** in demand. Preferences are such that habitual consumers of certain products become desensitised to price changes.

Interactive question 7: Demand for a good [Difficulty level: Exam standard]

Under a health strategy, the UK government wishes to increase the purchase of organic food by consumers by 3% in volume terms. UK government economists have analysed data which reveal that the price elasticity of demand for organic food is –1.6.

By how much should the government encourage suppliers to change the price of organic food, assuming all other determinants of demand remain the same?

See **Answer** at the end of this chapter.

7.5 Income elasticity of demand

Definition

Income elasticity of demand: An indication of the responsiveness of demand to changes in household incomes.

$$\text{Income elasticity of demand} = \frac{\text{\% change in quantity demanded}}{\text{\% change in household incomes}}$$

- Demand for a good is **income elastic** if income elasticity is greater than 1, so that quantity demanded rises by a larger percentage than the rise in income. For example, if the demand for downloads will rise by 10% if household incomes rise by 7%, we would say that the demand for downloads is income elastic. These are **luxury goods**.
- Demand for a good is **income inelastic** if income elasticity is between 0 and 1 and the quantity demanded rises less than the proportionate increase in income. For example, if the demand for baked beans will rise by 6% if household incomes rise by 10%, we would say that the demand for baked beans is income inelastic. These are **normal goods** or **necessities**.
- Demand for a good is negatively income elastic where, in response to an increase in income, demand actually falls. These are **inferior goods**. An example could be coach travel, where passengers might switch to faster, but more expensive, trains as their income rises.

7.6 Cross elasticity of demand

Definition

Cross elasticity of demand: A measure of the responsiveness of demand for one good to changes in the price of another good.

$$\text{Cross elasticity of demand} = \frac{\text{\% change in quantity of good A demanded}^{*}}{\text{\% change in the price of good B}}$$

*(given no change in the price of A)

Cross elasticity depends upon the degree to which goods are substitutes or complements.

- If the two goods are **substitutes**, such as tea and coffee, cross elasticity will be positive, so a rise in the price of one will increase the amount demanded of the other.
- If the goods are **complements**, such as real coffee and cafetieres, cross elasticity will be negative, so a rise in the price of one will decrease demand for the other.
- For **unrelated goods**, such as tea and oil, cross elasticity will be 0.

7.7 Price elasticity of supply

Definition

Price elasticity of supply: A measure of the responsiveness of supply to a change in price.

$$\text{Price elasticity of supply (PES)} = \frac{\text{\% change in quantity supplied}}{\text{\% change in price}}$$

- Where the supply of goods is fixed whatever price is offered, for example in the case of antiques, vintage wines and land, supply is **perfectly inelastic** and the elasticity of supply is zero. The supply curve is a vertical straight line.
- Where the supply of goods varies proportionately with the price, there is **unit elasticity of supply** and the supply curve is an upward slope passing through the origin.
- Where the producers will supply any amount at a given price but none at all at a slightly lower price, elasticity of supply is infinite, or **perfectly elastic**. The supply curve is a horizontal straight line.

7.7.1 Elasticity of supply and time

As with elasticity of demand, the elasticity of supply for a product varies according to the time period over which it is measured. Three lengths of time period may be considered.

(a) **The market period** is so short that supplies of the product in question are limited to existing inventory. In effect, supply is fixed.

(b) **The short run** is a period long enough for supplies of the product to be altered by increases or decreases in current output, but not long enough for the long-term plant and machinery used in production to be altered. This means that suppliers can produce larger quantities only if they are not already operating at full capacity; they can reduce output fairly quickly by means of lay-offs and redundancies.

(c) **The long run** is a period sufficiently long to allow suppliers' long-term equipment to be altered. There is time to build new factories and machines, and time for old ones to be closed down. New suppliers can enter the industry in the long run.

8 Types of market structure

Section overview

- The market for a good may be structured on the following lines: perfect competition; monopoly; monopolistic competition; oligopoly (including duopoly).

Definition

Market structure: A description of the number of buyers and sellers in a market for a particular good, and their relative bargaining power.

8.1 Perfect competition

Perfect competition is characterised by:

- **Many** small (in value) buyers and sellers which, individually, cannot influence the market price
- **No barriers** to entry or exit, so businesses are free to enter or leave the market as they wish
- **Perfect information** such that production methods and cost structures are identical
- **Homogeneous** (identical) products
- **No collusion** between buyers or sellers

The consequences of perfect competition include:

- Suppliers are '**price takers**' not 'price makers', that is they can sell as much as they want but only at the market-determined price
- All suppliers only earn '**normal**' **profits**
- There is a **single selling price** (see Figure 13.7)

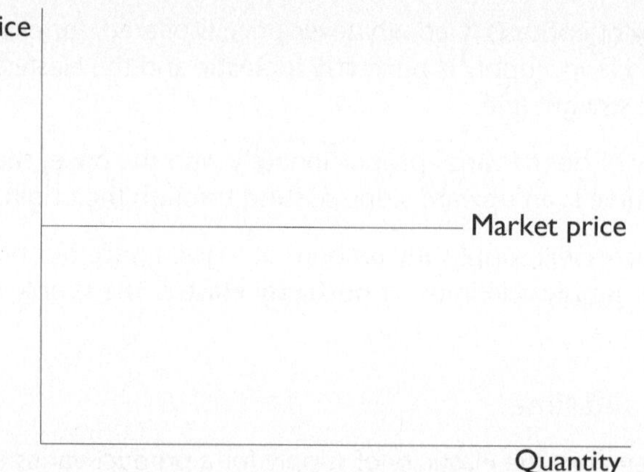

Figure 13.7: Perfect competition – demand curve

Perfect competition is often seen as an ideal state (for consumers) but very rarely if ever occurs in practice, mainly due to the fact that:

- There are often **barriers to entry**
- There is **asymmetric information** (see Chapter 12 for an example of this in the financial markets)
- Goods are **differentiated**
- There may be **collusion**

We shall see more about these issues a little later.

8.2 Monopoly

Monopoly is characterised by:

- **One supplier** (or one dominant supplier)
- **Many buyers**
- **Barriers** to entering the industry, for instance the capital cost of setting up a national grid of electricity would be prohibitive for most businesses. Other barriers include:
  - Patent protection
  - Access to unique resources
  - Unique talent
  - Public sector monopoly
  - Size domination of market

The consequences of monopoly include:

- The fact that businesses can EITHER **set the selling price** OR **determine the quantity supplied**, but the market will determine the other factors
- Monopolists can earn greater than normal profits ('**supernormal profits**')

Monopolies can be further classified as follows:

- A **pure monopoly** is a monopoly by virtue of there being only one supplier in the market
- An **actual monopoly** is a monopoly by virtue of there being one supplier with a dominant market share
- A **government franchise monopoly** is a pure monopoly that has arisen specifically by virtue of a government deciding to operate in that way
- A **natural monopoly** is a monopoly that arises by virtue of the market displaying such high levels of fixed costs and low marginal costs (eg public utilities) that economies of scale are such that there is no fear of entry into the market from others

Monopolies are usually (but not always) seen as operating against the interests of consumers, so there is extensive **regulation** to control them (see Chapter 14).

8.3 Monopolistic competition

Monopolistic competition is characterised by:

- **Many** buyers and sellers (as in perfect competition)
- **Some differentiation** between products (not homogeneous as in perfect competition)
- **Branding** of products to achieve this differentiation
- Some (but not total) **customer loyalty**
- **Few barriers** to entry
- Significant **advertising** in many cases

Examples include:

- Pubs
- Hairdressers

In both cases, customers display a loyalty or preference to one supplier so that they will not switch purely on price, as they would do in perfect competition.

Consequences include:

- Increases in prices cause loss of some customers
- Only normal profit earned in the long run (as in perfect competition)

8.4 Oligopoly

Oligopoly is characterised by:

- **A few large sellers but many (often small) buyers**
- Product **differentiation**
- A high degree of **mutual interdependency**

Examples include:

- The oil industry (Shell, Esso, BP)
- Banking (Lloyds, HSBC, Barclays)
- Washing powder (Procter & Gamble, Unilever)

Consequences include:

- Businesses compete through **non-price competition**, particularly advertising and branding
- **Price cuts** are generally **copied** by competitors but
- **Price increases** are not always copied.

8.4.1 Duopoly

Duopoly is characterised by:

- **Two** dominant suppliers who between them control prices
- A temptation for the two suppliers to act in **collusion** (which is an illegal breach of competition laws in most countries)

Consequences include **higher prices** as competition is very limited.

9 The failure of perfect competition

Section overview

- Free markets are often seen as efficient in resource allocation.
- This efficiency may be allocative or productive.
- However, markets can and do fail because of: market imperfections (monopoly, monopsony, asymmetric information, and slowness of response); externalities; public goods; economies of scale (internal and external).
- Internal economies of scale arise from: specialisation of labour; division of labour; larger and more specialised machinery; dimensions; buying economies; indivisibility of operations; holding inventory.

9.1 Is perfect competition (a free market) the best structure?

The following arguments are put forward by **advocates of the free market**.

- Free markets are **efficient**. Suppliers and buyers react fairly quickly to changes in market conditions in making their output and purchasing decisions; **resource allocation** within the economy is quick to adapt to the new conditions.
- Free markets are **impersonal**. Prices and levels of output are arrived at as a result of numerous decisions by consumers and suppliers, and not as the result of regulation or central planning
- The market forces of supply and demand result in an efficient **allocation of economic resources.**
  - Buyers will want lower prices and suppliers will want higher prices, and a balance of supply and demand is struck in the market through the price mechanism
  - Suppliers will decide what goods to supply, and in what quantities, by relating their prices to the costs of production (and the costs of the scarce resources needed to produce them)
  - If the price of a product is too high, buyers will want to buy less of it. If the price is too low, producers will make less of it and switch their production resources into making something different

In this context, there are two **types of potential efficiency**:

- **Allocative efficiency** is achieved when goods and services that are wanted by buyers are produced in optimum quantities. Allocative efficiency occurs when resources are allocated in such a way that it is impossible to re-allocate factors of production to increase overall benefit
- **Productive efficiency** is achieved when the economy produces its goods and services at the lowest factor cost. It occurs when factors of production are organised in such a way that the average cost of production is at its lowest point

However, the arguments in favour of a free market are based on the assumption that there is **'perfect competition'**, including:

- A **large number of competing suppliers**, each producing a **homogeneous product** and each having only a **small share of the market**
- Buyers and suppliers having **perfect information** about markets and prices
- There is **perfect mobility of factors of production**, which can be switched easily from making one type of good into making another
- There is **free entry and exit** of suppliers into and out of the market

In reality, these assumptions are often not valid. Instead, the **free market often fails to allocate resources efficiently.**

9.2 Market failure

Definition

Market failure: A situation in which a free market mechanism fails to produce the most efficient (the 'optimum') allocation of resources.

Market failure is caused by a number of factors:

- **Market imperfection** with one, or a few, suppliers exerting **market power**
- **Externalities**
- The existence of **public goods** and benefits that are gained by third parties
- **Economies of scale**. Large-scale production leads to reductions in costs per unit, which are not matched by price reductions. This leads to above-normal profits and enables large companies to dominate smaller companies

9.3 Market imperfection

Market imperfection describes any situation where actual behaviour in the market differs from what it would be if there were 'perfect' competition in the market. The following are examples of market imperfection.

- If a **monopoly** supplier controls a market, it might prevent other suppliers from entering the market (for example, by claiming patent rights, or launching a strong marketing campaign with the intention of keeping customers away from the new suppliers). By restricting supply in this way, the monopolist may keep prices higher than they would be in a competitive market, and/or may cause customers to have to put up with poorer goods than might be available in a competitive market.
- Just as monopolies are suppliers which dominate supply to a market, **monopsony** buyers are large individual buyers who dominate demand in a market. Monopsonists may exert control over the market, extracting low prices or other favourable conditions from suppliers. An example sometimes quoted is the immense buying power built up by large supermarkets.
- Consumers may make bad purchasing decisions because they have **incomplete** and **inaccurate**, or **asymmetric information** about all goods and services that are available.
- It takes time for the price mechanism to work. Firms cannot suddenly enter a new market or shut down operations. The **slow response of the price mechanism to changes in demand** creates some short-run inefficiency in resource allocation.

9.4 Externalities

In a free market, suppliers and buyers make their output and buying decisions for their own private benefit, and these decisions determine how the national economy's scarce resources will be allocated to production and consumption. Private costs and private benefits, as opposed to social costs and benefits, therefore determine what goods are made and bought in a free market.

- **Private cost** measures the cost **to the supplier** of the resources it uses to produce a good
- **Private benefit** measures the benefit obtained directly by a supplier or by a buyer
- **Social cost** measures the **cost to society as a whole** of the resources that a supplier uses
- **Social benefit** measures the total benefit obtained, both directly by a supplier or a buyer, and indirectly (at no extra cost), by other suppliers or buyers

It can be argued that a free market system would result in a satisfactory allocation of resources, **provided that** private costs are the same as social costs and private benefits are the same as social benefits. In this situation, suppliers will maximise profits by supplying goods and services that benefit customers, and that customers want to buy. By producing their goods and services, suppliers are giving benefit to both themselves and the community.

However, there are instances when either:

- Suppliers or buyers do things which give benefit to others, but no reward to themselves, or
- Suppliers or buyers do things which are harmful to others, but at no cost to themselves

When private cost is not the same as social cost, or when private benefit is not the same as social benefit, an allocation of resources which reflects private costs and benefits only may not be socially acceptable. Here are some examples of situations where **private cost and social cost differ.**

- A supplier produces a good and, during the production process, **pollution** is discharged into the air. The private cost to the supplier is the cost of the resources needed to make the good. The social cost consists of the private cost plus the additional 'costs' incurred by other members of society, who suffer from the pollution.

- The private cost of transporting goods by road is the cost to the haulage company of the resources used to provide the transport. The social cost would consist of the private cost plus the social cost of **environmental damage**, including the extra cost of repairs and maintenance of the road system, which sustains serious damage from heavy goods vehicles.

Here are some examples of situations where **private benefit and social benefit differ.**

- Customers at a café in a piazza benefit from the entertainment provided by professional musicians, who are hired by the café. The customers of the café are paying for the service in the prices they pay, and they obtain a private benefit from it. At the same time, other people in the piazza, who are not customers of the café, might stop and listen to the music. They will obtain a benefit, but at no cost to themselves. They are **free riders**, taking advantage of the service without contributing to its cost. The social benefit from the musicians' service is greater than the private benefit to the café's customers.

- A large firm pays for the training of employees as accountants, expecting a certain proportion of these employees to leave the firm in search of a better job once they have qualified. The **private benefits** to the firm are the benefits of the training of those employees who continue to work for it. The total **social benefit** includes the enhanced economic output resulting from the training of those employees who go to work for other firms.

9.4.1 What is an externality?

Definition

Externality: The difference between the private and the social costs, or benefits, arising from an activity. Less formally, an 'externality' is a cost or benefit which the market mechanism fails to take into account because the market responds to purely private signals. One activity might produce both harmful and beneficial externalities.

Interactive question 8: Externality **[Difficulty level: Exam standard]**

Much Wapping is a small town where a municipal swimming pool and sports centre have just been built by a private company. Which of the following is an external benefit of the project?

(a) The increased trade for local shops
(b) The increased traffic in the neighbourhood
(c) The increased profits for the private company
(d) The increased building on previously open land in an inner city area

See **Answer** at the end of this chapter.

9.5 Public goods

Some goods, by their very nature, involve so much 'spillover' of externalities that they are difficult to provide except as **public goods** whose production is organised by the government.

In the case of public goods, the consumption or use of the good by one individual or group does not significantly reduce the amount available for others. Furthermore, it is often difficult or impossible to exclude anyone from its benefits, once the good has been provided. As a result, in a free market individuals benefiting from the good would have no economic incentive to pay for it, since they might as well be 'free riders' if they can, enjoying the good while others pay for it.

National defence is perhaps the most obvious example of public good. It is obviously not practicable for individuals to buy their own defence systems. Policing is another example, although the growth of private security firms illustrates how some areas of policing are becoming 'privatised'.

9.6 Economies of scale

When large companies are able to produce goods at a low unit cost because of economies of scale, but either do not pass these savings onto buyers, or use the advantage to dominate smaller companies, there is a market failure to allocate resources efficiently.

9.6.1 Reasons for economies of scale

The economies of scale attainable from large scale production may be categorised as:

(a) **Internal economies**: economies arising within the business from the organisation of production, or

(b) **External economies**: economies attainable by the business because of the growth of the industry as a whole

Internal economies of scale arise from the more effective use of available resources, and from increased specialisation, when production capacity is enlarged.

- **Specialisation of labour**. In a large undertaking, a highly skilled worker can be employed in a job which makes full use of their skills. In a smaller undertaking, individuals must do a variety of tasks, none of which they may do very well ('Jack-of-all-trades – master of none').
- **Division of labour**. Because there is specialisation of labour there is also division of labour, ie work is divided between several specialists, each of whom contributes their share to the final product. A building will be constructed, for example, by labourers, bricklayers, plumbers, electricians, plasterers and so on. Switching between tasks wastes time, and division of labour avoids this waste.
- Large undertakings can make use of **larger and more specialised machinery**. If smaller undertakings tried to use similar machinery, the costs would be excessive because the machines would become obsolete before their physical life ends (ie their economic life would be shorter than their physical life). Obsolescence is caused by falling demand for the product made on the machine, or by the development of newer and better machines.
- **Dimensional economies of scale** refer to the relationship between the volume of output and the size of equipment (eg storage tanks) needed to hold or process the output. The cost of a container for 10,000 gallons of product will be much less than ten times the cost of a container for just 1,000 gallons.
- **Buying economies** may be available, reducing the cost of material purchases through bulk purchase discounts
- **Indivisibility of operations**. There are operations which:
  - Must be carried out at the same cost, regardless of whether the business is small or large; **average** fixed costs always decline as production increases
  - Vary a little, but not proportionately, with size (ie 'semi-fixed' costs)
  - Are not worth considering below a certain level of output (eg advertising campaigns)
- **Holding inventory** becomes more efficient. The most economic quantities of inventory to hold increase with the scale of operations, but at a lower proportionate rate of increase.

External economies of scale occur as an **industry** grows in size. For example:

- A large skilled **labour force** is created and educational services can be geared towards training new entrants
- Specialised **ancillary industries** develop to provide components, transport finished goods, trade in by-products, provide special services and so on – for instance, law firms may be set up to specialise in the affairs of the industry

The extent to which both internal and external economies of scale can be achieved will vary from industry to industry, depending on the conditions in that industry. In other words, large-sized firms are better suited to some industries than others.

- **Internal economies of scale** are potentially more significant than external economies to a supplier of a product or service for which there is a **large consumer market**. It may be necessary for a supplier in such an industry to grow to a certain size in order to benefit fully from potential economies of scale, and thereby be cost-competitive and capable of making profits and surviving.
- **External economies of scale** are potentially significant to smaller businesses which specialise in **ancillary services** to a larger industry. For example, the development of a large world-wide industry in drilling for oil and natural gas off-shore led to the creation of many specialist suppliers, making drilling rigs and various types of equipment. Thus, a specialist business may benefit more from the market demand created by a large customer industry than from its own internal economies of scale.

Summary and Self-test

Summary

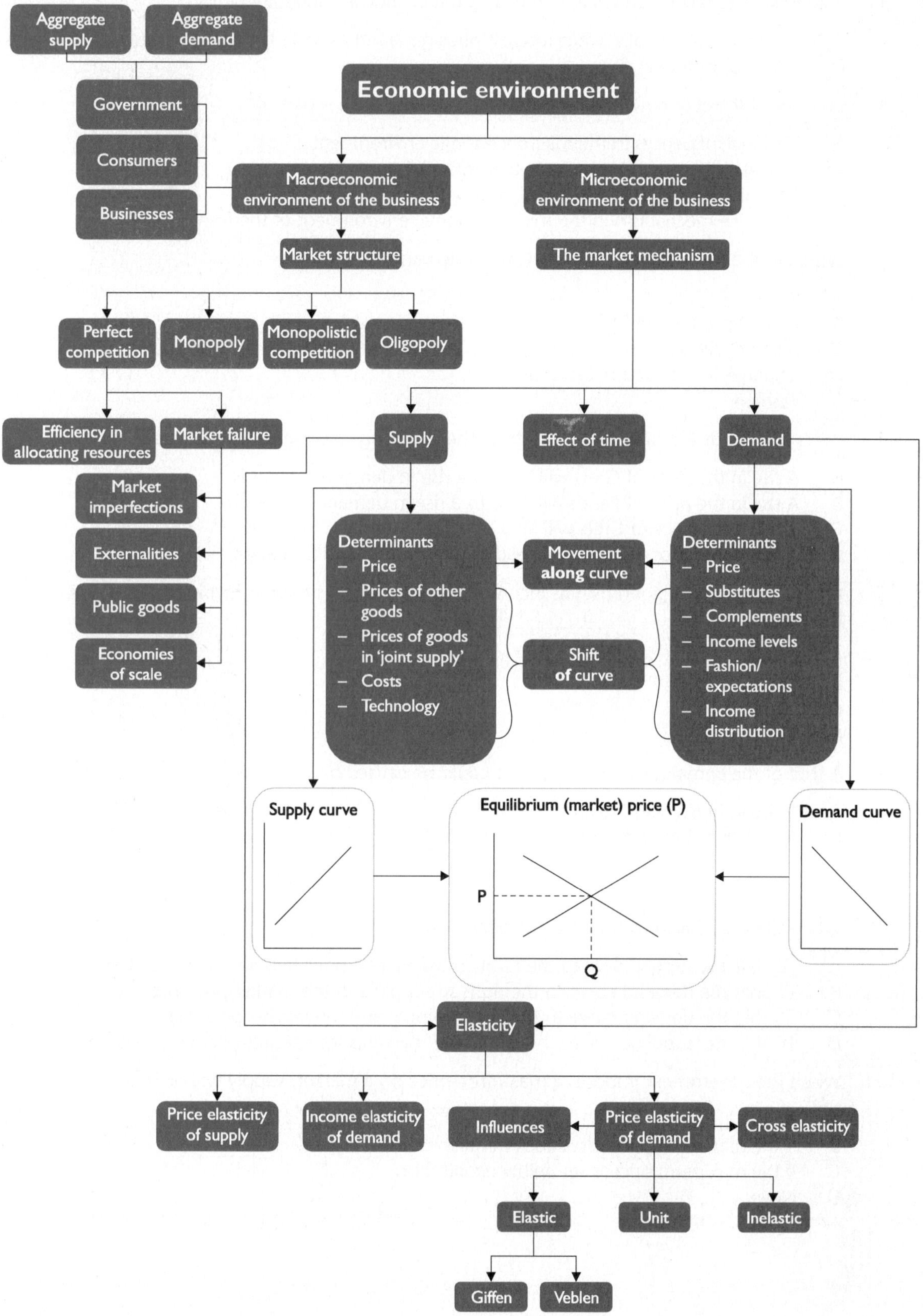

Aggregate supply
Aggregate demand

Government
Consumers
Businesses

Economic environment

Macroeconomic environment of the business
Microeconomic environment of the business

Market structure
The market mechanism

Perfect competition
Monopoly
Monopolistic competition
Oligopoly

Efficiency in allocating resources
Market failure
Market imperfections
Externalities
Public goods
Economies of scale

Supply
Effect of time
Demand

Determinants
- Price
- Prices of other goods
- Prices of goods in 'joint supply'
- Costs
- Technology

Movement **along** curve
Shift **of** curve

Determinants
- Price
- Substitutes
- Complements
- Income levels
- Fashion/ expectations
- Income distribution

Supply curve
Equilibrium (market) price (P)
P
Q
Demand curve

Elasticity

Price elasticity of supply
Income elasticity of demand
Influences
Price elasticity of demand
Cross elasticity

Elastic
Unit
Inelastic

Giffen
Veblen

Self-test

Answer the following questions.

1 Why might an investor not wish to hold surplus funds in a currency in which interest rates offered are the highest available?

2 Is monetary policy mainly concerned with government spending and taxation?

3 If interest rates have risen what, in effect, is the change in monetary policy?

4 Suppose that inflation falls, while interest rates remain the same. Is that good news or bad news for (a) lenders (b) borrowers?

5 In terms of the economic environment, the business cycle is part of

A National influences in the macroeconomic environment
B Global influences in the macroeconomic environment
C The microeconomic environment of the firm
D The price mechanism in the microeconomic environment of the firm

6 Which of the following are determinants of demand?

A Price
B Cost of production
C Income levels
D Changes in production technology
E Fashion

7 Grets and Pands are substitutes. Which of the following statements will be true?

A A rise in the price of Grets will lead to a rise in demand for Pands
B A rise in the price of Pands will lead to a rise in demand for Pands
C A fall in the price of Grets will lead to a rise in demand for Pands
D A fall in the price of Pands will lead to a fall in demand for Pands

8 When demand for a good rises as incomes rise but then falls back as incomes pass a certain point, the good is termed

A Giffen
B Normal
C Inferior
D Veblen

9 A shift of the demand curve to the right could be caused by which of the following conditions?

A A rise in household income
B A negative change in tastes for the goods
C A fall in the price of a substitute
D A rise in the price of a complement

10 When there is a fall in factor costs the effect will be

A To shift the supply curve to the right so the market price falls and demand rises
B To shift the demand curve to the right so supply and the market price rise
C To shift the demand curve to the left so supply and the market price fall
D To shift the supply curve to the left so the market price rises and demand falls

11 When the government imposes a maximum price on a market, supply will be reduced

A Always
B If the maximum price is set above equilibrium
C If the maximum price is set below equilibrium
D Never

12 The price of a good is £1.50 and annual demand is 50,000 units. Research has shown that dropping the price to £1.40 will increase demand by 5,000 units. What is the PED of the good at £1.50?

A 0.10
B 0.67
C 1.50
D 1.96

13 The price of Seagrims has fallen by 5% in the last month, and in the same period demand for Halcets, where there has been no price change, has risen by 8%. What is the cross price elasticity of demand between Seagrims and Halcets?

A –1.600
B –0.625
C 1.600
D 0.025

14 The oil industry is an example of which kind of market structure?

A Perfect competition
B Monopoly
C Duopoly
D Oligopoly

Now, go back to the Learning Objectives in the Introduction. If you are satisfied you have achieved these objectives, please tick them off.

Answers to Interactive questions

Answer to Interactive question 1

(a) Domestic freezers and perishable products are complements because people buy freezers to store perishable products.

(b) Perishable products are supplied either as fresh produce (for example, fresh meat and fresh vegetables) or as frozen produce, which can be kept for a short time in a refrigerator but for longer in a freezer. The demand for frozen produce will rise (the demand curve will move to the right), while the demand for fresh produce will fall (the demand curve will move to the left).

(c) Wider ownership of freezers is likely to increase bulk buying of perishable products. Suppliers can save some packaging costs, and can therefore offer lower prices for bulk purchases.

Answer to Interactive question 2

Under assumption 1, the demand for swimming pools will be confined to household 1. Even if this household owns three or four properties, the demand for swimming pools is likely to be less than under assumption 2, where potentially all five households might want one.

Answer to Interactive question 3

The supply of shares in a particular company is relatively static, although new shares will be issued from time to time. Demand for a company's shares will depend largely on how well the company is performing, although broader economic considerations are also influential. The price mechanism responds very rapidly – a share price may fluctuate up and down at very short intervals, often undergoing several changes in the course of a single day.

Answer to Interactive question 4

(a) **A retail fruit and vegetable market**

The market will probably consist of many small traders, each with their own stall and competing with each other.

The supply conditions affecting prices are:

(i) **Costs**: the main cost to traders will be the cost of their own wholesale supplies, although there will also be costs of renting a stall and costs of wages/labour. Even so, costs will be lower in a market of this kind than in a shopping centre

(ii) **The availability of stalls**: the prices that traders can charge will depend to some extent on the number of stalls that there are and the ease with which new traders can acquire a stall and enter the market.

The demand conditions affecting price are:

(i) The price of **similar goods in shops**

(ii) **Shopping habits** – for example whether householders are accustomed to buying their food from markets

(iii) The **quality** of the goods on the market and how they compare with similar goods in shops

(iv) How much **money** shoppers have to spend

(b) **An auction of antiques and paintings**

The items up for auction will probably have a reserve price. Once the price bid during the auction rises above the reserve price, the seller cannot supply more of the items. They can only sell the item at whatever the maximum bid price happens to be.

The supply of items for auction is unlikely to be influenced by cost of the items. The factors which are relevant to the supply decision are:

(i) The reserve price – the minimum price the supplier will accept

(ii) The expected price – the supplier might put an item up for auction in the expectation of receiving a certain price

(iii) Other circumstances (such as personal factors) influencing the supplier's decision to sell at all

The price obtained at an auction is mainly determined by demand. Factors influencing demand are:

(i) The number of potential customers at the auction and the amount of money they have to spend
(ii) The investment value of the items
(iii) The tastes of customers and the artistic value they perceive in the items up for sale
(iv) The price of similar items at recent auctions elsewhere

Broadly speaking, it could be argued that prices in a retail fruit and vegetable market are influenced mainly by costs (wholesale prices), while in an auction of antiques and paintings the main factor influencing price will be demand. Different conditions have varying degrees of importance between one type of market and another.

Answer to Interactive question 5

We can use the same price/quantity change data, assuming that the demand curve is a straight line, although we are now looking at a different point on the curve.

At a price of £1.30, annual demand is 730,000 units.

For a price fall from £1.30 of 10 pence:

% change in demand $\frac{70{,}000}{730{,}000} \times 100\% = 9.59\%$ (rise)

% change in price $\frac{10\text{p}}{130\text{p}} \times 100\% = 7.69\%$ (fall)

Price elasticity of demand $= \frac{9.59}{-7.69} = -1.25$,

or 1.25 ignoring the minus sign.

Demand is even more *elastic* at this point than it was at £1.20.

Answer to Interactive question 6

(a) Product A

At price £5:

Change in quantity $\frac{300}{1,700} = 17.6\%$

Change in price $\frac{-40p}{£5} = -8\%$

$$PED = \frac{17.6\%}{-8\%} = -2.2$$

Demand is elastic and a fall in price should result in such a large increase in quantity demanded that total revenue will rise.

	£
Revenue at old price of £5 × 1,700	(8,500)
Revenue at new price of £4.60 × 2,000	9,200
Increase in total revenue	700

(b) Product B

At price £8:

Change in quantity $\frac{500}{9,500} = 5.3\%$

Change in price $\frac{-50p}{£8} = -6.25\%$

$$PED = \frac{5.3\%}{-6.25\%} = -0.85$$

Demand is inelastic and a fall in price should result in only a relatively small increase in quantity demanded. Total revenue falls.

	£
Revenue at old price of £8 (× 9,500)	(76,000)
Revenue at new price of £7.50 (× 10,000)	75,000
Fall in total revenue	(1,000)

Answer to Interactive question 7

As demand for organic food is elastic, the government can expect a strong response to a reduction in price, that is an expansion of demand down the demand curve as the price drops. This can be calculated as follows:

Target increase in demand: 0.03
PED: –1.6

Percentage change in price needed to achieve target increase: 0.03/1.6 × 100% = 1.875%

Answer to Interactive question 8

Item (b) is an external cost of the project, since increased volumes of traffic are harmful to the environment. Item (c) is a private benefit for the private company which built the complex. Item (d) would only be an external benefit if a building is better for the people in the inner city area than the use of open land, which is unlikely. Item (a) is correct because the benefits to local shops are additional to the private benefits of the sports firm and as such are external benefits.

Answers to Self-test

1 Because its exchange rate may depreciate.

2 No. The description given is of fiscal policy.

3 Monetary policy has been tightened: money is more expensive.

4 Lower inflation is good news for lenders, since the real value of the loan will deteriorate more slowly. Conversely, it is bad news for borrowers, since the value of their debt will be relatively higher.

5 A

6 A, C, E

7 A

8 C

9 A

10 A

11 C

12 C (5,000/50,000)/(£0.10/£1.50)

13 A +0.08/-0.05

14 D

CHAPTER 14

External regulation of business

Introduction

Learning objectives

Tick off

- Specify the principal effects of regulation upon businesses ☐
- Show how the needs of different stakeholders in a business (eg shareholders, the local community, employees, suppliers, customers) impact upon it ☐
- Specify the effects of international legislation on businesses ☐

Specific syllabus references are: 6d, e. f.

Syllabus links

Regulation is developed further as a topic in Business Strategy at Professional level and at the Advanced level.

Examination context

You will almost certainly encounter a question on business regulation in your exam.

Exam questions are likely to be set in multiple choice style and in a scenario context, though knowledge-type questions on key points and principles are also possible.

1 Why is regulation of businesses necessary?

Section overview

- Regulation of businesses addresses market failure and protects the public interest.
- Governments intervene in markets to address market failure caused by market imperfection, externalities, asymmetric information and lack of equity.
- Regulation also aims to protect the public interest of employees, suppliers, customers, the local community and the public at large from the self-interest of shareholders, directors and managers.
- Effect of regulation: facilitation of competition; protection of public from abuse of power; flexibility; fair enforcement; transparency.
- Forms of regulation: legislation/delegated legislation; self-regulation plus oversight; a combination.

Regulation of business is needed:

- To address **market failure** and **externalities**
- To protect the **public interest**

Definition

Regulation: Any form of state interference with the operation of the free market. This could involve regulating demand, supply, price, profit, quantity, quality, entry, exit, information, technology, or any other aspect of production and consumption in the market.

1.1 Addressing market failure

As we saw in Chapter 13, market failure is said to occur when the market mechanism fails to result in economic efficiency, so the outcome in terms of allocation of resources is sub-optimal.

Government often seeks to intervene in the case of market failure, and has several alternative ways of doing so:

- Providing **public goods** such as street lighting
- Providing **merit goods** such as education which are in the long-term interests of society
- Controlling the means of production through **state ownership** of industries
- Re-distributing wealth through the system for **direct taxation of income**
- **Creating demand** for output that creates jobs, such as defence contracts or major public works such as road-building
- **Influencing supply and demand** through:
  - **Price regulation** (minimum or maximum prices)
  - **Indirect taxation** on expenditure on some goods and services, so that supply is restricted as the price to consumers includes the tax but suppliers only receive the net-of-tax price (the supply curve shifts to the left)
  - **Subsidies** paid by the government to suppliers (shifting the supply curve to the right), in order:
    - To encourage more production
    - To keep prices lower for socially desirable goods whose production the government wishes to encourage
    - To protect a vital industry such as agriculture

- Influencing markets through **persuasion**
- **Regulating** markets through **legislation** and other means

In this chapter we shall be concentrating on **legislation and regulation of markets.**

Of the various forms of market failure, the following are the cases where regulation of markets can often be the most appropriate policy response.

- **Market imperfection** – where monopoly power is leading to inefficiency, government will intervene through controls on, say, prices or profits in order to try to reduce the effects of the monopoly
- **Externalities** – a possible means of dealing with the problem of external costs and benefits is via some form of regulation. Regulations might include, for example, controls on emissions of pollutants, restrictions on car use in urban areas, the banning of smoking, compulsory car insurance and compulsory education
- **Asymmetric information** – regulation is often the best form of government action whenever informational inadequacies are undermining the efficient operation of markets. This is particularly so when consumer choice is being distorted. Examples here would include: regulation of financial reporting and financial services; legally enforced product quality/safety standards; consumer protection legislation; the provision of job centres and other means of improving information flows in the labour market
- **Equity** – the government may resort to regulation to improve social justice. For example, legislation to prevent discrimination in the labour market; regulation to ensure equal access to goods such as health care, education and housing; minimum wage regulations and equal pay legislation

We shall come back to regulations with respect to market imperfection and externalities shortly.

1.2 Protecting the public interest

Just as regulation of the accountancy profession is needed to provide the public interest with protection and assurance, so too with businesses, which are the source of most wealth creation and economic power, but which are focused as we have seen on meeting the interests of:

- Shareholders
- Directors and managers

External regulations on businesses of many different forms are designed to ensure that the **needs of the other stakeholders can be met.**

1.3 Functions of the regulation of business

People find it difficult to trust business entities that exist to make profits for the benefit of one very select group of people, the shareholders. Experience has taught society that this objective has historically been pursued at the expense of the public interest, so society has increasingly demanded that business activities should be externally regulated, to **restore the balance of power.**

2 What form does the regulation of businesses take?

Section overview

- Business is subject to a great deal of formal legislation/regulation from the EU, Parliament and other statutory bodies.
- Regulation is efficient where the total benefits to some people outweigh the total costs to others.
- Outcomes of regulation: market failures are addressed; social standing of some groups is enhanced; the collective desires of society are enacted; particular preferences in society are developed; irreversibility is dealt with.
- Business responses to regulation: non-response; mere compliance; full compliance; innovation (the Porter hypothesis).

2.1 What is regulation?

In a legal sense, a **regulation** is a rule created by the government, an administrative agency or another body which interprets a statute, or the circumstances of applying the statute. It is a form of secondary or **delegated legislation** which is used:

- To implement a primary piece of legislation appropriately
- To take account of particular circumstances or factors emerging during the gradual implementation of, or during the period of, a primary piece of legislation

2.2 Outcomes of regulation

Regulation has **costs** for some and **benefits** for others. **Efficient regulation** exists where the total benefits to some people exceed the total costs to others.

Regulation is justified using various reasons and therefore can be classified in several broad categories according to its intended outcome. Regulations may be put in place to:

- Address **market failures** (see above)
- Increase or **reduce** the **social standing** of various social groups
- See through the **collective desires** of a significant section of society
- Enhance **opportunities** for the formation of diverse preferences and beliefs in society
- Affect the development of particular **preferences** across society as a whole
- Deal with the problem of **irreversibility** (current activities will result in outcomes from which future generations may not recover at all)

Interactive question 1: Irreversibility **[Difficulty level: Intermediate]**

Try to think of at least two ways in which regulations of which you are aware from your general business knowledge seek to deal with the problem of irreversibility.

See **Answer** at the end of this chapter.

2.3 Business responses to regulation

Businesses can respond in a variety of ways to regulation:

- Entrenchment of a particular practice (nil or **non-response**)
- **Mere compliance**, so that the desired regulatory outcome is met simply by passing on the cost of compliance to clients and consumers
- **Full compliance**, so that behaviour is changed and products and processes are adjusted to comply with regulations
- **Innovation**: the Porter hypothesis (see below)

We shall deal with compliance in the next section of this chapter.

2.3.1 The Porter hypothesis

The economist Michael Porter formulated the hypothesis that strict environmental regulations trigger the discovery and introduction of cleaner technologies and environmental improvements, **the innovation effect**. This makes production processes and products more efficient, and the cost savings achieved are sufficient to compensate for both the compliance costs directly attributed to new regulations and the innovation costs. Overall therefore commercial competitiveness is improved.

2.4 Regulatory compliance

Definition

Regulatory compliance: Systems or departments in businesses which ensure that people are aware of and take steps to comply with relevant laws and regulations.

Interactive question 2: Compliance in banks [Difficulty level: Intermediate]

Try to identify what types of regulation are monitored by the compliance sections of a bank.

See **Answer** at the end of this chapter.

2.5 The role of regulatory bodies

There is a considerable level of business regulation in the UK, some of which arises from the EU, and there are a great many regulatory bodies which oversee and enforce these regulations. Examples include the FRC, the PRA and the FCA, which we saw in Chapter 10 plus:

- The **Information Commissioner**, who is responsible for enforcing rules brought in by the Data Protection Act 1998 and the Freedom of Information Act 2000
- The **Office of Fair Trading (OFT)**
- The **Competition Commission**

We shall look at the work of these last two regulators now. Note that following the Enterprise and Regulatory Reform Act 2013 a new single Competition and Markets Authority (CMA) will take on the functions of the Competition Commission plus the OFT's competition functions and consumer enforcement powers by Spring 2014.

3 Direct regulation of competition in a market

Section overview

- The level of competition in a market is regulated because the closer a market gets to perfect competition, the more efficient the allocation of resources in that market.
- Anti-competitive agreements and the abuse of a dominant position are prohibited in the UK.
- Anti-competitive agreements result from collusion between 'competitors' in the same market, and result in price fixing, production limitation, sharing markets, and different trading conditions and supplementary obligations for consumers.
- A dominant position arises where one business is able to behave independently of competitive pressures. As a result it may: impose unfair prices; limit developments; apply different trading conditions and supplementary obligations on consumers. A business will not be considered dominant unless it controls 40% of the market.
- A cartel of businesses is involved in collusion on prices, discounts, production etc.
- A business that is party to an anti-competitive agreement or a cartel or that abuses a dominant position may be fined up to 10% of its worldwide annual revenue. Cartels may lead to criminal sanctions.
- Regulation of competition is effected by the OFT, the Competition Commission, and the Takeover Panel (which enforces the Takeover Code).

3.1 Why is the regulation of competition important?

In a market economy the allocation of resources is generally determined by the price mechanism. In Chapter 13 we saw that the uninhibited and rather idealised operation of the price mechanism is called **perfect competition**, but we also saw that there are plenty of circumstances where competition is far from perfect, and conditions exist for monopolies to take over.

Generally monopolies are not in the public interest as they do not allocate resources efficiently. The government seeks to diminish them by fragmenting an industry via UK and EU legislation, so that market share is not concentrated in the hands of one or two producers. The same effect is also achieved indirectly sometimes, for instance in the case of new pharmaceutical products, where stringent testing and government approval are required before they can be marketed.

3.2 How is competition regulated in the UK?

The Competition Act 1998 (which derives from but is not completely identical to Articles 101 and 102 of the Treaty on the Functioning of the EU (TFEU), previously Articles 81 and 82 of the Treaty of Rome) prohibits agreements, business practices and conduct that damage competition, namely:

- **Anti-competitive agreements** (Chapter I of the Act, and Article 101 of TFEU)
- **Abuse of a dominant position** (Chapter II and Article 102 of TFEU)

In addition, the Enterprise Act 2002 makes **cartel activity** a criminal offence.

The laws apply to all businesses, of whatever size, although there are provisions for immunity, exception and exemption.

3.3 Prohibiting anti-competitive agreements

Both informal and formal agreements, whether or not they are in writing, are prohibited if they are agreements resulting from **collusion** between businesses that have as their object or effect the prevention, restriction or distortion of competition. Many different types of agreement may fall within the prohibitions; Chapter I and Article 101 provide an identical illustrative list of examples of agreements to which the prohibition applies:

- **Fixing** purchase or selling prices or other trading conditions
- Agreeing to **limit or control** production, markets, technical development or investment
- **Sharing** markets or supply sources
- Applying **different trading conditions** to equivalent transactions, thereby placing some parties at a competitive disadvantage
- Making conclusion of contracts subject to acceptance of **supplementary obligations**

Market conditions that lead to increased collusive behaviour are covered under the section on cartels below.

Agreements will only fall within the Chapter I prohibition and Article 101 if they have an 'appreciable effect on competition'; whether this is so in a particular case depends on a number of factors, such as the market share of the businesses involved in the agreement. Note though that agreements:

- To fix prices
- To impose minimum resale prices or
- To share markets

will generally be seen as capable of having an appreciable effect regardless of how small the businesses involved are.

A business that is found to be party to an anti-competitive agreement can be fined up to 10% of its annual worldwide revenue.

3.4 Prohibiting the abuse of a dominant position

Chapter II/Article 102 prohibit the abuse by one or more businesses of a **dominant position** in a market.

Definition

Dominant position: One where the business is able to behave independently of competitive pressures, such as other competitors, in that market.

Both Chapter II and Article 102 give examples of specific types of conduct that are particularly likely to be considered as an abuse where the business is in a dominant position. These include:

- Imposing **unfair** purchase or selling prices
- **Limiting** production, markets or technical development to the prejudice of consumers
- Applying **different trading conditions** to equivalent transactions, thereby placing certain parties at a competitive disadvantage
- Attaching unrelated **supplementary conditions** to contracts.

Factors that help to determine whether there is dominance by a business include:

- Its **market share** – generally, a business is unlikely to be considered dominant if it has less than 40% of the market
- The number and size of **competitors**
- The **potential** for new competitors to enter the market

A business that is found to be abusing a dominant position can be fined up to 10% of its annual worldwide revenue.

3.5 Prohibiting cartels

Definition

Cartel: An agreement between businesses not to compete with each other. The agreement is usually verbal and often informal.

Cartel members typically agree or collude on:

- Prices
- Output levels
- Discounts
- Credit terms
- Technology
- Which customers they will supply
- Which areas they will supply
- Who should win a contract (bid rigging).

Cartels can occur in almost any industry and can involve goods or services at the manufacturing, distribution or retail level. Some sectors are more susceptible to cartels than others because of their structure or operations. Cartels or collusive behaviour in general are more likely to occur in industries or sectors where:

- There are **few competitors**
- The products have **similar characteristics**, leaving little scope for competition on quality, service, or cost
- **Communication channels** between competitors are already established
- The industry is suffering from **excess capacity**
- There is general **economic recession**

A business that is found to be a member of a cartel can be fined up to 10% of its annual worldwide revenue. In addition, participation in agreements between undertakings at the same level in the supply chain (horizontal agreements) may expose individuals responsible for those agreements to criminal sanctions under the Enterprise Act 2002.

Businesses and individuals in a cartel who end their involvement and confess may be granted immunity or a significant reduction of any fine.

3.6 The Office of Fair Trading (OFT)

The OFT has strong powers to investigate businesses suspected of breaching the Competition Act 1998 or the Enterprise Act 2002, and to impose tough penalties on those that do. Key implications for businesses are that:

- OFT officials can **enter premises** and **demand relevant documents** to establish whether any of the prohibitions has been infringed
- The **fine** can be up to 10% of annual worldwide revenue
- Third parties may be able to **claim for damages** from the business if it has been found to breach any of the prohibitions
- There will be **adverse publicity**
- Competition Disqualification Orders may be made against the **directors**

3.7 The Competition Commission

The Competition Commission is an independent public body established by the Competition Act 1998 which conducts **in-depth inquiries into mergers, takeovers, markets and the regulation of major industries**. The Commission has no power to conduct inquiries on its own initiative; every inquiry is referred to it by another authority, usually the OFT. Ministers or regulators under sector-specific legislative provisions relating to regulated industries may also make a reference to the Competition Commission.

In most merger, takeover and market references the Commission is responsible for making decisions specifically on competition issues and for making and implementing decisions on appropriate remedies. It does not have to determine whether matters are against the public interest. The **public interest test** is replaced by tests focused specifically on **competition issues**.

There are specialist panels on the Competition Commission for utilities (including gas and electricity inquiries), telecommunications, water and newspapers.

3.7.1 The Takeover Code

The main principles and rules governing the planning and day-to-day conduct of a takeover offer for a UK public company are covered by a non-statutory set of general principles and rules set out in the **City Code on Takeovers and Mergers**, usually known just as the **Takeover Code**. These are designed to ensure that takeover and merger activity does not undermine competition in the UK. The Takeover Code is enforced by the Takeover Panel, an independent public body.

4 Direct regulation of externalities

Section overview

- Externalities (external costs and benefits) are regulated by a variety of methods designed ultimately to affect the level of supply: price regulation; direct taxation or tariffs; subsidies to suppliers; quotas, standards and fines.

To intervene in the level of supply in a market where there are problems of external costs and benefits, such as pollution and other environmental damage, the government can use:

- **Price regulations** (setting maximum or minimum selling prices, as we saw in Chapter 13)
- Direct or indirect **taxation** or **tariffs**
- **Subsidies** to suppliers, for instance to encourage exports
- Regulation, by means of:
  - **Quotas**, that is physical limits on output so that output is set at the social optimum
  - **Standards** that must be complied with
  - **Fines** for those businesses that do not meet the necessary standards

Worked example: Regulation of pollution by emissions trading

As part of government **environmental and sustainability policies** many businesses are set **standards** for pollution control and **quotas** for emissions (which may be bought and sold as **tradable permits** on the **emissions trading market**), plus they may be **fined** if they create unacceptable levels of pollution. It is hard however to preset pollution fines and output quotas without having accurate and reliable estimates for private benefits, private costs and external environmental damage arising from pollution. In addition, compliance with environmental regulations is costly to enforce, and it may be impossible to monitor all businesses accurately because of imperfect information. Finally, setting the levels of the fines can be difficult: some businesses may not cut their emissions of pollutants if the fine they receive is less than the private benefit they derive from polluting. Fines must have some impact, which is perhaps best determined by setting them as a percentage of revenue or gross profit.

5 Direct regulation of people in business

Section overview

- Directors and other people engaged directly in managing companies are subject to direct regulation:
  - To prevent insider dealing and market abuse, if the company's shares are listed.
  - To prevent wrongful trading if the company is insolvent, and fraudulent trading whether or not the company is insolvent.
  - To control the activities of directors who have been involved with insolvent companies, or who have committed some other forms of misdemeanour
  - To prevent money laundering

It is not only businesses as entities that are subject to regulation. **Individuals** too are regulated in the way they manage and deal with listed and insolvent businesses, in order to protect the public interest and the interests of company creditors.

5.1 Insider dealing of a listed company's shares

People 'in the know' commit a crime under the Criminal Justice Act 1993 if they use knowledge they have as business 'insiders' to **make a profit or avoid a loss** when buying or selling shares on the back of that knowledge and at the expense of open dealings in the market. Significant inside knowledge – of a takeover, an oil strike or a massive fall in profits – will affect the share price when it becomes known, so insiders who benefit from dealing in advance of the knowledge becoming generally known are guilty of **market manipulation**. The crime of **insider dealing** extends to getting someone else to deal, and to disclosing the relevant information at all.

5.2 Market abuse

Following the EU Market Abuse Directive people engaged in the stock market are expected to observe the Code of Market Conduct issued by the FCA, which embodies the **standard of behaviour** that is reasonably expected of such a person. If they fail to do so they may be subject to an unlimited fine for **market abuse** under the Financial Services and Markets Act 2000.

The **Code of Market Conduct** covers:

- **Insider dealing** including
  - **Improper disclosure** creating an unfair market place
  - **Misusing information** as an insider
- **Manipulating transactions** and thus creating a false or misleading impression about supply, demand, prices and values in the market
- **Manipulating devices** – trading and then employing fictitious devices or any other form of deception or contrivance, such as spreading misleading information, to distort the price
- **Dissemination** – giving out information that conveys a false or misleading impression where the person who disseminates the information knows it to be false or misleading
- **Distortion and misleading behaviour** to induce another person to act in a particular way in the market

5.3 Fraudulent trading

Directors of companies must be very careful of the danger of continuing to trade when the company is insolvent – that is, when the company **cannot pay its debts as they fall due**. If a company that is being liquidated as insolvent is found to have been carried on with the **intent to defraud creditors**, or indeed for **any fraudulent purpose**, directors and managers who were knowingly party to this are said to have

engaged in **fraudulent trading**, and can be personally liable for the company's debts under the Insolvency Act 1986.

Directors of any company that engages in fraudulent trading may also face **criminal sanctions,** whether or not insolvency is involved, under the Companies Act 2006.

A business may be carried on fraudulently just by making one transaction or by paying off debts rather than making trading contracts.

5.4 Wrongful trading of an insolvent company

Even if there is no fraud involved, a director engaged in **wrongful trading** may still be required by a liquidator to make a contribution to an insolvent company's assets under the Insolvency Act 1986. This may arise where the director knew, or should have known, that there was **no reasonable prospect of the company avoiding insolvent liquidation**, or where the director took **insufficient steps to minimise the potential loss to creditors**. Professional accountants are more at risk of falling foul of these rules than anyone else, as their skills, knowledge and experience mean they are judged by **higher standards** than those applied to non-professionals. This is true even if they are accountants employed as sales or marketing directors, for instance, rather than as finance directors.

5.5 Disqualification of directors

To protect the public in general and creditors in particular, a person may be disqualified from acting as director or manager of companies for a wide range of reasons under the Company Directors Disqualification Act 1986. These include:

- **Insider dealing**
- **Fraudulent or wrongful trading**
- Violating **competition laws**
- Being convicted of an **offence** in connection with the promotion, formation, management or liquidation of a company or with the receivership or management of a company's property
- Being the **director of an insolvent company**
- Being **unfit** to act as director or manager, such as failing to read the company's accounts
- Being **consistently in default** regarding company law requirements, such as failing to keep proper accounting records
- Being a **threat to the public interest**
- Making **loans** from company funds that were unlikely to be repaid.

5.6 Money laundering

There are very extensive regulations on **money laundering** that have been made following the Proceeds of Crime Act 2002, particularly the Money Laundering Regulations 2007. The CCAB issued the Anti-Money Laundering Guidance for the Accountancy Sector in August 2008, which has been approved by the Treasury as 'relevant guidance' within the meaning of the Money Laundering Regulations 2007. Courts must consider relevant guidance when determining whether an accountant's conduct gives rise to certain offences under either the Act or the Regulations.

It is this guidance which practitioners must implement and comply with if they are not to fall foul of the anti-money laundering requirements.

6 The effect of international legislation

Section overview

- International legislation regulates some markets more than others; the effect is generally not global.
- International legislation for the regulation of business is driven to a great extent by: international bodies (WTO, UN, IMF, ICC); governments (especially the US, regional trade groups such as EU and NAFTA); businesses (especially US corporations).

The emergence of global regulation does not necessarily happen at the same time as the globalisation of either markets or business organisations. Gambling, for example, via the internet, is a global market, but it is regulated in different ways by different states. By contrast, regulations relating to prescription drugs are now largely global in effect, but national markets are kept isolated from one another by differences in government policy on medicine as a welfare benefit.

The processes that result in developments in global regulation are complex and vary from industry to industry. But some common features emerge.

- The **US** has huge influence over the globalisation of regulation; the **EU** has similar influence.
- **International organisations** such as the World Trade Organisation (WTO), International Monetary Fund (IMF) and International Chamber of Commerce (ICC) also have extensive power to influence the development of regulations
- **US corporations** are very effective at enrolling the power of their own government and international bodies to promote their interests

Regulation has great potential both to further and to frustrate business plans. The adoption of one company's patented technology as a global standard confers huge benefit; conversely, regulations relating to pollution or working conditions have great potential to drive up costs. It is therefore in the interests of businesses to **remain alert to the general thrust of regulation** as it affects their industries, and to participate in the processes of lobbying and representation that underpin it.

7 International regulation of trade

Section overview

- The benefits of industrialisation have been sought by most economies via either import substitution or exports.
- International free trade supports the efficient allocation of resources in the world by encouraging: specialisation; evening out of surpluses and deficits of resources; competition; economies of scale; closer political links.
- Barriers to free international trade (protectionism) are formed by: tariffs; customs duties; quotas on imports; embargoes; hidden subsidies; import restrictions; exchange rate manipulation.

7.1 What are the economic advantages of international free trade?

The doctrine of **comparative advantage** states that countries should stick to what they are best at, which may suggest preserving the *status quo*. Nevertheless the benefits of industrialisation have been sought by many nations via two main routes.

- **Import substitution**: a country aims to produce manufactured goods which it previously imported. It does this by protecting local producers

- **Export-led growth**: relying on cheap labour, businesses ensure economic growth by exporting. The success of this particular strategy depends on the existence of open markets elsewhere

Although export-led growth has meant that global trade has opened up, the existence of global free trade and markets should not be taken for granted in terms of all products and services, or indeed in all territories. Services in particular are still subject to managed trade (for example, some countries prohibit foreign firms from selling insurance) and there are some services which by their very nature can never be exported (eg hairdressing).

Encouraging international free trade has the following advantages.

- Countries **specialise** in items they produce comparatively most efficiently so resources are allocated efficiently.

- Some countries have a **surplus** of raw materials to their needs, and others have a **deficit**. A country with a surplus (eg of oil) can take advantage of its resources to export them. A country with a deficit of a raw material must either import it, or accept restrictions on its economic prosperity and standard of living.

- **Competition** is increased among suppliers in the world's markets. Greater competition reduces the likelihood of a market for a good in a country being dominated by a monopolist, and will force businesses to be competitive and efficient, producing goods of a high quality.

- **Larger markets** are created for a business's output, and so some businesses can benefit from **economies of scale** by engaging in export activities. Economies of scale improve the efficiency of the use of resources, reduce output costs and also increase the likelihood of output being sold to the consumer at lower prices than if international trade did not exist.

- The development of **trading links** provides a foundation for closer **political links**. An example of the development of political links based on trade is the EU.

Note, however that high transport costs can negate the advantages of specialisation and international trade.

7.2 Barriers to free international trade

In practice many legislative and other barriers to free trade exist because governments try to protect home industries against foreign competition. This '**protectionism**' can be practised by a government in several ways:

- Tariffs or customs duties
- Import quotas
- Embargoes (bans on certain imports or exports)
- Hidden subsidies for exporters and domestic producers
- Import restrictions
- Government action to devalue the nation's currency (reduce its foreign exchange value)

7.2.1 Tariffs or customs duties

Tariffs or **customs duties** are taxes on imported goods. The effect of a tariff or duty is to raise the price paid for the imported goods by domestic consumers, while leaving the price paid to foreign producers the same, or even lower. The difference is transferred to the government sector.

An *ad valorem* tariff is one which is applied as a percentage of the value of goods imported. A *specific* tariff is a fixed tax per unit of goods.

7.2.2 Import quotas and embargoes

Import quotas are restrictions on the *quantity* of a product that is allowed to be imported into the country. The quota has a similar effect on consumer welfare to that of import tariffs, but the overall effects are more complicated.

- Both domestic and foreign suppliers enjoy a higher price, while consumers buy lower quantities at the higher price

- Domestic producers supply more

- There are fewer imports (in volume)
- The government collects no revenue

An **embargo** on imports from one particular country is a total ban, ie effectively a zero quota.

7.2.3 Hidden subsidies and import restrictions

An enormous range of government subsidies and assistance for exports, and deterrents against imports, have been practised.

- **For exports** – export credit guarantees (insurance against irrecoverable debts for overseas sales), financial help (such as government grants to the aircraft or shipbuilding industry) and administrative assistance
- **For imports** – complex import regulations and documentation, or special safety standards demanded on imported goods and so on

When a government gives grants to its domestic producers, for example regional development grants for new investments in certain areas of the country or grants to investments in new industries, the effect of these grants is to make unit production costs lower. These give the domestic producer a cost advantage over foreign producers in export markets as well as domestic markets.

Summary and Self-test

Summary

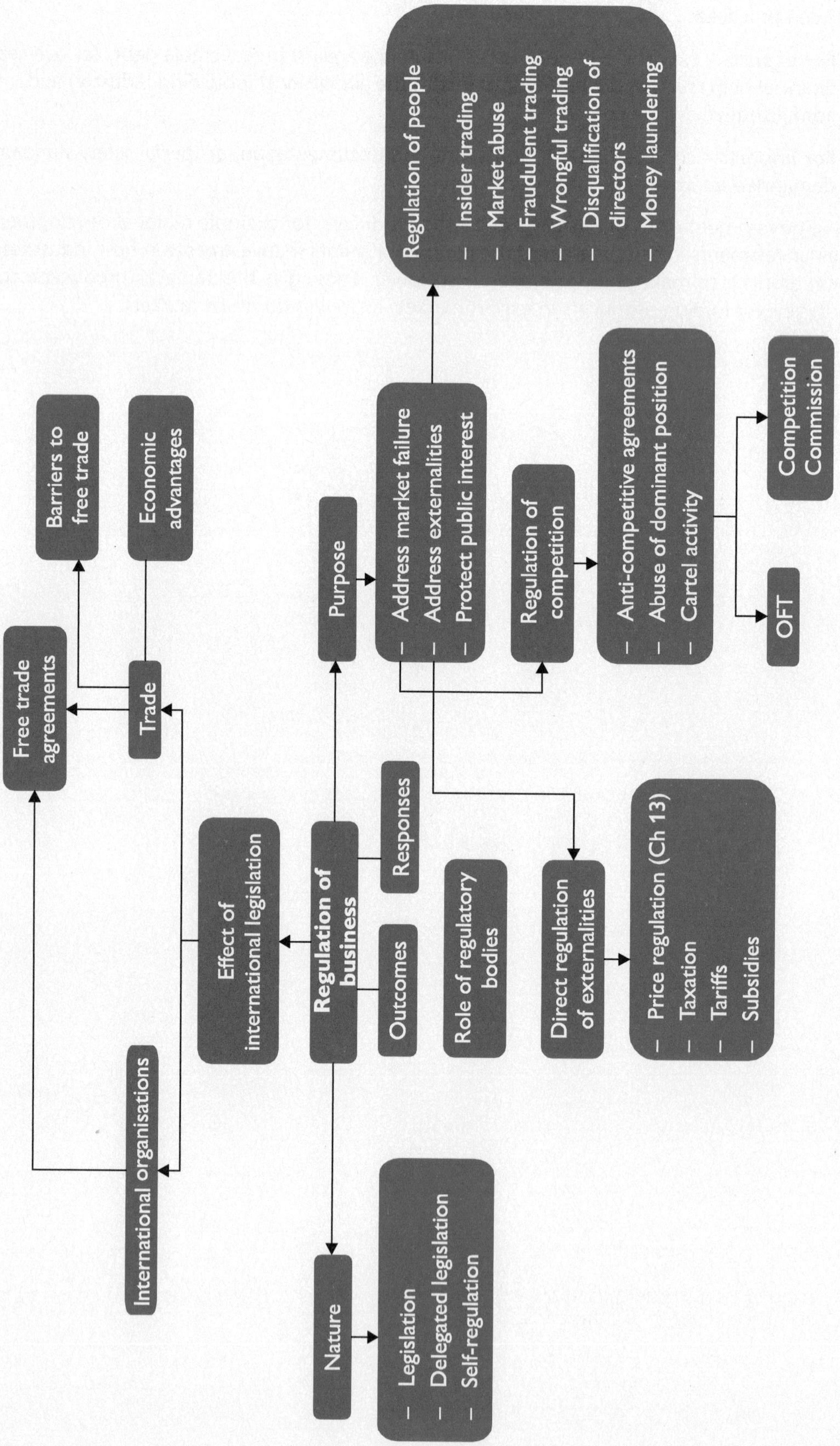

Regulation of business

Nature
- Legislation
- Delegated legislation
- Self-regulation

Effect of international legislation

International organisations

Trade

Free trade agreements

Barriers to free trade

Economic advantages

Purpose
- Address market failure
- Address externalities
- Protect public interest

Regulation of people
- Insider trading
- Market abuse
- Fraudulent trading
- Wrongful trading
- Disqualification of directors
- Money laundering

Regulation of competition
- Anti-competitive agreements
- Abuse of dominant position
- Cartel activity

OFT

Competition Commission

Direct regulation of externalities
- Price regulation (Ch 13)
- Taxation
- Tariffs
- Subsidies

Outcomes

Responses

Role of regulatory bodies

Self-test

Answer the following questions.

1 The provision of public goods by government is an example of intervention to address market failure caused by

A Market imperfection
B Externalities
C Asymmetric information
D Lack of equity

2 By the direct taxation of income government is seeking to

A Provide public goods
B Provide merit goods
C Redistribute wealth
D Create demand

3 Regulation of financial reporting is an example of intervention in order to alleviate market failure caused by

A Market imperfection
B Externalities
C Asymmetric information
D Lack of equity

4 Grando plc operates in a market where compliance with EU regulations has added £1.50 to the cost of each unit produced. As a result, Grando plc has raised its price from £12.60 per unit to £14.10. It has not made any other changes. Grando plc's response is an example of

A Mere compliance
B Full compliance
C Non-response
D Innovation

5 Of a market worth £12.5m, Topping plc has a £2m share and Bartholomew plc has a £3.5m share. They require customers to sign an agreement that they will pay a £10,000 penalty if the customer terminates the contract within two years. This is an example of

A An abuse of dominant position by both companies
B An anti-competitive agreement between the two companies
C A cartel of the two companies
D All of the above

6 In-depth inquiries into the regulation of major industries are conducted by

A The Financial Conduct Authority (FCA)
B The Competition Commission
C The OFT
D The Takeover Panel

7 A UK industry has been lobbying Parliament to require goods bought from three Asian countries for sale in the UK to be subject to additional safety checks. From the perspective of supporting free trade the UK government may be reluctant to agree as this would be an example of

A A tariff
B A quota
C Dumping
D An import restriction

Now, go back to the Learning Objectives in the Introduction. If you are satisfied you have achieved these objectives, please tick them off.

Answers to Interactive questions

Answer to Interactive question 1

There are many possible examples. One of the most obvious is government regulations on emissions, which seek to prevent the destruction of the natural environment – a pretty important irreversible effect of current activities on future generations! Another important example is the regulation of pensions, which should seek to prevent erosion of the funds available for future pensioners.

Answer to Interactive question 2

Banks need to comply with the Basel Accord (Basel III), and with regulations produced by the PRA and FCA. As with any other business, they will also need to comply with employment and health and safety regulations.

Answers to Self-test

1 B

2 C

3 C

4 A

5 B As neither company has 40% of the market, neither is in a dominant position

6 B

7 D

Index

A

B

N

O

S

REVIEW FORM – BUSINESS AND FINANCE STUDY MANUAL

Your ratings, comments and suggestions would be appreciated on the following areas of this Study Manual.

	Very useful	Useful	Not useful
Chapter Introductions	☐	☐	☐
Examination context	☐	☐	☐
Worked examples	☐	☐	☐
Interactive questions	☐	☐	☐
Quality of explanations	☐	☐	☐
Technical references (where relevant)	☐	☐	☐
Self-test questions	☐	☐	☐
Self-test answers	☐	☐	☐
Index	☐	☐	☐

	Excellent	Good	Adequate	Poor
Overall opinion of this Study Manual	☐	☐	☐	☐

Please add further comments below:

Please return completed form to:

The Learning Team
Learning and Professional Department
ICAEW
Metropolitan House
321 Avebury Boulevard
Milton Keynes
MK9 2FZ
E learning@icaew.com